D1741502

SWEDEN AND THE 'THIRD WAY'

This book is dedicated to Rudolf Meidner and the members of the Swedish labour movement for giving us a glimpse of an achievable better society.

Sweden and the 'Third Way'

A macroeconomic evaluation

PHILIP WHYMAN
University of Central Lancashire, UK

ASHGATE

© Philip Whyman 2003

All rights reserved. No part of this publication may be reproduced, stored in a retrieval system or transmitted in any form or by any means, electronic, mechanical, photocopying, recording or otherwise without the prior permission of the publisher.

Published by
Ashgate Publishing Limited
Gower House
Croft Road
Aldershot
Hampshire GU11 3HR
England

Ashgate Publishing Company
Suite 420
101 Cherry Street
Burlington, VT 05401-4405
USA

Ashgate website: http://www.ashgate.com

British Library Cataloguing in Publication Data
Whyman, Philip
   Sweden and the 'third way' : a macroeconomic evaluation
   1. Macroeconomics - Mathematical models 2. Sweden - Economic
   policy
   I. Title
   339.5'09485

Library of Congress Cataloging-in-Publication Data
Whyman, Philip.
   Sweden and the "third way" : a macroeconomic evaluation / Philip Whyman.
      p. cm.
   Includes bibliographical references and index.
   ISBN 0-7546-1797-1
      1. Sweden--Economic policy. 2. Socialism--Sweden. I. Title.

   HC375.W456 2003
   339'.09485--dc21   2002043696

ISBN 0 7546 1797 1

Printed and bound by MPG Books Ltd, Bodmin, Cornwall

Contents

List of Tables

List of Figures

Acknowledgements

There are a large number of people I wish to thank for their assistance, directly or indirectly, in the preparation of this book.

Firstly, I must thank my family for their forbearance during the endless sunny days locked in my study. I thank Claire for her patience throughout this process and Barbara for proofreading my text and quality controlling my bibliography – proof that two minds are better than one.

I thank Kirstin Howgate and her colleagues at Ashgate for their patience during the almost inevitable over-runs. I hope you are pleased with the final product, and agree that it was worth the wait!

Thanks go to the Swedish Institute for providing me with a Visiting Scholarship, which facilitated much of my background work on this topic. In this regard, I would additionally wish to offer my appreciation to the faculty and staff at the Statsvetenskapliga institutionen (Stockholm University) for providing me with a stimulating research environment. I am grateful to Professor Olof Ruin for allowing my affiliation to his department, and to Michele Micheletti for acting as my informal mentor during this time. Furthermore, thanks are also due to the Arbetslivsinstitutet (National Institute for Working Life), formally the Arbetslivscentrum (Centre for Working Life), for allowing me liberal use of their facilities and for helping me with more recent enquiries.

I must thank the countless individuals who were kind enough to be interviewed during my time in Sweden – many of their observations both filled gaps in my knowledge and raised additional questions to research. The multiple kindnesses shown to a humble researcher have nurtured my deep affection for the country and its people.

Thanks also go to Professor Philip Arestis, Professor Murray Milgate and Dr. Brian Burkitt, for their guidance and input into this project, particularly in its embryonic state. Furthermore, I offer my thanks for the comments made by two anonymous referees on the initial book proposal – some of which were extremely insightful and have improved the text that you see before you.

Despite the help and assistance freely given by all those individuals named, I personally translated all quotations from Swedish text and therefore, in this, and in all other matters, all errors are entirely mine.

I hope I have repaid all your kindness with a work that you will enjoy, and which will, in some small way, contribute towards a saner political economy in the future.

Phil Whyman
Chorley, Lancashire

List of Abbreviations

ATP   National Pension Fund System (Allmänna pensionsfondens) – there were ten funds in 1984-1991; three restricted to bonds, two AP-Funds and five WEFs.

EFO   Economic model estimating justified wage increases according to sheltered and competitive sectors – named after the first initial of the three authors.

EMU   Economic and Monetary Union – introduction of a single currency, the Euro, between participating EU member states.

EU   The European Union, formerly The European Communities (EC).

LO   The Swedish Trade Union Confederation (Landsorganisationen i Sverige).

MBL   The Co-Determination (in Work) Act (1976).

RRV   The National Audit Bureau of Sweden (Riksrevisionsverket) – the government body that administers the state pension fund system.

SACO/SR   The Swedish Confederation of Professional Associations/Federation of Civil Servants (Sveriges Akademikers och Statsjänstemännens Riksförbund Centralorganisation).

SAF   The Swedish Employers' Confederation (Svenska Arbetsgivareföreningen, SAF).

SAP   The Swedish Social Democratic Labour Party (Sveriges Socialdemokratiska Arbetarpartiet, SAP).

SI   Swedish Industrial Employers' Organisation (Sveriges Industriförbundet).

TCO   The Central Organisation for Salaried Employees (Tjänstemännens Centralorganisation).

TNCs   Trans-National Corporations.

TWEP   Third Way Economic Programme – the macroeconomic strategy implemented by the 1982-1991 SAP government.

VP   Left Party (Vänsterpartiet).

WEFs   Wage Earner Funds (Löntagarfonderna).

Introduction

The creation of a 'Third Way' between unfettered capitalism, on the one hand, and old-style Keynesian-corporatist forms of social democracy, on the other, has become the driving force behind the policy programmes of many left-of-centre political parties in the industrialised nations of the world today. This 'Third Way' approach is distinct from previous versions of social democracy in that it rejects the Keynesian consensus that aggregate demand management is an essential feature of a successful macroeconomic strategy. In its stead, 'Third Way' theorists concentrate upon reforming social and economic policy to enhance their competitive edge within a world dominated by globalisation and technological change, and which render previous forms of social democratic strategy powerless.

This book seeks to critically evaluate the 'Third Way' version of 'new' social democracy, and to use for its case study the experience of Sweden, formerly the prototype old-style social democracy, but more recently undergoing a profound shift towards the 'Third Way' synthesis of neo-liberalism and elements of traditional social democracy. In order to accomplish this task, the theoretical features of a 'Third Way' model are first developed. The famous 'Swedish Model', developed by labour movement economists Gösta Rehn and Rudolf Meidner, is outlined, in some detail, in order to contrast this with contemporary forms of economic policy. Moreover, the internal and external challenges to Swedish macroeconomic policy, including globalisation, European integration, post-Fordist technological change and the relative empowerment of capital, are all analysed to discover the extent to which they constrain national economic autonomy.

The economic programmes of successive governments can then be analysed, over a couple of decades, in order to illustrate the breadth and depth of changes identified in macroeconomic stance. Finally, the book concludes by establishing the degree to which contemporary social democratic policy in Sweden can be considered to be a variant of the 'Third Way' model, before examining the plausibility of revising the core elements of the 'Swedish Model' as an alternative to the prevailing macroeconomic platform.

PART I
THEORETICAL
BACKGROUND

Chapter 1

The 'Third Way' – Explored

Introduction

The term, the 'Third Way', has been used to describe various innovative policy programmes, which occupy middle ground in-between two polarised positions. It may have first been used as long ago as the late nineteenth century, by Pope Pius XII, as part of his campaign for an alternative to both capitalism and socialism (Gould, 1998:236). It was utilised to legitimise anti-democratic variants of extreme right-wing politics in the 1920s, most notably including the fascism of Franco. Moreover, it has also been applied to Yugoslavia, under the communism of Tito, resulting from its pioneering synthesis of elements of worker participation and state ownership (Estrin, 1983).

Social democracy, itself, has been presented as a third way between free market capitalism and Soviet command socialism-communism (Przeworski, 2001:312). One of the most notable examples was the 'middle way' popularised by Marcus Childs (1936), when contrasting the full employment and developing welfare state in Sweden in the 1930s with the Great Depression in the orthodox capitalist economies and the repression associated with Stalin's regime. Furthermore, the term 'Third Way' has been utilised by Ota Šik and advocates of market socialism.

In this book, however, the concept of the 'Third Way' is used in accord with contemporary terminology, relating to the manifestation of a 'new' form of social democracy that is partly defined by contrast to a 'traditional' social democracy that has arguably lost its relevance and/or policy potency. This fact alone is not extraordinary, since Przeworski (2001:312) notes that all new social democratic strategies share the presumption that new external constraints rendered traditional strategies ineffective, and therefore new policy instruments and/or strategies had to be developed in order to maintain effectiveness and to meet new challenges. What distinguishes the contemporary identification of 'Third Way' from previous examples is due to the fact that it involves a middle way between neo-liberalism and *social democracy* itself, or at least its more traditional forms (Freeden, 1999; Tsakalotos, 2001:38).

It is important to bear in mind that the 'Third Way' approach is a practical phenomenon, developed to solve perceived problems from a centre-left perspective, and not derived from an established theoretical perspective. As a result, it is not surprising that such approaches vary from country to country, which makes it difficult to develop a unified theory. Nevertheless, there are sufficient elements that all variants share, to enable them to be encompassed within a common definition that embodies elements of a common strategy.

This chapter outlines the main features of this new social democracy, including identification of certain ideological and philosophical influences, before deriving its main policy consequences. In effect, this chapter will attempt to develop a recognisable 'Third Way' programme, based upon a synthesis from the leading theorists of the 'new' social democracy and practical adherents to this form of political economy. This programme will subsequently be utilised as a benchmark against which to measure the evolving 'Swedish Model', in order to determine the extent it has shifted in the same direction, and the degree to which it remains a distinctive economic and political strategy.

A 'New' Social Democracy?

The past decade has witnessed the development of a 'new' form of social democracy, which may be distinguished from a more 'traditional' version due in part to a number of philosophical differences, but predominantly because of their acceptance of many tenants of neo-liberal economics. This 'new' social democracy has perhaps been most notably identified with the fortunes of Tony Blair and 'New Labour' in Britain.

Responding to a devastating electoral defeat in 1983, involving "an internationally unprecedented collapse in the popular support for the main left-of-centre party", 'modernising' faction sought to re-orientate the party towards its vision of a European social democratic party (Gould, 1998:20-22). For the modernisers, the 'project' would involve the rejection of contemporary support for unilateral nuclear disarmament, withdrawal from the European Community, public ownership and an active fiscal policy associated with a Keynesian strategy rejected as inflationary and problematic to implement due to the consequences of globalisation. The rationale was based upon

> ...a simple thesis: Labour lost the twentieth century and allowed the Conservatives to govern for seventy of the last hundred years because it failed to modernise; it forgot the people that it had been created for. It took the modernisers to save the Labour Party (Gould, 1998:xii).

In its place, 'New Labour' would create "a dynamic capitalism" whose benefits were experienced by *all* citizens (Rustin, 2001:15).

The remodelling of the British Labour Party borrowed significantly from the changes that had been introduced in other progressive political parties. This included the Australian Labour Party, which governed between 1983 and 1996 under the leadership of Hawke and Keating, and which combined the deregulation of the economy with a corporatist 'Accord' negotiated with organised labour (Harcourt, 2001:201).

Other examples of social democratic parties adopting elements of 'Third Way' strategy include the Spanish socialist government, 1982-1996, based upon an orthodox economic programme; the PASOK Greek socialist party whose economic programme shifted from Keynesian to a more orthodox policy stance; and elements of Italian left-of-centre coalition governments in their combination of labour market deregulation, privatisation programmes and orthodox economics (Ferreiro and Serrano, 2001; Skouras, 2001; Graziani, 2001). A 'Third Way' mode of rethinking social democratic strategy could, furthermore, be viewed within the German SPD

'Innovation and Justice' (*Innovation und Gerechtigkeit*) programme, together with the 'Strong and Caring' (*sterk en sociaal*) approach by the Dutch PvdA.

The development of 'New Labour' and the 'Third Way' approach was further influenced, to a considerable extent, by the Clinton presidency of the USA, and in particular by his reinvention as a "New Democrat" following the Republican electoral successes in the 1994 congressional elections (Pollin, 2001). Borrowing elements of his analysis from the Republican critique of 'big government' and their 'contract with the people', Clinton accepted the case that a New Deal social contract, based upon the co-operation of the "big institutions" of state, big business and trade unions, was no longer sustainable. In its place, government should alternatively seek to create the conditions facilitating innovation, investment, education and training, in order to promote growth and productivity, and thereby provide jobs, rising incomes and a degree of security within a global economy (Giddens, 2000:2). This strategy involves the reform of the welfare system, promoting work rather than passive receipt of benefit transfers, together with fiscal conservatism and abdication of monetary policy to the Federal Reserve and its charismatic Chairperson, Alan Greenspan (Green and Wilson, 2000:428).

The electoral success of these re-positioned 'new' centre-left parties generated considerable interest in other European social democratic movements, including most notably the German SPD under the leadership of Gerhardt Schröder. Indeed, British Prime Minister, Tony Blair and German Chancellor, Gerhard Schröder, published a joint paper entitled *Europe: The Third Way – die Neue Mitte*, which advanced a general framework for social democratic parties within Europe (Blair and Schröder, 1999). Although the specific programmes instituted by each of these individual parties are by no means identical, there is enough of a common theme at their heart to identify their distinctive contributions. Thus, the German SPD (1999) 'Basic Values Commission' distinguished between the market-orientated strategy pursued by 'New Labour', with the Dutch 'market-and consensus- oriented' alternative, whilst the Swedish 'reformed welfare state' approach retained far greater continuity with previous policy, as was the more traditional 'state-led' programme preferred by the French socialists (Giddens, 2000:31).

A Reaction to Globalisation?

The 'Third Way', at its heart, is derived from the attempt to develop alternative strategies to pursue many (but not all) social democratic objectives, but starting from acceptance of the proposition that globalisation has fundamentally altered the international climate in which countries and governments operate (Skouras, 2001:181). 'Third Way' theorists share the perception that globalisation has undermined the attempts made by nation states to regulate and tax financial capital, trans-national corporations (TNCs), together with mobile, highly educated, managerial and professional employees. Therefore, globalisation has imposed limitation upon fiscal redistribution (Kitschelt, 1994). It has furthermore limited or ruled out a whole range of policies previously forming a central part of a social democratic-Keynesian economic strategy (Arestis and Sawyer, 2001a:5). This viewpoint was perhaps most memorably expressed by former British Labour Prime Minister, James Callaghan, in the following terms;

We used to think that you could spend your way out of a recession and increase employment by cutting taxes and boosting government spending ... I tell you in all candour that the option no longer exists, and that in so far as it ever did exist, it only worked on each occasion since the war by injecting a bigger dose of inflation into the economy, followed by a higher level of unemployment as the next step (Callaghan, 1988).

Financial market integration limits the ability of national economic autonomy, as perceptions of 'excessive' fiscal expenditure would generate fears of inflation and devaluation, and, irrespective of whether these expectations proved rational or in line with economic fundamentals, the economy in question would be penalised by rising interest rate 'risk' premiums, a process likely to undermine economic growth. The perception of the financial markets, and the result of their subsequent actions, is likely to prove to be a self-fulfilling prophesy. The ability of the 'electronic herd' to discipline governments, corporations and trade unions, is imposed through the cumulative effect of individual movements of physical and financial capital across the world, according to the norms established by the financial markets. Capital has increased its dominance over society due to the 'disembedding' of activities from constraints of time and space, whereby financial capital is instantly mobile and corporations can relocate their activities with a minimum of cost, and can therefore undermine the bargaining position of nationally located workers, suppliers and governments. As a consequence, globalisation is therefore viewed as "one of the key challenges for social democracy" due to its limitation of national state autonomy, and is central to the analysis of the 'Third Way' (Giddens, 1998:30-2; Arestis and Sawyer, 2001a:5).

The 'Third Way' response to globalisation involves government seeking to "equip people to deal with the travails of the new risk society, in which stable employment and other traditional forms of job security can no longer be taken for granted" (Corea, 1998:14). This involves the provision of life-long education and training programmes that facilitate the adaptation of individual skills to a dynamic labour market, together with a modified welfare system providing portable benefits (i.e. pensions, health care) due to the necessity for frequent job changes. In addition, the 'Third Way' strategy requires the creation of a favourable environment for transnational investment, whether through lowering general taxation, generation of a more flexible and highly skilled labour force, deregulation of the economy, providing monetary incentives to encourage inward FDI and so forth (Arestis and Sawyer, 2001a:6).

This view of globalisation is not universally held, and many theorists propose that most of its supposed consequences are actually caused by other phenomenon, including changes from Fordist to flexible forms of technology (Przeworski, 2001:330).[1] The freedom of action for governments may have been reduced by globalisation, but autonomous action remains possible. Most investment is domestically financed, and even where foreign direct investment is a significant element of capital formation, it is more closely associated with access to profitable

---

[1] For further discussion of the consequences for social democracy emanating from globalisation, European integration and post-Fordism, these are covered in more detail in Chapters Seven, Eight and Nine of this book.

markets, access to skilled labour and the absence of economic and political instability, and is relatively insensitive to government policies in general (Porcano, 1993). Similarly, although financial globalisation has increased the constraint upon economic policy autonomy posed by the likely reaction of investors to government policies, the factors determining capital flows are difficult to determine and often have multiple equilibria (Przeworski, 2001:330). Under normal circumstances, a rise in interest rates should increase inward capital flows in search of higher returns. However, if it causes increased expectations of an imminent devaluation, it may have the opposite effect, circa the ejection of Sterling and the Swedish krona from the European Exchange Rate Mechanism in 1992.

Nation states remain the most powerful actors in the international economy due to their ability to determine the conditions pertaining to economic activity within the boundaries of their territory. TNCs do not control territory, legitimate military force and nor do they have the ability to make laws, together with the apparatus needed for their implementation. Governments have the ability to regulate financial markets, productive activity and introduce taxation, such as a 'Tobin tax',[2] in the attempt to steer the behaviour of private economic agents. As a result, Giddens (1998:30-2) accepts the proposition that national government remains strong, has not been rendered impotent by globalisation, and retaining the ability to impose its priorities upon global capital through transnational collaboration. However, supporters of the 'Third Way' wish to utilise transnational regulation to maximise gains from increased trade and capital flows, in terms of a predicted enhanced rate of growth, optimum allocation of scarce resources, and facilitating the development of the Asian sub-continent, whilst limiting less palatable consequences such as increased unemployment and rising inequality. Indeed, Giddens (2000:159) argues that, "taking globalisation seriously means emphasising that democratisation cannot be confined to the level of the nation state", thereby reinforcing support for supra-national institutions, such as the EU, to provide a focus for progressive response to globalisation.

Rojas therefore points to "the unparalleled advances of the past 30 years", which, he argues, have demonstrated the "enormous potential" of the global economy to alleviate underdevelopment, and that therefore government policy should be to "transform more and more countries into dynamic parts of this expansive economy" (Rojas, 1999:12). Instead of opposing further extension of globalisation, 'Third Way' proponents suggest that supranational authorities could concentrate upon the surveillance of financial transactions, to prevent destabilisation caused by excessive capital flows, together with the provision of international liquidity to facilitate the expansion of the world economy (Giddens, 2000:126-7).

Pro-Market Philosophy and the Restricted Role of the State

The 'Third Way' takes a markedly different approach to the role and scale of the state than traditional social democracy, which has generally favoured its expansion into social and economic matters in order to create new policy instruments and

---

[2] For further discussion, see Chapter Seven.

thereby more efficiently enact social democratic strategy. The state has therefore been viewed as the principle instrument for the redistribution of income and power, the regulation and taming of capital, together with the ability to better manage the capitalism to produce full employment, rapid growth economy (Padgett and Paterson, 1991:49).

Neo-liberal critics of the 'big state' have argued that it has become too impersonal, threatens individual liberty and is less efficient than market forces. Consequently, state activities should become limited, and its size dramatically reduced, in order to free resources for more efficient market allocation. Thus, 'Third Way' theorists adopt a position closer to the neo-liberals, in that they favour reconstruction of the state in order to create "the state without enemies" (Giddens, 1998:70).

This approach shares with the neo-liberals their criticism of an over-expansion in state power leading to moral hazard, dependency, reduction in incentives, bureaucracy, "clientism", fiscal irresponsibility, a tendency towards authoritarianism and a lack of accountability, even potentially corruption and fraud (Offe, 1998). As a result, 'Third Way' literature promotes the idea of freezing at its present level, or reducing, the scale of the state through engineering a decline in the ratio of public expenditure as a proportion of GDP (Giddens, 2000:7; Arestis and Sawyer, 2001a:6).

In place of the 'strong state', the 'Third Way' philosophy relies upon an optimistic conception of the ability of the civil society to act as a "self generating mechanism of social solidarity", thereby reducing the need for the state to form a conduit for corporatist frameworks (Giddens, 1998:11). Nevertheless, this does not imply a total disregard for the state to play a positive role in the new 'Third Way' economy (Rustin, 2001:22). Indeed, the state is expected to swap its activist Keynesianism for a role as a "social investment state", providing education and training programmes in order to enable individuals to gain the skills and abilities they need to successfully compete in the global labour market.

Redefining education and labour market policies as 'human capital investment' narrows the conception of the benefits derived from public expenditure, but does provide a financial case for certain types of increased spending. By inference, however, it condemns other areas of public provision to a continual tightening of resources and cutback in provision in the absence of hard won productivity gains. Similarly, the reform of the welfare state is intended to strengthen a drive to get people into work, by increasing incentives, and thereby reducing social exclusion (Tsakalotos, 2001:39). Giddens (2000:6) describes this change in emphasis as one where "the state should not row, but steer: not so much control, as challenge".

Macroeconomic Strategy

The economic strategy advocated by 'Third Way' theorists involves a rejection of the Keynesian policies required to pursue full employment, and replaces these with an "iron commitment to macroeconomic stability and financial prudence" (Routledge, 1998:222). Government no longer utilises all of the economic policy instruments under its control in order to pursue multiple objectives simultaneously, the most important of which being to maintain the full employment of all resources in the economy. The new definition involves the creation of a stable framework for business activity, implying price stability having become the new principle goal of economic strategy (Gould, 1998:244; Tsakalotos, 2001:33). Government activism is restricted to supply side policies, particularly improving the "employability" of the unemployed, and thereby enhancing their capability to compete for jobs created in the new flexible labour market (Blair, 1998; Finn, 2000:386).

The 'Third Way' economic programme is built upon the acceptance of a number of theoretical positions, either consciously or in ignorance of the finer points of the economic literature. For example, the replacement of full employment by low inflation as the principle goal of macroeconomic strategy, together with a passive fiscal stance and the detachment of monetary policy from a co-ordinated policy stance, suggests an acceptance of the natural rate of unemployment hypothesis. This holds that unemployment is ultimately determined by structural factors, such as the wage flexibility of the labour market, rather than the result of aggregate demand. Therefore, the level of unemployment pertaining in the economy is set according to supply-side factors in the labour market, together with the preference of individuals within the labour force to either choose to work at existing wages or choose to consume leisure time instead.

Thus, there is no Phillips curve trade-off between lower unemployment and higher inflation, and governments that seek to lower the unemployment rate below the natural rate, can do so only temporarily, and at the cost of faster rising prices. Hence, the policy solution is for governments to deflate the economy to lower prices, since market clearing theory will have at worst only a temporary impact upon output and prices, because these are determined in the labour market, not by aggregate demand. Unemployment should instead by tackled by measures such as reducing the generosity of benefits and the length of time they are paid, introducing inspection regimes upon the economically non-active – to help reduce job search time and deter fraud – reduce the power of unions to push up wages and hence increase unemployment, together with the introduction of tax incentives for low paid work, and so forth.

This is a theoretical and policy stance associated with the monetarist and 'New Keynesian' schools of economics – the latter representing a synthesis of neo-liberalism and elements of Keynesian policy activism in the short-run. This is a position that causes most post-Keynesians to regard 'New Keynesianism' as illdefined and not forming part of the body of thought associated with Keynes, Kaldor, Robinson and Kalecki.

Fiscal Policy

Fiscal policy becomes a largely passive economic instrument under the 'Third Way', with its main role being to ensure that a tight control is kept upon public expenditure, which is kept constant in real terms such that it declines as a proportion of national income as the economy grows. There is no concept of the need for management of aggregate demand, either through a process of 'fine tuning' or even 'coarse tuning'. Therefore, the 'Third Way' approach must be based upon the Say's Law hypothesis, namely that the economy always tends towards the full employment of its resources because economic activity is set by the supply side of the economy and the level of effective demand adjusts to the appropriate level. Thus, the economy is relatively stable, and any shock, which does cause a temporary deviation from full employment equilibrium, will be self-adjusting, through price flexibility rather than via variations in output and employment. Consequently, the budget should be balanced over the economic cycle, and counter-cyclical policy is not required, save for the operation of automatic stabilisers during a temporary downturn in activity.

Monetary Policy

Monetary policy is dedicated to meeting the new prime objective of price stability, rather than undertaking a more balanced role in stabilising the domestic economy, complete with full employment and a favourable rate of growth. Moreover, there is an increasing tendency, particularly within the EU, to transfer into the hands of an independent central bank, which is given policy autonomy subject only to inflation targets established by government for the ECB to meet.

The idea of making the central bank independent, rather than a part of a democratically controlled and co-ordinated economic strategy, was suggested by a new body of research which purports to demonstrate that, removed from government control, central bankers can and will target lower inflation (Rogoff, 1985). However, there is a considerable danger in placing one of the most important macroeconomic policy instruments into the hands of central bankers, whose preferences are likely to be more 'conservative' in terms of their preference for very low rates of inflation irrespective of the impact upon growth rates and unemployment. The evidence supporting this change is statistically weak, and there is almost as much data to predict that independence would result in relative economic stagnation (Cukierman, 1992; Posen, 1995).

Labour Market Programmes

The supply-side orientation of 'Third Way' policy places great emphasis upon the labour market, in terms of reducing unemployment and ensuring that wage formation is consistent with low inflation targets. This approach concentrates upon increasing the incentives to work, through reducing benefits and transferring the emphasis to minimum wages paid in employment, together with enhancing the skills and abilities of individual workers. It ignores the major contribution played by aggregate demand, and that employment is directly associated with productive capacity. This is due to the adaptation of these policy proposals from within a neo-liberal framework, when the level of employment is assumed determined by Say's Law. Consequently, the 'Third Way' strategy is based upon a non-Keynesian theoretical base – one that roots all the problems of unemployment, a poor level of investment and industrial growth, low growth rates and social inequality, as originating within the labour market.

One 'Third Way' solution involves the re-skilling of the labour force, through an expansion in educational and training programmes to make the unemployed more employable. Much of this analysis is based upon the work of Richard Layard, who argued that "the main thing that determines the number of jobs is the number of 'employable' people in the economy" rather than the level of aggregate demand (cited in ESC, 1996:340). Furthermore, a more educated pool of labour, better fitted to the job vacancies being advertised, reduces supply bottlenecks in the economy and thereby reduce the inflationary pressure generated by employers raising wages to attract scarce labour. It focuses upon the problems of long-term and youth unemployment, in addition to seeking to curb tendencies towards 'Eurosclerosis', whereby an overdeveloped welfare state reduces incentives to work and hence is associated with rising unemployment and falling rates of growth (Nickell, 1997; Siebert, 1997).

As human capital is regarded as the major driver of economic growth in the information age, this element of 'Third Way' thinking is in line with the new endogenous growth theories, which claim to have found evidence that long-term economic growth rates are closely associated with a nation's combination of both physical and human capital. Therefore, educational expenditure should make a positive contribution towards enhancing the growth rate (Harcourt, 2001:215). The welfare state should, then, be reconstituted into a 'social investment state', for precisely this purpose (Giddens, 2000:52).

To take one example, the British 'New Labour' government claims that their emphasis upon 'Education, Education, Education', together with the training provision included in the 'New Deal' labour market programmes, is intended to "build security through employability" through skill enhancement and enabling individuals to adapt to changing needs of the labour market (DfEE, 1997). In terms of the 'New Deal', introduced by the 'New Labour' British government, a recent report by the NISER found a reduction in youth unemployment by 30,000 in its first year, equivalent to a 40% reduction in long-term youth unemployment. However, the overall impact of the programme on the economy as a whole would be marginal (Anderton et al, 2000). In the absence of sufficient job opportunities available in the economy, retraining programmes suffer deadweight costs as the unemployed move from one temporary project to another with minimal consequent reduction in unemployment (Turok and Webster, 1998:325).

Retraining programmes can help to reduce a skills mismatch, but do very little about demand deficient unemployment, which the European economy has arguably been suffering for over a decade. Thus, Solow (1998:30-1) claims that, in the absence of near full employment, retraining programmes may result in the retrained unemployed competing with low-skilled workers in employment, leading to a fall in related wages and may, therefore, encourage employers to replace semi-skilled workers with the now more competitive, less skilled alternatives.

One additional feature of the 'Third Way' approach is a marked preference to discuss targets of 'high' rather than full employment. Indeed, Giddens (1998:126) rather pessimistically suggests that this may be a rational response to his perception that global capitalism no longer generates sufficient work to accommodate a full employment strategy. Nevertheless, the steady decline in unemployment has caused the New Labour government to abandon caution and begin discussing their long-term objectives in terms of a return to full employment. This is despite the fact that UK unemployment figures tend to under-estimate the number of individuals temporarily excluded from the labour market, but who may return if opportunities increased and wages rose.

Industrial Relations

It is difficult to identify a distinctive 'Third Way' approach to industrial relations. Even within specific national programmes, dualistic tendencies can be noted. For example, New Labour emphasises the notion of social partnership between employers and trade unions. In addition, the position of individual employees within the workplace is strengthened, to a small but significant degree, through incremental increases in job security, health and safety and minimum wage legislation (Guest and Peccei, 1998:8). However, many of these measures arise from EU social legislation, which seeks to provide a minimum acceptable level of social protection for European workers far below the rates that most of the advanced nations already offer but which provide additional benefits to the relatively low levels of regulation covering UK workers.

These measures sit oddly with the emphasis New Labour place upon the deregulation and flexibility of the labour market. Hence, this dualism within New Labour's approach to industrial relations may be explained by the remnants of previous 'old' Labour policy remain within a predominantly neo-liberal New Labour programme (Undy, 1999:333). The significance of this explanation relates to its inference that the underlying New Labour strategy is far more neo-liberal than the trace elements of a previous policy stance would make it seem, at first glance.

Social Policy Reform

The 'Third Way' approach to social policy centres upon the belief that employment is the only secure and sustainable means to social inclusion (Rustin, 2001:20). It concentrates upon the expansion of individual opportunities, which can be maximised through work and a programme of continual reskilling, rather than the redistribution of income and wealth. Moreover, it promotes equality of opportunity, but says little about the inequity of outcomes and the obstacles within society preventing many from taking full advantage of the opportunities on offer (Faux, 1999). Social policy reform is perceived as providing a potential contribution towards the 'Third Way' work-centred programme through a reduction in the level of payment and duration of unemployment benefits, together with an associated improvement in take home income when in work.

The well-known study conducted by Layard et al (1991) found that these features were associated with higher unemployment, through a reduction in work incentives. Moreover, Giddens (1998:122) suggested that high levels of unemployment are linked with the provision of "generous benefits that run on indefinitely and to poor educational standards at the lower end of the labour market – the phenomenon of exclusion". Consequently, 'Third Way' policies tend to include an element of benefit reduction – whether through the British government's practice of uprating in line with prices and not average wages, or through actual cuts in entitlements. Hence, increased reliance upon national minimum wages, together with the introduction of tax credits modelled upon US precedence, have tended to provide greater incentives for individuals and families to seek employment, even if it is low skilled and low paid (Arestis and Sawyer, 2001b:52-6). Undy (1999:332) argues that this second element, namely the targeted schemes to boost the disposable income of low paid workers, distinguishes the 'Third Way' strategy from neo-liberalism.

The development of the welfare state was one of the proudest achievements flowing from traditional social democracy. Indeed, utilising a concept most closely associated with T.H. Marshall, the welfare state has been presented as part of a gradual extension of citizenship rights, from legal and political rights, to social and ultimately economic rights (Marshall, 1963). In this regard, the welfare state decommodified labour and thereby provided individuals with enhanced choices about how to live their lives (Esping-Andersen, 1990).

Giddens (2000:103), however, argues that this approach has become unsustainable, both in terms of cost and fundamental concept. Welfare programmes create dependency and introduce moral hazard through the provision of perverse incentives (Giddens, 1998:115). Therefore, instead of seeking to insulate and protect individuals *from* the consequences market mechanisms, the 'Third Way' aims to enhance the position of individuals *within* the global market system.

Achieving fundamental reform of the welfare system is not easy to achieve due to the reliance of entrenched interest groups upon welfare transfers. However, Giddens (2000:104) points to the development of new social tensions, including taxpayer resistance to further growth in public expenditure, differences between generations relating to the generosity of the welfare system and conflict between those who benefit from the system and those who are net contributors, all increase the possibility of forming coalitions for reform. Thus, New Labour Prime Minister, Blair, claims that, with more than £50 billion currently allocated through social transfers to people of working age, his "greatest challenge" will involve the "welfare to work" programme, which aims to "refashion our institutions to bring the new workless class back into society" (cited in Finn, 2000:388).

One obvious consequence of the 'Third Way' approach to welfare reform relates to the impact this is likely to have upon the distribution of income. Measures to increase employability and the provision of minimum wage legislation have equalising effects upon the national distribution of income, whilst the promotion of low paid jobs, reduction in benefits in terms of average wages and reductions in progressive taxation, all have regressive effects. Hence, the Gini coefficient for disposable income indicated rising inequality in the UK during the first term of office of the New Labour government (Atkinson et al, 1996:225-6). In the absence of income redistribution, "one generation's inequality of outcome is the next generation's inequality of opportunity" (Tobin, 1999).

European Integration

The 'Third Way' strategy amongst European economies is identified closely with the process of European integration. Part of the reason for this is due to the neo-liberal foundation that has been established for the single internal market (SIM) and economic and monetary union (EMU) that are forming the basis for the 'new' European economy (Whyman, 2001). In particular, the Stability and Growth Pact (SGP) maintains and reinforces the convergence conditions created to ensure fiscal conservatism amongst potential EMU participants, and which has contributed to a decade or more of economic stagnation across the majority of the European continent (Holland, 1995; UNCTAD, 1996).

The policy framework embodies a distrust of politicians to successfully manage economic policy, so that the supranational European Central Bank (ECB) has been created wholly independent of all democratic influence and/or control, and there has been no comparable European Ministry of Finance created to counter its dominance over the European economy. The ECB's sole policy objective is price stability, which it defines within a range of 0–2%, and the bank is instructed to avoid all consideration of other factors, such as employment and growth, if these detract from meeting this objective. Thus, there is no balanced portfolio of macroeconomic goals established for the new Europe, only the monetarist preoccupation with low inflation, assuming a natural rate of unemployment and the policy ineffectiveness of Keynesian counter-cyclical intervention.

Tsakalotos (2001:38) argues that the EU macroeconomic strategy should not be considered a purely neo-liberal approach due to its championing of the social chapter and the fact that social partnership in the industrial relations sphere has been retained in many member states. However, these facts are equally consistent with the proposal that the economic stance is inherently neo-liberal, but that the social policy advocated by the EU Commission enhances the primacy of federal determination over wider areas of formally national policy, and with it the role and importance of the Commission itself. The social chapter is, at best, a minimalist construction, whose operation is in many respects in contradiction to the overall neo-liberal economic structure created at Maastricht (Whyman, 2001). Moreover, the social partnership maintained by many nation states is restricted to ensuring a social consensus for contentious cuts in welfare programmes, due to the requirements of the SGP, and/or the moderation of real wages to facilitate a transition to EMU. Furthermore, suggestions that the EU might provide the necessary economic muscle to introduce a form of Euro-Keynesianism is neither very likely within the preset institutional arrangements, and nor is this an example of 'Third Way' thinking, because advocates of this initiative are more readily associated with 'traditional' forms of social democracy.

Critique of the 'Third Way'

The 'Third Way' has attracted a considerable amount of criticism. For example, Faux (1999:75) describes it as "an intellectually amorphous substance" with parameters "so wide that it is more like a political parking lot than a highway to anywhere in particular". The Economist (1998:49) remarked upon its "fundamental hollowness", whilst Hall (1998) dismissed it as "the great moving nowhere show". Rustin (2001:13) suggests that the version of the 'Third Way' being developed by New Labour in Britain was initially a concept discussed by political strategists, before only latterly being provided with any theoretical foundation. In practice, he claims that this has provided a political platform, which closely mirrors the failed agenda associated with the now defunct SDP of the 1980s. Marquand (1998:19) agrees that it is "patently not socialist...not even social democratic or social liberal".

Ryan (1999) claims that the approach contains little original analysis, as it adopts many ideas from the form of 'New Liberalism' that existed in Britain at the beginning of the twentieth century. Furthermore, Green and Wilson (2000:428) suggest that it is intended to "legitimate a seismic shift in social democratic policy towards neo-liberalism". This viewpoint is disputed by White (1998:18-21). He claims that, although it is vague in terms of detailed analysis, the 'Third Way' strategy combines individual opportunities and civic responsibility in such a way that it promotes an "asset based egalitarianism". Finally, Giddens (2000:22-5) cites criticisms that the project is "amorphous", lacking direction, ignores environmental issues and has no effective economic programme apart from an uncritical adoption of neo-liberalism and the promotion of marketisation.

Power and Social Class

One powerful criticism of the 'Third Way' approach is that it is too accepting of the existing structures of power within capitalist society. For example, Giddens does not allow for the market being a principle means of widening social inequality (Finlayson, 1999:76). Moreover, the fact that the 'Third Way' prefers to focus upon social exclusion rather than inequality represents a limitation of analysis and a reduction of traditional social democratic objectives (Tsakalotos, 2001:41). In addition, it also ignores the Kaleckian argument that capitalism may be incompatible with sustained full employment in the absence of corporatist-institutional reform, due to the fact that tight labour markets empowers labour, reduces the impact of industrial discipline and is likely to be opposed by organised capital (Kalecki, 1943; Henley and Tsakalotos, 1993).

Giddens' (2000:37-8) counter-argument states, that, "the struggle to sustain and extend democratic mechanisms, control corporate power, and protect cultural minorities is fundamental to the third way, as it has been to previous forms of social democracy". However, this point sits awkwardly with his later argument, that;

> The division between left and right reflected a world where it was widely believed that capitalism could be transcended, and where class conflict shaped a good deal of political life. Neither of these conditions pertains today (Giddens, 2000:39).

Economic Democracy

The 'Third Way' places great emphasis upon an active civil society providing a viable constraint upon the power of both markets and governments (Giddens, 2000:64). However, Marquand (1997:336-8) suggests that this vision is notably narrower than the traditional social democratic promotion of "citizen empowerment", in that:

> The citizenship ideal is one of participation, activity and self-development and, by the same token, of accountability, transparency and scrutiny. Good citizens debate, argue and question; they don't simply accept what is handed out to them. And they cannot switch off their citizen selves when they go to work. That, of course, is what the early social democrats meant by social democracy. A democracy confined to the political sphere was no democracy; it had to embrace the social sphere as well. Citizenship was indivisible.

In addition, the 'Third Way' project has little or nothing to say about the traditional social democratic demand for economic democracy; in other words, the extension of democratisation from the social to the economic sphere (Tsakalotos, 2001:41). The promotion of employability as a means of empowerment of individual workers in the global labour market is an individualistic and distinctly different concept to the previous social democratic notion of economic citizenship through collective organisation and labour market institutions. Furthermore, the 'Third Way' is almost completely silent upon the potential of social ownership to further social and economic goals associated with social democracy. Instead, government regulation of private sector corporations is the preferred option, based upon the neo-liberal assumption that private ownership will inevitably lead to greater efficiency.

Evaluation of Clintonomics

Pollin (2001:60) notes that it is the record of the US economy that is often used to provide evidence to justify the superiority of the 'Third Way'. Indeed, at first glance, the performance of the US economy does appear impressive, with an average 3.7% growth rate, productivity of 1.8%, inflation of 2.5% and unemployment averaging 5.6% over the eight year Clinton administration. They are certainly an improvement over the Reagan-Bush periods. However, they are decidedly weaker figures than the Kennedy-Johnson 'Keynesian' period, despite the contributions made by the IT revolution (Pollin, 2001:65).

Fiscal policy played little active role in the Clinton period, being utilised to reduce budget deficits and, in the process, reducing public expenditure as a share of national income from 21.9% to 18.6% of GDP (Pollin, 2001:63). Moreover, the facilitating role played by the Federal Reserve, by maintaining relatively low interest rates, were the consequence of the "heightened sense of job insecurity and, as a consequence, subdued wages" (Greenspan cited in Pollin, 2001:73,76). Thus, economic growth depended upon an expansion in private consumption, encouraged by the wealth effects resulting from dramatic increases in stock market prices, rising at an unprecedented average of 13.9% growth above that of the real economy, being partly driven by the development of an investment bubble relating to 'dot.com' internet company shares. Consumer borrowing additionally rose from 77.8% to 94.2% of disposable income during the Clinton period (Pollin, 2001:67). Therefore, the underlying reality of 'Clintonomics' concerned an unsustainable asset boom, deriving from the stock market, together with private consumption financed via increasing personal debt (Pollin, 2001:61). Hence, Clintonomics failed to construct a viable economic model, that could sustain economic expansion into the medium and long-term, due to its over-reliance upon the rapid acceleration in personal debt to finance private consumption.

Is it Social Democracy?

Giddens (1998:26) claims that the 'Third Way' represents an attempt to "transcend" neo-liberalism and "old-style social democracy" by providing a "framework of thinking and policy-making that seeks to adapt social democracy to a world that has changed fundamentally over the past two or three decades". Indeed, social democracy once provided an alternative to command communism and free market capitalism, combining a concern for equality, social solidarity, social protection and full employment, with democratisation, economic efficiency, together with the combination of regulated capital and the social ownership and control of resources (Rustin, 2001:12; Glyn, 2001:3). However, Dahrendorf has subsequently announced the "end of the social democratic century", whilst Giddens claims "the death of socialism", and therefore that social democracy has lost its ability to transform society because "no one any longer has any alternatives to capitalism" (Giddens, 1998:3,43; 2000:19-20).

The rise of globalisation and subsequent decline of national economic self-management, together with the growth of post-Fordist production and with it the homogenised working class, have weakened the Keynesian-social democratic paradigm. Whether traditional social democracy methods retain the ability to deliver desired objectives remains to be seen. However, the solution of the 'Third Way' is to reject those traditional goals it cannot in any case achieve because of the inadequate policy instruments allowed by its neo-liberal foundations. Thus, full employment becomes regulated to a long-term aspiration, equality is restricted to opportunity and not outcome, whereas social policy is defined in terms of reducing social exclusion through the promotion of low paid employment opportunities.

The democratic control over a citizen's own life has become a non issue, with even the democratic control over national macroeconomic policy reckoned to be suspect due to acquiescence to capital mobility and acceptance of the EU's neo-liberal economic regime. Indeed, Arestis and Sawyer (2001b:58) claim that the macroeconomic stance pursued by leading 'Third Way' regimes, including the New Labour government, can be perceived as the "final triumph of (new) monetarism and the defeat of Keynesian economic policies"; at least, if not challenged by a renewal of the post-Keynesian-social democratic synthesis. Therefore it is an interesting question as to whether the 'Third Way' approach is really a modernised version of social democracy, or a new phenomenon, more closely related to classic political liberalism. This is one of the questions that this book will seek to answer through the consideration of the Swedish case study.

PART II
THE TRADITIONAL
'SWEDISH MODEL'

Chapter 2

Laying the Foundations of the Swedish Model

Introduction

This chapter establishes the background to the development of the 'Swedish Model'. It highlights the importance of Sweden's late and rapid industrialisation, its tradition of political rights and freedoms, a popular culture of self-education and participation in collective movements, together with the necessity for innovative analysis and organisation of a small nation, situated on the Northern periphery of the European continent, and ever reliant upon international trade for its prosperity. These features proved significant in creating the conditions for a thoughtful and creative social democratic labour movement, less tied to defending traditional privileges of a skilled-craft labour elite or revolutionary politics, than to an acceptance of a gradualistic path to social transformation and open to the latest ideas in political economy.

Capital, likewise, proved far-sighted in recognising that permanent opposition to a moderate labour movement might be in contradiction to its fundamental interests, and that co-operation between the social partners in managing the labour market may potentially deliver a positive-sum gain for all participants. Together with a proto-type Keynesian macroeconomic government strategy, using counter-cyclical fiscal policy to reduce unemployment, this combination of factors facilitated the development of what became known as the 'Swedish Model'.

A detailed examination of the traditional social democratic programme is essential in order to answer the subsequent question concerning whether or not the current platform developed by the Swedish Social Democratic and Labour Party (*Sveriges Socialdemokratiska Arbetarpartiet, SAP*) is in essence a continuation of this earlier 'Swedish Model'. Or, alternatively, whether it is a distinctive strategy, more closely resembling essential elements of the 'Third Way' as advocated by Blair-Clinton-Schröder governments, and in turn based loosely upon ideas developed by sociologists like Giddens, together with economists of the new monetarist and new Keynesian schools.

Development of the Social Democratic Movement

The development of the 'Swedish Model' is, first of all, the story of the growth and adaptation of the social democratic labour movement in Sweden. Without the establishment of the SAP in political office and the dramatic growth of trade union representation, primarily under the co-ordination of the blue collar Swedish Trade Union Confederation (*Landsorganisationen i Sverige, LO*), there would not have existed the secure platform on which the 'Swedish Model' was constructed. Consequently, it is worthwhile briefly recounting the major factors which lay behind the development of the Swedish labour movement, and which influenced its gradualistic strategy to achieve social transformation.

Democracy not Revolution

The first feature of Swedish history, which facilitated the relatively straightforward development of the social democratic labour movment, concerns the long tradition of political rights and freedoms, including laws safeguarding freedom of the press and of association. In the Feudal period, a free peasantry largely governed itself through democratically elected village councils, and farmed fields they collectively owned, thereby ensuring a relative independence from noble authority (Milner, 1989:50-1). The absence of a tradition of centralist despotic rule and emphasis upon decentralisation of decision-making helped to ensure that the SAP escaped the repression many other socialist movements faced. Furthermore, the fragmentation of the bourgeois parties facilitated labour movement development by preventing united and coherent political opposition.

Rapid Industrialisation

The second factor favouring the establishment of an organised labour movement concerned Sweden's relatively late and "remarkably rapid" industrialisation (Therborn, 1992:8). In 1870, agriculture and forestry still employed three-quarters of the working population with only 9% in building, mining and manufacturing, whilst by 1910 manufacturing accounted for over one quarter of total employment and it was only after 1930 that manufacturing exceed agricultural employment (Korpi, 1978:55-6). Industrialisation was financed by imported foreign capital equivalent to 5% of GNP between 1870-1910, funding the construction of a state owned railway network. Domestic capital concentrated upon private long term investment (Himmelstrand, 1981b:16).

   Economic development was further enhanced by a substantial emigration of surplus agricultural workers, making labour relatively scarce and thereby encouraging capital investment in labour saving devices. Between 1853 and 1930 approximately 1.5 million people emigrated from Sweden, which compares to the 1850 total population of only 3.5 million (SCB, 1993). However, the dynamic fueling Swedish industrialisation involved export-led growth (Lindbeck, 1975:7). This was initially dependant upon exports of minerals (including iron ore and uranium) and forestry products, before being overtaken by innovation and sophisticated manufacturing production.

   Rapid industrialisation facilitated the emergence of the labour movement in Sweden. Two hundred and sixty trade unions were already formed by 1890, whilst in 1889 more than 70 unions and workers' political clubs unified to form the SAP (Figure 2-1). The party's two initial priorities were to agitate for universal suffrage, which was a prerequisite for democratic control over the political and economic sectors, whilst simultaneously pursuing *uppfostran*, establishing education and self-teaching through study circles[1] to secure "organisational, intellectual and moral superiority" over their opponents (Branting, 1926viii:125).

Table 2-1: SAP membership 1889-1991

Year	No. of Members	Population (December 31)
1889	3,194	
1890	6,922	4,774,409
1900	44,100	5,136,441
1905	67,325	
1907	133,388	
1910	55,248	5,522,403
1915	85,937	
1920	143,090	5,904,489
1930	227,017	6,142,191
1940	487,257	6,371,432
1950	722,073	7,041,829
1960	801,068	7,497,967
1970	890,070	8,081,229
1980	1,205,252	8,317,937
1983	1,233,166	
1986	1,207,383	
1989	1,014,565	
1990	838,822	8,590,630
1991	259,077	

Source: Misgeld et al (1992:449).

Alongside maintaining the pressures for democratic reforms, the SAP consolidated their organisational structure through development of 427 labour communes (*arbetarekommunen*), opened by 1911 (Gidlund, 1992:102). These local party branches supported campaigning work and strikes, but also initiated cultural activities. They founded a complementary system of People's Halls and Parks (*Folkets Hus* and *Folkets Park*) providing facilities for libraries and cultural activities, in addition to political meetings. Socialist youth and women's movements were founded in 1892, whilst party newspapers and journals provide channels for information and debate. The Workers' Educational Association (*Arbetarnas Bildningsförbund, ABF*) was founded in 1892 to provide education and training for party members (Gidlund, 1992:102). Furthermore, the Swedish Co-operative Union

---

[1] Study circles are a form of self-education where between five and twenty participants provide a mutual educational experience from study materials provided without a teacher. In 1981, one-third of all Swedes were regular participants in adult education and 12% frequent participants (Milner, 1989:167). For further discussion see Blid (1989).

and Wholesale Society (KF) was established in 1899 to provide food and the essentials of life to workers at affordable prices.

The range of co-operative services eventually grew to include insurance products, domestic energy provision, a travel agency, housing co-operatives and a co-operative construction company, in addition to becoming the largest food retailer in Sweden (Milner, 1989:77-8). Thus, the SAP responded to its isolation from political power by constructing a popular set of labour movement organisations without retreating into its own "empires of workers' welfare societies" within worker ghettos (Esping-Andersen, 1992:40).

Non-political movements, including the evangelical church and temperance movements, also encouraged the organisation of self-education through study circles and supplied the labour movement with many of its leading members. They additionally legitimated changing conditions through collective organisation.

The industrial arm of the labour movement, the Swedish Trade Union Confederation (*Landsorganisationen i Sverige, LO*), was formed in 1898 by representatives of 24 national trade unions, 13 local unions and 19 co-operating organisations, together representing over 50,000 organised workers (Ullenhag, 1971). Though primarily a defensive organisation, LO were persuaded by the SAP to organise a general strike, in 1902, involving 120,000 strikers, in order to demand universal suffrage. The strike was defeated when 11 large companies instituted a lockout and the Swedish Employers' Confederation (*Svenska arbetsgivareföreningen, SAF*) was subsequently formed to counter increased labour movement strength.

This proved a pyric victory for the SAF because, despite a lock out of 18,120 workers for 135 days in 1905, the Swedish metal working employers were forced to concede trade union recognition, minimum wages in the industry, together with the reluctant acceptance of the principle of collective bargaining. Through organisation, trade unions had achieved 45% membership density in the metal working industry, and had thereby reduced the power resource difference with capital and this encouraged further industrial unrest (Korpi, 1981:192; 1983:45).[2]

---

[2] Power Resource Theory defines power as the activation of power resources of one actor in relation to those of other actors; effectiveness depending upon the cost of resource mobilisation and application, together with the degree of 'investment' converting high- to low-cost resources. The two central types of power resource within capitalist economies are capital and labour, with the former retaining permanent superiority by virtue of its wide application and low mobilisation costs. Labour's relative disadvantage varies over time, depending upon the extent it can increase its power resources – through control of government, maintaining full employment, decommodifying labour through the welfare state, increasing trade union density and the permeation collective values – or reduce capital's power resources through financial market regulation and exchange controls (Stephens, 1979; Himmelstrand, 1981b; Korpi, 1983).

The 1906 'December Compromise'

Rapid manufacturing employment expansion facilitated LO membership growth, averaging 22% per annum over its first six years (see Figure 2-2). Swedish trade unions had already become the "most comprehensive" such movement in the world (Therborn, 1992:9). The SAF's strategic response was to centralise industrial relations through negotiating a general settlement with a reluctant LO, thus bypassing individual unions by threatening a general lockout.

The resulting 1906 'December Compromise' ensured trade union recognition at the cost of the LO's abandonment of the closed shop. Both parties were "mutually accepted as representatives for their respective members" (Hufford, 1973:8). This committed the SAF to pressure its member companies to recognise LO unions and bargain in good faith, whilst LO unions had a comparable responsibility to threaten industrial action against rogue employers who refused to join the SAF.

The main contentious issue was the SAF's insistence that all collective agreements should contain a clause (paragraph 23)[3] stating that employers had the right to "freely appoint and dismiss employees, and to assign jobs and manage production" (de Geer, 1992:34). The LO begrudgingly accepted this "symbol of employers' prerogatives" if exercised within the boundaries established by collective agreements. The class compromise reflected the balance of power pertaining at that time. The SAF believed it had institutionalised its ability to "effectively combat and control" organised labour by forcing trade unions to negotiate "within the existing framework of society" (Hufford, 1973:8). However, the LO secured negotiating rights which it could utilise to expand membership.

Initially, the assumption that the institutionalisation of conflict would reduce industrial unrest proved false, as employers responded to a 1908-9 strike-wave by imposing industry-wide lockouts. The LO's response was to call a general strike. However, despite support from 300,000 workers, representing 90% of those employed in the affected industries, even 11,071,400 lost working days and 25 million kronor in lost output failed to defeat employer resolve and the simultaneous debilitating impact of the 1908 economic recession. Eventual defeat resulted in a serious setback for the unions, which, together with the impact of rising unemployment, resulted in a membership loss of 57% by 1911. The observed limitations to a radical use of the strike weapon did, however, present the LO with the opportunity to undertake a major restructuring of the union movement in order to enhance unity and cohesion between constituent unions. Consequently, by 1912 it had embraced industrial unionism as its "main organising principle" (Korpi, 1978:46,64). In the process, the LO strengthened its position as co-ordinator of union activity and as the pre-eminent think-tank for the union movement.

---

[3] Later renumbered clause 32.

Table 2-2: LO membership, affiliated unions and % average annual change, 1899-1990 (Source: LO, 1991e)

Year	No. TU's	Sections	Men	Women	Total	Change
1899	16	664	37,497	26	37,523	–
1900	21	787	42,546	1,029	45,575	+16.1
1905	30	1,291	79,888	6,747	86,635	+18.0
1910	27	1,576	79,461	5,715	85,176	-0.3
1915	27	1,502	104,652	6,056	110,708	+6.0
1920	31	2,799	247,242	32,787	280,029	+30.6
1925	34	3,901	349,749	34,868	384,617	+7.5
1930	37	5,064	495,649	57,807	553,456	+8.8
1935	42	6,318	597,629	103,557	701,186	+5.3
1940	46	7,602	813,199	157,904	971,103	+7.7
1945	46	8,622	922,004	184,913	1,106,917	+2.8
1950	44	8,886	1,037,986	240,423	1,278,409	+3.1
1955	44	8,739	1,090,891	293,565	1,384,456	+1.7
1960	44	7,930	1,150,895	334,840	1,485,735	+1.5
1965	38	5,193	1,168,431	396,183	1,564,614	+1.1
1970	29	2,425	1,199,603	480,532	1,680,135	+1.5
1971	29	2,305	1,215,616	517,523	1,733,139	+3.2
1972	27	2,086	1,223,352	548,133	1,771,485	+2.2
1973	25	1,931	1,236,604	571,006	1,807,610	+2.0
1974	25	1,886	1,250,324	613,157	1,863,481	+3.1
1975	25	1,837	1,257,978	660,107	1,918,085	+2.9
1976	25	1,792	1,262,062	699,165	1,961,227	+2.3
1977	25	1,729	1,269,765	748,026	2,017,791	+2.9
1978	25	1,684	1,272,526	784,764	2,057,290	+2.0
1979	25	1,629	1,273,502	815,888	2,089,390	+1.5
1980	25	1,582	1,271,346	855,447	2,126,793	+1.8
1981	24	1,530	1,263,899	876,915	2,140,814	+0.7
1982	24	1,460	1,258,024	902,958	2,160,982	+0.9
1983	24	1,392	1,270,217	925,556	2,195,773	+1.6
1984	24	1,266	1,282,427	956,161	2,238,588	+2.0
1985	24	1,201	1,286,747	976,082	2,262,829	+1.1
1986	24	1,178	1,282,604	994,683	2,277,291	+0.6
1987	24	1,149	1,276,786	1,003,099	2,279,885	+0.1
1988	24	1,100	1,267,710	1,008,010	2,275,720	-0.2
1989	23	1,038	1,252,093	1,008,111	2,260,204	-0.7
1990	23	1,011	1,225,766	1,004,635	2,230,401	-1.3

Universal Suffrage and the Dilemma of Proletarian Electoralism

Under relatively favourable circumstances, assuming universal suffrage could be secured, it is not surprising the SAP chose a gradualist or evolutionary approach to achieving socialism (Hamilton, 1989:156). However, universal suffrage was only reluctantly conceded by the bourgeois parties. As late as 1908, only 9.4% of Swedish citizens were entitled to vote and, even amongst this elite group, inequitable restrictions on election to the first chamber meant that every vote from the very rich was worth *forty* times that of the rest (Milner, 1989:48).

The introduction of proportional representation and moderate extension of the franchise did enable the SAP to gradually increase its parliamentary representation, gaining 28.5% of the popular vote in the 1911 general election, 36.4% in 1914 and 39.4% in 1917. However, it was ultimately the threat created by the Bolshevik revolution in Russia, and its popularity amongst significant sections of the Swedish working class, rather than the growing strength of liberal and social democrat parliamentary representation, that forced the bourgeois parties to reluctantly concede universal suffrage (Misgeld et al, 1992:451; Therborn, 1992:16). Universal suffrage was subsequently adopted in 1919.

Despite the SAP forming three minority governments, an electoral breakthrough was not immediately forthcoming and little was achieved. Bourgeois propaganda created fears about nationalisation amongst many ordinary Swedes, frustrating SAP electoral ambitions whilst the end of the wartime boom resulted in unemployment rising to 34% in January 1922 (trade-off between class purity and electoral success was required when the working class are not a majority of the electorate. The party thereby increasingly presented itself as a 'people's party', and this change in emphasis was encapsulated in the desire to transform society into a 'peoples' home' (*folkhemmet*) built upon democracy and national solidarity. Social and economic barriers dividing citizens into privileged and deprived members were to be eliminated. The good society was to be based upon democracy and solidarity. Thus, it was a device to criticise contemporary Swedish society. SAP leader Per Albin Hansson expressed his vision of social transformation, thus;

> If Swedish society is going to be a good citizens' home, class differences must be eliminated, social services developed, economic equalisation achieved, workers provided a role in economic management, democracy carried through and applied both socially and economically (Hansson cited in Berkling, 1982:227).

The *folkhemmet* approach prepared the ground for the electoral breakthrough of Swedish reformism because it introduced the idea that socialism could be advanced through social reforms inaugurated by the state (Hentilä, 1978; Olsen, 1992:98). The image of national solidarity facilitates the formation of a cross-class progressive coalition necessary for the SAP to secure a majority government, despite reservations from Wigforss who remained concerned that the 'people's home' might be misrepresented as unduly paternalistic by their political opponents.

Enhancing the basis of electoral support was insufficient, however, without coherent economic policies which could reduce unemployment and thereby consolidate labour movement strength in the long-term. The onset of the Depression, with unemployment rising from 12.2% in 1930 to 23.7% in 1933, together with the fragmentation of the bourgeois parties and the ineffectiveness of eight minority governments in the 1920s, had paralysed state policy and highlighted the need for an alternative economic strategy (Hamilton, 1989:169).

Developing the 'New' Economics

The shadow Finance Minister, Wigforss, used the forum of the Commission of Enquiry into Unemployment, which the SAP government established in 1926, to develop a proto-Keynesian strategy in conjunction with a group of young economists who became known as 'The Stockholm School' (Uhr, 1977:92). The 'new economic strategy' was publicly adopted by the SAP in a 1930 SAP Riksdag motion which asserted that unemployment was a permanent, not a temporary, feature of the business cycle (Landgren, 1960:60-2).

Instead of relying upon markets clearing through price and wage flexibility, the new policy identified a shortfall in purchasing power as the cause of unemployment. The state should therefore actively stabilise the economy by stimulating production *and* demand via increased public expenditure through extensive public works programmes and enhanced welfare provision. Market wages paid to workers employed in public works and increased welfare benefits were justified because they boosted demand. Wage cuts were rejected as a cure for unemployment. The SAP programme foreshadowed what later became known as Keynesian economic policy even though it predated the publication of *The General Theory* (Sainsbury, 1993:43).

There has been considerable debate about whether the Swedes *independently* developed an aggregate demand strategy similar to Keynesianism (Hicks, 1965:77; Sandelin, 1991:211), or whether they were influenced by the ideas that Keynes was already advocating but had not yet systematically developed (Rock, 1986:185). It is unlikely that Swedish economists were unaware of the vocal criticisms made by Keynes of orthodox economic policy, and nor the fact that the 1909 Minority Report of the Poor Law Commission, written largely by Sydney and Beatrice Webb, had recommended public works schemes to absorb the unemployed. However, SAP leaders, Branting and Möller, had themselves previously proposed achieving full employment through public sector expansion and fiscal policy as early as 1913 (Johnpoll, 1972:553; Ginsberg, 1983:112).

The difference in 1932 was that the SAP had sufficient strength to implement their ideas, whilst the depression caused many to reject the orthodox assumption that markets automatically return to full employment through price adjustments. Disequilibrium, or equilibrium at less than full employment, was equally, if not more likely, to occur than full employment equilibrium in a capitalist market economy (Lindbeck, 1975:31). Nevertheless, irrespective of the precise lines of influence, the fact remains that the combination of academic theory and practical success in their application thereby constructed a power justification for proto-type Keynesian policies.

The 'Cow Deal' and Keynesian Consolidation

The SAP fought the 1932 election on its crisis programme aimed at reducing unemployment which provoked vigorous opposition from bourgeois politicians, including the Liberals, as well as mainstream economists and bankers (Weir and Skocpol, 1985:131). The head of the Central Bank, Ivar Rooth, dismissed deficit finance as catastrophic since it would generate runaway inflation, whilst orthodox economists argued public sector expansion would 'crowd out' private sector investment. They claimed that rising public expenditure would not be reversed, creating a ratchet effect which squeezes private enterprise out of existence (Standing, 1988:2). Nevertheless, economic failure in office undermined bourgeois claims of economic competence.

The result of the election was a significant victory for the new strategy, with the SAP increasing their share of the vote to 41.7%, which meant that the socialist block received a majority of votes for the first time. However, a bourgeois majority in an upper Chamber protected by a longer election cycle, meant the SAP needed bourgeois parliamentary support to implement its crisis economic programme (Stephens, 1982:143). Nevertheless, the SAP formed a minority government and appointed a new Commission on Unemployment, directed by the leading figures in the Stockholm School; Myrdal, Ohlin and Hammarsköld. Their conclusions formed the basis of a 100 page motion placed before the Riksdag in 1932, containing analysis, calculations and practical proposals to deal with the crisis (Weir and Skocpol, 1985:131).

The parliamentary stalemate was broken after six months of negotiation when the Agrarian Party supported the crisis programme in return for $10 million in long term agricultural support and price stabilisation; a compromise which became known as the *kohandeln* ('cow trade'). Thus, the crisis package was enacted by May 1933 with only slight concessions, including minor reductions in expenditure plans and no initial agreement on unemployment insurance (Odhner, 1992:195). However, this did not alter the fundamental principle behind the measures; namely that loan-financed public works and welfare benefits increase demand and reduce unemployment.

One hundred and sixty million kroner were dedicated to create public relief jobs in construction, road building and forestry between 1932 and 1934, representing a two-and-a-half fold increase in these programmes. Central government expenditure almost doubled in real terms between 1930 and 1939, whilst revenue was planned to rise more slowly, thereby relying upon deficit financing to stimulate aggregate demand. Moreover, public work schemes began to pay market wage levels rather than the previous 15–25% below the going rate (Rock, 1986:185-6). The multiplier effect was calculated to stimulate the economy to the value of SEK300 million and create approximately 90,000 jobs (Trehörning, 1993:9-10). Bergström (1992:143) argues this budget was the "first conscious implementation of Keynesian economic policy in the world" and it appeared to succeed, with unemployment falling from 164,000 in 1933 to 36,000 by 1936 and 18,000 a year later.

Keynes or Exports?

There is considerable disagreement amongst economic historians concerning the impact of the 1930s crisis measures upon the Swedish economy and the extent they helped Sweden escape the depression. Hufford (1973:19) argued the crisis programme "played an important role in the recovery" whilst Trehörning (1993:11) considered its impact "not entirely clear". Bergström (1992:143), Lindbeck (1975:23) and Trehörning (1993:11) believed it had a "limited" impact compared with the export-led growth resulting from the maintenance of an undervalued currency throughout the 1930s. Unga (1976) argued the new policy was not consistently applied and deficit-financed programmes were viewed as a necessary evil in an extraordinary situation, not as valuable in themselves to stimulate expansion. Furthermore, whilst Heclo and Madsen (1987:48) agreed that the SAP had "some Keynesian impulses", they claimed that total public spending was too small to have a significant influence upon the economy. Central government budget expenditure almost doubled in real terms between 1930 and 1939, but as a percentage of GDP, this only represented an increase from 8% to 12% (Rock, 1986:185-6). Over the same period, government revenue rose from 8% to 9% of GDP, signifying the SAP *deliberately* stimulated the economy through deficit financing, even though the sums were modest when spread over the decade.

When evaluating the contribution the crisis package made to Sweden's recovery, however, it is important to place the policies in context. Deficit financing was previously unknown in modern industrial economies and viewed with distrust by orthodox economists as akin to debasing the currency. Four years before Keynes published his General Theory and gave theoretical justification to the new economics, the SAP's programme represented a considerable achievement, particularly when compared to the "ineptitude" of contemporary labour parties, including Britain in 1931 (Therborn, 1984:123). In this respect, the SAP were fortunate to achieve power after the bourgeois parties had been forced off the Gold Standard and were consequently free to undertake economic experimentation during a period of neo-liberal weakness. Nevertheless, the fact that the party had an appropriate strategy in place at this point is an achievement of some significance. Wigforss's election pamphlet *'Har vi råd att arbeta?'* [can we afford to work?] demonstrated that it was a *deliberate* Keynesian-type reflationary strategy which established the case for increased public spending to offset a shortfall in private investment and anticipated what later became known as the 'multiplier effect' (Wigforss, 1941:304-20).

It is, furthermore, a mistake to consider reflation and devaluation as distinct, opposing policies. Withdrawal from the Gold Standard certainly presented the Swedish export industry with the competitive advantage of an under-valued currency. However, *maintaining* this in the longer term would have been less likely under conventional policy since Keynesianism promoted flexibility and autonomy in economic decision making which orthodoxy dismissed (Rehn, 1984:160). The crisis programme also ensured the domestic conditions required to sustain export-led recovery (Möller, 1938:57-62). Reflation and agricultural support stabilised demand and enabled Swedish firms to export from a firm domestic market position (Lundberg, 1981:9-12).

Perhaps the primary significance of the crisis programme, however, was "the stable basis it laid for continuing Social Democratic Governance" by legitimising and institutionalising active government policy to maintain full employment and promote welfare by using all available economic tools (Olsson, 1991:149; Weir and Skocpol, 1985:132). In this sense, it mattered more that the SAP were *seen* to assert the power of government to defeat unemployment than what *actually* happened (Heclo and Madsen, 1987:48). Prior to the success of the 1932 crisis packages, the SAP had been unsure of itself and feared office "because it did not know what to do with it". Consolidating its successful crisis policies, the SAP claimed an "undisputed leading position" in Swedish politics, thereby raising the standard of democracy in the process (Molin, 1992:392).

The successful adoption of Keynesianism furthermore laid the basis for continuing social democratic government. The substantial support for the SAP programme resulted in a 46% share of the vote at the 1936 election and formation of a formal coalition government with the Agrarians. This provided a secure platform to develop Keynesian economic policies and insulate its achievements from reversal after future elections (Ginsburg, 1983:112). It also gave the SAP a new "ideological identity and a role in the country's mythology" as "the agents of Sweden's delivery from the Depression" (Olsson, 1991:149).

Thus, full employment was accepted as the prime economic policy goal, with public works augmented by an under-valued, managed-floating kronor, infrastructure development, low interest rates, a more progressive taxation system combined with selective tax benefits to stimulate production and employment, together with tax-based investment funds intended to influence the timing of investment decisions to reinforce counter-cyclical macroeconomic policy. Under these policies Sweden's real aggregate GDP rose by over 40% between 1932 and 1940, whilst unemployment fell continually throughout the decade (Rock, 1986:188). Renewed prosperity "helped to institutionalise the legitimacy of both active full employment policy and social democracy itself" (Esping-Andersen, 1992:44).

The Road to Saltsjöbaden

Consolidation of SAP executive power and two decades of uninterrupted trade union membership growth reduced labour's relative power resource disadvantage *vis a vis* capital. However, it additionally provided an alternative means for trade unions to seek a more egalitarian distribution of income rather than through the strike weapon. The pursuit of wage militancy had already made Sweden the country most prone to industrial conflict in the years up to the mid-1930s, and yet the unions knew that their gains were subject to the maintenance of union strength which could dramatically diminish if mass unemployment returned. Thus, the new political and economic environment had created conditions favourable to the agreement of a new class compromise (Korpi, 1981:185).

LO recognition that SAP control of the executive could ensure sustained full employment and transfer the distributional struggle into the fiscal system made it willing to discipline its own constituent unions to prevent industrial action undermining the SAP Keynesian full employment programme (Korpi, 1983:47). Thus, the LO accepted the principle of wage moderation to enhance international competitiveness if accompanied by SAP economic and social reforms; in effect to put "society first" rather than promoting sectional interests (Hufford, 1973:16). Likewise, the SAP required the continuation of economic success to maintain its electoral support. This relied upon a stable labour market and minimal industrial disruption to secure its ability to manage the economy effectively and deliver the jobs that would determine its ultimate political future.

Domestically-orientated capital[4] was equally prepared to co-operate with labour if it produced wage moderation, a stable labour market and higher profitability due to Keynesian reflation (de Geer, 1992:85). The LO's new moderation and 'society first' strategy strengthened the position of the SAF's new leadership, who realised the dangers inherent continuation of their militant opposition to social democratic government as they were likely to remain in power for the foreseeable future. The threat that a hostile social democratic government could pose to organised capital caused the SAF leadership to prudently adopt political neutrality in order to avoid unwelcome government intervention in the labour market (Swenson, 1989:47). Thus, all actors recognised their mutual interest in avoiding zero-sum conflicts in favour of increased welfare through enhanced productivity and economic growth.

The precise form of the labour market co-operation was established by the 1935 SAP-appointed Mammoth Commission (*Mammutredningen*) report, which proposed centralisation of labour market negotiations in order to improve national economic performance and material welfare (Swenson, 1989:50). With the SAF and the LO preferring to avoid government intervention in industrial relations, they forged a formal framework for rule-based collective negotiations; the 1938 Saltsjöbaden 'basic agreement' (*Huvudavtal*).

Despite its symbolic importance, the document was "surprisingly modest" since it largely codified existing labour market practices, establishing rules and procedures for negotiations and regulating strikes and lockouts (De Geer, 1992:87-9; Gourevitch et al, 1984:198; Olsson, 1991:24). The SAF accepted negotiations over a greater range of issues as long as the LO did not utilise its political influence to achieve by legislation what it could not get through bargaining, thereby confirming the primacy of negotiation (de Geer, 1992:88).

The new class compromise resulted from a decrease in the power differential between capital and labour primarily due to the entrenchment of the SAP in government. It relied upon both sides being "willing and able to assume responsibility for developments on the labour market" (de Geer, 1992:87-8; Korpi, 1981:195; 1983:47). However, it not only institutionalised conflict resolution but also recognised the advantage in avoiding zero-sum conflicts in favour of increased welfare through economic growth.

Centralisation of wage bargaining empowered the LO relative to its constituent unions and made "the strike weapon an instrument of the labour movement as a whole" (Gourevitch et al, 1984:199; Swenson, 1989:51). Moreover, workers, through association, could negotiate about wages and working conditions. However, management retained the right to manage and Keynesianism *favoured* capital by providing conditions for investment and expansion of production (Olsson, 1991:24). Thus, the class compromise was founded upon an assumed "stable division of

---

[4] Different factions of capital disagreed over the optimal allocation strategy for the SAF to pursue. Whilst domestically-orientated capital predominantly favoured accommodation with organised labour, the 'Directors Club' owners of the large export-orientated multinationals preferred an aggressive anti-SAP offensive and wage structures determined by international competitive factors. However, the failure of the 'great lockout of 1925' caused the SAF leadership to conclude "it was no longer feasible to crush or seriously weaken the labour movement" (Westerståhl, 1945:146, 154).

economic power and governmental power between opposing classes" whereby capital institutionalised its power superiority so that any challenge to it would be difficult within the Saltsjöbaden system (Korpi, 1983:48).

Problems with Stage One Keynesianism

Simple Keynesian demand management and deficit-financed reflation provided an economic policy framework which restored and maintained full employment during the 1930s. However, it was not designed to respond to unexpected inflationary pressures caused by excess demand in the aftermath of the Second World War. Consequently, wartime emergency controls over foreign exchange and imports, the rationing of scarce commodities, together with wage and price controls were reintroduced in the short term to "repress" inflationary pressures without eliminating their causes (Hamilton, 1989:185-6; Rock, 1986:190). However, the LO rejected long term reliance upon incomes policy as unacceptable and unsustainable in the over-heated post war period because it required trade unions to persuade their members to accept increases beneath those determined by market forces (Lindbeck, 1975:28-31; Meidner, 1986:63).

As voluntary organisations, whose stated aim is to secure the best possible wages and working conditions for their members, continued wage restraint, which may redistribute income from labour to capital, strains union organisational cohesion and threatens membership support (Robinson, 1973:51-2). In these circumstances, the union dilemma is either to pursue a militant wage policy with inflationary consequences or lose its members' confidence (Rehn, 1985:66). Wigforss (in Levin 1947) stated the problem thus;

> Nothing can prevent a whole population from granting increased monetary income – nothing except the realisation that it will not necessarily lead to a real rise in living standards. The difficulty with allowing such an insight to determine actions lies not least in the difficulty of finding one amongst all the recognised norms for a just distribution of the national income. Striving for social/economic balance is thus conjoined with attempts to find such mechanisms within economic life which take account of the need to promote enterprise and thrift, and at the same time, give various groups of citizens the feeling of receiving their just proportion of the results of production.

Full employment fundamentally increases the bargaining power of labour. Therefore persuading or compelling workers to refrain from securing an increased share of national income under such conditions is "futile" (Rehn, 1987:67). For unions to accept "unconditional responsibility" for "economic stability" would destroy their organisational authority (LO, 1951). Yet without solving inflationary instability, full employment may be threatened (Meidner, 1993a:214; Rehn, 1957). Indeed, Meidner (1987) argued that "*there can be no strong labour movement unless the government guarantees full employment*" [author's emphasis]. Thus, the trade union movement can only "survive as an independent and democratic organisation" whilst full employment is maintained by means compatible with a stable currency and free collective bargaining (Meidner, 1988:456).

Inflationary pressure associated with 'bastardised' Keynesian policy in action, had unintentional effects upon distribution, thereby itself causing tensions between different groups of wage earners and thereby threatening the internal cohesion of the Swedish labour movement (Erixon, 2001:16). Thus, the long-term health and vitality of the labour movement depended upon the maintenance of full employment by means other than those which presupposed "having to discipline their own working-class base to the degree that political support is lost" (Esping-Andersen, 1985:193). This was the basis behind the Rehn-Meidner Model developed by LO economists. This is discussed in the next chapter.

Chapter 3

The Rehn-Meidner Model

Introduction

Keynesian counter-cyclical aggregate demand management, combined with the maintenance of a competitive exchange rate, proved successful in reducing Sweden's unemployment rate when implemented during a period of international recession. However, once this 'new economics' had achieved its primary goal, namely the restoration of full employment, it was always obvious that this same strategy would have to be further developed to deal with the different problems created by an economy already at or near full employment. This was recognised by Keynes (1936:375-8) himself, together with William Beverage (1944:207), co-architect of the UK's post-war Keynesian-welfare state social contract.

International examples of institutional reform intended to accommodate the new pressures created by full employment have included incomes policies and/or wage bargaining co-ordination, industrial policies and the socialisation of investment through public ownership. However, in none of these cases did institutional reform go as far as in Sweden where, at the initiative of the trade union movement no less, the first attempt was made to devise a truly 'post-Keynesian' solution. Thus, whilst maintaining full employment as the over-riding goal of public policy, and endorsing the need for a sufficient level of aggregate demand to prevent involuntary unemployment, the burden placed upon simple demand management was partly alleviated by the introduction of a range of additional policy instruments, the combination of which was to be treated as a self-reinforcing new strategy. This new approach has been designated as the 'Rehn-Meidner Model', after its two principal architects, Gösta Rehn and Rudolf Meidner. Outside Sweden it forms the basis of what we term the 'Swedish Model'.

Rehn-Meidner – Theory

The fact that the Rehn-Meidner model was devised during a period characterised by an over-heated economy, helped to determine its disposition. Rehn and Meidner argued that *maintaining* full employment requires a different combination of policies than 'simple' (or 'bastard') Keynesian demand management required to eliminate mass unemployment.[1] Demand management's "inherent limitation" is that

---

[1] The Rehn-Meidner approach provided the framework for the 1951 LO Congress report entitled 'Fackföreningsrörelsen och den sysselsättningen' [Trade Unions and Full Employment] (Rehn, 1948). See LO (1953) for the English-language version.

it is too blunt an instrument to adapt to the economy's differentiated structure (Martin, 1992:29). Even when total demand equals total resources, dis-equilibrium is still implied within, and between, different sectors due to the dynamism of the economic process (OECD, 1963:20). Thus, whilst aggregate demand must be maintained at a level sufficient to sustain near-full employment, selective and locally applied policies can reduce residual and structural unemployment without creating inflationary pressures (Gourevitch et al, 1984:208).

The Rehn-Meidner approach was a "conscious break" with oversimplified Keynesian policy and therefore represents an evolution to a second stage Keynesianism (Martin, 1979). It therefore represents one of the few coherent economic post-Keynesian macroeconomic strategies (Erixon, 2001:13). In the short-term inflation was tackled by restricting private demand through fiscal and monetary policy, whilst in the long-term productivity must increase to make room for average wage rises without negative macroeconomic effects (Pontusson, 1992:60). The strategy was to construct an expansionist policy which "dampen[s] inflation instead of enhancing it" (Rehn, 1985:84). Consequently, it rejected the idea of a rigid trade-off between inflation and unemployment. The Rehn-Meidner model contains four essential components:

1. restrictive aggregate demand which squeezes profits,
2. **selective labour market policy** promoting structural adjustment,
3. **solidarity wage policy** favouring the competitive sector,
4. **increased public savings** compensating for the profits squeeze.

These instruments are intended to be complementary in terms of their ability to secure social democratic goals of full employment, compatible with low rates of inflation and inequality, and all contributing towards enhancing economic growth.

Restrictive Demand Policy

The Rehn-Meidner approach used Keynesian demand management to achieve full employment in the most efficient sectors of the economy but *less* than full employment over the whole economy. Maintaining sufficient aggregate demand to create employment in the least profitable sectors of an economy produces excess demand for labour in highly profitable activities (Martin, 1992:29). Limited short-term mobility and bottlenecks in labour and product supply imply that maintenance of full employment *solely* by demand management results in inflationary pressures and "unavoidable" wage explosions. To reduce pockets of excess demand, Rehn (1952:34) proposed combining selective measures with more restrictive aggregate demand:

> Purchasing power should be pumped away so that the demand surface sinks. The islands of unemployment which then must appear must not be flooded over again by re-raising the 'demand-surface', but instead must be removed.

Restrictive aggregate demand was intended to squeeze profits to prevent inflationary wage increases triggered by over-tight labour markets or distributional concerns (Rehn, 1987:67). Low average profits encourage employers to resist inflationary wage demands as the scope for price rises is small, whilst restrictive demand prevents excessive competition for scarce labour. Moreover, since past profits influence workers' mobilisation and bargaining attitudes, high profits may "increase worker demands for pay rises, regardless of other economic circumstances" (Olsson, 1991:92-3).

Bargaining theory predicts that trade unions will seek to share economic rents accruing to their company, and which would otherwise be declared as high profits and part distributed to shareholders. Thus, higher profits may encourage higher union wage claims (Blanchflower et al, 1996). Therefore, the Rehn-Meidner model concluded that profits should be constrained, in the medium and long run, in order to exert continual restrictive pressure on inflationary tendencies (Erixon, 2001:23). Furthermore, a high wage share of national income was considered essential to avoid inflationary wage demands. However, in the absence of wage formation in the interests of society (i.e solidaristic wage formation), rather than sectional groups, this may still prove insufficient to ensure non-inflationary wage growth.

The profit squeeze was additionally intended to enhance industrial rationalisation and provide the incentive for companies to innovate, in terms of product and work organisation, in order to reduce possible X-inefficiencies and thereby maintain competitiveness. The profit squeeze would, therefore, contribute towards structural change in the economy and hence towards higher levels of economic growth. Hence, restrictive demand management both creates the need to use active labour market policy in order to reduce pockets of unemployment remaining at a given level of aggregate demand, and also contributes towards its success in enhancing structural transformation.

Despite discussion of a restrictive demand management strategy, it is important to note that neither Rehn nor Meidner were against the adoption of a traditional, counter-cyclical Keynesian response to periods of prolonged recession. Moreover, the Rehn-Meidner strategy viewed labour market policy as a useful tool around the margin, but it was still the place of the Finance Minister to ensure a sufficient level of demand in the economy just short of the full employment level. In these circumstances, this more targeted, restrictive aggregate demand policy should prove more efficient in restraining inflation, during periods of weak as well as strong growth. Thus, aggregate demand management should therefore represent the policy norm (Erixon, 2001:21-3).

Hysteresis theory indicates the importance of Keynesian measures in reducing the rate of unemployment, since this is likely to have a long-term impact upon the future level of unemployment due to persistence effects (Elmeskov, 1994; Assarsson and Jansson, 1998). Endogenous growth theories suggest that unemployment can reduce long-run growth rates, due to its depressing impact upon capital formation, and therefore Keynesian measures to reduce unemployment could have positive effects upon economic growth (Daveri and Tabellini, 2000). Furthermore, long-term investment is dependant upon future expectations, and therein upon the general orientation of macroeconomic policies (Notermans, 1992:9).

Labour Market Policy

Meidner (1985:2) states that, whilst "it is obvious that the task to realise the full employment commitment is mainly the responsibility of general economic policy", *selective* manpower strategies, applied *locally*, are "supporting and complementary".

Table 3-1: Different types of labour market policies

Matching	Supply	Demand
Public employment services • Information • Job placement • Counselling	• Subsidised geographical mobility • Free labour market training • In-house labour training	• Public relief work • Recruitment wage subsidies • Youth teams • Sheltered employment

Labour market policies incorporate both demand- and supply-side measures (Table 3-1). The former reinforce counter-cyclical stabilisation, whilst the latter ease market adjustment by achieving a higher employment level at a given rate of inflation and promote structural change by reducing structural rigidities, search and transaction costs (Johannesson and Niklasson, 1974:4). Examples of demand measures include public works schemes, employment subsidies to individual firms, control over the release of tax-exempt private investment funds and state purchases placed with firms and in localities where unemployment would otherwise increase.

Supply-side measures, in contrast, ease the market adjustment process by achieving a higher employment level at a given rate of inflation, whilst simultaneously accommodating structural change. The dynamic nature of the labour market gives rise to constantly changing stocks and flows of vacancies and workers, whilst adjustment processes are weakened by job heterogeneity and segmentation of the labour market. Supply-side measures include reducing transaction costs through the provision of comprehensive information, alleviating the job-search process through an efficient labour exchange service, providing incentives for workers transferring to activities or localities where they are most required, and providing extensive training and retraining services to facilitate voluntary movement to new activities.

Criticisms of manpower policies focus upon *displacement* and *dead-weight* effects. It is argued that employment creation measures displace labour elsewhere in the economy or substitute for other workers in the same firm or sector. This assumes that demand for labour is limited; Layard et al (1991:64) reject this assumption as "almost totally misconceived". Manpower policy is applied in the belief that *structural rigidities*, rather than deficiencies in aggregate demand, are the main problems in targeted areas. Furthermore, dead-weight effects – that is when money is spent on employment which would have occurred anyway – are estimated to be a "smallish issue in the overall social cost-benefit calculus of most active labour market policies" (Layard et al, 1991:65).

One further criticism of manpower measures claims that they are inflationary since they prevent the open unemployment necessary to reduce wage costs (Calmfors, 1990:46-7). Such studies indicate that, at very low levels of unemployment, labour market policies may empower "insiders" by lowering the threat of unemployment, and thereby tolerate more wage pressure than a rise in open unemployment (Newell and Symons, 1987; Calmfors and Nymoen, 1990:399; Calmfors and Forslund, 1991).

These findings are, however, criticised by Layard et al (1994) on technical grounds. They are also contrary to the larger body of studies, which find that labour market programmes exert downward pressure upon wages by promoting competition for jobs through reducing skills bottlenecks and active search behaviour (Layard et al, 1991). However, there is a more fundamental point at stake here, because arguments that unemployment should be increased to reduce inflation are *inconsistent* with the full employment goal upon which the Rehn-Meidner Model is based. For as long as full employment remains the crucial objective, the question becomes whether stage two Keynesian policy efficiently achieves it in combination with rapid economic growth and low inflation. Furthermore, Meidner (1983:9) argues "there is simply no evidence" that manpower measures increase "the rigidity of the labour market, counteract mobility and influence wage formation in an inflationary way".

Labour market policies increase flexibility, facilitating adaptation to structural and industrial change. Without comparable promotion of structural mobility, a commitment to preserve jobs at all costs could result in economic stagnation and prevent adjustments necessary to maintain international competitiveness. Labour mobility moderates the high pay rises otherwise necessary to attract scarce labour to sectors experiencing high demand and bottlenecks in the supply of skilled labour. Therefore, labour market policy should lead to an inflation-dampening effect. However, as labour market policy also prevents a unemployment from rising, it may thereby limit wage reductions during recession periods. The overall impact of labour market policy upon inflation is, therefore, indeterminate and depends upon which one of these two effects predominates in practice (Erixon, 2001:20).

Katzenstein (1985) argues small countries with open economies require greater flexible adaptation to international market changes than larger nations. Reducing uncertainty and socialising costs borne by those affected by changing employment patterns reduces opposition to modernisation (Rock, 1986:193). Trade unions can actively promote modernisation to increase productivity and hence maintain full employment and rising living standards. Therefore, active labour market policy is a "necessary element of an economic policy that aims at full employment, stable money and a higher standard of living" (OECD, 1963:20).

Solidarity Wages Policy

First proposed at the 1936 LO Congress, solidarity wage policy demands 'equal pay for equal work' irrespective of the employing firm's ability to pay (Figure 3-1). Based upon the assumption that an unjust distribution is inherently unstable, rational wage policy requires unions to internalise a generally acceptable range of differentials according to skill, hardship or training (LO, 1951:96; Robinson, 1973:48). In practice, formulating a 'just' distribution of wages proved too difficult for the trade union movement, especially when including professional and white-collar income differentials. In its absence, the solidarity wages policy promoted preferential treatment for low paid workers who, "almost by definition", cannot benefit from decentralised bargaining (Robinson, 1973:50).

Solidarity wage policy promotes economic efficiency in three ways. Firstly, Holmlund (1988) argues that a comprehensive union organisation, capable of influencing the entire economy, has a greater vested interest in achieving efficient wage settlements. Unlike a fragmented wage bargaining framework containing multiple small unions, each only bargaining for a small proportion of an industry or craft-skill base, a monopoly union organisation cannot ignore the impact on jobs and inflation resulting from its wage bargaining demands. Therefore centralised wage bargaining is more likely to be associated with a superior trade-off between inflation and unemployment. This conclusion is consistent with the influential Calmfors and Driffill (1988) study.

Figure 3-1: A comparison of the solidarity wage policy and a wage strategy dependant upon the firm's ability to pay

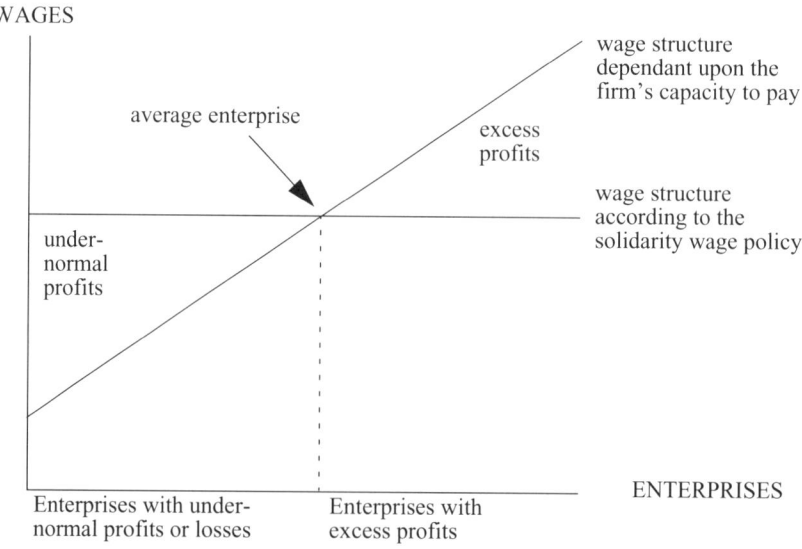

Source: Öhman (1985:31).

Secondly, it reinforces active labour market policy[2] by promoting structural change and labour market mobility. Elimination of 'wage dumping' means inefficient firms are not subsidised by paying lower wages to their employees for equivalent work to higher-waged posts in other firms in the industry. Moreover, moderate wage-cost pressure increases the substitution of capital for labour, accelerating business restructuring and rapid introduction of new technology; thereby stimulating greater labour and capital productivity (Bergström, 1980:6).[3] In the process, solidaristic wages would encourage economic growth (Erixon, 2001:18). Narrow wage differentials can additionally aid labour mobility, by minimising any loss of earnings if workers transfer from a high to low wage sector (Rehn, 1987:76).

Finally, solidaristic wages were considered to be less inflationary than the alternative, namely a reliance upon wage differentials to encourage labour to transfer to areas of skill shortage. Inertia in job preferences, and time lags involved in training programmes, contributes to the fact that wage differentials must be quite large in order to successfully attract employees from other sectors of production or to re-join the labour market from education, childcare and/or retirement. However, such large differentials would cause greater social inequality, and hence may create additional inflationary pressures due to the resultant distributional conflict between groups of workers. Rehn and Meidner both considered that the development of 'fair wages' would minimise such inflationary wage-price spirals. The solidarity wages policy should therefore be a constraint upon inflation (Erixon, 2001:18-19).

Collective Savings and Investment Policies

The rapid modernisation of Swedish industry envisaged by the Rehn-Meidner Model depends upon an enhanced supply of risk capital to compensate for lower self-financing caused by the profits squeeze (Rehn, 1952:52-3). Government ineffectiveness in altering private savings patterns, and the high levels of tax required to fund labour market policies and welfare state expansion, mean household savings are unlikely to fill this gap (Bosworth and Lawrence, 1986:107-110). Consequently collective savings must expand, either through enlarging the size of the public sector or increased supply of credit to private enterprises. Rehn

---

2   Solidarity wage formation and active labour market policy are mutually reinforcing. The former depends upon low levels of employee uncertainty and mobility costs to sustain membership support, whilst Meidner states that solidarity wage policy will "not function unless the government is willing and able to carry out an active labour market policy" and manage aggregate demand (Meidner, 1983:15; 1987a).

3   The Efficiency-wage hypothesis proposes that firms and industries may find it profitable to pay wages exceeding those that clear the labour market because the wage, or total compensation, stimulates productivity (Leibenstein, 1957; Solow, 1979). This effect may occur due to increased effort or human capital investment by labour, but could also occur because high wage pressure encourages increased capital investment which stimulates productivity (Perelman, 1995:145). In this context, the OECD found that Sweden had twice as many robots in industry as Japan, in 1983, and six times more than USA and Germany (Bächström, 1988:245).

(1952:53-4) suggested a supplementary pension scheme incorporating a fund to finance housing and stimulate economic growth, since:

> The membership of trade unions cannot be expected to accept private capitalists as the owners of all new capital....Thus, if we wish to avoid inflationary wage increases the increase of the national wealth must be, to a rather large extent, the result of collective saving done by the masses on the basis of high wages and high taxes.

Bosworth and Lawrence (1986:107-110) calculated that reliance upon collective saving to finance productive investment, warranted a 4% budget surplus to ensure adequate growth in long-run Swedish capital stock investment. Thus, the Rehn-Meidner strategy required a mechanism to steer investment allocation "as part of the role of accumulation would be transferred to public agencies" (Rock, 1986:193). The precise form of collective capital formation was the subject of debate in the following years, with Rehn advocating a supplementary pension scheme, whose funds were to finance housing construction and productive industrial investment, and thereby contribute to the stimulation of economic growth (Rehn, 1952:53-4). Alternative forms of collective capital formation were advocated, by Meidner, at subsequent LO congresses, but it was not until the late 1960s that the issue became a significant feature of macroeconomic debate (Tilton, 1990:203; Pontusson, 1992:61-2).

Delayed Implementation

The Rehn-Meidner Model was not initially implemented by the SAP because the conditions required were not present. The first impediment concerned the absence of parliamentary support for stage two Keynesianism, since the Agrarian coalition partners would not support the measures. Secondly, the Minister of Finance, Per Edvin Sköld, strongly opposed the programme (Wadensjö, 2001:9). Finally, the decentralisation of wage bargaining frustrated aspirations to enact the new strategy (Gourevitch et al, 1984:211-3).

Centralised Wage Bargaining

This last constraint was progressively relaxed throughout the 1950s as the SAF forced a reluctant LO into central negotiations (Pontusson, 1992:64). The return to decentralised wage bargaining after wartime regulation was marked by large wage demands and increased instability as pent-up labour frustration was worsened by international inflationary pressures due to the Korean War. Therefore, centralised bargaining, for employers, presented the best available method of achieving moderate wage demands and ensuring a low level of industrial conflict. It also interfered less with "managerial prerogative at the point of production" than workplace negotiation (Streeck, 1992:1).

Centralised bargaining, however, additionally provided the LO's leadership with the opportunity to implement its solidarity wage policy, demanded by the low paid unions, strengthening the centre against shop floor organisation and reinforcing the "primacy of the 'external' over the 'internal' union" (Streeck, 1992:2). Central negotiations, undertaken on behalf of all affiliated unions, enabled the LO to embody a shared collectivity, psychologically enhancing electoral support for the SAP (Martin, 1992:16-17). Bargaining co-ordination also reduced the risk of unforeseen wage explosions undermining the SAP's stabilisation measures. Accordingly, from the 1958-1959 wage round onwards, a degree of solidarity in wage increases was secured in return for a degree of moderation. Through these agreements, the LO enhanced its reputation amongst its members, the employers stabilised the labour market through one agreement and the government benefited from the removal of labour market uncertainty.

Supplementary Pension Scheme and the End of Coalition Government

Securing the political consensus needed for the adoption of the Rehn-Meidner model required the extension of SAP electoral support to enable the party to govern without the continuation of the coalition with the Agrarian Party. The latter remained very critical of the expansion of public spending and 'big government' associated with the Keynesian approach to macroeconomic management (Wadensjö, 2001:6).

Stung by rising criticism, the decline of the rural vote and haemorrhaging electoral support, the Agrarian Party sought a new policy profile. Whilst the SAP wanted to attract sufficient white-collar support to facilitate implementation of a distinctive range of policies. Thus, both coalition partners concluded they were damaged by their close association (Gourevitch et al, 1984:215). Therefore, following the Agrarians withdrawal from the coalition in 1957, the SAP responded aggressively by pursuing an electoral strategy which sought to create a *wage-earners front* (*löntagare*) around second stage Keynesianism, together with a series of social reforms aimed to appeal to white-collar workers (Åmark, 1992:81).

The main issue which facilitated a major increase in SAP support concerned the struggle for *comprehensive* earnings-related pensions (Gourevitch et al, 1984:217). Fifteen years of government commissions, a referendum and a deadlocked parliament was only narrowly overcome to introduce the National Pension Fund System (*Allmänna pensionsfondens, ATP*) (Heckscher, 1984:117). The support for the ATP by the white-collar trade union confederation, TCO, proved crucial and a majority of lower- and middle-level white-collar voters accordingly supported the SAP in the 1960 election, which proved a resounding success for the party. It received 48% of the vote and a one-seat majority over the bourgeois block, enabling the party to govern with the acquiescence of the VPK. LO pressure and a strengthened electoral base empowered the SAP, and, due to the gradual conversion of Prime Minister Tage Erlander, these factors facilitated the implementation of the Rehn-Meidner Model (Erlander, 1976; Wadensjö, 2001:9).

Rehn-Meidner Model – In Action

The recession of 1957-8 provided the opportunity for the SAP to expand labour market programmes rather than providing a general boost to aggregate demand. This policy switch was facilitated by the newly appointed Director General of the National Labour Market Board, Bertil Ohlsson, who strongly favoured an expansion of active labour market policies to target temporary increases in unemployment, rather than an indiscriminate increase in the overall level of aggregate demand (Wadensjö, 2001:9).

Labour Market Policy

Accordingly, public works schemes were expanded eight-fold and targeted training programmes four-fold (Rehn, 1985:70). Thus, whilst representing only 0.4% of the labour force, the significance of a reorientation in macroeconomic policy, towards reliance upon targeted manpower programmes, was unambiguous. Labour market measures continued to expand almost continuously throughout the period 1961-73 in terms of the share of GNP and government spending, with the most rapid increases during periods of recession (see Figure 3-2).

Figure 3-2: National Labour Market Board Expenditure as % of total government expenditure and as a % of GNP, 1949-1977

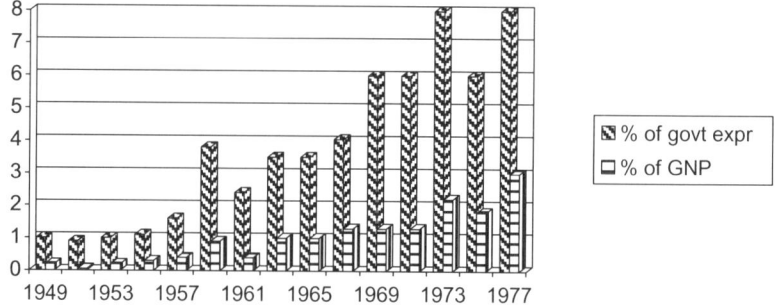

Source: Johannesson and Persson-Tanimura (1978:6).

Supply-side programmes steadily increased in importance, facilitating labour market participation, for women and disadvantaged groups especially, and labour mobility through a series of grants to persuade people to relocate to profitable, efficient companies; the latter were known as the 'moving van policy'. These measures combated structural problems which were becoming apparent in the Swedish economy, whilst increasing the range of employment opportunities to those not traditionally active. One consequence of the new strategy was that, between 1963 and 1975, labour force participation for women aged between 16 and 74 rose by 10%, with a similar increase during the following decade (Gladh and Gustafsson, 1981:93). Largely through these measures, Sweden achieved the highest labour force participation rate in the world (Tehörning, 1993:29).

There are two general criticisms of labour market policy. Firstly, that devaluation and expanding public sector employment were more significant factors in maintaining full employment in Sweden (Lindbeck et al, 1993b:236). Secondly, that manpower measures are inflationary because they prevent the open unemployment necessary to reduce wage costs (Calmfors, 1990:46-7). The first criticism is accurate although it misunderstands that labour market policy was intended to supplement, not displace, macroeconomic strategy. However, the second criticism implies that unemployment should be increased to reduce inflation which is *inconsistent* with the full employment goal upon which the Rehn-Meidner Model is based. If full employment remains the central objective of government policy, the issue becomes whether stage two Keynesian policy efficiently achieves it in combination with rapid economic growth and low inflation.

Evaluation of labour market policy found "strongly favourable" effects for intensified placement assistance, compulsory notification of vacancies and geographic mobility grants (Björklund, 1991; Johannesson and Persson-Tanimura, 1978). The efficiency of public works and training schemes proved generally positive, although studies disputed their precise impact. Training had the greatest benefits for those in a weak labour market position – women, immigrants, disabled and those without vocational training – than for skilled individuals. It is therefore *at least probable* that Sweden's adaptation to economic change was facilitated by manpower policy, preventing mass unemployment and labour market rigidity suffered by other European countries (The Economist, 1987). Moreover, these policies paid for themselves since the amount spent on active and passive measures was no higher than the European average (Layard, 1991:4-5).

In a thoughtful summary of the effective role of labour market policies, Meidner (1997:95-6) argues that it has played a key role despite its limited volume accommodating between 3–4% of the labour force, particularly during periods of very low unemployment. Labour market programmes were, however, conceptualised as part of the overall macroeconomic strategy and not a stand-alone measure. Thus, over-reliance upon manpower measures would inevitably reduce their effectiveness (Forslund and Kruegaer, 1995; Jackman, 1994). Nevertheless, even here, labour market policies contributed towards the avoidance of long-term unemployment and thereby prevented the process of hysteresis from maintaining high levels of unemployment, together with ultimate exclusion from the labour market.

Solidarity Wages Policy

The expansion of labour market measures provided the necessary conditions for the LO to pursue a solidaristic wage policy in negotiations with the SAF; offering a degree of wage moderation and labour market stability in return. Advocates of the solidarity wages policy argued that by reconciling "divergent interests within the labour movement", LO could exercise voluntary wage restraint without suffering organisational disintegration (Higgins and Apple, 1983). Solidaristic wages became an "integral part of LO's entire strategy of conflict, a rallying principle" and increased efforts were made to improve the relative wages of low-paid workers (Olsson, 1991:112) (Figure 3-3). TCO bargaining cartels typically followed LO's lead on this issue because most trade union leaders shared "a deep ideological commitment to equality" (Hibbs, 1990:20).

Figure 3-3: LO wage distribution 'cone' – % variance of average wages *within* *contract areas* from the average nationally negotiated wage

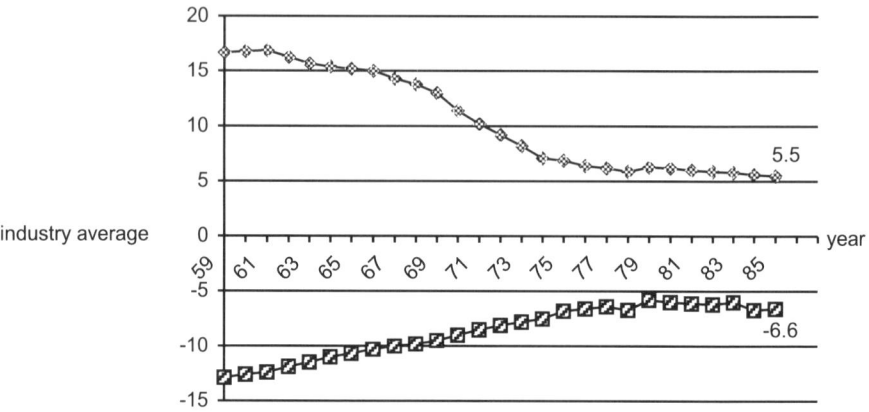

Source: Elvander (1988:36).

The main criticism of solidarity wage formation is that relative wages are distorted by not reflecting local conditions and skill differences, thereby hampering economic efficiency and labour mobility (Lindbeck et al, 1993b:226-252) (Figure 3-4). However, this can be rejected on three main grounds.

Firstly, Sweden's inter-industry wage structure replicates neo-classical norms more closely than the decentralised, largely non-bargaining, labour market of the USA (Hibbs, 1990:19). Secondly, Labour mobility is enhanced "precisely because the wage structure had become so compressed" as firms benefit from relatively inexpensive skilled workers (Rehn, 1987:76).[4] Thirdly, because real wage flexibility is associated with the *degree of centralisation* in wage bargaining.

---

[4]   High marginal tax rates may have facilitated acceptance of the wage moderation element of the solidarity wages policy for high paid workers, whilst high payroll taxation may explain minimal employer resistance to lower differentials as this meant lower costs for enterprise (Hibbs, 1990:17).

Figure 3-4: Discounted lifetime salary dispersion for occupational and income groups within Sweden (skilled manual worker-welder = 100)

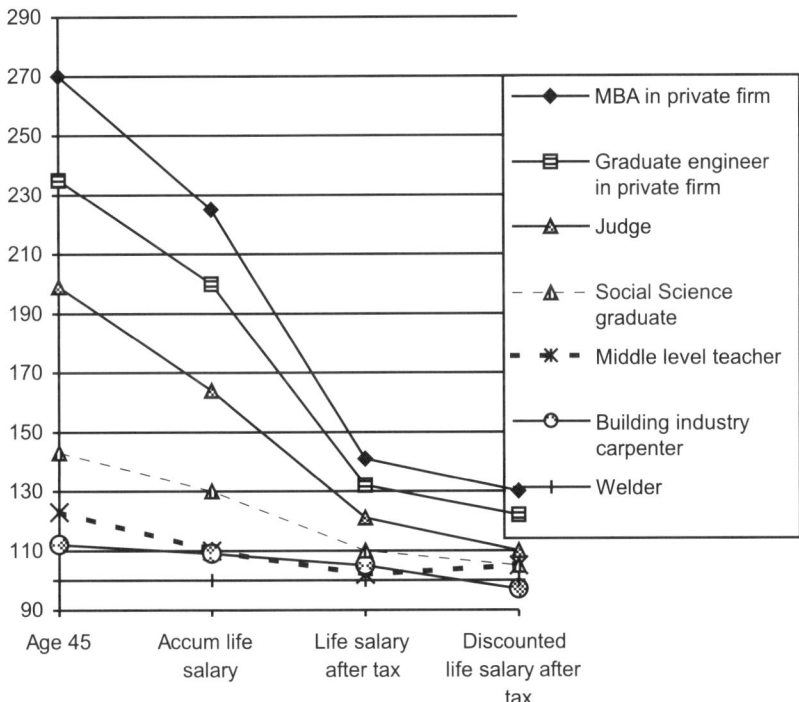

Source: Lindbeck (1983:238).

The pioneering study by Calmfors and Driffill (1988) found that high- as well as low-centralised structures adapted more flexibly to market conditions, leading to a superior inflation:unemployment trade-off. This result was largely confirmed by Amoroso and Jespersen (1992:79-80) and Calmfors and Nymoen (1990). However, a number of other studies suggested a more linear relationship, with higher levels of corporatism, centralised and/or co-ordinated wage bargaining internalising negative externalities, reducing social conflict and assisting economic performance. This corporatist literature includes Cameron (1984), Bruno and Sachs (1985), Crouch (1985), Rowthorn and Glyn (1990), and Henley and Tsakalotos (1995:186-9) (Figure 3-5). A subsequent study, undertaken by Iversen (1999) claimed that the macroeconomic impact of the degree of co-ordination of wage bargaining depended upon its interaction with the extent to which the national monetary authority pursued an accommodatory or non-accomodatory policy stance.

Figure 3-5: Corporatism, unemployment and real wage flexibility

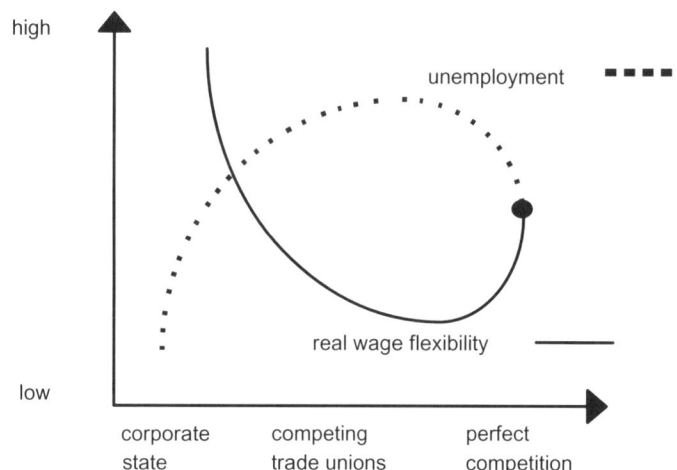

Source: Amoroso and Jespersen (1992:80).

Sweden's wage bargaining system kept real wage increases close to productivity gains, achieving the lowest level of Western industrial conflict outside Switzerland, and enhanced a superior inflation-unemployment trade-off (Bosworth and Rivlin, 1986:44; Layard et al, 1991:98,398) (see Figures 3-8 and 3-9). Söderström (1985) concludes that stabilisation of employment in exchange for union wage moderation is Pareto superior to alternative accommodation or non-accommodation strategies.

Collective Savings and Investment

The state earnings-related pensions system (*Allmänna pensionsfondens, ATP*) included three buffer stock 'AP-funds' which initially fulfilled collective savings requirements. They accounted for a majority of equity capital and long term credit, and for 35% of the total credit market at their peak between 1970 and 1973 (Pontusson, 1984:5; 1992:80). The public sector's share of total savings increased faster than in any other OECD country between 1962 and 1972, rising from 35% to 44% (Erixon, 2001:28). However, as pension payments grew, the significance of the funds declined. Moreover, their restriction to the bond market prevented them being used as instruments of industrial policy and investment steering. Rigorous foreign exchange controls were alternatively employed to ensure that excess profits and savings were reinvested in the Swedish economy rather than seeking higher returns in other countries (Amoroso and Jespersen, 1992:82). Nevertheless, by definition, restrictions are a blunt instrument when seeking affirmative action.

Investment Funds

One reform which the SAP were able to accomplish in 1955 concerned a comprehensive overhaul of the tax-exempt investment funds Wigforss introduced in 1938. Corporations could deposit up to 40% of their annual profits in these funds, 40% of which remained in a blocked, interest-free account at the Central Bank in order to lower liquidity during boom periods. Depreciation allowances were tightened so the investment funds became the most efficient way for tax avoidance and considerable corporate funds became deposited within this system.

Figure 3-6: Statutory and effective profits taxation for industry, 1953-1975

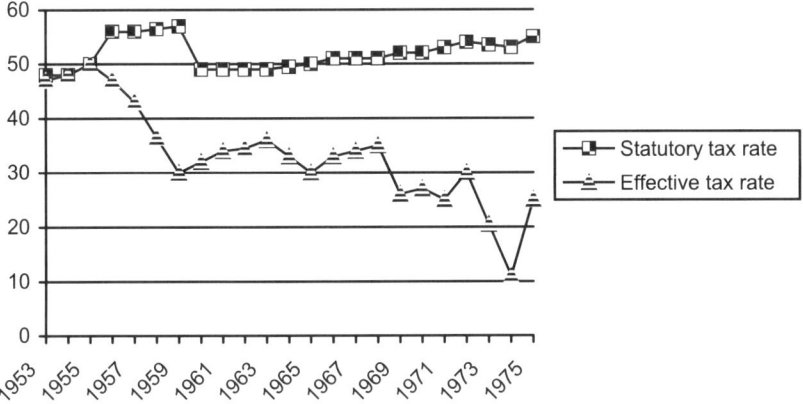

Source: Pontusson (1992:73).

Between 1956 and 1965, the number of firms with investment funds rose from 640 to 2566, whilst their total volume increased from SEK0.25bn to SEK3.3bn. Investment fund savings accounted for 3.2% of GDP in the 1960s (SOU, 1977:294). These funds were extremely favourable for capital, reducing effective corporate tax rate considerably below the statutory rate (Figure 3-6). Whilst total taxes set by local and central government rose from 26% of GDP in 1955 to 41% in 1970 and 52% in 1979, taxes levied upon corporate profits fell from 11% in 1955 to 3% in 1970 and 1979 (Bergström, 1982:12). As long as profits were reinvested, corporations faced a generous taxation regime.

Investment funds were released during the recessions of 1957-8, 1962-3 and 1967-8, for counter-cyclical stabilisation. Though the first release was delayed until the recovery had already begun, Pontusson (1992:78) calculated that during the 1960s the investment fund system "appears to have been effective as an instrument of macroeconomic management". Henning (1977:76-82) found that almost all corporations informally negotiated with the government concerning releases of investment funds and the effects of such releases were significant. In 1968, for example, releases from investment funds accounted for 25% of total industrial investment and 12% of gross capital formation. For the period 1956-70 as a whole, they financed an average of 5% gross fixed capital formation when general releases were allowed, whilst only 2.6% at times of selective releases (Pontusson, 1992:77).

Whilst a powerful tool for general economic stimulation, investment funds did not significantly *steer* investment. Pontusson (1992:79) suggested the government never effectively used them for industrial or regional policy and that their effectiveness was limited by their dependence upon voluntary business participation. Greater firm- or region-specific releases were allowed during the 1960s and 1970s, resulting in weaker economic stabilisation and corporate profit subsidisation. Simultaneously pursuing counter-cyclical and industrial or regional policy goals through this one instrument proved incompatible.

Macroeconomic Stance

Productivity growth in Swedish manufacturing industry was high, compared to other industrialised economies, during the first two decades of the Rehn-Meidner model (Erixon, 2001:26). Indeed, manufacturing productivity averaged 7.5% per annum between 1964-9, whilst value-added rose by over 5% (Ministry of Finance, 1990:45). Structural change in manufacturing was notably rapid during the 1960s and the first half of the 1970s, especially when compared to the larger industrialised economies (Andersson et al, 1998). Exports claimed an increasing proportion of world trade disproportionate to Sweden's population size, whilst GDP per capita increased steadily, remaining second only to Switzerland during this period (Hufford, 1973:24; *Svenska Handelsbanken*, 1990:4). Calculated by way of purchasing power parities, Sweden's GDP per capita ranked third amongst OECD nations in 1970, 8% above the average (Ministry of Finance, 1993:46).

In terms of the key economic variables, the Swedish economy also performed admirably. The Economist (1991:65) stated that Sweden had achieved "one of the best trade-offs between unemployment and inflation of any industrial economy". Unemployment remained low (Figure 3-7), whilst inflation rates were certainly no worse than the average for European Union countries (Figure 3-8).

Stage two Keynesian policy was designed to achieve sustainable full employment without damaging labour movement coherence. In this, it certainly succeeded, as economic success reinforced continuous SAP government and LO membership expansion. It provided the labour movement with a coherent approach to economic management and established the LO's "pivotal role" within the "success of labour reformism in Sweden" (Pontusson, 1992:96). At the high point of stage two policy, the SAP received 50% of the vote in the 1968 election (Rehn, 1985:80). Thus, the Swedish Model contributed towards the maintenance of the political support essential for the furtherance of its social democratic goals.

Despite its association with economic success, the Rehn-Meidner second stage Keynesian strategy was not fully implemented. This was partly due to the fact that the SAP found it more difficult to impose fiscal restraint than to expand welfare and public services (Meidner, 1987a:7; Olsen, 1992:105). Tax increases were often wrongly timed, not applied sufficiently early in economic upswings and occasionally accompanied by "a trace of 'vulgar Keynesianism'" (Pontusson, 1992:78; Rehn, 1985:80; Söderström, 1990:63-7).

Figure 3-7: Unemployment rates in Sweden and the EU (12), 1964-1991

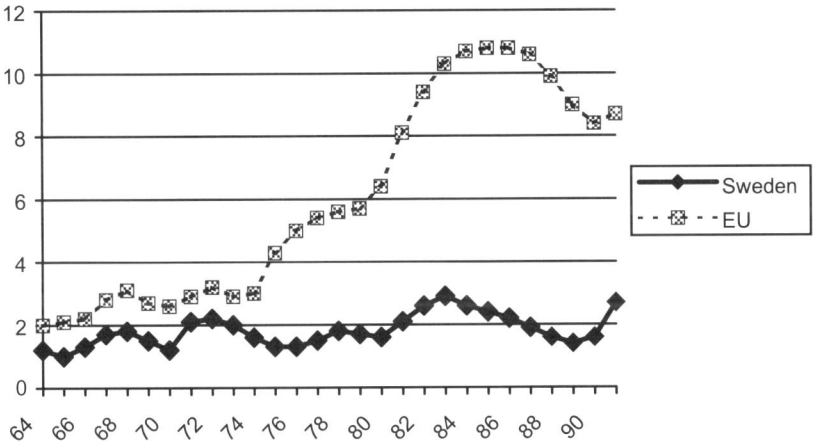

Sources: Layard et al (1991:528); OECD data.

Figure 3-8: Inflation rates for Sweden and the EU (12) average, 1963-1991

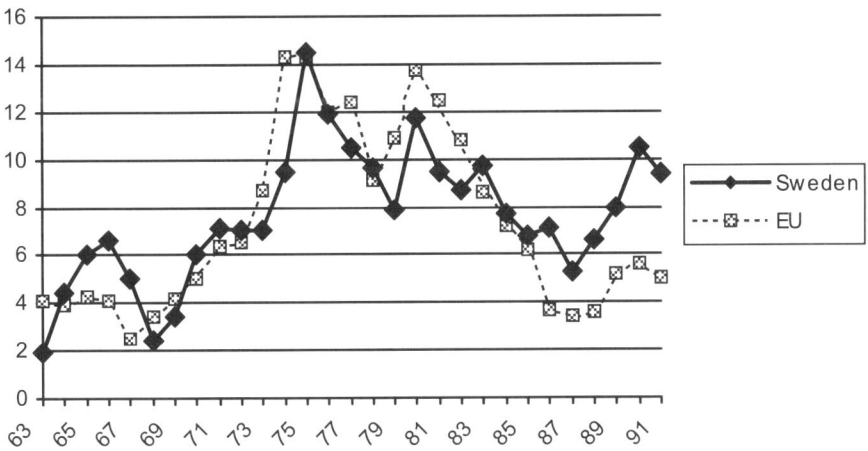

Sources: Layard et al (1991:532); OECD data.

Erixon (2001:29) argues that the deflationary effects of macroeconomic policy during the 1966-8 and 1970-2 mini-recessions owed more to the "difficulties of implementing Keynesian fine-tuning" than the reliance upon the restrictive aggregate demand portion of the Rehn-Meidner model. The reduction in general profit levels was due more to an increase in international competition than the squeeze demanded by the Rehn-Meidner strategy (Södersten, 1971:324-9; Erixon, 2001:29). Moreover, Rehn (1985:82) states labour market policy "suffered from 'ideological lags'" so insufficient consideration was taken designing programmes to be "effective instruments against inflation".

Conclusion

The Rehn-Meidner model was a remarkable innovation in economic strategy, constructing, as it did, a viable post-Keynesian framework that went beyond simple Keynesian demand management, but one that was based upon the needs and objectives of a social democratic labour movement. Each element of the model was intended to complement all other elements, so the strategy should be viewed as a holistic approach, rather than simply being the sum of individual policy instruments. Each element of the model had multiple goals, although this difficulty was eased by the fact that the work of individual tools were complemented by other instruments. Thus, it was the sum of these individual policies that were intended to make maintain full employment, consistent with international competitiveness, low inflation and high growth rates, together with a reduction in income in equality, the development of the welfare state and a reinforcement of trade union solidarity through a sympathetic wage bargaining system. Moreover, the approach appeared to be rather successful in terms of its objectives, certainly during its first fifteen years. Swedish inflation, productivity, growth and structural change rates compared favourably with other industrialised nations, whilst unemployment was squeezed to very low levels, inequality was progressively reduced and a comprehensive welfare state consolidated.

The performance of the Rehn-Meidner model remains contentious. In part, this is due to theorists' differing viewpoints, often coloured by the allegiance of the commentator to one or other economic school of thought, either in sympathy with, or opposed to, the basic tenants of the strategy. Indeed, Swedish economic development is currently being subjected to the type of historical revisionism that has been applied to the 1930s depression and the contribution of Keynesian policies to its ultimate solution.

The fact that the theory was imperfectly applied appears to be uncontrovertible. Yet, the economy did appear to work rather well during this period, and Sweden furthered its varied objectives better than most comparable nations. Thus, when all the factors are considered, Milner (1989:110) is probably correct in his assertion that the Rehn-Meidner Model "undoubtedly contributed substantially toward making Sweden a model of stable growth and full employment". Nevertheless, despite its obvious successes, stage two Keynesianism was increasingly strained through tensions inherent within the strategy itself. These limitations of the Rehn-Meidner model are considered in the next chapter.

Chapter 4

Limitations to Stage Two Keynesianism

Introduction

The Rehn-Meidner model represented an evolution or adaptation of Keynesian theory and strategy. In so far as it was ever fully implemented, the Rehn-Meidner approach sought to utilise a wider range of instruments in order to target interventions upon supply side bottlenecks in addition to demand management intended to maintain a high, but not quite full, level of employment, consistent with a low rate of inflation and the maintenance of international competitiveness.

This strategy worked well during its first two decades of operation, when measured by most macroeconomic variables, relative to other OECD countries. Nevertheless, by the mid-1970s, there were a number of identifiable problems that second stage Keynesianism found increasingly difficult to solve. Certain of these issues were driven by changes in the external economy. Others were caused by tensions inherent within the model itself.

Tensions in the Rehn-Meidner Model

The three most prominent contributory factors were:

- *Democratic* – demand for workplace influence weakens Saltsjöbaden approach;
- *Macroeconomic* – insufficient industrial investment to sustain full employment in the long-term, combined with insufficient restraint upon inflation;
- *Egalitarian* – investment-constrained limits to redistribution.

Employee Demands for Influence at the Workplace

Rationalisation, high occupational and geographical mobility, together with an intensification of work, imposed unanticipated "substantial burdens" on many workers and fuelled demands for improved working conditions (Haas, 1983:21-2; Hamilton, 1989:196-7; Rosenblum, 1980:269). Second stage Keynesianism had secured "substantial gains" for employees but "at a high cost to workers themselves" (Esping-Andersen, 1981:124). Employees were increasingly frustrated with the limitations placed upon their influence over their working lives within their immediate working environment, due to their continued acceptance of the terms of the 1930s class compromise and the centralisation of bargaining in the hands of a remote union bureaucracy (Ahrne and Clement, 1992:476). Affluence and sustained full employment empowered labour and hence encouraged demands for an improved working environment and greater work fulfilment (Crouch, 1979:14).

Discontent was dramatically manifested by a wave of wildcat strikes which swept over Sweden in 1970, with 250 recorded disputes causing 155,000 lost working days, compared to only thirty five in 1967 (Andersson, 1969; Swenson, 1989:89). This was symbolised by the state-owned LKAB iron ore mine strike, where the strikers expressed dissatisfaction with their own union as with management. Perceptions of a distant and unresponsive union bureaucracy were clearly articulated during the dispute (Heclo and Madsen, 1987:53).

The two specific demands made by the strikers, namely for higher wages (in order to narrow differentials with white-collar workers) and increasing employee influence within the workplace, both created problems for a union movement content to operate within the Saltsjöbaden class compromise. This held that managers had the right to manage at local level, restrained only by the increasing scope of negotiated agreements. Moreover, LO unions were incapable of ensuring a narrowing of differentials with white-collar workers without demanding substantial wage rises for the highest paid blue collar workers, a strategy which would undermine the solidarity wages policy as this would increase inequality within the LO sphere (Swenson, 1989:87).

'New Factories' or Industrial Democracy

The sudden outburst of shop floor frustration took central union officials and senior management representatives by surprise, because their elite level collaboration had worked to their mutual advantage. However, in response to this demonstration of dissatisfaction, unions and management both sought to re-establish their credibility with their own membership-employees, and sought to craft reforms that could encompass demands for increased employee participation within the workplace.

The SAF initiative became known as the 'New Factories' approach, after their report of that name. This involved replacing linear production methods by work teams, task rotation and a lengthening of work cycles to give greater autonomy in an attempt to humanise work and increase efficiency (von Otter, 1986:9-12). The Volvo-Kalmar factory, opened in 1974, embraced many of these concepts. This approach, whilst making work more tolerable, remained Taylorist[1] and gave employees the appearance of greater freedom at work whilst increasing managerial control (Higgins, 1986). It also explicitly refused to contemplate the enlargement of local union responsibility to bargain over non-wage workplace issues. However, whilst the LO conceded the need for enhanced workplace participation, they were adamant that any formal mechanism should centre upon existing union organisational frameworks, and not be used by management as a means to bypass collective representation (Haas, 1983:22). Thus, desperate to satisfy grassroots union members and maintain its internal organisational coherence, the LO ignored the Saltsjöbaden compromise and demanded that the social democratic government introduced industrial democracy legislation (Gourevitch et al, 1984:257).

---

[1] Frederick Taylor's 'scientific management' divided the work operation into its smallest segments, facilitating its inspection, measurement and control. Employee initiative remained subject to detailed managerial control over the work process (Taylor, 1947).

The resulting reforms, included; employee representation on company boards, a job security act, prior notification of dismissals, rights for shop stewards, a work environment act, equal opportunities legislation and a co-determination act (*MBL*) (Åmark, 1988; Edlund and Nyström, 1988). These reforms were supported by 75% of the electorate and prompted the centre parties to advocate firm-level industrial democracy as an alternative to elite-level social democratic corporatist collaboration (Petterson, 1977:89-91). The SAP believed the reform package reinforced its 'wage-earner' coalition and Prime Minister Olof Palme described it as "the greatest diffusion of power and influence...since the introduction of universal suffrage" (Carnoy and Shearer, 1980:261; Hancock and Logue, 1984:252).

The reforms were intended to strengthen labour's position within the labour market and provide workers with a direct influence in corporate decision making. However, by leaving managerial prerogatives unchallenged, the industrial democracy initiative was ultimately a disappointment for the trade unions (Hancock et al, 1991:153; Holzhausen, 1982:91). Whilst they undoubtedly improved the working environment for Swedish employees and secured union access to corporate information, the reforms largely codified existing employee participation as practised in larger Swedish companies (Hanami and Blanpain, 1987:194).

Macroeconomic Problems: Excess Inflation and Insufficient Investment

Micro-level problems for the labour movement were augmented by macroeconomic tensions that stage two Keynesianism was failing to resolve. The first occurred towards the end of the 1960s when the "allocative outcomes of private investment decisions began to diverge from labour's interests" causing insufficient investment in productive industry to sustain full employment in the long-run (Pontusson, 1992:98). Balance of payments current account deficits in 1965 and 1969-70 signified structural problems which second stage Keynesianism had failed to prevent. Indeed, the 1970 government 'Long-Term Survey' calculated that restoring long-term equilibrium required annual domestic industrial investment growth of 6.5% over five years (Gourevitch et al, 1984:268-9).

Bergström (1980:17) estimated that replacement investment, as a proportion of gross investment, had risen from 50% in 1950 to 65% in the 1970s. Thus, a given volume of investment contributed less to capacity expansion than two decades earlier, necessitating higher investment levels than previously required to sustain full employment output. Moreover, insufficient domestic savings, exacerbated by budget deficits restricting collective savings, caused interest rates to rise and increased international borrowing, thereby reducing Swedish macroeconomic policy autonomy (Olsen, 1992:68) (Figure 4-1).

International instability compounded Sweden's problems as the global inflationary boom of the early 1970s, together with a corresponding surge in demand for raw materials, resulted in extraordinarily high industrial gross profits of 23% in 1974 (Erixon, 1985). The strong imbalance so generated was, of course, intensified by the supply shock caused by the rise in oil prices. Economists had predicted a recession, so the LO had negotiated a low one-year deal, but instead found that excess profits remained high, and hence wage drift rose to record levels. Aggregate demand management was not sufficiently restrictive to prevent the very large excess profits, and, as predicted by the Rehn-Meidner model, this high level of high industrial profitability presented problems for the LO's solidaristic wage strategy. It proved impossible to restrain trade unions demanding their fair share of the economic rents which would otherwise have all accrued to capital owners, thereby worsening the unequal distribution of income (Lundberg, 1985:25).

Figure 4-1: Swedish national savings and investment, % of Swedish GDP, 1961-1988

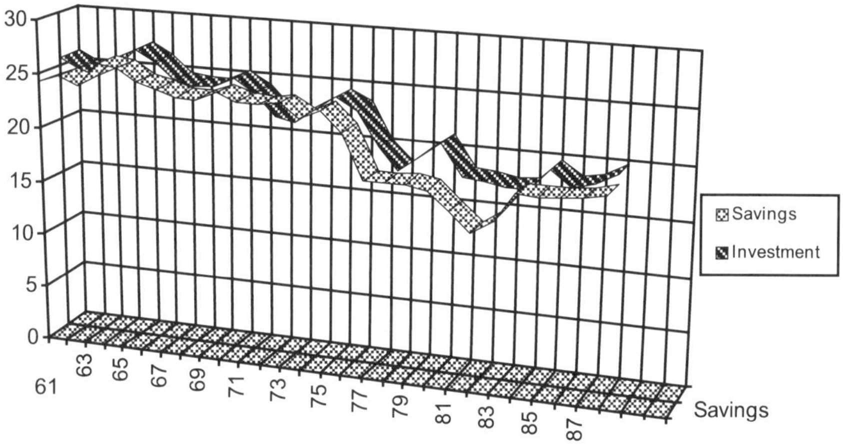

Source: Dean et al (1990:13).

Rather than dampen demand by revaluing the exchange rate, as leading economists had suggested, the threat to macroeconomic stability led to the 'Haga' tripartite agreement, which introduced a new economic policy, namely income tax concessions for those groups of workers who maintained wage moderation (Milner, 1989:95). The tax shortfall was to be counter-balanced by raising employer taxes upon the size of their wage bill (in the UK, this is termed employer national insurance fees). This would have the twin effect of reducing excess profits, whilst taxing wage costs presented employers with an additional incentive to oppose high wage rises, as the tax take would similarly rise.

The net effect was a substantial increase in centrally negotiated wages, with total employee costs for the firm rising by 22% between 1974 and 1975, and by a staggering 40% over a two year period (Martin, 1984:294). Critically for the Swedish economy, these cost increases were introduced just as the economy slid into the delayed international recession. The decline in demand for Swedish exports was intensified by monetarist governments in the UK, Germany and USA choosing to deflate their economies to reduce inflation rather than participating in a general reflation of the international economy. These were difficult circumstances for a suddenly uncompetitive Swedish economy, as documented in the next chapter.

Demands for Equality

The contradictions faced by the Swedish labour movement were further complicated by research findings that, despite solidarity wage bargaining and constant SAP tenure in government, there had been no significant change in income distribution between 1948 and the late 1960s (Rosenblum, 1980:268; Panitch, 1977). These results appeared to confirm the charge, levied at social democrats, that their brand of gradualist reformism was not capable of significantly transforming capitalist society (Miliband, 1961). Hence, it provoked the SAP to promise a "new era of equality" by increasing marginal taxation and fiscal transfers whilst the LO intensified solidarity bargaining (Esping-Andersen, 1992:56). However, although labour's share of national income rose during the early 1970s, it did so in most OECD nations during this period (Keohane, 1984:31) (Figure 4-2). Moreover, it represented no greater fluctuation than Bergström (1980:4) previously observed, leaving the long-term stability of income distribution unaltered.

Figure 4-2: Domestic factor income shares in Sweden as % of net national income at factor prices, 1950-1983 (labour share includes collective contributions including pensions and insurance premiums whilst capital includes enterprise operating surpluses)

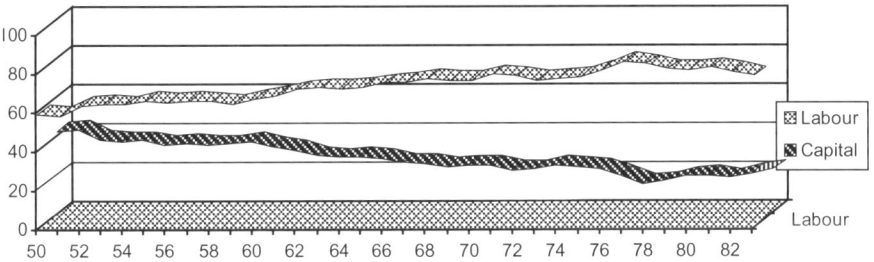

Source: Rock, 1986, 352.

Academic research also discovered that Sweden's already concentrated ownership of productive capital had intensified. Eleven thousand individuals or groups (representing 0.3% of all households) owned over half of all listed shares and the top 1.8% of stockholders increased their share of ownership from 50% to 62% between 1964 and 1975 (Lindström and Nordin, 1977:32; SOU, 1982; Spånt, 1980:53-7). Utilisation of high-voting 'A'- and low-voting 'B'-shares concentrated voting power. Hence, a voting majority typically required the agreement of between one and three people (Hadden, 1972:105; SIND, 1980:54). Rosenblum (1980:270) estimated that one hundred families controlled 95% of Swedish production through personal shares or control over institutional ownership, whilst other studies identified approximately seventeen ownership groups which dominated the Swedish economy (CIEC, 1976; Hermansson, 1965). The most powerful of these was the

Wallenberg group which controlled eleven of the fifty largest Swedish firms in 1976, employing 425,000 people, with assets of SEK40 billion and total sales of SEK70 billion, accounting for one-fifth of the sales of the two hundred largest Swedish companies.

The research concluded that Sweden was therefore amongst the most centralised, monopolistic capitalist economies with employment focused upon the largest corporations and with a concentration of capital "probably unparalleled in any capitalist society" (Isreal, 1978:347; SOU, 1968). The ten largest corporations employed 36.2% of all manufacturing workers in 1983 and the top forty corporations 57%, whilst the fifty largest companies produced 91% of Sweden's total exports (Jagrén, 1986:41; Skog, 1991:13). Consequently, the inequitable concentration of industrial ownership infringed not only trade union demands for greater equality but also frustrated the labour movement's goal of increased democratic influence over the economy.

Solutions?

Tighten Rehn-Meidner Model

The first, and most obvious solution to the problems facing the Swedish economy during the early 1970s, would have been to implement the Rehn-Meidner model in its entirety. In particular, inflationary pressures would have been more easily contained if the restrictive aggregate demand management policy had been fully operational. A tighter fiscal and monetary policy would have intensified the profits squeeze, and thereby removed one main cause of the inflationary pressures, together with cause of wage drift and a threat perceived to the future of the wage bargaining system. Thus, negotiated wage rises would have been more modest and the tax-based incomes strategy would not have imposed such large increases in the non-wage costs experienced by Swedish industry. In other words, the full implementation of the Rehn-Meidner strategy would have removed many of the worst problems facing the Swedish economy.

The solution to the other significant macroeconomic problem, namely the insufficient level of domestic risk capital and productive investment warranted by the maintenance of full employment, would not, however, have proved so easy to accomplish. Indeed, the neo-classical argument for relaxing the profits squeeze in the first place was based upon the supposition that retained profits provide a considerable proportion of the source of finance for industrial investment, and therefore profits should be allowed to rise to stimulate entrepreneurs to invest, thereby eliminating the structural shortfall. However, this ran the risk of re-introducing inflationary pressures and tensions in the system of wage formation.

The Rehn-Meider model's own prescription to end the shortfall in productive investment involved the expansion of social and collective savings. This provided an alternative to retained profits and private savings providing sufficient risk capital to finance the level of productive investment necessary to maintain full employment in the medium- and long-run. Since ATP pension funds had peaked in terms of their share of the Swedish credit market at this time, a new source of collective capital formation was required.

LO's 'Trilemma'

Employee militancy during a period of declining investment provided the LO with what Swenson (1989:114-5) describes as a 'trilemma'; how to pursue egalitarian objectives of wage levelling and a larger wage-share of national income without jeopardising full employment. Through wage regulation alone only two of the three objectives can be pursued simultaneously (Figure 4-3). Solidarity wage strategy could reduce differentials within the LO's sphere of influence whilst facilitating macroeconomic employment policy only as long as the government maintained a profit squeeze and thereby ensured a high wage share of national income. Failure to sustain this element of the Rehn-Meidner model in the early 1970s weakened grassroots acceptance of the solidaristic strategy.

Figure 4-3: Swenson's 'Trilemma'

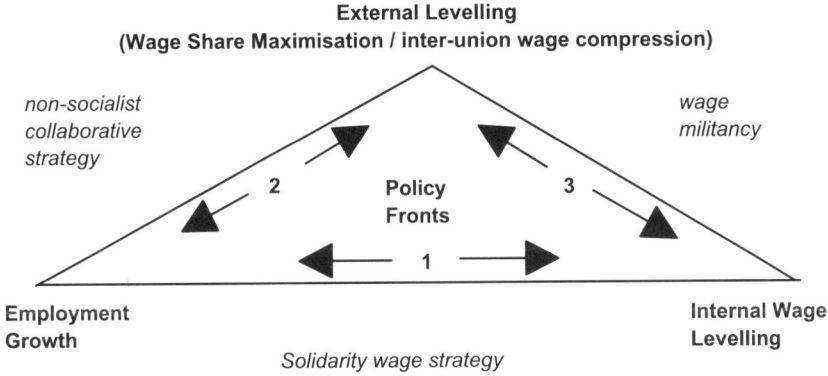

Source: Swenson, 1989:106.

Increasing inter-union competition meant that, unless the LO extended the scope of its pay bargaining to include the increasingly assertive white-collar unions, the solidarity strategy would result in wider differentials between skilled LO members and white-collar workers. White-collar union membership growth reduced the LO's relative importance from 81.5% of all organised employees in 1950, to 78% in 1960, 71% in 1970 and 64% by 1980 (Micheletti, 1985:30). Similarly, inter-union wage compression could only be achieved by abandoning either internal levelling or support for employment generation. With the trilemma(s) unresolved, the LO's wage strategy oscillated uneasily between solidarity and wage militancy throughout the mid-1970s (Swenson, 1989).

Organised labour is in a 'prisoners' dilemma' to the extent that, asymmetry of information can lead to sub-optimal solutions. Thus, whilst unions can squeeze profits until the point where investment declines, they cannot *guarantee* that wage moderation leads to increased investment (Martin, 1992:25-6). Lancaster (1973) called this the "dynamic inefficiency of capitalism".

If unions increase immediate consumption, future consumption is reduced and investment levels may be too low to sustain full employment. If, however, they restrain immediate consumption to free greater resources for productive investment, they cannot ensure these will not be used for capitalist consumption (Esping-Andersen, 1990:187). Capitalists face a similar dilemma since their consumption reduces future growth, but additional wealth created through increased investment may be claimed by workers. Thus, workers can be powerful and yet powerless simultaneously; controlling political power and determining present consumption, yet remaining powerless whilst capitalists retain power to determine investment. This highlights the asymmetry of union power (Gourevitch et al, 1984:248).

Two optimising solutions are available for labour; firstly, to collaborate with capital to achieve sufficient investment in return for a restricted wage share, or secondly to take control over investment (Hyman, 1975:38,368). The alternative is inflationary pressure resulting from wage struggle between labour and capital. Joan Robinson (1973:129-31) stated;

> It was an obvious rider to The General Theory that if we are to enjoy continuous near-full employment without changing the institutions and habits of industrial bargaining, we shall suffer from inflation. It is neither the fault of the trade unions, who are fulfilling their proper function of demanding their fair share in rising profits, nor of businessmen trying to preserve profits by raising prices when costs go up. It is the fault of an economic system inappropriate to the state of development of the economy.

Increased labour power resources, and the SAF's unwillingness to concede a further class compromise which moved beyond Saltsjöbaden, forced the LO to demand government action to achieve the redistribution of wealth and power it could not secure through labour market bargaining.

Investment-Constrained Limits to Redistribution

Conventional redistribution strategies are restricted by private control of the investment function because investment is a necessary but insufficient condition to maintain full employment in the long-run. Expected future profitability predominantly determines present investment, whilst realised past profits finance new investment (Kalecki, 1971). Contrary to the pre-Keynesian assertion that investment is constrained by the supply of savings, it in fact generates the savings (in the form of undistributed profits) needed for its own finance (Reynolds, 1987:199). Thus, the greater capitalist profit, the higher savings and accumulation of capital will be, *ceteris paribus* (Caporaso and Levine, 1992:117-8).

Profit expectations are largely determined by two influences; the *marginal efficiency of investment* and expected changes in profitable sales (Arestis, 1989:614). Keynes (1936:135-7,141) defined the *marginal efficiency of capital* (*mec*) as the point where current capital supply price equals future expected returns.

Investment is undertaken until the point where *mec* equals the market interest rate, so the aggregate investment schedule is interest-elastic. Expected development of future profitable sales stimulates investment intended to secure market share and expand capacity to take advantage of potential market growth (Arestis, 1989:614). Thus the following sequence can be identified;

$$P_{(t-1)} \rightarrow I_{(t)} \rightarrow P^*_{(t+1)}$$

where **P** *represents profit;* **t** *represents the current time period;* **I** *represents investment; and* **P*** *represents anticipated future profit.*

Figure 4-4: Kaldor's theory of distribution and the limit to redistribution

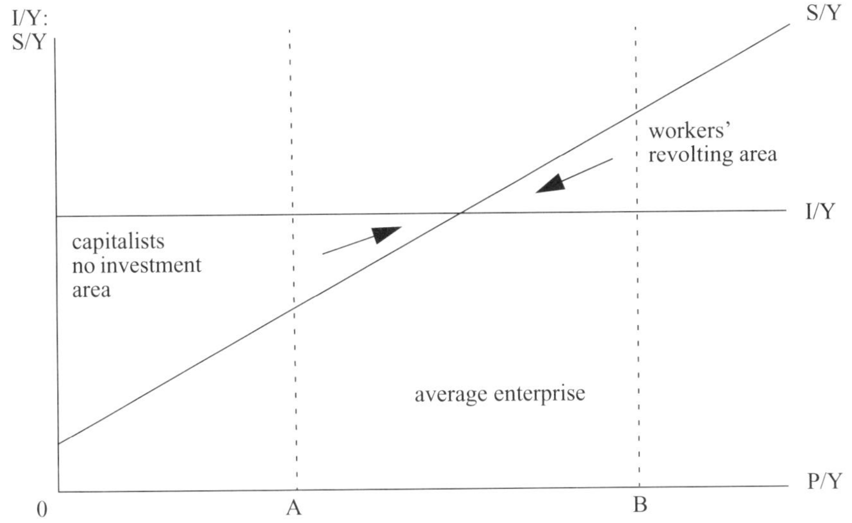

Source: Burkitt 1983a, 125.

[where Y = national income, I = investment, S = savings and P = profits. Assuming a state of full employment, national income is divided between two classes, labour (W) and capital (P), where the marginal propensity to save is higher amongst capitalists than workers. I/Y is autonomously determined, whilst S/Y is a function of P/Y, assuming workers' net savings to be negligible. Kaldor argued that P/Y settles between an upper limit at which workers revolt (B) and a lower limit where capitalists cease to invest (A).]

Whilst current profits remain high, and expectations of future returns provide incentives to accumulate, sufficient investment should be forthcoming to ensure capital accumulation consistent with full employment. However, this suggests a "fairly rigid lower limit to the profit share" beneath which profits cease to fulfil both functions, thereby severely limiting the income redistribution achievable by government or trade unions (Kaldor, 1966; Burkitt and Whyman, 1995:25-26) (Figure 4-4). Thus, wage bargaining alone cannot *permanently* shift the distribution of income between wages and profits over the long term beyond a "functional" level, nor achieve a more equal distribution of wealth (Robinson, 1966; SOU, 1979:74). That requires fracturing "the link between profits and personal income so enabling investment to increase without reducing equality" (Burkitt, 1983a:125).

Securing significant redistribution of wealth without reducing investment can be achieved by a permanent increase in employee savings. This can be derived from the following equations, employing the simplifying assumption that all non-wage factor incomes are included as profit. Thus;

> **National Income = wages + profit (including rent and interest)**

and,

> **Profit = Investment + Capitalist Consumption – Workers' Savings**

Redistribution from capital to labour can take two principal forms; reducing investment or capitalist consumption by raising wages or fiscal transfers or, secondly, a sustained increase in employee savings (Burkitt, 1984:179). The first option is limited whilst investment decisions remain in private hands because reducing current capitalist consumption reduces expectations of future consumption, leading to lower capital accumulation and thereby undermining full employment in the long run. Thus significant, sustainable redistribution requires a *permanent* increase in workers' savings. However, since savings are predominantly determined by the level of income, employees have little opportunity to permanently increase the proportion of national savings they provide. This requires a form of collective savings which grows independently of individual employee income and is protected from consumption.

Necessity for Socialisation of Investment

The principal restriction preventing a sustained redistribution of power and wealth concerns the private control over the investment function within capitalist economies. Consequently, the socialisation of investment would facilitate progressive redistribution. Indeed, Keynes (1936:375-8) advocated comprehensive socialisation of investment to "augment", or if necessary to replace, a majority of private investment to maintain full employment in the long-run. He did so for three main reasons:

1. Uncertainty and speculative 'animal spirits' ensured capital accumulation would be inherently unstable, so that capitalists were unlikely to undertake sufficient investment to sustain full employment in the absence of state intervention (Keynes, 1980:322; Skidelsky, 1979:57);
2. Inequality associated with capitalism, and the higher propensity to save of those with higher incomes, impedes economic growth (Keynes, 1936:373);

3. The high rate of investment and capital accumulation required to secure long-run full employment reduces the return on capital, either because its yield falls or increased demand causes its production price to rise, to the extent that the rate of interest and *mec* may decline towards zero within one or two generations (Keynes, 1936:136; Hyman, 1975:360). With the return on investment covering only the cost of capital production and normal profits to offset risk, together with supervision and administration, relative capital scarcity is replaced by capital abundance thereby minimising opportunity cost and social conflict (Smith, 1962:99). This would cause "euthanasia of the rentier" and the "euthanasia of the cumulative oppressive power of the capitalists to exploit the scarcity-value of capital" (Keynes, 1936:376). Given a low or zero *mec*, socialisation of investment provides the "only means" to secure sufficient investment, to maintain full employment and economic growth (Arestis, 1989:62; Keynes, 1936:376-8).[2]

Joan Robinson (1973:130) summarised;

> Keynes was arguing that, if a private enterprise system cannot deal with potential abundance, we must turn it into a system that can.

Post-Keynesian theorists suggested that a further refinement involved the incorporation of socialisation within a "social contract" forged between the state, industry and trade unions to provide a potentially superior framework that ensures efficient capital formation and full employment (Arestis, 1992:267-271; Tichy, 1984; Whyman and Burkitt, 1993c).

Economic Democracy

Tensions within second stage Keynesianism, and grassroots demands for increased workplace influence and an egalitarian distribution of income and wealth, caused the LO to promote an active investment policy intended to increase productive investment without regressive distributional consequences (Esping-Andersen, 1985:232). The traditional solution of increasing profits to raise investment would worsen inequality and was therefore unacceptable. Thus socialisation of investment appeared necessary to achieve *economic democracy*; particularly since organised labour's power resources had grown sufficiently to challenge core capitalist prerogatives (Ahrne, 1978:319; Korpi, 1983:212).

Economic democracy can be distinguished from industrial democracy since the former seeks to achieve control over the productive sector for labour and/or the community whilst the latter attempts to increase employee influence over their immediate work process (Figure 4-5). Whereas industrial democracy involves

---

[2] Westergaard and Restler (1975) found that profit levels *did* fall until the mid-1970s, appearing to confirm Keynes' prediction although it may alternatively reflect under-reporting profits during a high-tax period. However, abandonment of full employment enabled lower rates of investment to generate high *mec*'s, often through investment in non-productive, non-domestic asset portfolios (Bergström, 1980; Hyman, 1975:360).

expanding *microeconomic* restrictions upon management's right to manage arbitrarily, economic democracy seeks *macroeconomic* influence over the productive sphere through collective ownership. Economic democracy therefore complements and supplements industrial democracy. Whilst MBL sought to extend employee influence at the "immediate work situation within the restrictions set by capital owners, economic democracy would eventually abolish these restrictions" (Broström, 1982:9).

Figure 4-5: Differentiating between industrial and economic democracy

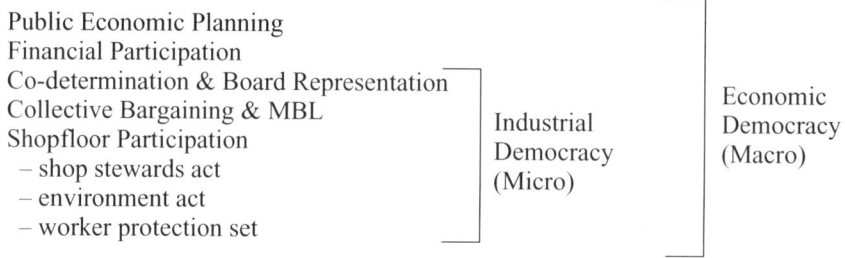

Public Economic Planning
Financial Participation
Co-determination & Board Representation
Collective Bargaining & MBL   Industrial   Economic
Shopfloor Participation   Democracy   Democracy
  – shop stewards act   (Micro)   (Macro)
  – environment act
  – worker protection set

Source: Asard 1986, 213.

The LO sought to achieve economic democracy through two principal means. Firstly, they demanded that the ATP funds be freed to invest in equity which would increase the supply of risk capital, lowering its cost, thereby creating favourable conditions for raising investment without increasing inequality. Opposition from the SAF led to a compromise solution with the establishment of a fourth pension fund in January 1974, which could purchase equity up to 5% of total pension fund capital (Gourevitch et al, 1984:271).[3] However, despite delegating a maximum 60% of its voting rights to local union representatives, this reform proved insufficient to satisfy trade union democratic objectives (Pontusson, 1992:190). Consequently, the LO decided to develop its own strategy to achieve economic democracy (Heclo and Madsen, 1987:266). WEFs constituted one method of its attainment.

---

[3] This limit doubled in 1976 and a 10% ceiling was set on permitted holdings in any company in 1979.

Chapter 5

Wage-Earner Funds:
Stage Three Keynesianism

Introduction

Macroeconomic problems stemming from the implementation of the Rehn-Meidner model, the political necessity to intensify redistributive policy objectives, combined with increasingly vocal demands made by employees for greater participation in work-related matters at the local workplace, established a challenging agenda for the Swedish labour movement. Reluctance to fully implement the Rehn-Meidner model had led to the partial unravelling of that combination of institutions and policy instruments. Consequently, a new initiative was required.

One response originated in the decision made by the 1971 LO Congress to establish an 'expert' group, chaired by the former Head of the LO's Economics Division, Rudolph Meidner, charged with investigating the possibility of reinforcing the solidarity wage policy through collective capital formation, via pension funds or an alternative approach. Following its considerations, the working group was mandated to prepare a technical feasibility report for the 1976 Congress (LO, 1973:10-13; Meidner, 1994INT).[1] This chapter provides a brief outline of the Meidner Report and the resulting intensive political struggle between organised labour and capital on the issue.

The Meidner Report

The research group report, written during 1974, was influenced by three principal factors:

1. Initiatives to secure a share of capital accumulation for workers, whilst preventing incomes policies increasing the inequality of wealth, were discussed by a majority of industrialised capitalist nations,[2] thereby providing the Swedes with a myriad of alternative models. Sweden was therefore relatively late in examining this issue;

---

[1] The 'INT' suffix is used to denote all interview material.
[2] Collective profit-sharing and/or investment-wage schemes were discussed in Austria, Belgium, Denmark, Finland, France, Germany, Italy, Netherlands, Switzerland, United Kingdom, United States of America, the Commission of the European Communities, the ETUC and as far afield as Peru (Whyman, 2002).

2. Swedish precursors included the 1920s committee of enquiry into industrial democracy and socialisation, together with a series of LO discussion papers between 1951 and 1966, which expressed interest in using the ATP system to steer investment (Heclo and Madsen, 1987:257-263). The academic economist, Villy Bergström (1973), proposed a hybrid WEF system comprised of national and industry funds, financed through a combination of investment-wage and profit-sharing mechanisms. Former Finance Minister, Wigforss, influenced by Guild Socialism, advocated an employee self-management alternative to nationalisation through "public enterprises without owners" (*samhällsförtag utan ägare*) (Wigforss, 1922; 1962);
3. The prevailing economic environment, dominated by LO member frustration at continued wage moderation during a large profit surge throughout 1973 and 1974, made redistribution a central feature of the report. This was despite Meidner initially stating that WEFs were *not* intended to alter power relations between capital and labour (Hamilton, 1989:205).

The frequency of debate legitimised economic democracy initiatives and enabled the LO research department's constant advocacy of this approach to establish a "strategic foothold" at the heart of the Swedish labour movement (Heclo and Madsen, 1987:262-3).

Remit and Aims

The Meidner report identified three aims for WEFs (Meidner, 1978:15):

1. complimenting the **solidarity wage policy**,
2. **counteracting the degree of wealth concentration** resulting from capitalist control of investment,
3. **increasing employee influence** over the economy.

Collective capital ownership and workplace self-management are **necessary but insufficient** conditions for employees to determine their own work situation. They reduce the power disadvantage between labour's rights to demand negotiations and seek modification of existing initiatives, and ownership rights to determine policy and control its implementation. Moreover, social ownership enhances democratic economic management without requiring expensive and regressive financial inducements to elicit investment behaviour in the social interest (Rosenblum, 1980:272). WEFs could therefore "greatly strengthen" the market economy and reduce market failure by harmonising private and social costs or benefits of production (Meidner, 1978:79-80).

Whilst noting the potentially significant contribution WEFs could make to economic management, the report emphasised that alternative tools, including national pension funds, should be used to stimulate capital formation and pursue active industrial policy. WEFs were designed to achieve a "long-term shift in the structure of ownership for the benefit of employees" (Meidner, 1978; LO, 1976:68-88). They were *supplementary* to other economic policy instruments and not a general panacea to solve all Sweden's problems (Meidner, 1981:315).

WEFs represent a 'Kaleckian' "institutional accommodation to full employment" by ensuring that employees share in accumulation, thereby securing high profitability and investment through enhanced corporate liquidity and the provision of additional risk capital (Esping-Andersen, 1990:184; Gourevitch et al, 1984:275). To maintain the balance between consumption and investment, and to avoid employers' responding to increased direct costs by increasing prices and therefore frustrating redistribution, WEFs were designed to be neutral regarding costs, wages and prices (Meidner, 1978:17).

WEFs were considered a gradualist reform and "logical part of the Swedish model" (Meidner, 1981:303; 1993a:217). Nevertheless, they also facilitated fundamental social transformation towards economic democracy and were consequently a *radical* reform (Rosenblum, 1980:273). Meidner (cited in Åsard, 1985:34) stated;

> We want to deprive the capitalists of the power they exercise by virtue of ownership. All experience shows that it is not enough to have influence and control. Ownership plays a decisive role. I refer to Marx and Wigforss: we cannot fundamentally change society without changing its ownership structure.

Rejection of Alternative Means

Alternative methods of achieving the aims given to the working group were dismissed because of unfavourable effects including:

- *Corporate profit taxation* – the working group claimed it was "illusory" that it could achieve major redistribution because profits and investment incentives would be reduced, thereby threatening full employment (Meidner, 1978:27);
- *Funds to redistribute wages from high to low wage sectors* – could hamper structural development and erode Sweden's competitive position;
- *Increasing private saving* – would be unlikely without large tax incentives (Meidner, 1978:63). Even if savings rose substantially, the resulting fall in aggregate demand would require compensatory state fiscal stimulation to protect employment which would raise profits and capitalist wealth;
- *Profit-sharing schemes* – for all employees to benefit, profit-sharing must *replace* part of wages and salaries, thereby undermining the solidarity wages policy whilst reducing employee security and the basic income from which pensions, sickness and unemployment benefits are calculated;
- *Inheritance, property and capital gains taxation* – would reduce wealth concentration but these options were outside the remit of the working group (Meidner, 1978:44).

Design of WEFs

The essence of the proposal was that a proportion of profits be transferred from the original owners to the company's collective employees through issuing additional company shares to an WEF which would remain within the company to fund future productive investment (Gourevitch et al, 1984:273). Profit-sharing rather than a wage-based contribution was selected to finance WEF development for two reasons (Meidner, 1978:32-4; Brems, 1975:34-40):

1. Only profit-linked contributions accomplish the transfer of a proportion of the company's asset growth to its employees,
2. To complement the solidarity wage policy, WEFs were designed to reduce the additional profits accruing from wage restraint in more efficient companies.

The intention was to regain for employees that element of profits which occurred as a result of egalitarian wage policy, not 'excess profits' due to economic fluctuations. This is what Nell-Breuning described as a "gift to owners of capital" and Meidner as "solidarity profits" (Meidner, 1978:33-4; 1991:294). However, in practice, it is difficult to distinguish between the components contributing to a company's profitability. Therefore the report assumed that all firms making large profits derived some benefit from the solidarity wage policy and should consequently contribute to the WEF system. Moreover, to prevent under-reporting of profitability through account manipulation or multinational shadow-pricing, the report proposed a pre-tax profit calculation defined as the difference between the company's assets (including subsidiaries) at the beginning and end of the accounting period (Meidner, 1978:56-60).

The report proposed that the profit-sharing contribution should be at least 20% of estimated profits (Meidner, 1978:58-9). However, contributions would be tax exempt to maintain company liquidity and promote capital growth (Gourevitch et al, 1984:273; Rehn, 1983:8). Multinational companies would only be liable for the proportion of profit generated within Sweden.

The profit-sharing contribution was to take the form of newly issued company shares; the number depending upon the value of existing shares. To equalise treatment between companies and avoid manipulation of the relatively small Swedish stock market to temporarily inflate share prices, the report suggested calculating share value by dividing the total assets of the company by the number of issued shares. Thus the number of shares issued to WEFs would then be determined by the change in company assets over the year divided by share value. Furthermore, the report recommended modification of the Swedish Companies' Act to prevent companies issuing WEFs with shares carrying lower-voting rights, whilst existing owners retained shares with higher-voting rights, to reinforce their dominant position in corporate governance. It further suggested that WEFs be able to veto mergers or other transactions which would alter its share of ownership (Meidner, 1978:48-50).

Assuming WEFs received equity equivalent to 20% of annual profits, the report estimated fund growth, as a proportion of an average participating company, on the basis of different realised profit rates (Table 5-1). For example, if a company made 5% profits per year it would take seventy five years for WEFs to control 52% of the company, whilst if it made 20% profits per year it would take only twenty years to achieve a majority shareholding. Individual funds could enhance or retard this process according to the extent they invested or consumed yields emanating from their shareholdings. This implies that the report's calculations were illustrative, not predictive, emphasising the *gradual* radicalism of the reform. It is not the "lemon socialism" of firms in crisis because it socialises the most profitable firms first (Tilton, 1990:231).

Table 5-1: WEFs share of a firm assuming 20% profit tax contribution

	Profits			
Year	5%	10%	15%	20%
1	0.01	0.02	0.03	0.04
5	0.05	0.09	0.13	0.17
10	0.09	0.17	0.24	0.30
15	0.14	0.25	0.34	0.42
20	0.18	0.32	0.43	0.52
25	0.21	0.38	0.50	0.60
35	0.29	0.49	0.62	0.72
50	0.38	0.62	0.75	0.84
75	0.52	0.76	0.88	0.93
100	0.74	0.85	0.94	0.97

Source: Meidner (1978:59).

Spread of the WEFs

The report stated that the solidarity principle necessitated that all employees benefit from the fund system, participate in its administration and share in its yields, irrespective of their place of employment. Thus, employees from smaller workplaces would receive a disproportionately large share of WEF resources for training and educational purposes. However, for technical and practical reasons, only organisations employing a minimum of either fifty or one hundred people would be required to contribute financially. This would treat the WEF reform on the same basis as most workplace regulation (Meidner, 1978:91). Although between 98.3% and 99.2% of firms would be exempt, approximately two-thirds of all employees would be covered by the fund system (Meidner, 1978:73-4).

All private economic organisations and producer co-operatives would be included in the WEF scheme. However, consumer co-operatives and the public sector were not intended to contribute towards WEFs as they are not privately owned and do not make profits. Transferring ownership from citizens and consumers, in the form of public sector and consumer co-operative organisations, to a particular group of employees via a WEF, was considered by Meidner to be a "retrograde step" of "re-privatisation" (Meidner, 1978:70-2).

Public and co-operative organisations should be "model employers" without recourse to WEFs, guaranteeing their workforce enhanced influence and participation rights without the need for employee ownership to secure such entitlement (Meidner, 1978:72). This viewpoint certainly presupposes significant reform of the public sector and co-operative organisations to make this participatory vision a reality. However, by narrowing the scope of the WEFs to employees working within the larger private sector companies, this consequently meant that the WEF reform would be of *minority* interest to the Swedish electorate and even within the labour movement itself. This fact would have significant consequences in the political debate over this initiative.

Fund Capital and Yield

Meidner recognised that significantly increasing employee asset holding involves the *permanent* saving of a share of profits which is unlikely to be achieved voluntarily (Meidner, 1981:310). Moreover, effective employee participation and influence through capital formation requires that employee assets remain *within* the participating enterprise as working capital to prevent increased consumption undermining investment, influence and redistribution (Meidner, 1978:45-6,82; Burkitt, 1985:275). Using the analogy that a co-operative can only flourish if all members maintain accumulated capital by deferring consumption, withdrawals from the WEF system reduce the capital necessary for economic growth and represent "illusory" profit-sharing (Meidner, 1978:45). The report states:

> Irrespective of who owns it, the total stock of capital forms the foundation of our economic and social progress. It is nothing less than a gross illusion to give the individual partner (the employee) the opportunity to dispose as he sees fit over 'his' or 'her' share. It is of doubtful value to the individual, and obviously harmful in the long run not only to the employees as a group but to the whole community.

Employees would, however, determine how to allocate the yields accruing to the WEFs. The report estimated that half of these yields may be required to safeguard fund growth by purchasing new share issues that prevent value-maximising firms diluting WEF capital through increasing the rate of new shares (Meidner, 1978:49; Hasko, 1990:21). If WEFs were unable to purchase their full quota of any new rights issue, the report suggested that AP-funds could do so. Therefore, the remaining half of the WEF yields could be distributed as individual dividends, used to purchase additional shares through the stock market or be devoted to collective consumption (Meidner, 1978:82). Other strategic options, included:

- Financing a trade union-based research institute to enable unions to compete with employers in the field of information provision and agenda setting;
- Education to raise employee competence to utilise enhanced participation opportunities provided through WEF ownership and the labour laws. This is a *prerequisite* for employees to assume efficiently the functions of ownership. It would also have the likely effect of increasing union activity and reducing the gap between union experts and the membership (Meidner, 1978:87);

- Hiring consultants to provide technical assistance which enables employee representatives to maximise gains from legal access to company information and participation on company boards (Eiger, 1983).

WEFs could perform the role of an agency promoting co-operative and labour managed firms[3] through provision of finance, professional assistance and other forms of mutual support which enable non-profit enterprises to survive in a hostile environment (Clayre, 1980:50; Vanek, 1970:317-8).

WEF Structure and Administration

There are four principal types of WEF; firm-centred, regional or industry-based, competing and centralised funds. Each has different propensities to stimulate labour productivity, enhance factor mobility, increase employee tolerance to profitability, minimise risk and maximise democratic influence (Brems, 1975:52-60; OECD, 1970:27). The Meidner Report sought to secure what it considered to be an optimum mix. Thus, a central clearing comprehensive fund administered and allocated dividend income, with membership drawn from national union nominees and representatives of the public interest to enhance social solidarity.

The initial 20% of corporate influence accruing through WEF ownership was delegated to local unions, supported by sector funds, to which additional voting rights would be transferred thereby avoiding over-centralisation (Meidner, 1978:93-98). The central fund is therefore a largely powerless body, administering assets which can never be realised and distributing dividends according to the democratic wishes of concerned employees. Membership plurality reduces group egotism and narrows group self-interest, whilst the central fund provides the necessary co-ordination for the efficient operation of the fund system (Meidner, 1978:101).

The Struggle for Economic Democracy

A False Start?

The Meidner Report was initially perceived as a solution to the macroeconomic problems faced by the Rehn-Meidner model, particularly relating to a means of providing additional risk capital to facilitate sufficient productive investment to maintain full employment, without this either exacerbating income inequality or requiring the relaxation of the profit squeeze inherent within the second stage Keynesian approach. However, the explosion of employee frustration at the technocratic management of their working lives, and the demand for a greater influence upon the economic sphere, particularly at the workplace, contributed to

---

[3] Labour management (LM) refers to a production unit whose economic decisions are made democratically by the entire workforce. Labour hires capital rather than vice versa, collectively performing the entrepreneurial role and receiving the surplus of revenue over cost to distribute according to democratic decision (Estrin, 1983; Vanek, 1970; 1971).

the ultimate presentation of the proposal as a means of complementing the SAP's industrial relations legislative reforms. Thus, the Meidner Plan was intended to strengthen macroeconomic management, whilst simultaneously advancing employee democratic influence over production issues through the means of collective share ownership.

A provisional draft of the Meidner Report received an enthusiastic response from eighteen thousand LO study group members, representing approximately one per cent of total LO membership, when it was circulated during the autumn of 1975 (Meidner, 1993a:224; Heclo and Madsen, 1987:270). Ninety percent of respondents believed ownership was essential for union influence, 97.8% thought excess profits were a significant problem and 91.6% opposed individual profit-sharing. Activist enthusiasm for the Meidner Report persuaded the LO leadership to present the WEF proposals to the June 1976 LO Congress with only minor modifications (Bergström, 1992:162-3).

Delegates proved similarly positive, submitting a large number of supportive motions. All fourteen speakers in the debate praised the idea or wanted a more radical scheme – only Meidner cautioned against rapid adoption of what he intended to be a provisional report (Bergström, 1992:162). Nevertheless, it was unanimously adopted "by acclamation" with the delegates standing and singing the *Internationale* (Åsard, 1993INT). WEFs were clearly an issue capable of vitalising the union movement, particularly during a climate especially favourable to radical reformism (Meidner, 1993a:224).

Economic democracy offered the trade union movement a potential solution to short-term macroeconomic and distributional problems, with simultaneously long-term system-transforming possibilities (Hamilton, 1989:206; Nilsson in LO, 1976). The LO newspaper proclaimed "we shall deprive the capital owners of their power" (*Fackföreningsrörelsens Tidningen*, 1975:19). Wigforss was quoted to be "enthusiastic" about the proposal, although he remained concerned that the labour movement may be insufficiently strong to achieve such a radical reform (Wigforss cited in Svenning, 1977:23; Meidner, 1991INTb).

The SAP leadership, however, reacted with surprise and "serious embarrassment" that the LO had adopted a "long-term and concrete" proposal immediately prior to a general election without consulting the SAP leadership (Åsard, 1980:383). The atypical breakdown in co-operation strained labour movement relations. Finance Minister, Feldt was quoted as stating that the proposals were "completely impractical and unworkable" and would generate insufficient investment, low productivity and an inefficient labour market (Feldt, 1991:28). Assar Lindbeck, a prominent social democrat as well as one of Sweden's leading academic economists, claimed that WEFs threatened democracy, replacing an economically efficient "pluralistic society" with a "Meidnerland" where citizens are clerks of an over-powerful monolithic "trade union state" (Abrahamsson and Broström, 1980:210-11; Meyerson, 1978:58).

The SAP was not, however, entirely consistent on this issue. Its 1975 programme emphasised economic democracy and, although vague on the question of ownership, it accepted the prerequisite of democratising production to empower citizens, wage-earners and consumers (Johansson, 1982; SAP, 1975). Moreover, Prime Minister, Olof Palme, had read the Meidner Report and believed it to be a "logical document".

Therefore, it could only have been union enthusiasm and the political consequences of the timing of the announcement, and not the content, which surprised the SAP leadership (Meidner, 1994INT).[4]

In particular, WEFs "exposed a serious cleavage" between the LO's aspirations and the "political calculations of the Social Democratic Party machinery" (Heclo and Madsen, 1987:270). The SAP was concerned about the reaction of the whole electorate, not a relatively homogeneous interest group membership, and feared the issue might alienate supporters more interested in traditional welfare and economic management objectives (Korpi, 1983:34-5; Åsard, 1980:380-2). Moreover, the LO's adoption of a radical, complicated proposal, three months prior to a General Election, led to SAP evasion of the issue and made the party vulnerable to bourgeois criticism, thereby being one (albeit minor) factor contributing towards the loss of executive power for the first time in forty four years.

Interestingly, the SAP actually received 78,000 *more* votes in the 1976 General Election than in 1973, but lost because their *share* of the vote declined by 0.9% (Misgeld et al, 1992:452). Election surveys suggested that WEFs did *not* significantly affect the election result, but that the loss of social democrat support was more related to a series of tax-related scandals which stimulated accusations of "bureaucratic high-handedness", together with criticism of too intimate co-operation with big business over nuclear power (Isreal, 1978:342; Himmelstrand, 1981a:160).

The failure of the SAP's *defensive* strategy and the narrow margin of defeat suggested that an *offensive* mobilisation around WEFs, similar to that achieved during the ATP struggle, could have won the election (Gourevitch et al, 1984,283-7; Meidner, 1991INTb). The SAP perhaps perceived this as a high risk strategy, requiring a "historically decisive struggle" with capital, and preferred to rely upon a traditional Keynesian-welfarist appeal rather than advocating economic democratisation to enhance its supportive wage-earner coalition (Esping-Andersen, 1981:138; Åsard, 1980:382). Nevertheless, with the benefit of hindsight, it proved to be a missed opportunity.

SAF Opposition to 'Trade Union Funds'

The labour movement's inability to unite around the WEF reform initiative weakened its political hegemony, whilst the resulting policy vacuum facilitated an ideological offensive undertaken by the Swedish Employers' Confederation (*Svenska Arbetsgivareföreningen, SAF*) and the Industrial Employers' Organisation (*Sveriges Industriförbundet, SI*) (de Geer, 1989:74). Although, viewed from today's perspective, it was perhaps inevitable that the Meidner Plan would become one of the most controversial issues in Swedish history, this was not immediately self-evident. Capitalists could benefit from the tax allowances accompanying the scheme, whilst *current* wealth was unaffected and profits could be enhanced by increased risk capital availability (Pontusson, 1988:51). Meidner (1975:97) consequently believed his proposals "should not be totally unacceptable to the

---

4   Palme preferred MBL but once WEFs were adopted by the LO he recognised they could
    not be ignored by the party (Meidner, 1991INTb; Åsard, 1993INT).

employers". Indeed, the initial response by organised business, namely the SAF and SI sponsored Waldenström report, was broadly sympathetic to the need for a fund-based reform, although preferring a firm-centred voluntaristic version (Eidem and Öhman, 1979:49; SI and SAF, 1976). However, despite initially favourable reactions from the SAF leadership, opposition from small firms and Wallenberg companies meant the Waldenström report was never officially adopted by either the SI or SAF (Schiller, 1991:151,160).

The complicated nature of WEF proposals meant it was easier to mobilise opposition than generate support around one plan amongst a plethora of alternatives (Pontusson, 1987:29). Leading employers derided WEFs as "pure and unadulterated socialism" and "the biggest confiscation ever seen in the Western world", arguing that they would cause the complete socialisation of Sweden (de Geer quoted in Olsen, 1992:80; Gourevitch et al, 1984:282). Marcus Wallenberg, the leading capitalist of the time, dismissed WEFs as "a half-cooked egg which sane politicians will never swallow", whilst the SAF claimed that WEFs could achieve majority ownership in all listed companies within *seven* years and would therefore have replaced the market economy with a "union planned economy" (Heclo and Madsen, 1987:269,304; Widén cited in Förtagareförbundet, 1982:26). Large employer's further threatened that employment and investment would be transferred overseas if WEFs were introduced. The intensity of feeling demonstrated by organised capital on this issue was described by Linton (1985:27) as "unrestrained hysteria" and appeared at odds with the increasingly moderate proposals being discussed by the LO and the SAP.

Mobilising Public Support

The struggle for economic democracy, between organised labour and capital, focused upon competition for public support on three levels:

• white-collar trade union support establishing a wage-earner coalition,
• political and interest organisations through the medium of a government commission,
• reaching the electorate via the media and measured in terms of opinion poll ratings.

TCO Neutrality

The Central Organisation for Salaried Employees (*Tjänstemännens Centralorganisation*, TCO) organises 1.3 million white-collar employees within the public and private sectors, covering both managers and staff. Its 85% membership density is the highest in the industrial world and it represents one-third of all Swedish union members (Micheletti, 1985:30; SCB, 1993:190). The TCO was interested in industrial and economic democracy long *before* the LO, publishing a report advocating a form of WEFs in 1972 a full year before the LO working group began its research (TCO, 1972; Wredén, 1976:105). Its approach was similar to the LO's, causing Elvander (1979:146) to suggest "there was almost a total meeting of minds" between the two union organisations on the issue. Both rejected individual profit-sharing as incompatible with solidarity wage formation, though WEFs could ensure sufficient capital formation to sustain long-term full employment, considered worker ownership would ease union acceptance for "capital formation based on higher profitability in business and industry", and could enhance employee influence (Eidem and Öhman, 1979:53).

The TCO rejected company-affiliated WEFs, which had little attraction for the 60% of its membership working in the public sector, but argued that collective funds must include *all* employees irrespective of employer (Olsen, 1992:109). However, despite the similarities, the TCO was less interested than the LO in the *macro* dimension of reducing the concentration of economic power, and more concerned in assisting *micro* level industrial democracy whilst simultaneously stimulating savings and capital formation (Elvander, 1979:154). Thus, the TCO proposals were less far-reaching than the Meidner report.

The broad membership base of the TCO made it a potentially decisive "arena for ideological battles" because it fractured capital's "social and political hegemony over non-manual employees" and thereby facilitated a power shift in civil society in labour's favour (Stephens, 1982:145; Micheletti, 1985; Åsard, 1985). However, the problem for the TCO concerned the fact that, once the issue became polarised, its weak class base inhibited the development of an ideology acceptable to all its members (Stephens, 1979:191-4). A dozen internal research reports, and a decade of membership consultation, failed to mobilise a majority for action (Micheletti, 1985:146-151; Albrecht and Deutsch, 1983:299).

The formation of 'TCO Members For Member Referendums On Wage Earner Funds' (*TCO:are för fondomröstning*), with a claimed membership of 70,000 and close contacts with the bourgeois media, intensified the pressure upon the TCO to avoid backing the WEF proposal. The group commissioned opinion polls which purported to demonstrate that 76% of the TCO membership opposed collective WEFs. Indeed, it even staged an 'alternative TCO Congress' the day before the official TCO Congress, where one hundred and thirty self-styled delegates passed resolutions calling for membership referendums within each affiliated union (Micheletti, 1985:159-161).[5] The end result was the effective neutralisation of the TCO on the issue (Pontusson, 1988:55; Öhman, 1985:9).

WEF Government Commission

The second focus for the political struggle was the Commission on Wage-Earner Funds and Capital Growth (*Utredningen om löntagarfonder och kapitalväxt*). Established in January 1975, the Commission's remit was to identify WEF variants and devise models which could be introduced in Sweden, together with the

---

5   It has proved difficult to substantiate whether 'TCO Members For Member Referendums' was funded by organised business, although links between the two were certainly close. Its leaders featured prominently in SAF-organised demonstrations, whilst SAF-owned *Timbro* published a book recounting the experiences of one of the protest organisations' leaders. Moreover, speakers at the 'alternative TCO Congress' included LWEF Widén who was active within SAF 'front' organisations (Ahlén, 1985; Micheletti, 1985:161-4).

necessary legal framework (Micheletti, 1985:145). It included representatives from the trade union federations (LO, TCO, SACO/SR), employer organisations (SAF, SI, *SHIO-Familjeförtagen*) and the largest political parties (SAP, Centre, Liberal and Moderate) (de Geer, 1989:317; Olsen, 1992:79). The conservative-Moderate Party and organised capital were predictably hostile to collective WEFs, whilst the Centre Party largely ignored the issue preferring MBL, redistribution through progressive taxation and individual share initiatives (Petersson, 1982:43-4; Öhman, 1985:11). The TCO was preoccupied by its internal debate. Thus attempts to forge a compromise solution focused upon the Liberal Party whose willingness to debate the issue was evident (Åsard, 1985:25; 1986:214-5).

The Liberal Party had previously demonstrated its interest through a 1974 Riksdag motion calling for a "statutory right for wage-earners to share in the company's profit" and capital growth (Helén, 1974; SOU, 1981:21). An internal working group, chaired by party secretary Carl Tham and including Anne Wibble (later to become Finance Minister, 1991-4) and Åke Wredén, produced a 1978 report advocating WEFs as "an instrument for increased capital formation in ways that were acceptable in terms of distribution policy" (de Groot, 1988:50; Öhman, 1985:10). Accordingly, the party adopted a decentralised, market-orientated system of 'citizen funds', competing on the basis of maximising long-term returns for individual holdings (Olsen, 1992:79).

The LO-SAP version was nevertheless rejected by the liberals because the absence of individual shares would cause an "unacceptable power concentration" (Folkpartiet, 1976:2). However, a compromise solution developed by one of the Commission chairpersons, Allan Larsson, was received "enthusiastically" by the centre parties, due to its combination of individual stakeholding in multiple locally based funds, financed in *cash* through a combination of excess profit-sharing, which would remain collectively owned, together with investment-wages, which would be released to individual employees after a waiting period. The funds would trade on the stock market in competition with private investors (de Groot, 1988:53,74). However, the LO were reluctant to concede individual shareholdings and market-orientated placements, arguing that it would turn WEFs into nothing more that a "local savings bank" (Åsard, 1985:76-7). Thus, the Commission was ultimately wound-up without a draft legislative proposal a majority could support (SOU, 1981:197-210; Åsard, 1993INT).

Defusing the WEF Issue

The 1976 election defeat convinced the labour movement of the importance of developing a joint position on WEFs, whilst Nilsson accepted that the LO must subordinate its interests to the political electoral victory needed to implement the resulting proposals (Åsard, 1978:191-2; 1980:383). However, whilst the party desired significant modification of the original proposal to develop a politically presentable solution, the LO was unwilling to abandon fundamental elements of the Meidner Plan (Åsard, 1985:46). Consequently, a series of modifications were made to the original proposal, by a series of LO-SAP working groups. Tactical changes intended to reduce external opposition by emphasising WEFs as an *economic* instrument to maintain full employment rather than redistributing power

(Abrahamsson and Broström, 1980:208-9; LO-SAP 1978,19-20; 1982:22). However, the complexity of the proposals attracted criticism, and a hesitant SAP leadership again refused to use it as a mobilising factor in the 1979 general election which the party lost by the narrowest of margins, one seat and 0.2% of the vote (Walters, 1983:38).

The 1981 WEF draft scheme was in many ways different from the preceding proposals, in that, although retaining the concept of collective funds financed through profit-sharing, it differed on the following points (LO-SAP, 1982:79-80):

1. County-based regional WEFs were to be located within the ATP system to reduce opposition. Fund objectives were modified to include enhancing collective savings and provide wage-earners with a recognisable stake in the reform through enhanced future pensions. WEFs were to pay a yield to the ATP for using their capital, which would be determined by the capital market (LO-SAP, 1982);
2. Profit-sharing was limited to 20% of *excess* profits, as first suggested by the Waldenström report, supplemented by a 1% payroll tax contribution. The report estimated that each WEF would receive an equal share of an approximate SEK2-3 billion total per year (LO-SAP, 1982:81-4,102);
3. Corporate contributions were to be paid in *cash*, not new share issues, and each fund would invest its resources through purchasing existing shares on the stock market, new share issues or shares in non-quoted companies (LO-SAP, 1982:84-92). Marketisation was justified as enhancing investment allocation between industrial sectors, whilst also reducing opposition to the fund reform (Pontusson, 1992:195). However, it abandoned the original principle that money should remain within the company (Feldt, 1980:411);
4. WEFs were viewed as a macroeconomic instrument, assisting employment and welfare rather than redistributing wealth and power. The funds were presented as part of a social contract to enhance economic performance by facilitating higher profits and investment through wage restraint (P-O Edin, 1981:368-373; Ministry of Finance, 1984b:13).

The deradicalisation of the WEFs proposal created opposition within large sections of the labour movement, criticising the "watering down" and "emasculation" of the original proposals (Lundberg, 1982; Swenson, 1989:166). However, the SAP leadership secured a "free hand" to negotiate the eventual form of WEFs with interested parties, without Congress imposing a binding resolution determining the *exact* design of a future system (Albrecht and Deutsch, 1983:306). It used that flexibility by continuing to water-down the proposals, with Palme repeatedly offering an "outstretched hand" to negotiate a compromise solution with the centre parties. He even raised the possibility that WEF boards could be elected by *all* Swedish citizens, which allayed fears of over-powerful trade union officials and met criticism of the labour movement's tendency to equate "wage-earner power" (*löntagarmakt*) with "people [or citizen] power" (*folkmakt*) (Feldt, 1991:155; Widén, 1991INT). This tactic partially neutralised the issue. Thus, despite the 1982 General Election becoming an effective referendum on the WEF issue, the SAP increased its vote by 2.7% and formed a minority administration, despite the opposition of all bourgeois parties and the organised business community.

The SAF spent an estimated SEK55-60 million intensifying its anti-WEF campaign, and "categorically" rejecting "**any** plan for the introduction of collective wage-earner funds in Sweden" [*my emphasis*] in an open letter to Palme, published in the *Expressen* newspaper prior to voting day (SI, 1983:6-7; Milner, 1989:133). This was a sum greater than the aggregated spending of all five political parties on the entire 1982 General Election (Boréus, 1994:112; Hansson, 1984). Edin estimated the resources available to SAF's anti-fund campaign, in terms of money and people, were *at least* ten times greater than for the LO (Olsen, 1991:134; 1992:82).

The new government was elected on a platform to introduce WEFs. However, its desire to reach a compromise solution led to the appointment of two 'expert' groups to advise on the preparation of final legislative proposals, including guidelines on profit-sharing and WEF investment (Adelsohn et al, 1983:5). They included representatives from the labour movement (Hedborg), the TCO, the Governor of the Central Bank (Dennis), the Director of the Fourth AP-Fund (Wikander), the Director of Scania (Wolrath), academia (Bergström) and public servant officials (Edin) (Ministry of Finance, 1984b:13-14). The bourgeois parties and the SAF refused to co-operate, with Curt Nicolin stating that capitalists "will not negotiate our own destruction" (*Dagens Nyheter* 20 September, 1982).

Opposition to the funds reached its climax with a demonstration in Stockholm which drew anywhere between twenty thousand and one hundred thousand people, depending upon who was doing the counting (George, 1990:17; Ivarsson, 1993INT). The intensity of the opposition was, by now, out of proportion to the de-radicalised 1983 proposals; their main purpose having now become a means of ensuring that devaluation generated lower real wages to increase international competitiveness and redistributed purchasing power from labour to capital, with only a small proportion retained for employees within WEFs (Milner, 1989:133). The new SAP administration sought to increase investment and economic growth through stimulation of corporate profitability and simultaneous public sector restraint, which was the antithesis of the Rehn-Meidner model (Pontusson, 1988:57). WEF legislation had become an *isolated* measure within an essentially orthodox economic framework rather than constituting part of a far-reaching democratisation initiative (Milner, 1989:134).

The Riksdag debate on WEFs was the largest and possibly most remarkable in Swedish parliamentary history, with eighty nine MPs making one hundred and twenty two speeches on three government motions and twenty motions opposing the scheme and lasting two full days; 20-21 December 1983 (*Riksdagens protokoll*, 1983; Åsard, 1985:9; 1986:207). Bourgeois speakers were considerably over-represented in the debate with 75.3% of all contributors. Moreover, the debate included elements of farse, when a photographer with a telephoto lens captured SAP Finance Minister, Feldt, scribbling a 'poem' during the parliamentary debate and reproduced it on the front page of the local Stockholm daily newspaper *Stockholms-Tidningen* the following day (Feldt, 1991:153). It went as follows (approximate translation on the right);

Löntagarfonder är ett jävla skit	WEFs are a damned load of shit
Men nu har vi baxat dem ända hit	But look how far we've shovelled it
Sen ska de fyllas med varenda pamp	Then shall they be filled with every VIP
som stött oss så starkt I våran kamp	who hurt us so strongly in our campaign
Nu behöver vi inte gå flera ronder	Now we do not need go several rounds
förrän hela Sverige är fullt av fonder.	before the whole of Sweden is full of funds.

Feldt angrily defended what he described as an "extremely private satire" which "reveals nothing about my views concerning the funds" (*Dagens Nyheter*, 22 December 1983:10). This embarrassing event, however, did not affect the eventual vote going according to party lines, and therefore an WEF system was established on 21st December 1983, after more than a decade of investigation and debate. The first appointments were made to the WEF boards in the following May and their began their operations soon thereafter (Hashi and Hussain, 1986:17).

The 1983 WEF Scheme

Aims

Four goals were established for the fund system (Ministry of Finance 1984b:7-16):

1. *reduction of distributional conflicts*, enabling higher profits without inflation,
2. *increased supply of risk capital*, stimulating investment, jobs and growth,
3. *increased employee influence* over production,
4. *redistribution of power and ownership* to reduce undue concentration.

These goals retained superficial similarity to those established by the Meidner Plan. However, distributional and economic democracy issues were given significantly less prominence. The 1983 plan emphasised the macroeconomic contribution that WEFs could make to facilitate higher profits without stimulating wage-cost inflationary pressure, whilst simultaneously reducing the cost, and increasing the availability, of risk capital to finance additional investment.

Organisation

The WEF system comprised five equal funds, each with a nominal regional affiliation reflected by their board members either living or working in the area to instil local knowledge within their operations.[6] Each board had nine members and four deputy members appointed by the government. These consisted of a chairperson, vice-chairperson, five board members representing wage-earners (three blue-collar and two white-collar), two representing social interests and at least two employee replacements. Their renewable term of office was one year, a deliberately

---

6   The five funds were Sydfonden, Fond Väst, Trefond Invest, Mellansvenska löntagarfonder and Nordfonden, representing the South, West, East, Central and Northern Swedish regions.

shorter mandate than the three years for ATP board members, in order to emphasise greater WEF accountability. The WEFs were located within the ATP system to ensure their legal independence whilst retaining parliamentary authority. This enhanced fund system flexibility since money not utilised by WEFs could be invested by another part of the ATP (*Finansdepartmentet*, 1983:52,66-78).

Finance

Finance derived from two sources; a payroll and a profit-sharing tax. The former was set at only 0.2% of wages and salaries, with the possibility of being increased to 0.5%, which in the event did not occur (Olsen, 1992:37). The profit-sharing element was set at 20% of *real profits*, after deducting tax and a "basic allowance" of *either* five hundred thousand kronor *or* 6% of the wage and salary bill according to company preference (George, 1990:15). The allowance was designed to avoid enterprises expanding on a small stock of capital making disproportionate contributions. The profit-sharing calculation establishing 'real profitability' was as follows (*Finansdepartmentet*, 1983:34-6,54);

```
Corporate taxable income
    + deduction for the previous year's local tax
    + deduction for losses in previous years
    + deductions for investments, research and export-credit allowances
    +/- changes in stock reserves reinstated, but not allocations to investment reserves
    - calculated national and local tax for the present year
    = NOMINAL RESULT
    - assets (stock, machinery, monetary assets) x inflation
    - inflation depreciation allowance (buildings and land improvements)
    + liabilities at year-start (including investment reserve) x inflation
    = REAL RESULT
    % total wage and salary bill
    = PROFIT-SHARING TAX BASE
20% profit-sharing tax – deductible for next year's income tax.
```

The Committee for Profit-Sharing estimated this calculation could be performed in most small and medium-sized companies between ten minutes to one hour, whilst the National Tax Board forecast that approximately fifteen man-years were required to examine the tax returns assuming five thousand enterprises participated in the scheme (Ministry of Finance, 1983:29). Companies excluded from compulsory profit-sharing contributions included sole traders, partnerships, family foundations, co-operative housing associations, municipal housing companies, life insurance companies, the Swedish National Lottery and the Football Pools (*Finansdepartmentet*, 1983:35).

Investment

Each WEF received an equal share of the capital provided by the ATP each year, until these payments ceased in 1990, to a ceiling of SEK400 million at 1983 prices (*Finansdepartmentet*, 1983:74-5). The five funds combined could, therefore, apply for an annual maximum of two billion kronor from the ATP to invest in equity. Additional income resulting from payroll or profit-sharing taxes accrued to the ATP not the WEFs. Thus, in 1983 prices, WEFs were predicted to receive a maximum SEK14 billion by 1990, representing between five and six per cent of the total value of listed shares. "Base amounts" used in calculating pensions and other government benefits were used to adjust the yearly ceiling by a cost of living index (*Finansdepartmentet*, 1983:14).

The draft legislation suggested that the funds should minimise risk by purchasing a wide portfolio of stocks (*Finansdepartmentet*, 1983:79). WEFs were restricted to investing in Swedish companies, particularly manufacturing industry, and have concern for long-term development not short-term share price fluctuation. They could provide risk capital for co-operatives and/or invest in bonds and securities, but the main focus for their investment was the purchase of existing shares via the stock market. Each fund had to pay the ATP a three per cent real rate of return for capital usage (*Finansdepartmentet*, 1983:8). This represented the advisory commission's estimation of Sweden's long-term growth rate and was intended to be an exacting target for fund managers, ensuring WEFs enhanced capital allocative efficiency.

Voting Rights

Half the voting rights accruing to the funds through share ownership were to be transferred to local trade union representatives at their request. In multi-union workplaces, failure to reach agreement resulted in the fund apportioning voting rights according to the number of members each union possessed at each site. In contrast to all earlier plans, the draft legislation restricted the aggregated collective funds to a minority of the voting rights in any company (*Finansdepartmentet*, 1983:65,82) (Figure 5-2). Subsequent amendments specified this overall limitation in more detail. Each WEF was only entitled to hold up to 8% of the voting stock of any individual *listed* company, with the Fourth AP-fund 10%, making the combined maximum 49.99% (Olsen, 1992:38). In view of the WEFs small size, significant co-ordinated holding was improbable. When a Fifth AP-fund was established in 1989, individual WEFs were further restricted to only 6% of the voting stock in *listed* companies to ensure combined voting power remained beneath 50%.

Time Limit

The WEFs were restricted to receive additional finance for only an initial seven year period. Once this experimental period had ceased, fund assets would decline unless yields exceeded the three per cent real rate of return payable to the ATP for the loan of capital (*Finansdepartmentet*, 1983:53). The restriction ostensibly provided a long-term planning base for companies, unions and citizens, although it was probably more concerned with further minimising opposition to the reform. The party took the position:

> Since the democratisation of economic life can be accomplished in a variety of ways, it seems appropriate that the influence exerted by workers through ownership should be clearly demarcated. This prompts the conclusion that the total scope of employee

investment funds should be limited. Thus their expansion is to be concluded with their attainment by 1990 of the intended volume (Ministry of Finance, 1984b:16).

Palme consequently stated "this proposal is not the first step – it is *the step*" [my emphasis] (*Riksdagens protokoll*, 1983:91). This emasculation of the proposal, by announcing its demise in 1990 *before* it had even been introduced, was controversial amongst the labour movement grassroots. Meidner (1994INT) regarded as "totally illogical" the idea of conducting an experiment you have a prior commitment to terminate regardless of its results.

Conclusion

The struggle for electoral support for the principles inherent economic democratisation ended with a major political setback for the social democratic labour movement. It is impossible to ascertain whether this would have still been the case had the policy been more wisely handled from the start, with time taken to present the ideas to the general population, and the labour movement taking full advantage of the activist enthusiasm for the proposal when first advocated in 1975-6 and championing the idea. Nevertheless, the fact remained that the WEF proposal contributed to perceptions of the government exhibiting general arrogance and elitist tendencies, amongst the electorate, partly due to the SAP's long term in office. It was this, together with the expressed view of 'give the others a chance', that contributed to the SAP remaining out of power for six turbulent years. During this time, the Swedish Model was tested by the difficult economic circumstances, whilst the SAP sought to use this period to develop a new strategy for new times. Confusingly for this book, they named their new strategy the 'Third Way' programme. This is the subject of the next chapter.

Table 5-2: Comparison of the main WEF proposals in 1976, 1978 and 1983

	1976	1978	1983
Goals	Solidarity wage policy. Reduce power concentration. Wage earner influence.	Solidarity wage policy redistribution. Wage earner influence. Increase capital formation.	Capital formation. Redistribute wages to investment. Wage earner influence.
Tax	20% pre-tax profits.	a) 20% profits. b) 3% wage bill.	a) 20% excess profit tax. b) 0.2% payroll tax.
Payment	Obligatory share issues, remain within company.	a) obligatory share issues. b) cash.	Cash to ATP, SEK2bn max. to WEFs.
Companies affected	More than 50 (or 100) employees.	Largest 200 firms.	All Plc's, public sector and econ. organisations.
Collective funds	Yes	Yes	Yes
Individual shares	No	No	No
Dividends	Purchase new shares. Union educational and welfare services. Support worker-directors.	Union educational and welfare services. Assist co-determination.	WEFs retain to help pay ATP 3% real return on capital.
Fund system	Dual: a) central clearing fund administers dividends. b) sector (industry) funds exercise influence.	Two separate systems: a) 24 county-WEFs. b) development funds. i) 2 national funds. ii) 24 county funds.	5 competing WEFs, nominally regionally based (North, South, East, West, Central), trading in shares through stock market.
WEF Board	a) Central – national union appointees. b) Sector – public reps, majority trade union reps: 50/50 split between industry/non-industry unions.	a) WEFs – local & regional wage-earners equal reps. b) Development funds. i) one with majority public reps & other with majority wage-earner reps. ii) unclear, possibly county council controlled.	9–member Board appointed by govt., with majority wage-earner representatives.
Company Director Entitlement	First 20% WEF capital-entitlement appointed by local unions; thereafter by sector funds.	Each fund appoints.	WEFs appoint – fund manager or outside expert. Local unions vote half WEF entitlement.
Restrictions on WEF development	None.	None.	a) SEK2bn. p.a. max. b) No new capital after 1990. c) 8% (later 6%) max. voting rights. d) No 'entrepreneurial responsibility'.

Chapter 6

Back to the Future

Crisis Keynesianism, 1976-1982

The fact that the SAP had lost the 1976 General Election, by the narrowest of margins was a shock to the entire Swedish political system. The SAP had been in office for 44 years, and their values had become almost synonymous with perceptions of Swedish society – certainly when viewed from the outside. Despite the fact that reform of the Swedish constitution had weakened the dominance of the largest political party, by increasing the proportionality of the electoral system, together with shortening the frequency of the electoral cycle from four to three years, and irrespective of the fact that the 'left' and 'right' political bloc's had exactly the same number of seats since the 1973 election, the SAP defeat was still largely unexpected.

The bourgeois coalition that replaced it in government comprised the Liberal, Centre (formally Agrarian) and Moderate parties – the latter being the conservative party in Sweden. This coalition was led by Thorbjörn Fälldin, the ex-farmer leader of the Centre Party, whose popularity owed much to his principled stance against Sweden's continuation of nuclear power generation. This issue proved problematic for the SAP, because their support for economic growth, to facilitate full employment and finance welfare programmes, became associated by many as forming a 'cosy' relationship with Sweden's large, and powerful corporations.

The change of government, however, led to an inexperienced coalition government taking office at a time of international economic crisis. The raw material supply shock to the international economy, caused by a sharp rise in oil prices, destabilised the Swedish economy and caused a wage-cost eruption between 1974 and 1976 (Lundberg, 1985:25). This weakened the coherence of the wage bargaining system, and presented a difficult choice for the Rehn-Meidner strategy; to intensify the profit squeeze in order to reduce inflationary pressure and assist wage moderation, or to stimulate profit margins to facilitate a higher level of investment necessary to maintain full employment and international competitiveness in the long-term.

By the time the bourgeois government had actually assumed office, the Swedish economy had experienced a downturn, and the increases in non-wage tax costs implemented by the previous government had contributed to a profitability crisis, which lasted for several years, and had a severe impact on exports, production and investment. Moreover, in the aftermath of the sharp deterioration in international competitiveness caused by the sudden increase in wage-cost push inflation, the Swedish crown became grossly overvalued.

The bourgeois government responded to the negative economic indicators by implementing a 'simple' form of Keynesianism, via a fiscal stimulation package, coupled with a 9% devaluation in 1977 (Calmfors, 1984). This proved to be insufficient, however, to restore former competitive conditions. Swedish business was increasingly priced out of a shrinking international market. Firms responded by announcing large-scale layoffs, whilst the volume of productive investment declined to 40% below its 1975-77 peak.

Productivity growth within the competitive sector stagnated, and even became negative during specific years (Lundberg, 1985:25). This had a dramatic impact upon Sweden's productive capacity. Compared with earlier trends in productivity growth, the economists at the SNS research institute estimated a capacity gap of between 10% and 15% during the years 1977-1978 (Lundberg, 1996:73). Consequently, there was clearly sufficient under-used economic resources for the government to attempt to close this gap, through a boost to aggregate demand and through measures to facilitate export-led growth. However, the problem for the new government concerned the timidity of their Keynesian stimulus package when related to the scale of the problems facing industry. In the absence of a competitive exchange rate, Swedish export-orientated companies proved unable to maintain their international market share, and thus continued to reduce current activity. Domestically orientated enterprise benefited from the fiscal stimulus package, but the combination of an overvalued exchange rate and excessive real wages, combined with structural problems in the Swedish economy, led to a sluggish response to the accommodatory policy stance (Lundberg, 1996:76).

Criticisms of the accommodatory stabilisation policy, due to its encouragement of "irresponsible" wage demands, ignores the evidence that the main problem facing the Swedish economy was a lack of demand. In such circumstances, the collapse of Swedish industry appeared a more realistic possibility than any potential damage that might be inflicted by wage-cost-push inflation.

In view of the worsening economic environment, the bourgeois government determined to protect employment and future production capacity through enacting a large scale industrial subsidy programme, aimed at those firms and manufacturing sectors experiencing particular problems, together with the nationalisation of declining industries (Rehn and Viklund, 1990). Selective subsidies to individual firms totalled 1.1 per cent of GDP in 1977-1978, rising to 2 per cent in 1982-1983 (Calmfors, 1993:44). The government additionally expanded the labour market programmes, as advocated by the Rehn-Meidner model in such circumstances, and in the process engaged up to 5 per cent of the labour force in a combination of public works, training courses, subsidised employment and/or sheltered workshops (Rehn and Viklund, 1990). Finally, the public sector was allowed to expand to become in effect an employer of last resort, and provided the means of expanding labour market participation, particularly for women, during adverse economic circumstances (Lindbeck, 1997:1311; Rojas, 1998:78,86). Thus, belatedly, the Swedish government introduced significant fiscal expansion, at least by comparative international standards (Bosworth and Rivlin, 1987).

This strategy succeeded in preventing official unemployment from rising beyond 3%, which was viewed as a political necessity for a new government, already charged by the social democratic opposition with ruining the economy and threatening the accomplishments of four decades. Moreover, it avoided the waste of resources, together with the negative material and psychological impact upon those individuals who would otherwise have been rendered unemployed. The economic theory of hysteresis, developed a decade after this time period, suggests that prevention of a large rise in unemployment has beneficial effects, because, once unemployment has taken hold, individuals find it harder to get back into the labour market and the reality of unemployment tends to perpetuate itself (Blanchard and Summers, 1986; Jenkinson, 1987).

There were, however, two main problems with this response to the international recession. Firstly, state subsidisation of mature industries, including shipyards, iron ore mining, together with iron and steel manufacturing, deferred the necessary rationalisation of the Swedish economy. It preserved old-style industries which had become 'price takers' in a highly competitive market for standardised products, and thereby prevented a reallocation of resources towards new, dynamic 'price makers' in emerging, high value-added markets (Erixon, 1984:115-124). This, weakness was similarly shared by the Rehn-Meidner model, in that it tended to lock resources into the already profitable companies, through the operation of the solidarity wage strategy in combination with tax incentives to re-invest retained profits as opposed to distribution to shareholders. Thus, although the booms of 1969-1970 and 1973-1974 were accompanied by large industrial investments, these were over-concentrated in such industries as iron and steel, petrochemicals, shipyards and shipping (Lundberg, 1985:25).

The second drawback with the policy of maintaining existing employment at all costs, related to the impact upon the government budgetary position, which declined dramatically due to the combination of fiscal policy expansion, industrial subsidies, labour market programmes and rising employment in the public sector, alongside a reduced tax-take resulting from lower corporate profits. The budgetary crisis additionally impacted upon capital formation, due to a sharp decline in collective savings without an offsetting rise in either corporate or household savings rates. The result was an extremely low rate of net savings, running at 4 per cent of GNP by the beginning of the 1980s, compared to a norm of some 12% to 15% (Lundberg, 1985:29). Reliance upon increased international borrowing, together with the current account deficit, reduced Swedish macroeconomic policy autonomy.

Low capacity utilisation, political uncertainty, high tax rates and an insufficient level of current profits, combined to lower the realised investment rate below the warranted level of investment required to maintain full employment in the long-run. Indeed, it appears that financial, rather than productive, investments yielded greater profits at this time than construction of new plant and equipment (Lundberg, 1985:29). A larger scale devaluation and reflation package could have been effective during the early period of the recessionary period. However, this strategy lost a considerable degree of its potency after 1979 because the low level of investment over the proceeding period, together with the scrapping of a considerable proportion of capacity, undermined the capacity for a sustained increase in economic activity, and therefore reinforced the structural immobility of resources (Lundberg, 1996:77).

The economic record of the bourgeois government was therefore rather mixed. Full employment was maintained, and compared with the almost universal failure amongst other industrialised economies, to deliver on this central tenant of social democracy, this achievement was significant in its own right. Nevertheless, the method by full employment that had been sustained was certainly not without cost.

Prevention of job losses had generated an unsustainable budget deficit, whilst industrial subsidies had locked scarce resources in amongst the least productive industries, rather than concentrate upon developing firms in predicted growth areas. Thus, capital formation and employee productivity stagnated during this period.

These failings cannot be blamed on the failure of the Rehn-Meidner model, because the economic strategy implemented by the bourgeois government owed little to the sophisticated package of policies developed by the LO economists. Instead, the economic strategy pursued was largely based upon stage one Keynesian principles. Due to the threat of recession, aggregate demand stimulation, via an expansive fiscal policy, became the main macroeconomic tool, supported by repeated devaluations – 9% in 1977 and a further 10% in 1981. Elements of second stage Keynesianism were retained, primarily labour market policy, which encompassed 5% of the entire labour force at the height of the recession. Moreover, the attempts to pursue a co-ordinated and solidaristic wage policy continued, and secured a 10% reduction in the real hourly income of industrial workers, from its 1976 peak, in under five years (Rehn and Viklund, 1990:301). Without such restraint, the economic record of the bourgeois government may have been far worse (Erixon, 1984; Ryner, 1999:57).

Critics who have subsequently claimed that the Rehn-Meidner model had already created the problems experienced during this period are dismissed by Lundberg (1985:33) as engaging in "the metaphysics of wishful thinking" and advancing "unscientific" conclusions. In particular, claims that the Swedish economy had already begun to indicate a significant deterioration in economic growth rates, as a result of stage two Keynesiansim, are incorrect, because there was no apparent deviation in Sweden's growth record from the OECD average until the mid-1970s. Consequently, the economic problems experienced in the second half of the 1970s, and their subsequent effects in latter decades, can be identified as due to a combination of unfortunate external shocks destabilising the Swedish economy, amplified by an incorrect strategic response implemented cautiously by an inexperienced government.

Reconstructing the Rehn-Meidner model, 1982-1991

The record of economic stagnation proved to be a major factor in the defeat of the bourgeois coalition in the 1982 General Election. Thus, the SAP resumed office faced by a stagnant economy and with industrial production having declined by 6.2 percentage points between 1974 and 1982. Moreover, due to rising budget deficits during the bourgeois governments term of office, the SAP inherited a foreign debt of 21.7% of GDP, representing a sharp deviation from the 5.3% of GDP net credit position pertaining in 1974 (Ryner, 1994:247). Furthermore, the long duration of the economic recession had led to surplus capacity being scrapped rather than temporarily 'mothballed', thereby imposing capacity constraints upon a rapid recovery in industrial production (Lundberg, 1985:25).

In view of the economic difficulties facing any new administration, the SAP advanced a distinctive economic strategy they termed the 'Third Way' economic programme (TWEP). This was intended to signify a middle road between the monetarism of British Prime Minister Margaret Thatcher and the type of 'simple' Keynesianism associated with the previous bourgeois government and/or the Mitterand government in France, which had sought to combine demand management with extensive nationalisation (Ross and Jenson, 1994:172). The TWEP was presented as a return to traditional social democracy after the radicalised 'red' 1970s (Bergstrom, 1987; Åmark, 1988).

Initial Phase – The Recovery Programme

The TWEP sought to reverse Swedish industrial decline through the combination of a substantial devaluation to restore the international competitiveness of Swedish industry, together with a tightening of aggregate demand management and co-ordinated restraint in wage formation, to restrain inflationary pressures. Labour market policies would additionally deal with any resultant unemployment (Ryner, 1994). The timing of the shift to an export-orientated strategy proved, with the benefit of hindsight, to be fortunate as it coincided with a recovery in the international economy. Therefore, it facilitated an expansion in Swedish exports, and hence prompted an economic recovery. The current account started to improve and unemployment, which had risen to a post-war high of 3.1% in 1982, started to decline (Iversen, 1996:420).

The essential component of the TWEP was the use of a 16% devaluation as an offensive policy instrument utilised to secure a competitive exchange rate, rather than as a defensive measure (Lundberg, 1985:25). Thus, the strategy depended upon the restoration of price competitiveness leading to export-orientated Swedish industry recapturing market share and expanding production to meet additional overseas demand, thereby securing export-led growth. Together with an earlier 10% devaluation in 1981, the 1982 devaluation contributed to a total 35% reduction in the value of the Swedish krona between 1976 and 1983 (Gros and Thygeson, 1992:17; Hansen et al, 1991:148-9). However, it was the acceptance of a 10% reduction in real wages by the trade union movement, in the attempt to reverse rising unemployment, that enabled industrial costs to be reduced by a substantial 45% below the levels pertaining during 1973-4.

In order to achieve a real exchange rate devaluation, however, the strategy had to secure a shift in productive resources throughout the Swedish economy, from consumption to savings, to thereby provide sufficient national funds for industrial productive investment and the shift resources from the sheltered to the competitive sectors. This required a relative shift in prices in favour of export goods (Henrekson, 1990:93). In turn, this necessitated trade union consent to a further decline in real wages, whilst the government pursued a restrictive fiscal and monetary policy, to facilitate the transfer of resources toward the internationally competitive sector (Ahlén, 1989; Pontusson, 1992:116-7). According to the Marshall-Learner condition, a devaluation only secures an improvement in the current account if the sum of the price elasticities of import and export goods and services is greater than unity. Empirical estimates suggested that the long-term values for Swedish produce were in the magnitude of 1.5-2 and 0.8, respectively, thus producing a Marshall-Learner value of between 2.3 and 2.8, thereby indicating that devaluation was an effective policy option for the (Goldstein and Khan, 1985).

The devaluation strategy appeared to work well, with an increase in net exports leading to a positive balance of trade in the first year of its implementation, thereby overturning a trade deficit equivalent to 3.7% of GDP in 1984 (OECD, 1989:45-6). Fiscal and monetary policy restraint, a reduction in the growth of the public sector and co-ordinated wage moderation, all contributed to export-led stimulation to the Swedish economy feeding through to enhance the profit levels of Swedish industry and thereby encourage a rise in business fixed investment. Ryner (1994:254) reports that, one year into the programme, the ratio of profits to value added had already recovered to between 0.30 and 0.35, which represented a level approximately the same as enjoyed during the 'golden years' of the 1950s and 1960s. Relative unit costs were reduced, and Swedish industry responded by expanding output and increasing the size of the manufacturing workforce for the first time in a decade (Calmfors, 1993:48).

One criticism levelled at the devaluation policy concerned the fact that relative prices only declined by about one-third of the amount of the nominal adjustment in the currency. Firms preferred to absorb two-thirds of the impact through a rise in their profits, rather than attempting to increase their sales by taking full advantage of the devaluation and lowering their prices in foreign currency by the maximum amount. However, this assumes two things. Firstly, that the only factor preventing a large increase in Swedish export activity concerned relative price competitiveness, which could be cured by devaluation, rather than issues of quality and reliability, which may require higher retained profits to finance additional investment in new technology and improved distribution networks. Secondly, faced with economic conditions where corporate profitability and investment had been squeezed to artificially low levels for the better part of a decade, some increase in profit levels would appear to be perfectly reasonable. Indeed, even the Rehn-Meidner approach, with its preference for profits to be squeezed, recognised that firms had to make a minimum level of profit unless their future expectations would be harmed and with them, their willingness to investment in productive capacity (Henrekson, 1990:94; Ryner, 1994:256).

Interesting, the 1982 devaluation, whilst a necessary component of the package of measures, was viewed as a necessary evil, and not a policy instrument that the SAP government wanted to utilise if future circumstances determined its usefulness. The policy was discussed as "the" devaluation, and immediately upon its completion, the government adopted a hard currency policy (Bieler, 2000:42). Thereafter, they sought to establish the credibility necessary to convince trade union negotiators and representatives of big business that government would no longer accommodate inflationary wage claims or price rises, and that these would result in unemployment and lower profits rather than be painlessly offset through devaluation. SAP officials further argued that devaluations are anti-worker because they reduce living standards. However, the attempt to establish a new consensus around this change in policy was only moderately successful, as it was clearly at odds with the evidence that the economic success being enjoyed by the new administration was in large part due to the very policy the government were now denouncing.

The fiscal policy restraint accompanying the TWEP additionally led to the substantial improvement in the government's budgetary position, as industrial subsidies were phased out and increased industrial activity resulted in higher levels of corporate taxation revenue (Ryner, 1994:251). The budget deficit had growth from 2% of GDP in 1976 to 13% in 1982 (Bosworth and Lawrence, 1987). However, economic recovery enabled its reduction to 4% of GDP by 1996, with two thirds of this sum due in equal measure to tax increases and reductions in public spending (Lindbeck, 1997:1306).

The increase in international borrowing, caused by the budget deficits tolerated by the bourgeois government, had caused Sweden to become more closely linked with the international financial market. Therefore, the SAP government no longer had quite the degree of autonomy over its monetary and exchange rate policies. Financial regulation and restrictions of capital movements had facilitated Swedish governments to pursue counter-cyclical economic policies intended to pursue domestic objectives, including full employment, a low rate of inflation, decent levels of economic growth and reduced rates of social inequality. This, too, had been weakened by Sweden's foreign borrowing, and provoked demands from leading Swedish banks for financial deregulation (Olsen, 1994:208). Financial regulation facilitated the steering of economic resources into productive investment in the tradable sector (Calmfors, 1993:50). This element of the strategy also worked well in its early stages, with a full 77% of the increase in Swedish GDP being channelled into capital formation, between 1981 and 1984, with only 17% being realised in net consumption (Henrekson, 1990:96). Nevertheless, the TWEP accelerated the process of deregulation started by the previous bourgeois government, with thirteen controls abolished between 1974 and 1985. This included the ending of liquidity quotas and credit ceilings, together with liberalisation of controls over new bond issues and restrictions governing bank lending rates (Olsen, 1994:209).

The final element of the recovery programme involved the utilisation of labour market policies to reduce residual unemployment not otherwise dealt with by the expansion of employment in the internationally competitive sector. Approximately 5% of the labour force were enrolled on labour market schemes during 1982/83, with almost half of these employed by temporary public works schemes. Expenditure on labour market policy accounted for approximately 4% of GNP (Johannesson, 1991).

The Secondary Phase – Building upon Economic Success

The TWEP proved to be a considerable success, providing the economic conditions for Swedish industry to take full advantage of an upswing in the international economy, and provide export-led growth. However, three years into the project, and another General Election victory secured, the SAP government had the opportunity to move from a recovery strategy towards strengthening the economy for the medium to long-term. They had a number of choices. Firstly, they could have reinstituted the full Rehn-Meidner strategy, complete with concentration upon traditional social democratic goals such as continued expansion of the welfare state. However, the perceived necessity to continue re-building the industrial sector, after its period of deindustrialisation, necessitated further transfer of resources from the sheltered to the tradable sectors, thereby limiting the resources available for welfare development. The LO had accepted this in their 1986 LO Congress report 'Fackföreningsrörelsen och Välfärdsstaten' [the trade union movement and the welfare state], which suggested that the welfare state was now fully developed in terms of its overall share of national resources, and therefore additional benefits must accrue from initiatives to improve its efficiency of operations and service delivery.[1]

Other elements of the Rehn-Meidner model had, of course, never been abandoned, most notably the reliance upon labour market policy to remove bottleneck unemployment. The tighter aggregate demand management regime that accompanied the 1982 devaluation could be represented as a return to the Rehn-Meidner approach, even through this was not intended to squeeze profits in the trading sector. Indeed, one sizeable objective pursued by the post-1982 strategy was to restore former levels of profitability to Swedish export-orientated companies, and thereby stimulate investment levels necessary to maintain full employment in the long-run. This part of the recovery strategy had worked well, and the SAP government were unwilling to restore the profit squeeze so quickly after devoting part of their strategy to raising profits. Moreover, the Rehn-Meidner reliance upon collective capital formation had become a politically sensitive issue after the WEF debate, and this was one issue the SAP did not want to re-open. Therefore, private savings and retained profits had to provide resources for productive investment. This, in turn, required an acceptance of higher profits in manufacturing industry, and/or a relaxation in tax disincentives to save.

The second option open to the SAP government was to use their mandate to pursue the third stage post-Keynesian strategy advocated by proponents of economic democratisation, but to pursue this in a different guise to prevent unwanted political fallout. The rationale for this course of action was equally pressing in 1985 as a decade earlier, since the problems identified with other forms of Keynesian strategy had not disappeared over time. Nevertheless, this option was always unlikely due to the lack of enthusiasm from Finance Minister, Feldt, and the ideological exhaustion of the trade union movement, together with the desire to avoid issues which might damage the party's delicate electoral popularity.

The SAP government therefore began to evolve its programme in perhaps a surprising direction, namely to incorporate elements advocated by the neo-liberal, orthodox economics, internationally dominant at this point of time. In particular, the government began a process of financial deregulation, closely followed by the lifting of exchange controls in 1989.

The lifting of controls that had shielded the Swedish economy from the dictates of the international money markets for the entire postwar period was clearly a controversial strategy. However, the government argued that economic autonomy had been weakened by the greater international borrowing caused by the bourgeois government's large budget deficits and trade imbalances, and therefore the deregulation was simply accepting what had de facto already occurred. The attempt to maintain low interest rates, simultaneously with internationally high levels of inflation, had arguably undermined the institutional capacity of the Riksbank to

---

[1]   The restrictions imposed upon public expenditure and the reforms in the public bargaining system weakened the bargaining power of public sector unions, resulting in public sector wages declining from 97% of the private sector average during 1971-79, to 89% by 1980-88 (Suack, 1991).

control the money supply through credit controls, when excess demand for debt drove financial innovation to evade regulation. It was this that prompted the major banks to press for deregulation (Notermans, 1993:142-6).

With the progressive removal of administrative controls, the Riksbank argued that the application of internationally determined interest rates remained the only effective method to control inflation. Monetary policy thus became "norm based" in that it adapted to international interest rates (Bergström, 1993:159-60). This would, in turn, prevent inflationary wage-cost pressures by exposing wage bargainers to market discipline (Horngren, 1993). Abolition of exchange controls reinforced this process by giving credibility to the new monetary policy, reinforced by the 'hard' fixed exchange policy (Horngren and Westmand, 1991:26-7).

This strategy was founded upon the assumption that all economic actors possess rational expectations, in that, on average, they understand the likely consequences of their actions, and will therefore change their behaviour accordingly. In this case, unions and employers internalise an understanding of increased interest rate sensitivity to the consequences of their actions, and therefore behave more 'responsibly' if government refuses to accommodate inflationary wage claims (Bergström, 1993; Horngren, 1993). In practice, however, the adoption of a non-accommodatory 'conservative' monetary policy has resulted in the government abdicating its responsibility to pursue a discretionary macroeconomic strategy in order to maintain an domestic stability, consistent with full employment (Ryner, 1994:252).

One reason why the government had become so concerned about controlling the behaviour of wage bargaining agents, arose from the fact that the co-ordinated wage bargaining system was in the process of fragmenting after pressure for decentralisation from the SAF (for further discussion, see Chapter Nine). Government attempts to restore a measure of co-ordination through tripartite meetings and incomes policy norms were only partially successful, despite the determination on behalf of the LO to restore a form of managed wage formation system. However, in practice, the decentralised system has proved to be prone to inflationary 'leap-frogging' of wage demands and has not exercised the same degree of restraint as the central organisations were able to achieve. Of course, this is in line with bargaining theory (Calmfors and Driffill, 1988; Iversen, 1999). However, given the unstable vacuum left by the collapse of the co-ordinated system, the government sought to get the unions to accept 'caution' and 'responsibility' (Rehn and Viklund, 1990:303). Other options were tried, including a tax-based incomes policy in 1985, but the results proved disappointing.

Wars of the Roses

The synthesis of elements from traditional Keynesianism, the Rehn-Meidner approach and latterly neo-liberal ideas, was presented to the Swedish voters and labour movement members as 'adapting the Rehn-Meidner model to new times' (Palme, 1987). However, a significant proportion of this new cocktail of policies had little in common with traditional social democratic ideals. For example, the reforms of the welfare state owed more to ideas emanating from the USA than to the Rehn-Meidner approach (World Bank, 1997; Stiglitz, 1998). Taxation underwent a major reform process in 1991, and this reduced the progressivity of income taxation lower than it had been three decades earlier.

The LO additionally opposed the deregulation of the financial markets as this increased the difficulty involved in managing the economy. The Rehn-Meidner model, in common with its Keynesian heritage, presupposed the continuation of credit and exchange controls. The government, however, were persuaded that deregulation would increase the allocative efficiency of the credit market; a necessity if the state no longer wished to follow the Rehn-Meidner model prescription of increasing the share of risk capital provided by collective savings (Ministry of Finance, 1984a). Similarly, instead of the 'norm based' monetary policy, the LO preferred the Rehn-Meidner approach to the restraint of inflation, namely a tight macroeconomic stance combined with collective savings. The latter may perhaps involve investment funds financed by a form of 'excess profit' taxation, thereby resembling the Fourth ATP Pension Fund and/or the Waldenström Report (see Chapter Four) (Ryner, 1999:65).

The 1980s were a very different decade to the 1970s, however, and the LO were no longer the ideological powerhouse of the labour movement. Instead, the Ministry of Finance tended to set the economic agenda for the government. Thus, policy makers were able to resist increasingly vocal criticism from the trade union wing of the labour movement that their policies were deviating from the traditional social democratic heritage. This public disagreement between Finance Ministry and LO leadership became coined the 'war of the roses', after the shared symbol of both political and industrial sectors in the social democratic labour movement.

There are a number of different explanations that have been presented to explain this untypical public argument. Criticisms of the LO, whether accurate on the basis of the harm that this did to the electoral prospects of the SAP, nevertheless fail to account for their main charge, which is that the SAP shifted its economic strategy towards neo-liberal ideas, and did so whilst continuing to maintain that it had remained faithful to the Rehn-Meidner approach.

Other factors included the fact that the Finance Ministry tends to have fewer routine contacts with interest groups than other ministries and might therefore be expected to have less immediate sympathy for the objectives favoured by these organisations (Petersson, 1989). Furthermore, Ryner points to the interaction of a "transnational elite" on economic matters, where regular meetings between central bankers and government economists facilitate the transmission of the latest thinking on the subject, which, at the time, enhanced the spread of neo-liberal theoretical approaches (Ryner, 1999).

Ryner notes that there is at least a superficial appearance that both the Rehn-Meidner and monetarist approaches both call for a restrictive macroeconomic framework to deter inflation, and that this represents "an important bridge from one discourse to the other" (Ryner, 1999:66-8). Of course, there is a clear and decisive difference between a more restrictive form of counter cyclical aggregate demand management, intended to ensure a profit squeeze in order to facilitate a co-ordinated solidaristic wage bargaining system, and a monetarist approach which emphasises market determination of all allocative outcomes. Nevertheless, this "Popperian falsification of Keynesian ideas" facilitated the shift towards neo-liberalism within the SAP government's evolving programme (Ryner, 1999:68).

Three Problems: Deregulation, Inflation and Capital Flight

The deregulation of the financial markets was, with the benefit of hindsight, badly timed, irrespective of whether it was theoretically justified or not. The sudden relaxation of controls that had closely regulated most aspects of credit control, the degree of competition in the sector, the provision of minimum deposits for mortgage business and so forth, had the inevitable consequence of stimulating new competition in the sector. Indeed, this was the desired result of deregulation.

The macroeconomic logic of implementing deregulation must therefore be questionable, with its predictable expansionary consequences, at precisely the moment when the Swedish economy was already experiencing admirable rates of export-led growth, but whilst capacity constraints, inherited from the preceding period of stagnation, had not yet been eliminated. Thus, a 20% expansion of bank credit fed directly into other areas of the economy, leading to an "explosion" of asset prices, particularly property and shares quoted on the Swedish stock market. The prices of purchasing office buildings increased fourfold between 1980 and 1990, whilst private houses experienced a five-fold increase. Consumer goods experienced a doubling of prices, whilst share prices rose by a staggering ten times over this decade.

The consequence was a reversal of the recovery strategy's success in channelling additional resources into the rebuilding of Swedish export industry, as 102% of additional resources fed directly into consumption between 1985 and 1988 (Henrekson, 1990:96). Sweden embarked upon a remarkable asset price inflation, and this switched scarce resources away from the tradeable sector before capacity constraints could be successfully addressed. The intensity of consumer demand is reflected in the fact that the personal savings ratio fell by a dramatic seven percentage points between 1985 and 1988 (Glyn, 1998:8).

Growth switched to being generated primarily in the non-tradable sector. This consequence could have been at least partially negated if aggregate demand policy were made more restrictive (Franzen and Horgren, 1989; Bergman et al, 1990; 1991). However, this would have squeezed profit margins in the tradable sector and undermined their investment programme, at least in the absence of cheap risk capital generated through collective savings. Unfortunately, since this option had been seemingly ruled out in favour of a market orientated strategy, and therefore the full beneficial impact of the 1982 devaluation was never allowed to take full effect (Henrekson, 1991). Thus, Ryner (1999:64) argues that "one cannot but conclude that capital deregulation and the strategy to increase Sweden's interest rate sensitivity seriously backfired".

Failure to fully implement the Rehn-Meidner strategy was always likely to undermine the co-ordinated wage bargaining system. Tight labour markets combined with ineffective central union organisational control over its members, enabling unions in sheltered sectors of the economy to exploit their bargaining position and ratchet wage demands upwards during negotiations, thereby free riding on more responsible bargaining partners (Notermans, 1992:26). Indeed, Ryner (1999:65) suggests that:

> It is quite remarkable that the Ministry of Finance could have thought that they could stabilise bargaining by blatantly violating the conditions LO required for wage co-ordination.

Accordingly, Swedish competitiveness deteriorated rapidly, with unit labour costs rising more rapidly than in most OECD countries (Iversen, 1996:420).

The final weakness with the TWEP involved its central key assumption that higher profits would inevitably lead to higher levels of investment in domestic productive capacity. In the absence of controls over the movement of capital this, however, appears to have been only weakly realised. Swedish foreign direct investment (FDI) represented a mere 10% of total business investment in 1985, but this had risen to 28% by 1989, the year foreign exchange controls were finally abolished (OECD, 1990:25).

As a proportion of GDP, Sweden's FDI rose from less than 1% in 1982, to in excess of 6% by 1990. The latter was the highest rate amongst all industrialised nations. Indeed, during the decade of the 1980s, the outward flow of productive investment capital rose more than forty-fold. As can be seen from Table 6-1, net direct investment outflow increased substantially from relatively small amounts in the 1970s, to $12.6 billion in 1990. Had this money been invested in productive capital within Sweden, the economy is unlikely to have had such inflationary difficulties, as its capacity utilisation would not have been such a tight constraint upon expansion in demand.

The loss of a substantial proportion of Swedish productive investment overseas, proved to be the ultimate weakness of the government's strategy. Without additional jobs and investment being channelled into domestic plant and equipment, there remained no reason why Swedish unions should continue to exercise wage restraint if the profits retained as a consequence were to be used to finance a more rapid transfer of their jobs abroad. Support for FDI was always conditional, for the unions, upon its ability to strengthen the viability of Swedish-located companies, and therefore secure jobs in the long-term. The circumstances in the 1980s did not represent a strengthening of manufacturing in Sweden, but rather represented capital flight, facilitated by the removal of exchange controls.

A Strategy Out Of Control?

The government reaction to the growing inflationary pressures, generated by a consumer boom feeding off the wealth effect arising from the unprecedented explosion in asset prices, involved a sudden tightening of the macroeconomic policy stance. A cross-party agreement was forged with the Centre Party, whereby 3% of all wages would be "obligatorily saved" from September 1989 until the end of 1990, to slow the growth in private consumption. However, inflation had by now reached double figures and with trade and budget deficits forecast, Finance Minister Feldt tabled an austerity package aimed at reducing economic overheating.

This package involved a temporary freeze of rents, local taxes, dividends, prices and wages. It was initially supported by the LO leadership, however this support was ultimately withdrawn after opposition from rank-and-file union members to a temporary ban on strikes, which was also included in the crisis package. Friendless, the austerity measures were defeated in parliament, and the government resigned – albeit reluctance by the opposition parties to take over a deteriorating economy, close to a general election, led to Carlsson forming a new government within the week. Feldt, however, resigned from party politics.

Table 6-1: Direct investment, 1970-1995 ($US million)

Year	Outflow	Inflow	Net Outflow
1970	213	108	105
1971	176	84	92
1972	265	65	200
1973	293	84	209
1974	430	77	353
1975	434	80	354
1976	596	5	591
1977	737	81	656
1978	415	70	345
1979	618	112	506
1980	625	251	374
1981	825	181	644
1982	1212	355	857
1983	1458	226	1232
1984	1497	290	1207
1986	3963	1083	2880
1987	4780	639	4087
1988	7471	1673	5798
1989	10296	1812	8484
1990	14629	1982	12647
1991	7262	6351	911
1992	419	-5	424
1993	1471	3705	-2234
1994	6596	6241	355
1995	10733	14273	-3540

Source: IMF (1996).

This new administration signed a compromise austerity pact with the Liberals, which substituted a rise in VAT and the delaying of a promised extended minimum holiday entitlement for employees for the controversial ban on strikes. The Swedish stock market declined rapidly, due to the combination of political instability and the problems the economy was experiencing. The outflow of capital intensified. Interest rates were raised by 5% inside a week, and additional austerity measures were discussed. It was within this austerity package being introduced to parliament that a pledge to apply for European Union (EU) membership was inserted, in a footnote (Aylott, 1999:126).

The SAP government broke with another traditional policy position by announcing that it had substituted a low inflation rate as the "overriding" (overgripande) economic objective pursued by the government, thereby relegating full employment to that of secondary importance (Lindbeck, 1997:1303). In so doing, new Finance Minister Allan Larsson emphasised the prioritisation of reducing inflation over all other goals, "which in fact meant nothing less than that the SAP abandoned its long-standing goal of full employment" (Notermans, 2000:31). In the process, the government announcement had confirmed what had for so long been the trend of economic strategy, namely the replacement of a Keynesian framework with neo-liberal orthodoxy.

An Evaluation

The TWEP sought the "renewal of the private sector as the engine of economic recovery" (Walters, 1985:368). Accordingly corporate profitability was promoted via a 16% devaluation at the expense of consumption, which was restrained by public expenditure control and wage constraint, in the hope that higher profits would stimulate higher investment and capital accumulation. Increased profits were immediately forthcoming, rising by an average of 60% in the year 1982/3 (Affärsvärlden, 9 November 1983:6). The profit share of value added in manufacturing rose from 15% in 1978 to 33% by 1984, approximately the same level as in the 1950s and 1960s (Lawrence and Bosworth, 1986:62; Ryner, 1993:8).

Profits and Capital Formation

The strategy assumed that higher current profitability causes higher future profit expectations that, in turn, stimulate higher investment, facilitated by a pool of collective savings. Increased availability of risk capital, through retained earnings together with the fledgling WEF system, was intended to lower the cost of capital, hence raising investment (Atkinson, 1972; 1974; Hasko, 1990:60-1). In the event, the TWEP succeeded in significantly raising investment expenditure, which was a considerable achievement after a decade of real stagnation (Table 6-2 and Figure 6-1).

Table 6-2: Comparing gross and real capital formation, 1964-1991

Years	Gross capital formation (% change)	Real capital formation (% change)
1964-1973	8.34	2.85
1974-1983	10.34	-0.01
1984-1990	12.1	5.5
1984-1991	10.1	3.4

Figure 6-1: Percentage change in real fixed capital formation in Sweden, 1964-1991

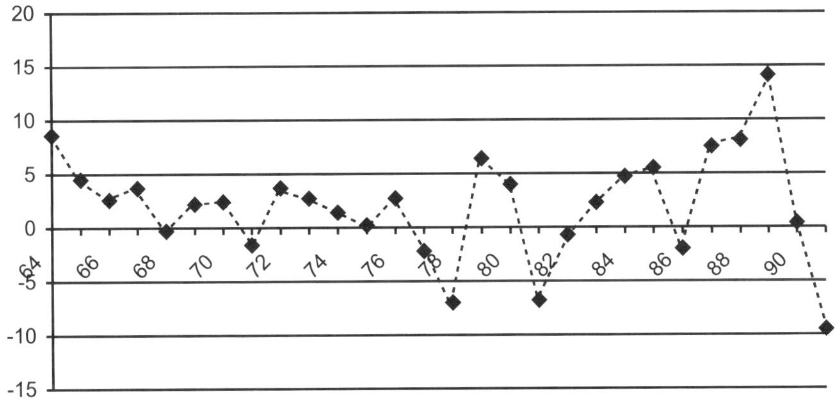

Source: OECD, 1993.

Fixed business investment rose from 10.5% of GDP in 1982 to 15% by 1990, facilitating Swedish industry to regain two-thirds of the world trade it had lost during the period 1975-82 (Lawrence and Bosworth, 1986:62; Ryner, 1993:8). Moreover, if WEFs had been introduced a decade earlier, and capital accumulation had occurred at the rate achieved during the observed WEF period (1984-1991), productive capital would have been 52% higher by 1991. This represents a substantial potential loss of economic growth and employment opportunities during this period. For example, if the rate of capital formation had increased by an average 5.5% between 1974 and 1991, as achieved during 1984-1990, productive capital would have been 132% higher at the end of this extended period.

Economic Growth and Employment

In terms of economic growth, the TWEP sought to stimulate capital formation in order to shift the Swedish economy to a higher rate of growth and secure the long-term maintenance of full employment. This was partially achieved as Sweden's average growth rate increased to 2% between 1982 and 1990. However, this falls to a disappointing 1.7% per annum if extending the time period to the re-formed 1991 SAP administration, when the TWEP had all but collapsed (Rivlin, 1986:4).

Figure 6-2: Comparative standardised unemployment rates, 1974-1991

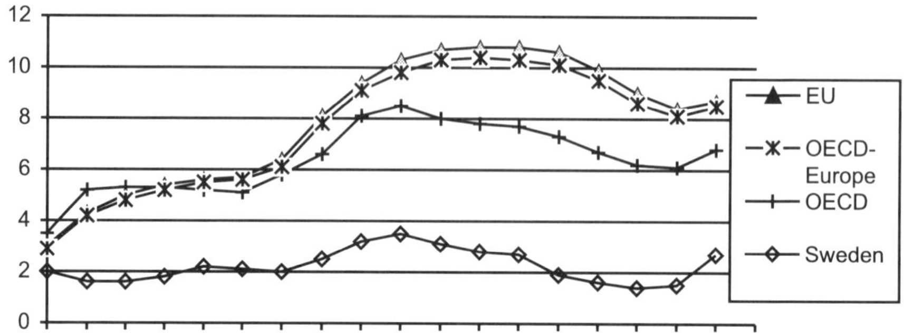

Source: OECD, 1993.

The TWEP sought to boost employment through growth and investment, rather than industrial subsidies and deficit finance. This programme was undoubtedly a more sustainable strategy to maintain low rates of unemployment, but within a stronger economy. Unemployment fell back from just over 3.5% when the SAP took office and was reduced to 1.6% in 1990, before the TWEP began to unravel. This was all the more impressive because other EU and OECD nations were suffering from mass unemployment during this same period (FIG 6-2). Thus, whilst unemployment increased by an average exceeding 50% across the EU between 1982 and 1991, Swedish unemployment was reduced.

The maintenance of full employment throughout a period of international deflationary pressure was a significant achievement, particularly when associated with increased labour market participation. Indeed the OECD found Sweden to have the highest labour force participation in the world in 1990, comprising approximately 85% of the total working age population (Trehörning, 1993:29). Furthermore, the TWEP was associated with an increase in total employment, from 3.89 million to a peak of 4.23 million people in 1990, before recession reduced this to 4.17 million in 1991.

Wages

The TWEP was based upon the need for wage moderation to facilitate expansion in corporate profits, investment and capital formation. WEFs were intended to resolve distributional conflict by securing for employees a share of capital accumulation without wage militancy. However, this assumes that employees are indifferent as to whether they hold equity wealth or enjoy higher immediate consumption, otherwise WEF collective savings would exert little significant effect on trade union wage pressure. Nevertheless, academic studies have inferred that employee ownership is positively associated with depressed bargained wages, lower wage drift and provides an alternative to incomes policies (Hasko, 1990:4). Examination of wage developments and labour costs can reveal whether Swedish experience confirms these predicted results.

The TWEP period followed a depressed economic environment where real wages had declined by approximately 10% between 1977 and 1982 (Arestis, 1986:720). Consequently, the success of the strategy in tightening labour markets and facilitating high profitability would have been expected to cause a real wage explosion as employees 'caught up' prior living standard deterioration. Instead, the 1982 devaluation exacerbated the previous reduction in real wages, because WEF introduction and increased welfare provision persuaded the LO to accommodate devaluation by demanding average wage increases of only 2.5%, implying significant purchasing power reductions for most employees (Calmfors and Forslund, 1990:91; Elvander, 1988). Consequently, between 1982 and 1991, real manufacturing labour costs and earnings expanded more slowly than in previous periods (Table 6-3). Indeed, it took the loss of around one-fifth of Swedish industrial employment, during the 1991 to 1994 recession, to achieve smaller real wage increases.

Table 6-3: The development of Swedish manufacturing earnings and labour costs

Years	Manufacturing hourly labour costs		Manufacturing hourly earnings	
	Nominal	Real	Nominal	Real
1969-1973	12.0	5.9	10.3	4.2
1974-1983	12.3	2.0	10.2	-0.1
1969-1983	12.2	3.3	10.2	1.4
1969-1981	12.9	4.1	10.6	1.8
1982-1991	8.4	1.4	7.9	0.9
1984-1991	8.6	2.2	7.9	1.4
1992-1994	4.8	1.1	4.0	0.3

Source: OECD (1993).

Inflation

During the TWEP period, Sweden's inflation rate remained one per cent higher than OECD and EU averages. Critics pointed to this as evidence of failure. However, this is slightly unfair. The economic strategy was intent upon boosting investment and economic growth, in order to sustain full employment, and do so with as lower inflation rate as possible, rather than concentrating upon the sole task of minimising inflation. Therefore, relative changes in Sweden's inflation-unemployment trade-off are arguably a more significant indication of the relative success of the economic programme. On this basis, Sweden achieved a clear advantage over other EU and OECD nations, reducing inflation by 3.9% whilst maintaining full employment against the international trend.

Relative macroeconomic superiority is highlighted by compiling indexes measuring the 'misery' caused by unemployment and inflation, and secondly the 'sacrifice ratio' in terms of lower inflation achieved at the cost of higher unemployment (Dawson, 1992:60-74) (Table 6-4). The first index represents the sum of both the unemployment and inflation rates, whilst the second doubles the unemployment rate weighting based on the assumption that unemployment generates greater disutility and social disruption than inflation. This still underestimates the real cost of unemployment, however, since Dawson's (1992:86;193) estimated that a change of 1% in the unemployment rate would result in a change equivalent to 1% of GDP, whereas a change of 1% in the inflation rate would lead to only a 0.108% change in GDP. Thus, the costs incurred through higher unemployment were almost ten times greater than an equivalent percentage change in inflation. Furthermore, this omits additional evidence that unemployment causes additional social, psychological, health and crime costs (Dawson, 1992:87-97; Michl, 1995:72-3; Sawyer, 1995:15-16).

Table 6-4: Comparison of inflation, unemployment, misery indexes and sacrifice ratios, between the TWEP and previous periods

Years		Countries			
		Sweden	Total OECD	OECD Europe	EU
1974-83	Inflation	10.4	10.0	12.1	11.9
	Unemployment	2.3	5.9	6.1	6.3
	Misery (I+U)	12.7	15.9	18.2	18.2
	Added Misery (I+2U)	15.0	21.8	24.3	24.5
1984-91	Inflation	6.5	4.7	6.3	5.0
	Unemployment	2.2	7.1	9.5	9.9
	Misery (I+U)	8.7	11.8	15.8	14.9
	Added Misery (I+2U)	10.9	18.9	25.3	24.8
	Sacrifice Ratio	-0.03	0.23	0.59	0.52

Source: OECD (1993).

Increased misery indexes for most EU and OECD countries implies that the cost of reducing inflation by increasing unemployment created more misery than existed before, whilst Sweden's economic approach improved the welfare of its citizens

(Table 6-4). The 'sacrifice ratio' emphasises this conclusion. Defined as the cumulative rise in unemployment divided by the fall in inflation, the 'augmented' misery index illustrates that, whilst OECD and EU nations suffered a high real cost as a result of their deflationary policies during the 1980s, Sweden actually achieved a net gain (Figure 6-3). Thus, between 1982 and 1990, the TWEP could be considered an unqualified success.

Figure 6-3: Comparative augmented 'misery' indexes, 1974-1991

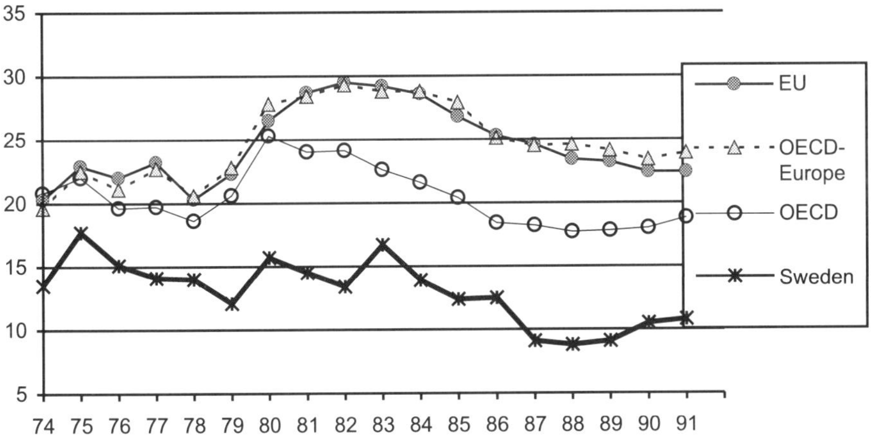

Source: OECD, 1993.

Perceived Weaknesses with the 'Third Way' Strategy

Two inherent weaknesses, became apparent later in the TWEP. Firstly, for a nominal devaluation to facilitate industrial restructuring and regeneration, a relative expansion of the traded sector must occur through a rise in the relative price of its products. This real devaluation was significantly weaker than the nominal variation in exchange rate, so that only a modest relative expansion of the traded sector occurred (Henrekson, 1990:97). Indeed the sector most favoured by the nominal devaluation was Sweden's primary industries, particularly forestry-related products, thereby locking resources into mature industries at the expense of firms based upon new technology and innovative techniques (Erixon, 1989:187-93). Consequently, despite increasing industrial activity, productivity growth only rose by an average annual rate of 1% between 1982 and 1990 (Ryner, 1993:9).

The second problem was the absence of an effective means to ensure that increased profitability was consistently channelled into increased investment in domestic productive resources. Deregulation of Sweden's financial markets and exchange control abolition encouraged companies to invest their increased profits in property, financial securities or foreign assets, rather than domestic productive capital. In 1981, for example, Sweden's direct investment abroad was around the OECD average of one per cent of GDP, whereas immediately after exchange controls were abolished in 1989 it exploded to 6.2% of GDP in 1990, before stabilising at four per cent in 1991. This was considerably more than any other OECD country. Consequently, by 1990 approximately 55% of Sweden's investment stock was located in EU countries (OECD, 1992:9,18). Thus "the increases in profitability created by the devaluation and by the wage restraint of Swedish workers has largely been used to finance operations outside Sweden", or to take-over competitors to achieve market dominance (Ryner, 1993:10). Therefore, relatively little of the additional capital formation made possible by wage restraint actually benefited Swedish employees.

Under such circumstances, trade unions were unable or unwilling to accept lower wages than dictated by market forces when the only beneficiaries appeared to be wealthy shareholders. Consequently, the logic of the TWEP proved flawed and the Rehn-Meidner assertion correct. In the long-run it is difficult, if not impossible, to combine full employment and high profitability with sustainable wage restraint because the unions' ability to deliver is continually undermined by market forces and distributional disquiet (Pontusson, 1992:118-9). WEFs were intended to solve this problem. However, their restricted size and scope effectively emasculated their ability to become a significant macroeconomic instrument. Wage pressure therefore increased and the economy severely overheated in 1990, whilst the SAP minority status in parliament prevented corrective measures being introduced. The result was a political crisis and the replacement of the social democratic government in 1991.

Political difficulties cannot disguise the fact that the TWEP had become unsustainable and that deregulation of the economy had withdrawn many policy instruments previously deployed to stabilise the economy in the advent of external shocks. Reliance upon managers and capitalists to invest higher profits in domestic productive capital proved an inefficient method of stimulating economic growth and employment. Unions were unwilling to continually moderate their wage claims when the benefits were largely going to already rich shareholders or being invested abroad. Therefore, in the absence of a means to transfer increased corporate profits directly into productive investment, the TWEP failed as a long-term strategy. WEFs were prevented from fulfilling their initial macroeconomic goals because of the restrictions imposed upon them by the SAP in a vain attempt to minimise opposition to their existence. Consequently, the funds did exactly what could be expected of them according to the scale of activities their limited resources allowed. Furthermore, whilst the macroeconomic balance had been restored for a while, the failure to turn high corporate profits into productive investment in the domestic economy failed to secure the growth in productivity that was anticipated. Indeed, productivity growth averaged only 1% per annum between 1982 and 1990 (Ryner, 1994:396). Unemployment, meanwhile, was forced extremely low, with the state acting as "employer of last resort" due to its failure to encourage the private sector to significantly expand its employment (Alogoskoufis, 1995:70; Gylfason, 1997:49).

The TWEP ultimately faltered because the anticipated stimulation to domestic productive capacity expansion and productivity growth were not realised, and the implicit incomes policy failed. A basic fallacy of the policy was the premise that increased private profits and investments would regenerate GDP and productivity growth. Despite increased profits, investments and paradigmatic labour process innovation in some enterprises a dynamic 'post-Fordist' growth and productivity trajectory was not realised, but these growth rates remained at the levels of the late 1970s (Ryner, 1994:396). Apart from the success of pharmaceuticals, there was little growth in new dynamic sectors and enterprises. Instead the strategy benefited existing firms, which had a 'golden decade' despite the lack-lustre performance of Sweden's economy (Erixon, 1989). These firms disproportionally located high value added activities in continental Europe. Apart from precluding domestic growth rates, this also led to large deficits on the capital account. This may have taken place for the 'defensive' purposes of buying up competitors to ensure a price-making privilege (Erixon, 1989). Alternatively, foreign direct investments may have fulfilled part of an 'offensive' strategy, where the purpose was to achieve customer and market proximity (Bergholm and Jagren, 1985; Andersson, 1993). This last point is consistent with post-Fordist 'just-in-time' production.

PART III
PARADIGM SHIFT?

Chapter 7

Globalisation and National Economic Self-Determination

Introduction

The well documented difficulties facing the 'Swedish Model', in the aftermath of its peak during the early 1970s, have been in large part the consequence of successive economic policy mismanagement. This included mistimed fiscal interventions, inappropriately lax policies that did not suppress excess profits, and consequently, failure to prevent compensatory, yet inflationary wage increases that undermined international competitiveness. Nevertheless, even if these had been avoided, there is considerable evidence to suggest that the social democratic strategy would have experienced significant internal and external challenges, which threatened the future development of traditional solutions (Ingebritsen, 1998:60).

The internal problems relate to those inherent within the 'Swedish Model' itself, together with the impact of a more specialised, flexible-specialisation form of production, with its inevitable consequences for employment and wage formation. These factors will be examined in detail in the following chapters. In addition, changes in the international economic environment posed potential problems for a nationally-orientated approach to the development of social policy and economic management. In particular, the trend towards regional economic integration, together with the impact of globalisation, have both had a marked impact upon the behaviour of Swedish industry and both the design and implementation of economic policy by successive Swedish governments. Consequently, before continuing the evaluation of Swedish economic strategy, consideration should be made concerning the degree to which these external forces constrained national economic autonomy, and contributed to an observed shift in policy.

Globalisation – A Definition?

There are many different definitions of globalisation. At its most fundamental, it refers to an evolving pattern of cross-border activities of firms involving international investment, trade and collaboration for purposes of product development, production, sourcing and marketing. It involves an increasing flow of goods, services, technology and capital across national borders. The OECD (1996:9) describes it as an "evolving pattern of cross-border activities of firms involving international investment, trade and collaboration for purposes of product, development, production and sourcing and marketing". On a 'micro' level, Ruigrok and Van Tulder (1995) discuss globalisation in terms of corporate strategies to establish a global intra-firm division of labour, to complement an inter-firm division of labour. Alternatively, Hirst and Thompson (1996) refer to a stronger version of the globalisation concept, involving the development of a new economic structure, where they agree that TNCs are the principle actors, and where distinct national economies are subsumed into the global system.

The fact that the present international system is characterised by a relatively high degree of interdependence among nations and societies, when measured in historical terms, is an insufficient definition of globalisation. The latter is denoted by the combination of the "transnationalisation of finance and production at the ideological level" (Cox, 1993:259-67; Bieler, 2000:19).

A broad definition of globalisation incorporates both the internationalisation of economic production and capital flows, the growing dominance of foreign direct investment (FDI) and trans-national corporations (TNCs), together with a cultural aspect. It additionally involves "the rise of global cultural flows and 'deterritorialise' signs, meanings, and identities" (Amin and Thrift, 1994:4). Culture, according to this definition, includes corporate brands such as Nike, MacDonalds and Coca-Cola, alongside the global domination of Hollywood cinema productions. Thus, globalisation may be defined as the intensification of social relations throughout the world, such that distant localities are linked and local events are influenced by factors occurring in distant lands. Giddens (1994:4-5) makes the following point:

> Globalisation does not only concern the creation of large-scale systems, but also the transformation of local, and even personal contexts of social experience. Our day-to-day happenings are increasingly influenced by events happening on the other side of the world. Conversely, local lifestyle habits have become globally consequential.

Globalisation is often linked with discussion of an 'information society', whereby it is the power and cost-effectiveness of communication that has increased exponentially, and this facilitates the growth of global markets for products, specialised labour and especially financial assets. The 'dot-com' revolution is a good example of this practice, whereby internet sites provide a new gateway to an existing marketplace, whether relating to the purchase of cut-price airline tickets, purchasing CDs or selling shares. Call centres provide a similar service for those less computer literate, but at an equally rapid speed – at least, in so far as site capacity expands as quickly as consumer demand. The low costs of communications and transportation, as a proportion of the total cost of goods and services, facilitates the geographical diversification of corporation production facilities (Rustin, 2001:18).

Globalisation, then, relates to the multiplicity of interconnections between nations and societies, and described the means by which phenomena occurring in one area of the globe impact upon the activities of individuals in a geographically distinct region. It therefore involves a spatial linkage, together with an intensification and interdependence between nations and social groupings. It incorporates the growth of international consumer markets in cultural, as well as consumer, products. Finally, the globalisation thesis infers a reduced role for national government policy, and an increased potential for supranational economic regulation (McGrew and Lewis, 1992:22).

Supporting Evidence

Between 1970 and 1991, world GDP doubled, global exports nearly tripled in real terms and FDI quadrupled, with rates of real increase exceeding 25% p.a. during the latter half of the 1980s (UNCTAD, 1993:17). In 1991, world exports of goods and services were valued at US$4 trillion, one-third of which was intra-firm trade, whilst exports represented approximately 19% of global GDP (Lazar, 1996:274-5). Furthermore, corporations are increasingly becoming global institutions – adopting strategies which transcend the influence of the small and medium-sized nations of the world. Indeed, it is estimated that the largest 500 TNCs perform a majority of world trade. UNCTAD (1995) estimates that there are some 40,000 companies with headquarters in more than three countries; the hundred largest responsible for turnover valued at US$1.4 trillion dollars per annum.

Taking all of these TNCs into consideration, their output exceeds US$5.5trillion and their share of international trade rises to two-thirds of the total, with almost half of this amount occurring internally and therefore not being subject to external competitive market pressures (Martin and Schumann, 1996:112; Lazar, 1996:274-5). In fact, merely focussing upon the top five TNCs in the world market, in the mid-1990s, research indicates that these firms control 70% of the consumer durables market, more than half of the car, airline, electronic components and steel industries, together with more than 40% of the market share in the oil, personal computer and media industries (Korten, 1995).

TNCs are one of the key driving forces of globalisation, as information technology and low transportation costs facilitate production becoming part of a unified process, despite being spread across different regions of the globe. The aggregate stock of foreign direct investment was estimated to be US$180 billion, in 1991 (Lazar, 1996:274-5). However, FDI flows are different from trade flows in that they do not end with the initial transactions, but rather construct long-term relationships between economic agents in different locations. To take one example of this process, the former Swiss-Swedish TNC, Asea Brown Boveri (ABB), is truly trans-national, with one thousand subsidiaries in forty countries. This diverse production matrix enables output to be diverted from one plant to another within a short space of time, and therefore the corporation is less subject to the particular regulations of any one government or affected by instability within isolated parts of the world. Moreover, the fact that subsidiaries occur in more regions of the world is likely to have a depressing effect on the export trade of the 'home' nation, as the demand for their produce are fulfilled by the subsidiary in the 'host' nation in substitution for the original flow of exports. Thus, the evidence points to capital movements and trade flows evolving in opposite directions (Bairoch, 1996:183-4).

The feature that perhaps most signifies a significant shift towards globalisation, however, relates to the extraordinary expansion in short-term financial capital flows. Since 1970, internationally managed money has increased by 1,100% globally, relative to other forms of capital (Giddens, 1998:36). Thus, disconnected capital has increased in volume and importance to the future stability of the world economy.

The daily volume of trading across the major foreign exchange markets reached approximately US$1.5 trillion by mid-1990s, a figure more than fifty times the equivalent value of international trade and four times the total world expenditure on crude oil. Furthermore, the rapid increases in computer capacity has facilitated the growth of derivatives trading, which has grown so rapidly as to become almost completely autonomous. Indeed, the nominal value of derivatives contracts has increased eight-fold, between 1989 and 1995, and reached a staggering US$41 trillion worldwide in 1996 (Martin and Schumann, 1996:48-52).

This statistic illustrates the significance of the change in the nature of financial transactions, as between only 2% and 3% of the total value is intended to provide protection to international trade and industrial production. The remainder of the contracts are affectively a form of gambling between market transactors, with the advantage that only a small amount has to be put up as the original stake; the promised sum is only transferred when the contract is due, and by then most transactors will have limited any potential losses through offsetting contracts. However, the significance of this market lies in the fact that, divorced from the real economy, even small movements of capital lead to large price movements, such that transactors' expectations become the driving force behind the market and acquire their own momentum. In this process, "the financial world has emancipated itself from the real sphere" (Martin and Schumann, 1996:52-3). Thus, futures markets, which were created to reduce the risk farmers and other producers faced when agreeing contracts in advance of delivery, due to fluctuations in currencies, raw materials of other costs, has been transformed itself into the type of 'casino' Keynes was so scathing about in his writings.

Is Globalisation New?

Having established that globalisation appears to be a real phenomenon, the next question concerns the originality of this effect, or whether it represents evidence gathered from a peak period within a series of periodic fluctuations. Accordingly, historical analysis indicates that the economy of the gold standard, from 1870 to 1914, was internationalised to a very high degree and, indeed, in many respects the world economy is only just beginning to realise a similar degree of interdependency.

In terms of international trade, the UK's trade accounted for 44.7% of GDP in 1913, and after a dramatic decline between 1914 and 1945, it had only risen to 40.5% in 1993. Similarly, France remains beneath its 1913 levels of openness (35.4%), with Germany only narrowly surpassing its 1913 figure of 35.1% by 3.2% in 1993, and with Japan recording a sharp fall from 31.4% per cent in 1913 to 14.4% in 1993 (Hirst and Thompson, 1996a:60; Bairoch, 1996:176). Western Europe exported 18.3% of GDP in 1913, rising only slightly to 21.7% in 1992, whereas the USA exported 6.4% of GDP in 1913 and 7.5% in 1992. The comparable figures for Japan demonstrated a fall in the importance of international trade from 12.5% to 8.8% of GDP (Bairoch and Kozul-Wright, 1996:6). Thus, although the volume of trade has increased substantially over the seventy years covered by these statistics, the international economy does not seem demonstrably more open today than during the gold standard era (Hirst and Thompson, 1996a:37-8).

Capital mobility was similarly a feature of the gold standard period, with one estimate calculating that the stock of FDI was around 9% of global output, in 1913 (Bairoch and Kozul-Wright, 1996:10). Moreover, the growth in portfolio investment, particularly from France, Germany and the UK, exceeded expansion in output, and financed the industrial expansion of North America, Argentina, Australia, South Africa and Nordic European nations like Sweden. Indeed, the UK exported an average 4% of GDP between 1870 and 1914, with the absolute annual figure having risen to an incredible 9% of GDP by the end of the gold standard epoch (Hirst and Thompson, 1996a:37-8). Obstfeld and Taylor (1997), together with Taylor (1996), estimated that capital movements represented 5.3% of global GDP at the end of the gold standard epoch, whereas this figure only averaged 2.3% of world GNP between 1989 and 1994. Thus, when compared to relative GDP, capital flows are smaller than seven decades ago, indicating that perhaps capital markets are not as tightly integrated as is typically perceived (Roderik, 1998:4). One difference between the two time periods concerns the fact that most capital flows took the form of portfolio investment in 1913, rather than foreign direct investment (FDI), with the debt typically issued by governments and utilised to finance infrastructure investment, including railway construction, harbour development and telecommunications (O'Rourke and Williamson, 1999:211-2).

The preceding analysis is not intended to substantiate a claim that the world economy is essentially similar to the period immediately preceding 1914. It is a profoundly different place. Indeed, one only has to drive to work, and spend time accessing the internet via laptop computer, and responding to urgent faxes and text messages on a mobile phone, to illustrate the point. Nevertheless, Hirst and Thompson (1996a:37-8) note that the international economy is still dominated by the same handful of nations. Moreover, they point out that, to date, no major international trading and monetary regime has exceeded four decades, and therefore advocates of the globalisation thesis may suffer from a short memory if they do not appreciate the fact that periods of openness and growth have oscillated with periods of closure and decline. Consequently, it would be "naïve" to project the continuation of current trends as if this were an unreversible inevitability.

Is it a Good Thing?

Economic theory predicts that internationalisation is inherently positive for all participants in the system, assuming that the terms of trade are set correctly, because trade enables specialisation in the economy to be taken further than would be possible under conditions of self-sustainability. Specialisation in the industry or service in which a nation has a competitive advantage, reduces costs for consumers and increases global output, resulting in a surplus after trade has occurred; the relative distribution of this surplus depends upon the terms of trade. Furthermore, the internationalisation of financial markets is predicted to increase competition, increase the quality of service for customers, whilst increasing banking efficiency. Risks can be pooled internationally, and nations subjected to temporary recessions or other economic problems, together with developing countries with a surplus of investment opportunities over scarce capital resources, have the ability to borrow abroad. In both cases, economic growth should be enhanced and global savings are allocated to its most efficient usage (Obstfeld, 1994). Moreover, international capital markets have the ability to discipline governments who may seek to pursue "unsound" policies, such as excessive borrowing or inflationary fiscal expenditure (Rodrik, 1998:10).

Finally, FDI provides developing markets with the combination of scarce capital and knowledge-intensive organisational resources, which, when combined, provide the TNC in question with their international competitive advantage.

This view of globalisation, however, has a distinctly neo-liberal bias. Critics dismiss many of the supposed benefits, arguing that instead of producing greater international competition, the dominance of TNCs results in a concentration of power, increasing social inequalities, the weakening of democratic accountability and environmental damage (Leisink, 1999:2).

Many researchers dismiss the concept of 'globalisation' as an exaggeration, whereby the real growth has occurred amidst a 'triadisation' of regional blocs; Europe, North America and Asia. South-Saharan Africa has failed to experience any significant benefit from the supposed 'global' forces. Indeed, the World Bank (1997:134) notes that, "despite spreading trade liberalisation, the share of trade in GDP fell in forty-four of ninety-three developing countries between the mid-1980s and mid-1990s". Furthermore, a significant section of the literature concludes that the "national system of innovation" is far more significant than the global trends described in this chapter (Porter, 1990; Patel and Pavitt, 1991).

The Decline of the Nation State?

Globalisation has additionally been implicated in a decline in the ability of the nation state to determine its own economic policies. One aspect of this postulated weakening of state power relates to the fact that financial deregulation has provided additional exit options for private capital. Thus, corporations can relocate more easily than in the past, and hence governments may not find it as easy to tax more mobile assets as highly as previously. It is not a large step to move towards a system of global tax competition, where corporations threaten to relocate unless governments reduce their tax burdens, or provide them with a variety of subsidies – i.e. rent rebates, provision of 'greenfield' sites for development and infrastructural investment predominantly benefiting the company but financed by tax-payers. Similarly, nation states may use tax competition as one incentive to attract FDI, thereby further driving down tax revenues (eg. Ireland).

This is important from a social democratic perspective, because reducing taxation on mobile capital either requires it to be redirected onto less mobile labour, thereby increasing social inequality, or being forced to reduce public expenditure and with it prized welfare programmes. Tanzi (1996) argues that a trend towards lower corporation tax rates has become identifiable across OECD countries, during the last decade. However, Roderik (1998:5) notes that comparable tax rates still vary widely across the industrialised nations, and moreover, the evidence used to predict convergence is, at best, limited. Indeed, Eichengreen (1990) points out that the variability of state tax rates remains significant even in an integrated economy such as the USA, albeit at a little over half the level between EU nation states. Therefore, it would appear from the available data, that capital taxation may be squeezed because of increased mobility, but the potential for significant variation is likely to remain.

A second issue concerns the argument that transnationalisation of the economic environment reduces the economic space left to be controlled by the nation state.

Susan Strange (1994) perceives a hollowness of state authority and a "retreat of the state". Nation states are increasingly being forced to bargain with TNCs over their conditions of operation, rather than regulate their activities (Stopford and Strange, 1991). However, this claim neglects the fact that markets are not natural phenomena, but are always established in some form of legal and institutional context that defines the conditions under which transactions occur. Ultimately, the power of the nation state creates the conditions for markets to operate, for example, by creating legal protection for most transactions, employing inspection teams to ensure the integrity of the trade (i.e. checking weights and measures, the accuracy of advertising, and the safety of the product or service).

The intensification in globalisation is closely associated with the rise of neo-liberal economics during the late 1970s and early 1980s, which led to the deregulation of the UK and US economies, and through this process dramatically increased the mobility of international capital. Furthermore, the use of the General Agreement on Tariffs and Trade (GATT), and latterly the World Trade Organisation (WTO), has created an international climate receptive to FDI and trade. Consequently, globalisation depends upon the continued acquiescence of nation states in order to expand. The World Bank acknowledges this point, and challenges the "overloaded government" thesis, by calling for states to enlarge their role in protecting and correcting markets. Indeed, according to this perspective, the state is viewed as a necessary "partner, catalyst, facilitator" to the long-term sustainability of globalisation (World Bank, 1997:41). Hence, it is possible to portray this shift in viewpoint as a tentative movement towards the social democratisation of globalisation.

It is a misunderstanding, then, as Panitch (1994) states, that globalisation equals the end of the nation-state. Indeed, the constraints upon national policy are exaggerated. Admittedly, it has become impossible to sustain a policy of fixed exchange rates together with an independent monetary policy, but the alternatives of a floating currency or a system of adjustable peg, semi-fixed rates, are viable alternatives (Roderik, 1998:5).

Financial integration has resulted in an increased probability of contagion from financial crises elsewhere in the international community (i.e. Mexico, Russia, South East Asia, Argentina, Brazil, etc.), due largely to a substantial increase in short-term liquidity through financial capital flows. However, this may caution against closer integration in the absence of sufficiently tight supranational regulation to prevent occurrences of this kind. Furthermore, transnational capital is not a homogeneous class, but contains different fractions, some benefiting from short-term volatility in financial markets and others from longer-term investment in manufacturing. Moreover, as one final point, it is interesting to read of the end of the nation state when there are currently more nation states in the world today than during any previous period in history.

A slightly different version of the 'weakened state' thesis predicts that globalisation is changing its "nature and role" (Rhodes, 1996:308). Cerney (1994) argues that the nation state is forced to consider the interests of mobile capital in order to increase its attractiveness as a location for production. This gives rise to reduction in business taxes, deregulation and the establishment of a low inflation, market-orientated neo-liberal macroeconomic programme. Cerny described this process as "regulatory arbitrage", where government policy shifts from the development of a welfare state that protects people from the worst features of market determination, to one that seeks to provide citizens with the skills and abilities to be able to compete successfully in the global marketplace.

Globalisation is thus causing a shift away from 'welfare' states to 'competition' states. Deregulation has indeed become a useful indicator for the award of top credit ratings from international agencies. Indeed, Sinclair (1994) argues that Moody's Investors Service and Standard & Poors Ratings Group have thus become the "transmission belts" of deregulation practice, prompted by the globalisation process. Furthermore, Pauly (1995) notes that the international organisations, including the OECD and IMF, have expended considerable energy in promoting the "capital mobility norm"; namely, the concept that the unrestrained free flow of capital delivers superior economic outcomes, and therefore national regulation of capital is an inefficient practice.

Globalisation and Social Democracy

The End of Social Democracy?

Social democracy traditionally places great importance upon the ability of the nation state to manage the capitalist economy efficiently and thereby achieve sustainable full employment consistent with other social and economic objectives. Therefore, the claim that globalisation impairs national macroeconomic strategy undermines this national-orientated strategy. Indeed, Panitch (2001a:26) argues that, together with the fall of command communism, globalisation represents one of the two "central developments that define our era" that threaten the capacity of the social democratic labour movements to sustain their predominantly national institutional framework and strategies.

Capital mobility weakens Keynesianism, because a rise in fiscal expenditure either implies a rise in taxes, which threatens to cause capital flight, whilst increased borrowing would be viewed by the now-powerful international financial markets as leading to future inflationary pressure, and thereby resulting in an increased interest rate risk premium. The classic example, often used by supporters of the globalisation thesis, involves the failure of the 1981 Mitterand administration to maintain a radical economic programme, based upon Keynesian reflation and extensive nationalisation, and involving "a barrage of reforms without precedent in post-reconstruction Europe" (Ross and Jenson, 1994:172; Cameron, 1996). Thus, Rhodes (1998:313) feels able to argue that:

> The lessons of the 1980s is that socialism in one country is no longer possible. All the Social Democrats, like the British Labour Party, can realistically provide is a more humane variant of the neo-liberal state.

Deregulated capital flows additionally undermined the beneficial impact of social democratic versions of corporatism, which typically included powerful disincentives for domestic enterprises to move their operations abroad, together with restrictions upon foreign firms taking over domestic companies, and thereby encouraging domestic investment in productive capital (Kitschelt, 1994:4). As Kurzer (1993:12) notes, "the most persistent dilemma for labour is that increased mobility of capital has also increased the power resources of capital". Indeed, the ability to switch production to low-wage areas of the world, together with the desire to utilise payment as part of strategic management schemes to encourage productivity, improvement of skills and loyalty to the company, has reduced the attraction of nationally co-ordinated collective bargaining as a means of 'taking wages out of competition' (Jacoby, 1995:8). Furthermore, Glyn (1998:14-15) argues that the strategy adopted by capital, empowered by globalisation, echoes the prediction made by Kalecki in 1943, where he claimed that the maintenance of full employment would stimulate the opposition of organised capital, because it weakens industrial discipline and thereby encourage the assertiveness of workers demanding improvements in working conditions.

It is additionally claimed that social democracy is too generous in introducing too much equality, security and employment, into the capitalist economy, and therein undermines incentives to work hard, maintain a high level of private savings and results in inflationary pressures (Lundberg, 1985). Novak even goes so far as to claim that "social democracy is based on the same errors as socialism, but in a form that takes a little longer to effect self-destruction" (cited in Moene and Wallerstein, 1995:186). Jessop (1994) suggests that the model of the welfare state has to shift from a centralist-Keynesian to a Schumpetarian framework, orientated towards improving the competitiveness of the economy.

Finally, Radice (cited in Bieler, 1999:28) argues that globalisation represents more than any measured change in the internationalisation of trade, capital flows and cultural exchange, but, more insidiously, it provides "a powerful ideological framework within which big business pushes for a redistribution of income, wealth and power towards economic elite's". Hence, the decision to deregulate financial markets reflected "the policy shift from embedded liberal [neo-Keynesian] to neo-liberal frameworks of thought" (Helleiner, 1994:167). Moreover, "the neo-liberal concept projected a transition away from the welfare, social compromise state towards the night-watchman state of classical liberalism" (van der Pijl, 1989:66). Thus, Thurow (1996:180) felt able to declare that "capitalists declared class war on their workers – and they have won it".

Over-Exaggeration?

The globalisation thesis sounds convincing, when proclaiming the end of national economic self-determination, and with it the decline of social democracy. However, Notermans (1992:12) argues that this claim is "both theoretically and historically flawed". Instead, he suggests that the interesting question concerns why social democratic nations responded to this situation by increasing the exposure of their economies to international forces, through deregulation of financial capital and participation in fixed exchange rate regimes, and thereby tightening the constraints upon their own macroeconomic management. This response would seem illogical, when compared to the alternative of endeavouring to reduce the exposure to international pressures, through the strengthening of capital controls, financial regulation and lobbying for a new, decisive transnational regulation regime.

Glyn (1995) may provide one explanation for this apparent contradiction, in his argument that globalisation has been blamed for the inability of nation states to satisfactorily control social conflict and inflationary pressures. Lundberg (1985:28) suggests that a reliance upon foreign borrowing to finance public expenditure opens the national economy to the dictates of the international financial markets. Alternatively, Hay (1998:529) suggests that, although internationalisation has caused changes in the world economy, nevertheless, it is "only a distinct absence of political imagination and/or a severe dose of political fatalism" that causes analysts to conclude that this so narrows the range of potential strategies that traditional social democratic policies are consigned to a nostalgic memory. Thus, the so-called crisis of social democracy is based upon a combination of "political fatalism", "a lack of political imagination" and a failure to develop a viable alternative strategy (Hay, 1997; 1998).

The only other viable alternative to the re-nationalisation of economic policy involves the construction of supranational regulation of capital. The most visible example of this approach has been in the efforts of social democratic parties within the European Union, to replace national with community institutions to promote employment generation and to provide an element of regulation to labour and financial markets. The consequences of this approach are dealt with in the following chapter. However, for the purposes of this section, surfice it to say that, having embarked upon an economic and monetary union based upon monetarist principles, the European social democratic movement is ill-prepared to develop a distinct, social democratic alternative. Indeed, in this regard, Robert Solow suggests that the process of globalisation should be slowed down "until we can be more vigilant in compensating the losers" (cited in Pearlstine, 1997).

Capital Controls and the Re-Nationalisation of Economic Policy

An integral element of a social democratic alternative to the neo-liberalism, embedded in both European integration and globalisation, may involve a strategy to partially disengage national financial markets from international markets in order to provide enhanced room for national measures to be enacted. The reimposition of capital controls could facilitate a 'cheap money' monetary policy, where interest rates are deliberately set beneath the rates of international competitors, thereby providing a competitive bonus and promoting enhanced investment in productive capital, domestically located. Furthermore, restrictions imposed upon capital mobility would enable a greater use of fiscal policy as part of a counter-cyclical economic strategy. This would additionally encourage a corporatist consensus combining wage moderation in return for greater domestic investment, income growth and enhanced employment opportunities. Furthermore, through enhancing national economic policy alternatives, capital controls can be viewed as empowering national democratic self-determination (Glyn, 1986).

In view of these positive aspects to capital controls, it would appear perverse that virtually all OECD countries abolished these controls during the 1980s. Yet, it would appear that the re-imposition of exchange controls is unlikely, due to the balance of political forces, and it is this which helps to explain why this option remains subject to very little serious analysis. Indeed, exchange controls are often dismissed because of a number of economic reasons, including:

1. The increase in information technology increases the potential to evade controls – this is a strange argument, because this very same technology could be used to increase the efficiency of national supervision of financial organisations, especially since Block (1987:216) claims that "the reality is that such electronic transfers leave more traces than traditional currency transactions".
2. The domestic financial sector will be placed at a disadvantage in terms of global competition – this may be true for the UK, which has a significant international financial market share, although even here the use of exchange controls as part of a strategy to revitalise industry would be likely to provide a net benefit to the economy as a whole. However, the financial organisations in smaller countries would be likely to benefit from protection from the predatory instincts of larger financial agencies. Furthermore, the deregulation of the banking sector has proved particularly chaotic in Finland and Sweden, and therefore re-regulation should improve the situation for the economy at large.
3. All forms of controls are economically inefficient – this argument derives from neo-liberal theory, which postulates that the unhindered operation of market forces will secure optimal allocation, utilisation and distribution of scarce resources. Capital should therefore be free to move wherever it can receive its greatest reward, which in turn reflects its most efficient investment opportunity; restricting capital to the domestic market will reduce returns on capital and hence lead to a misallocation of resources. Of course, this argument ignores the distributional consequences of regulations, which would benefit domestic productive industry, employees and government, but at the cost to financiers. In these circumstances, governments might prefer a theoretical 'second best' solution, but one which is most likely to boost domestic investment, productivity, growth, jobs and rising incomes for most of its citizens.
4. Even if they worked, the transition to their application would create substantial capital flight, thereby itself weakening domestic production and creating the kind of economic destabilisation that the measure was intended to avoid – this is a practical problem and one that can be dealt with as with other pieces of economic legislation that are market-sensitive. For example, when the Bank of England was granted its independence, this was neither announced before the event, in electoral manifesto's or in other public statements, and was only indicated to senior bank officials hours prior to the actual enaction of the measures. Furthermore, even if this issue proved to be a problem in the re-imposition of exchange controls after they have been expunged from the legislative framework of the nation, it does not explain why nations, which had an extensive system of controls already in place, decided to dismantle, rather than reinforce, these measures. Nor does it explain how exchange controls were introduced during the depression years of the 1930s, when international capital integration was arguably as extensive, and government economic policy as market-sensitive, as it is today (Notermans, 1992:15).

In a plausible answer to the final issue, Scharpf (cited in Notermans, 1992:15) claimed that it was impossible to isolate Austrian and Swedish financial markets as long as the nations required capital imports to finance a current account deficit. However, this ignores the option of finance through official borrowing, which was a strategy first adopted, and then terminated specifically in order to create an external constraint upon the supposed profligate actions of government and trade unions. Furthermore, if the nations involved pursued a competitive exchange rate, combined with an easy monetary policy to encourage industrial investment, they could stimulate export-led growth and solve the problem of the current account deficit. Indeed, for Sweden in particular, outflows of domestic capital grew so large after the withdrawal of capital controls, that they significantly contributed to balance of payments weakness.

There are alternatives to the reimposition of national exchange controls that might prove as effective and perhaps less politically sensitive. The most well-known option involves the imposition of a small transaction 'Tobin tax' upon all spot foreign exchange transactions (Tobin, 1978; Haq et al, 1996). If tax rates were established at a mere 0.5%, this would equate to an annual rate of 4% on a three month round trip – 12% for a month and 365% for a day round trip – and this small tax thereby creates room for interest rates to be set with internal macroeconomic priorities in mind (Eichengreen et al, 1995:164-5). Smith (1997:766) argues that a 'Tobin tax' is a plausible means of raising substantial official revenues and potentially reduce the volume of currency transactions, but, in his opinion, is only feasible if introduced through international co-ordination, with prior agreement over the distribution of the revenue generated. Moreover, it should be perceived as only one instrument utilised to deter destabilising speculation and unsustainable short-term capital flows. However, Davidson (1997:685) introduces a note of caution, namely that, in 'normal' periods, the 'sand' of the Tobin tax may restrict international trade and arbitrage activities, in addition to reducing speculation, whereas during periods of instability:

> ...the sands of the Tobin tax will be merely swept away in whirlpools of speculation. Boulders are needed to stop the destructive currency speculation from destroying global enterprise patterns.

Instead, Davidson prefers an updated version of Keynes' famous 'bancor' system, where 'hot money' flows were prohibited and an international monetary system was established with the intention to maintain sufficient international liquidity and global effective aggregate demand (Keynes, 1980; Davidson, 1997:680-7).

Industrial Policy

A strategy to promote domestic industrial expansion could constitute a second element of an alternative national macroeconomic strategy. This might involve the creation of new industries, as per successful examples in Japan, South Korea and Taiwan, together with the provision of low-cost capital to corporations through a state-owned banking network (Henderson, 1993:34). Industrial policy may therefore develop additional reasons for corporations to wish to produce in the domestic economy.

Industrial policy could be additionally enhanced by the fact that there are many reasons why industries and firms are not as footloose as the globalisation thesis maintains. Indeed, there are a number of factors which will encourage firms to cluster in a particular region. These include the provision of a pool of specialist labour, supportive institutions, specialist suppliers and the benefits arising from inter-firm information flows stimulated because of closeness of physical proximity (Krugman, 1991; Kleinknecht and ter Webgekm, 1998:645).

Globalisation and the Swedish Economy

The impact of globalisation, then, upon a nation state, is often exaggerated, but has certainly been significant in a number of areas. Firstly, the expansion of international trade has meant a lessening of the significance of the domestic market for Swedish corporations. Thus, the proportion of total sales being exported rising from 25% in 1960 to 38% in 1975 and approximately 45% in 1982, whereas, for Swedish TNCs, this rise was even more significant, increasing from 52% in 1965 to 76% in 1983 (Erixon, 1985; Olsen, 1994:204-5). Nevertheless, it was the levels of foreign direct investment, flowing out of the Swedish economy, that proved to be particularly significant, especially after 1960, when in excess of three-quarters of all manufacturing subsidiaries were established abroad.

Initially, foreign production facilitated enhanced export activity by Swedish TNCs, and therefore had a positive impact upon the Swedish economy, in addition to strengthening the profitability of the corporations involved. However, even as early as 1974, this began to change, with production outside of Sweden increasing at a rate twice that of export growth, thereby increasing the importance of the foreign operations for the Swedish TNCs. From the mid-1980s onwards, increased investment abroad substituted for domestic expansion and involved the transfer of production and jobs out of Sweden (Andersson et al, 1996:126). Thus, the percentage of employees abroad rose by 11.4%, representing 42.7% of the overall increase between 1965 and 1990, and the percentage of turnover abroad by 9.1%, which is 35.7% of the overall increase between 1965 and 1990 (Braunerhjelm et al 1996:10). Moreover, the proportion of workers that Swedish TNCs employed abroad, rose from 33.9% in 1965 to 60.6% in 1990, whereas the share of corporate turnover increased from 25.9% to 51.4% over the same period (Bieler, 2000:42).

The principle reason for the relocation of a sizeable proportion of Swedish production abroad was due to the market-orientated reason of gaining access to markets protected in some way by trade barriers, such as the EU single internal market (SIM), and therefore forge closer ties with purchasers (Olsen, 1994:205). Indeed, the creation of the SIM provoked a substantial outflow of Swedish capital, increasing from US$ 1783 million to US$ 14,136 million between 1985 and 1990, increasing the share of Swedish FDI from 21.4% in 1985 to 70.4% at the end of this period (Figure 6-1) (Luif, 1996:208-9). However, the result of this relocation of production by Swedish TNCs was that, in 1989, investment abroad exceeded domestic investment for the first time in Swedish history (Kurzer, 1993:133).

This substantial increase in FDI flows was facilitated by the deregulation of financial and exchange controls in Sweden. Liquidity ratio requirements for banks were abolished in 1983, foreign banks were allowed to participate in the Swedish market in 1986, and foreign exchange controls were abolished in 1989 (Jonung, 1986:111). The result was a dramatic increase in the outflow of capital, including SEK25 billion within only one week (Schierbeck, 1990). Figures for 1987 and 1988 indicate that, once abroad, 61% of profits from foreign subsidiaries were reinvested abroad (Wilks, 1996:104).

The consequences of the internationalisation of Swedish capital is that it lacks its former stake in the domestic economy, thereby weakening capital-labour co-operation and increasing the difficulty in sustaining a social democratic welfare state, characterised by full employment (Meidner, 1993a). The fact that the Swedish economy has become internationalised increases the difficulty of maintaining national control. Owners of capital have become "a jury sitting in judgement on government policies", threatening to transfer their assets elsewhere if conditions do not favour their activities (Martin and Schumann, 1996:67-8). Corporations demanded the decentralisation of wage bargaining, the deregulation of the economy, tax cuts for business and higher rate taxpayers, a shift from Keynesian 'accommodatory' policies to neo-liberal, non-accommodation, together with a retrenchment in welfare expenditure caused by a fall in budget revenue arising from an increase in the unemployment rate (Mishra, 1996:324). Furthermore, the SAF lobbied for EU entry, which subsequently occurred, and this in turn has reinforced the transition for the Swedish economy towards European 'normality' of low inflation, low growth and high unemployment.

Lundberg (1985:27) argues that globalisation has reduced the policy autonomy available to the nation state, which has caused Sweden to "conform to the restrictionist policies of leading countries". Similarly, Van der Pijl (1989:66) asserts that the acceptance of neo-liberalism had begun a transition from a welfare state and towards the "night-watchman state of classical liberalism". Whilst productive capital had sought to compromise with organised labour and an entrenched social democratic national government in the 1930s in response to a depressed international environment, different fractions of capital were in ascendancy in the 1980s, and accordingly capital sought to escape the restraints imposed by the institutions of "organised capitalism" that were established to solve the earlier global economic crisis (Wilks, 1996:106).

Of course, even if this picture of a weakened Swedish state struggling against, or adapting to, the implications of globalisation is accurate, it does not explain why the Swedish social democratic government contributed towards the acceleration of this process by deregulating the Swedish economy. Nevertheless, once deregulation was undertaken, and the substantial flow of productive capital had flowed outside of the Swedish economy, the damage to national economic management was complete.

Conclusion

The increased incidence of foreign direct investment and short-term capital mobility has had a profound impact upon national economic management, causing a re-definition (or rejection) of traditional social democratic strategies, and an adoption of neo-liberal economics. This, in turn, has caused formerly distinctive social democratic states to become 'normalised' in terms of rising unemployment, low inflation, regressive income redistribution and underwhelming rates of economic growth. This is not, however, to suggest that globalisation inevitably leads to this eventuality, nor to imply that there are no viable alternatives remaining.

One of the joint architects of the 'Swedish Model', Meidner, argues that "full employment can only be regained through a fundamental change of priorities, from price stability to high employment", involving a "well-co-ordinated economic policy which aims at non-inflationary full employment and equality" (cited in Ginsburg et al, 1997:14). This may involve the re-imposition of exchange controls, financial re-regulation and/or an industrial policy aimed at providing a combination of incentives and penalties to encourage Swedish industry to expand production in the Swedish economy, to provide jobs and pay for the welfare state.

Chapter 8

European Integration
and the 'Swedish Model'

Introduction

The challenge globalisation posed to the pursuit of a traditional social democratic programme was further amplified due to the unforeseen intensification of regional economic integration during the second half of the 1980s decade. Throughout its post-war history, Sweden maintained its historical ambivalence towards the European Union (EU),[1] dismissing membership on the grounds that it would undermine Sweden's independence, sovereignty and policy of neutrality (Huldt, 1994:111).

This independence from political and economic alliances served Sweden well, both in terms of evading the destructive consequences of a geographical location placing the nation in between the Allies and Axis powers during the Second World War, and again between NATO and Warsaw Pact military blocs during the Cold War.[2] It enabled Sweden to pursue its policies of free trade, unemcombored by considerations of 'Fort Europe' protectionism behind high tariff walls. It also provided Sweden with a degree of international influence out of proportion to the nation's size, economic and military power, based upon its professed identification with world development issues, perhaps most associated with the pronouncements made by former Prime Minister, Olof Palme.

It additionally provided the opportunity for social democratic policies to become embedded in the national consciousness. Thus, "the nationalism of Swedish Social Democracy" evolved into a form of "welfare nationalism", whereby pride in the achievements of the 'Swedish Model' was popularly shared, albeit with predictable distrust of over-zealous tax officials, together with a reaction against the elitism arguably necessitated by a successfully functioning corporatist framework (Aylott, 1999:185).

---

[1] Prior to the signing of the Maastricht Treaty in 1992-3, the EU was formally known as the European Community (EC). However, for the sake of clarity of the terminology used in the book, the current title is used, even when reference is made to the earlier organisation.

[2] Sweden had negotiated an agreement with NATO that the alliance would provide assistance in case of Soviet invasion, a fact of which the potential aggressor forces were well aware (Andrean, 1991:79; Svenska Dagbladet, August 3rd and August 8th 1998). Consequently, the collapse of the command communism system did not present the opportunity to abandon former positions and join the EU nations, as embraced by Finland and Austria, but rather facilitated a subtle re-definition of the neutrality policy.

Nevertheless, whilst it remained accurate that Sweden maintained its autonomy outside the EU, British entry in 1973 and the intensification of European economic integration in the 1980s caused all Nordic nations to reconsider the possibility of closer co-operation with the EU. Indeed, elements of national sovereignty were gradually traded-off in favour of closer supranational regional co-operation (Ingebritsen, 1997:239). In particular, the renewed impetus provided for European economic and political integration by the introduction of the European Single Internal Market (SIM) initiative in 1985, significantly altered the balance of economic power across the continent, impacting upon members and non-members alike.

Large Swedish companies were greatly interested in their ability to benefit from the creation of a large EU market, free from barriers to trade. Its explicit intention was to encourage economies of scale through the regional rationalisation of European producers and service providers, and therein create internationally competitive 'European champions'. Telecommunications, construction and personal service sector companies were well placed to benefit from the de-regulation of public procurement procedures throughout the EU's SIM. Sweden's location outside the SIM potentially threatened the future profitability of Swedish TNCs, and therefore Swedish capital intensified its campaigning participation in the European integration process.

SAF wants EU Membership

Leading productive sectors are strategically important to the state, providing a significant share of national income, export earnings and providing highly productive employment. Consequently, the Swedish government is attentive to the preferences of manufacturing employer peak associations, namely the SAF and the SI. Paraphrasing the adage that 'what's good for General Motors is good for the USA', Ingebritsen (1998:37) quotes a member of the Swedish export council stating that "if Volvo accounts for 10% of your GDP, the preferences of the corporation are not insignificant." Thus, once Swedish TNCs advocated participation in the SIM, to avoid possible discrimination and to be geographically closer to the consumers of their products, the Swedish government was always going to have to reconsider their position on the issue (Bieler, 2000:73).

The employers' associations concentrated upon the economic advantages of EU membership, claiming that the SIM would stimulate competition and lower prices for consumers. It additionally provided the opportunity for securing lower costs through securing economies of scale, thereby improving the financial health of the firm and securing jobs. The harmonisation of standards and regulations was portrayed as stimulating trade and economic growth within the EU.

The secondary argument, that EU membership would present an ideal opportunity for eliminating the 'Swedish Model' was downplayed by the organisations of Swedish capital. This was partly because to do otherwise would have strengthened SAP opposition to EU membership at the time when its leadership were saying that it would prove the saviour of the very same 'Swedish Model'. However, it was also due to the fact that many considered the SAP to have already abandoned the Rehn-Meidner strategy at the beginning of the 1990s.

Nevertheless, elements of the business coalition expressed their belief that EU membership acted as a safeguard against future Swedish 'experiments' that involved diverging from the EU neo-liberal norm (Bieler, 2000:107).

The Swedish employers' arguments were reinforced by the economic and political pressure they could exert in pursuit of their preferred agenda. The first element involved a dramatic surge in foreign direct investment as, for each year between 1985 and 1988, Swedish industry doubled its investments in Europe (Olsson, 1993:33). Indeed, between 1986 and 1990 the proportion of Swedish direct investment destined for the EC rose from 24% to 73% (Wilks, 1996:105). In 1990, Swedish companies were involved in more than 135 take-overs and established themselves as 'Europe's top corporate raiders' (The Guardian, 16th October 1990). This concentration upon the SIM can be seen in Table 8-1.

Table 8-1: Regional distribution of outward FDI in Sweden (%) 1982-1990

	EFTA	EU	North America	Other	Total
1982-1985	8.2	29.9	22.0	39.9	100
1986-1988	14.0	40.7	16.8	28.4	100
1988-1990	6.7	62.1	7.0	24.1	100

Source: EFTA (1991: 27).

In addition to the economic pressure placed upon the Swedish government, Swedish industrialist Pehr Gyllenhammar formed the European Roundtable of Industrialists (ERT) as a focus for business to mobilise support for the Single European Act (SEA) at the EC level and within European states (Cowles, 1995b). In excess of one hundred business leaders joined a concerted campaign by complaining about the government's failure to promote a favourable climate for business, especially in light of the decision to decommission nuclear power stations and thereby threaten one source of cheap energy for Swedish industry (Aylott, 1999:195). As part of this lobbying for an improved business climate, Ericsson, Sweden's biggest export firm, moved part of its headquarters to London, claiming that income-tax levels made it unattractive for managers to live in Sweden.

Simultaneously, individual companies were taking advantage of the deregulation of the financial sector and removal of capital controls, by relocating a significant proportion of their production facilities out of Sweden and within the boundaries of the SIM. This unprecedented level of capital flight placed additional pressure upon the labour movement to respond by means of political initiative. Accordingly, from 1987 onwards, those unions operating within the transnational production sector, in particular the Metal Workers' Union, began to echo the concerns of leading export-orientated employers, including Ericsson, Electrolux and Volvo, who, in turn, pressed the SAP government for a response.

This contributed, at least partially, to the eventual government bill on 'Sweden and West European Integration', published in December 1987, which proposed increased co- operation with the EU. However, it regarded potential membership as unnecessary because it was important 'to keep national self-determination in certain important economic, social and security policies' (Bieler, 2000:70). The preferred position was to pursue closer relations through EFTA and the ETUC. Thus, when the newly established LO committee on relations with the EU concluded, in 1988, that participation in the internal market was crucial for Swedish economic development and exports, they advocated the compromise solution of negotiating a European Economic Area (EEA) between EFTA and the EU, rather than opt for full membership. The EEA agreement, which came into force on 1st January 1994, created an internal trading area of 18 countries and some 370 million people.

The European Economic Area (EEA)

The EEA provides for the free movement of goods (except agriculture and fisheries), services and capital, together with the creation of a single labour market, across the whole area. Participants are encouraged to co-operate in the fields of environmental protection, social policy, education and research and development programmes. The EEA therefore gave Swedish industry direct access to the SIM, and even provided the Swedish government with a limited influence over the rules which affect trade with EU nations; harmonisation legislation was supposed to be developed *jointly*, without the EU imposing standards arbitrarily, whilst EFTA member states retained the right to veto EU law if they feel that it operates against their national interest.

This all came at the price of a net transfer of income to the EU budget, although this fiscal burden was significantly lower than would be imposed by full membership. Furthermore, membership of the EEA did not require Sweden to participate in the Exchange Rate Mechanism (ERM) fixed exchange rate, nor from adherence to the convergence criteria established as entry criteria for ultimate participation in Economic and Monetary Union (EMU).

EFTA members remained conscious of a power imbalance with EU member states who had far greater opportunities to set the future agenda for co-operation through the EEA. Critics claimed that the EEA agreement implied the Swedish government accepting "regulation without representation", due to the acceptance of trade rules and the harmonisation of technical standards determined outside their borders (Ingebritsen, 1998:52). Nevertheless, it still represented an unprecedented reversal of foreign, economic and security policy, when the SAP government announced its intention to apply for EU membership, in a footnote to an austerity package it placed before the Riksdag, on 26th October 1990. The announcement stated that:

> Swedish membership of the [EU] with continued adherence to Sweden's policy of neutrality is in our national interest ...: the Government is seeking a new parliamentary decision on European policy which defines more clearly and in more positive terms Sweden's ambitions of becoming a member of the European [Union] (cited in Bieler, 2000:81).

Why Membership?

There are a number of plausible reasons for the dramatic shift in Swedish social democratic policy towards participation in European economic integration. The first of these relates to the claim that Sweden had to become a member because of its trade dependence on the EU (Miles 1996:63). Closely related to this factor, however, concerned the fact that Swedish enterprise was increasingly asserting the advantages of participation in the SIM. Thus, the significant element concerned the reaction of Swedish capital to the deregulation of domestic financial markets, including the abolition of exchange controls, combined with the increased opportunities for economies of scale represented by the SIM. This led to increased political pressure placed on government, whilst simultaneously ever larger proportions of productive activity was transferred from Sweden to within the EU member states. Indeed, the significance of these events caused many trade unionists to decide that they had no alternative than to accept and adapt to this trend (Bieler, 1999:24).

The second economic factor related to the immediate economic crisis that threatened the stability of the Swedish economy, and in the process that simultaneously undermined electoral support for the ruling SAP government only one year before a General Election. Bieler (2000:83) suggests that announcing an application for EU membership was a means of trying to regain economic credibility through portraying unpopular economic austerity measures as essential components of a closer relationship with the EU. If this was achieved, the government would have a useful means of distancing themselves from the consequences of their own preferred economic strategy, whilst utilising the popular belief that closer economic interdependence with the EU had become a necessary part of any economic strategy to preserve Swedish jobs and incomes. However, the decision taken was of a such fundamental nature that political expediency would hardly be the main determinant of the government's position, especially since the SAP had governed Sweden for an average of nine years in an average decade since the 1930s, and therefore they would expect to have to deal with the end result of any decision made in undue haste for short-term electoral considerations.

Aside from political manoeuvring, however, the 1990 economic crisis did cause a general loss of confidence in the ability of the SAP to successfully manage the Swedish economy. Bieler (2000:83) argues that it undermined the belief in a viable 'third way' between a Keynesian-based 'Swedish Model' and neo-liberalism. According to this argument, the international mobility of capital had fatally undermined traditional social democratic strategy in the same way as it had undermined the comparable national reflation in 1983 France, under the Mitterand administration. A small national government may therefore be powerless to regulate capital within a global financial market, and the attempt to do so could be penalised through higher interest rates charged on Swedish borrowing, due to the supposed higher risk of inflation and devaluation of the krona. Therefore, an independent Sweden would have to accept this charge upon productive investment, or adapt its economic policies to the preferences of the financial markets and adopt even harsher austerity measures.

This analysis can, however, be utilised to justify two mutually incompatible solutions. The first provides for the passive adaptation to the neo-liberal economic policies that form the basis of the varying economic programmes pursued across the EU. This approach may help to explain the progressive adaptation of Swedish economic strategy towards this approach throughout this period. Moreover, adherents to this switch in economic priorities considered that membership of Economic and Monetary Union (EMU) may represent one means of securing their preferred non-accommodating monetary policy, with credibility secured through the participation of the Bundesbank and the legally guaranteed independence of the newly created European Central Bank (ECB) from democratic control and/or influence (Aylott, 1999:172).

It is, however, the alternative solution that most social democrats focussed upon, namely the possibility of harnessing the economic power of a large regional bloc and use this to weaken the restraints upon Keynesian economic strategy that global financial integration had imposed. Thus, EU membership may facilitate a kind of Euro-Keynesiansim, through toleration of a more relaxed fiscal and monetary policy, which could be used to reduce unemployment, whilst the EU's social dimension demonstrated support for the maintenance of the Swedish welfare state (Bieler, 2000:103).

SAP Prime Minister, Ingvar Carlsson (1994:19-20), argued that "the Swedish model can, in my opinion, be safely recreated on the European level". Moreover, Carlsson (1994:19-20) argued that supranational politics was essential in a globalised world to "reassert the balance between the social economy and the business economy". He suggested that the European social democratic left requires "common democratic institutions so that our political ambitions can be realised". Indeed, Gustavsson (1988:114-5) claims that Swedish SAP Prime Minister, Ingvar Carlsson, was ultimately convinced in the merits of EU membership by a combination of political advisors, pressure from business representatives, and the suggestions made by other European social democratic leaders that the EU could provide a superior means of achieving traditional progressive objectives.

Senior trade unionists agreed with this analysis, claiming that, as the stronghold of social democracy and the welfare state, it was the duty of progressive political forces to struggle for a 'Red Europe' with the forces of conservatism (Edin, 1995; Randquist, 1995). EU membership provided the best option to regain an element of control over transnational capital (LO, 1994:4). Indeed, Bieler (1999:34) quotes one representative at the LO headquarters having claimed that there had actually *never been* an alternative between membership and staying outside.

It is notable that, by the beginning of the 1990s, that there had been a convergence of social democratic parties concerning EU integration, as even the most reluctant European social democratic movements had been persuaded to support the EU integration process (Ladrech, 2000:64). Despite a manifesto commitment to withdrawal from the EU, as recent as 1983, the British labour movement had, by this time, completed a complete policy reversal and regularly indicated its desire to be 'at the heart of Europe' (Strange, 1997; Whyman, 2001). Similarly, the Danish Social Democratic Party leadership had concluded that the costs of maintaining an independent stance far outweighed the potential benefits of this strategy (Haahr, 1993). Indeed, the social democratic consensus around the benefits of European integration reflected their belief in the limitation of national policy solutions to the problems they jointly faced as a consequence of globalisation (Butler, 1995).

The change in the international political environment, arising from the collapse of communism in Eastern Europe and the former Soviet Union facilitated a new definition of Sweden's neutrality policy. The termination of the 'cold war' provided neutral nations such as Austria, Finland, Ireland, Switzerland and Sweden, with an enhanced range of options. Consequently, a strict interpretation of neutrality from all political and military alliances was perceived, by influential individuals, as "a hindrance for international influence [rather] than an asset" (Pedersen, 1994:124). A more flexible interpretation of national security strategy does not, however, appear to have been the decisive factor in the decision to apply for EU membership. Nevertheless, the end of the 'cold war' tensions inevitably relaxed one of the major impediments to Swedish participation in the process of European economic and political integration (Aylott, 1999:17).

An additional political factor involved a general frustration with the slow progress of EEA negotiations, and the fear that this would limit Swedish influence upon the decision-making process in the fast-moving area of European regional integration. By the time the EEA finally came into force on 1 January 1994, proponents of full EU membership pointed to the fact that EFTA countries had failed to obtain co-decision making powers, but could "only influence the legislative process during the decision-shaping stage" (Laursen 1993:125; Luif 1996:151-68). Through the EEA, EFTA nations had failed to secure the right to initiate legislation and secured only limited access to EU committees, whilst opting-out of new EU legislation was restricted to collective EFTA decision. Thus, even the limited right to refuse unfavourable laws and rules of trade conduct were restricted to those occasions when a coalition for such action could be formed amongst EFTA nations, and no longer remained the prerogative of a sovereign nation state.

The pre-existing common rules of the EEA were to be treated as part of the Union's *acquis communitaire*, which requires all new members to automatically adopt the *entire* set of regulations, laws, institutions and procedures (Gstohl 1994: 358-9). This included acceptance of the establishment of an EFTA Surveillance Authority and Court of Justice, together with EEA law having gained primacy over national law. Furthermore, the EEA did not provide equitable access to the SIM for EFTA members because it essentially created a Free Trade Area, not a Customs Union, with the necessity of providing certificates of origin for all goods and services for all EFTA members, but not for EU member states. Thus, the EEA remained a limited compromise, which failed to provide Sweden with a significant influence upon the type of entity into which the 'new Europe' was intended to develop (Miles, 1996:64; Gstohl, 1996:61).

The final political factor encouraging the shift in policy related to the fact that, as Huldt (1994:119) noted, contemporary opinion polls published in May 1990 demonstrated a clear majority in favour of EU membership, with only 21% opposed and 20% undecided. To build upon this perceived 'window' of opportunity, Gustavsson (1998:182-6) claims that "Carlsson and Larsson *exploited the currency crisis* to secure their preference" for EU membership, by utilising the "atmosphere of crisis" to encourage government and party more willing to contemplate dramatic policy change. This strategy enabled the issue of EU membership to be discussed as an issue of macroeconomic stability, therefore emphasising the views of the pro-EU Finance Minister and marginalizing two sceptical cabinet members, Andersson and Gradin (Aylott, 1999:128).

The macroeconomic benefits, primarily in terms of access to the SIM, together with enhanced political influence as a full member of the EU, were then the primary factors that secured the dramatic shift in policy on behalf of the SAP leadership. It was a move that took the trade unions and party rank and file by almost complete surprise. Nevertheless, by the time of the announcement of the policy change, the mix of economic and political arguments had already convinced a formally sceptical LO leadership of the merits of EU membership. The social dimension was perceived as permitting membership to remain compatible with the traditional goals of the 'Swedish Model', if not all of its methods and policy instruments. Furthermore, the end of the 'cold war' permitted the redefinition of one of the remaining key articles of traditional social democracy, namely the policy of neutrality, withdrew a symbolic obstacle to participation in further economic and political European integration (Bieler, 1999:24).

Social Democratic Opposition to EU Membership

This viewpoint was not, however, consistently held throughout the Swedish labour movement. The supporters of "traditional" social democratic objectives and methods of attainment rejected the basic premise that lies behind the decision to adapt Sweden to the EU norm, rather than aim to solve its own problems through nationally located social and economic strategy. Accordingly, they argued that Sweden's economic problems were caused by a rejection of the Rehn-Meidner model, not its failure. In the absence of post-Keynesian techniques, aggregate demand could not be successfully constrained during an economic upswing, and which had led to the property boom and then collapse, beginning in 1990, together with the age-old problem of how to constrain excess corporate profits so as these did not cause regressive income redistribution, with its inevitable inflationary consequences.

The rejection of economic democratisation and the wage-earner funds meant that an alternative solution had to be invented to balance the competing distributional claims of workers and capital owners, whilst providing sufficient capital formation to sustain full employment over the long-term. The 1982-91 TWEP had sought to replace this novel mechanism with the 'simple' Keynesianism solution of boosting profits through competitive devaluation. However, whilst successful in the short-run, the deregulation of financial regulations enabled the majority of the subsequent resources to be transferred to productive activity abroad, and thereby undermining the wage moderation offered by Sweden's trade unions, which remained an essential element of any successful economic strategy in a country with such strong unionisation.

The alternative economic strategy, favoured by the 'traditional' social democratic supporters, involved a return to the main precepts of the Rehn-Meidner model, involving a boost to aggregate demand to reduce demand-deficient unemployment, before reintroducing the regulation that would return democratic control over capital, and with it a greater degree of national control over the Swedish economy. Thus, the social democratic opponents of EU membership preferred a post-Keynesian to a neo-liberal type economic programme, involving continued national autonomy in monetary policy, with provision for adjustable exchange-rates (Aylott, 1999:173-4).

Meidner (1993b:112) argued that "it is scarcely a coincidence that unemployment in Sweden has reached the EC's high levels at the same time as Sweden's powerful elites are preparing for EC membership." Indeed, the priority to be given to the maintenance of full employment would be more difficult in a small, open economy the greater the co-ordination of economic strategy with EU member states and the more integrated into the international financial markets (Kurzer, 1993). Moreover, the creation of a European labour market, where most participants tolerate high levels of unemployment, make it more difficult for individual nations to pursue full employment (Ingebritsen, 1994). Thus, Soren Wibe (1993:2000) could argue that economic integration with the EU, and particularly its plan for Economic and Monetary Union (EMU) "stands in direct conflict with what since the 1930s has been Social Democracy's chief goal, namely the maintenance of full employment".

A second argument against Swedish participation in the EU related to the fact that it might lead to tax competition amongst member states, leading to anticipated downward adjustments upon the Swedish welfare and taxation system (Meidner, 1994:345). Opposition from public sector workers related to a concern that the high tax levels needed to sustain the public sector would be untenable within the constraints imposed by EU membership (Lindström, 1994:46).[3] Aylott (1999:34) detects what he describes as "a peculiarly Swedish type of nationalism", combining folk myth, neutrality and "immense pride in a famously egalitarian society-that gave Swedish welfare nationalism a distinctly Social Democratic flavour". The division between social democrats, on this basis, related to those adopting an "isolationist" variant of welfare nationalism, against supporters of integration adopting a "missionary" variant, whereby "Sweden is a model that can be offered to EU countries, instead of being protected through isolation" (Aylott, 1999:70).

Garrett (1998:4) notes that "even if economic integration creates incentives for governments to use fiscal policy for redistributive purposes, they are constrained from doing so by the threat of capital flight. Governments cannot tax mobile capital to pay for spending. Therefore, they must either cut spending or shift the burden of taxation from capital to labour – undermining the net redistributive effects of fiscal policy". Since the EU fails to compensate for this loss of national policy instruments by developing comparable measures at supranational level, the welfare state is in danger of being "emasculated by both Brussels and the larger dynamic of globalisation" (Ladrech, 2000:24).

Organised labour is comparatively weaker at supranational level than in the Scandinavian nation states, and therefore a transfer of power and authority over

---

3   Supporters of integration countered by asserting that the public sector would be placed under greater pressure by remaining outside the EU because the tax burden would have to be reduced to attract FDI.

social and economic matters is a regressive step (Ingebritsen, 1997:240-1). This threatens the core social democratic objectives which have, together, formed a central element in the Scandinavian identity and threatens both the Scandinavian model and the end to Scandinavian exceptionalism (Moses, 1994).

The third factor associated with social democratic opposition to closer political and economic integration with the EU, concerned the impact this would have upon democracy. Support for national democratic self-governance, in the Swedish, *folkstyre* (translated as 'people's steering'), was in direct contrast to the undemocratic EU institutions and tradition of elite governance (Widfeldt, 1996:113; Ladrech, 2000:46). Thus, Korpi (1993:137) argued that Swedish social democracy is unlikely to have the degree of influence it assumes because "there are more than 50 bourgeois votes in the EC" for every Swedish social democrat supporter.

Prime Minister Ingvar Carlsson (1994:20-1) sought to justify EU membership by claiming that "democracy is more than discussing or negotiating – it is also being able to make decisions that matter." Yet, this is to confuse the manner in which decisions are made with the ability to achieve one's objectives in practice; thereby confusing democracy with power (Aylott, 1999:79). Nevertheless, even on Carlsson's own ground, opponents to EU membership claimed that the achievements made by the 'Swedish Model', in terms of Sweden's generous welfare system and high female participation in the workplace, would be threatened more within the EU than by remaining outside (Bieler, 1999:36).

Sten Johansson, a leading social democrat critic of EU integration, dismissed the EU's social dimension as a "little opening" that was insufficient to counterbalance the power of capital, whilst TCO economist Roland Spånt (1993:137) dismissed the social charter as "a gesture to the gallery". Moreover, a motion to the 1993 SAP congress suggested that, in its efforts to build the good society, "it is not necessary to convince twelve other [EU] countries first – we can start sooner than that" (Aylott, 1999:69).

The Campaign for EU Membership

The sudden introduction of the pro-EU strategy in the immediate run-up to the 1991 General Election provided a disciplining effect upon internal labour movement debate. Vocal opposition and fragmentation at this time would have hampered electoral prospects and the SAP has always been acutely aware of the necessity to maintain at least the appearance of a coherent message. Indeed, it is quite plausible that the SAP leadership deliberately manipulated the timing of the announcement of the policy shift, amidst an economic crisis and with opinion polls indicating a catastrophic electoral defeat, specifically in order to restrain opponents whose loyalty to the party would prevent their vigorous campaigning against the leadership on this issue. However, this strategy was eased by the almost complete unanimity on the issue amongst the political elites of all major political parties. Even the leadership of the Centre Party decided to support EU membership, against the opinion of many of their membership, whose association with forestry, farming and rural issues, made them natural opponents of EU interference in these matters (Bieler, 2000:112-3).

The Swedish trade unions overturned their previous opposition to the EU of 'big capital' and supported Sweden's application for membership, despite concerns over the impact upon employment and a generous welfare state (Bergquist,1969:9). Indeed, as already noted, it was largely the changing attitude of trade union elites that helped to convince the SAP to alter its policy on the issue (Jerneck, 1993:34: Miles, 1996:64). Thus, the Left Party (former communists) and the Green Party were the only political parties to consistently oppose EU membership, due to their shared concerns for the maintenance of Swedish independence, solidarity with developing countries and dismay over the future of democratic control within the EU (Widfeldt, 1996:113).

As a result of the near consensus amongst the political elite, EU membership remained a relatively minor issue during the 1991 national election campaign. The main issue concerned the economic competence (or otherwise) of the retiring SAP government, set against the 'New Start for Sweden' economic stance agreed by two of the opposition parties. Where the issue did arise, the SAP promoted the image of a social democratic Europe, where the EU could learn from the 'Swedish Model'. In contrast, the bourgeois opposition suggested that EU membership would result in lower rates of inflation, interest and taxation, whilst the SAF emphasised the supposedly superior performance of the Danish economy (lower inflation, but higher unemployment) and suggesting that this was the result of EU membership. Other memorable interventions in the debate included the publicity campaign waged by a prominent restaurant in Stockholm's fashionable, historic quarter (Gamla Stan), featuring "EG priser" (EC prices) on its menu to give the impression of how prices would fall if Sweden became an average EU nation (Ingebritsen, 1998:15).

The result of the 1991 election involved a significant defeat for the SAP, and a victory for a three party bourgeois coalition, with a small increase in popularity recorded by the anti-EU Left Party. Hence, the bourgeois coalition were left to negotiate Sweden's terms of accession to the EU. However, the Swedish constitution required decisions to be taken by two successive governments, with a general election in between, for changes in the constitution that would be required for Sweden to join the EU. Moreover, to reduce earlier opposition, all political parties had accepted the proposition that membership should first be agreed via a referendum before accession should occur. This was set for October 1994.

The pro-EU campaign featured the leadership of all of the major political parties, together with business leaders and trade unionists. Indeed, one fascinating feature of the Swedish debate concerned the fact that, unlike in the UK example, there was no organised opposition from nationally-oriented companies (Bieler, 2000:107). However, the scale of opposition to the EU within the SAP meant that they adopted the tactic first used by the UK Labour Party during the comparable 1974 referendum, whereas the party would remain officially neutral in the campaign, and therefore party members were free to campaign on both sides of the argument.

The trade union confederations remained concerned at the neo-liberal macroeconomic framework operated at federal European level, but they became convinced of the absence of any realistic alternative to participation in closer European economic and political integration, due to the pressures of globalisation. Thus, the joint analysis of the LO and TCO led them to believe that Sweden would ultimately be forced into the deregulation of its economy, due to the impact of globalisation, and consequently, both national government and trade unions would lose influence. However, an attempt to restore supra-national control over capital movements was perceived as possible, leading to the conclusion that regulation could be more effective if imposed at European level, and this would facilitate the protection of the benefits provided through the welfare state. Nevertheless, despite this shared analysis at the peak level, given the strength of opposition to EU membership amongst their affiliated member unions, neither the LO nor the TCO could officially campaign for a 'yes' vote in the referendum. They therefore contented themselves with the provision of educational study circle materials for their membership (Bieler, 1999:35).

The umbrella oppositional campaign organisation, *Nej till EG* (No to the EC), encompassed contributions from prominent social democrats and trade unionists, in addition to official support from the Left Party and Green Party, together with a number of social movements, with interests in the environment, public health and women's issues (Twaddle, 1997:189). *Nej till EG* encompassed a number of party groupings, including most importantly *Social Democrats Against the EC*, led by Sten Johansson, former head of Statistics Sweden, and whose 26–member executive included Rudolf Meidner, Soren Wibe (professor of economics at Umeå University), and Einar von Bredow (former foreign correspondent for the leading current-affairs programme, *Aktuellt*) (Aylott, 1999:147).

The social democratic group produced a book and newsletter, but was hampered by lack of resources, having been refused support from both the SAP and the LO. Indeed, the opponents to EU membership had to rely primarily upon government funding, shared between the major campaigning groups on both sides of the debate. This totalled SEK 26.5 million for *Nej till EG*, of which SEK 2.5 million went to the Social Democrats Against the EU. This was barely sufficient to employ two people to co-ordinate the group's activities. By contrast, Social Democrats For the EU claimed to have employed thirty people nation-wide, despite receiving a similar state grant for their activities, leading to the suspicion that the pro-EU groups benefited from additional funding from unidentified sources.

The trade unions organising industrial workers, particularly the Paper Workers Union and the Metalworkers Union, favoured EU membership, principally due to the fact that Swedish TNCs had already established themselves in the EU's SIM. Moreover, the engineering and paper sector are both export dependent, selling 50% and 80% of their products abroad respectively. Consequently, the unions adopted the worldview held by the dominant employers in these areas, arguing that remaining outside the EU was economically impossible. They furthermore claimed that EU membership would not involve a significant loss of national autonomy since this had already been eroded due to the acceptance of common regulations through the EEA negotiations (Bieler, 1999:35-6).

In sharp contrast, principal opponents of EU membership included the Commercial Workers' Union, Transport Workers' Union and the Municipal Workers' Union, all LO affiliates, whose opposition to EU membership revolved around the issue of potential job losses, especially in the public sector. Jobs, especially in the public sector, did not depend on exports or transnational production, and the increased structural power of transnational capital consequently, played a less significant role (Bieler, 2000:104). Furthermore, these three unions predominantly represented female blue-collar workers, and therefore the perceived threat to the future of the welfare state and gender equality, stimulated opposition to the neo-liberal EU. These unions argued that the utilisation of national policy tools offered a superior means of preserving the Swedish model. A similar 'export-sheltered' division was apparent within the TCO, with unions representing white-collar workers in the industrial and financial sectors supporting EU membership, whilst public sector workers were opposed. Finally, SACO considered the question of membership to be a matter of foreign policy and therefore beyond more limited 'trade union' issues (Bieler, 1999:36-38).

Last Minute Campaigning

A matter of weeks prior to the referendum, the opinion polls indicated that the nation was split almost evenly on the question of EU membership. The 'Yes' campaign was lifted by the fact that 57% of Finns voted to join the EU, and thereby created a bandwagon effect for their more sceptical Scandinavian neighbours. Furthermore, immediately prior to the Swedish referendum, nineteen of the twenty-two presidents of LO affiliated unions declared their support for EU membership in a joint newspaper article. This was significant for the referendum as many blue-collar workers remained doubtful about the supposed benefits of EU integration. Moreover, this stance was all the more important since the membership in many of the same unions was known to be less enthusiastic, or even hostile, to the EU.

Chief executives of Sweden's largest companies registered their support for the 'Yes' vote, in open letters and advertisements in major Swedish newspapers, containing an explicit threat of disinvestment and relocation to within the boundaries of the SIM if the referendum rejected membership (Fioretos, 1997:315). The financial markets additionally indicated support for EU membership, when an opinion poll suggested that the 'No' campaign might triumph, market-determined interest rates rose, indicating anticipated higher inflation and/or uncertainty if Sweden remained independent (Luif, 1996:321). Finally, the tacit agreement that the social democratic opposition campaign believed they had with the party leadership, namely that they would refrain from appealing to the loyalty of SAP voters, was dispelled when Carlsson and Sahlin published a joint article in *Aftonbladet*, stating that:

> Those who trust us and want to give us the best means to take Sweden out of the crisis and halt the dismantling of welfare – should vote Yes to the EU (Esaisson, 1996:41).

Furthermore, the then Finance Minister, Goran Persson, warned of higher interest rates and deep public spending reductions if the referendum rejected EU participation (Aylott, 1999:154).

The Result

The result, when it came on 13 November 1994, was that EU membership had been approved by a margin of 52.2% to 46.9%, with 0.9% spoilt ballot papers. The result was significant because it demonstrated the ability of the SAP leadership to swing their supporters behind their vision of EU membership. Represented from a Left-Right perspective, the political Right were substantially in favour of EU membership, anticipating lower taxation, more orthodox economic policymaking and limitations placed upon further social democratic experimentation, as Sweden became a 'normal' European country. The non-SAP Left similarly voted heavily against EU membership, because of its view that progressive economic and social policies would be more constrained within the EU than remaining independent from this political and economic bloc. However, the SAP vote split evenly, thereby facilitating the success of the 'Yes' vote (Table 8-2). Other divisions that are apparent from the voting data, relate to a split on gender lines, as women registered their concern that EU participation may threaten the public sector employment and welfare policies that facilitated the progress Sweden has made towards gender equality.

A second anticipated division arose between blue-collar workers, who typically enjoyed higher incomes than in comparable nations, due to unionisation, solidarity wage bargaining and the maintenance of full employment, and white-collar workers, who might benefit more from greater mobility across a unified labour market. Geographical location appeared to be significant, with urban and southern voters providing slightly greater disproportionate support for EU membership (Oscarsson, 1996). There also appeared to be a centre-periphery divide over the question of EU integration, with the better off, urban voters living in mid- or southern Sweden being more supportive than their less well off, rural and northern neighbours.

One perhaps surprising result was that younger voters were more sceptical of European integration than older citizens. If one accepts the stereotype that younger voters tend to be more idealistic, and older voters more conservative in outlook, this would imply that the 'Swedish Model' proved more inspiring to younger voters than the European alternative, whereas older voters, who had benefited from decades of these policies, favoured their replacement.

Of course, the true position is more difficult to establish, because Aylott (1999:86,98) found little difference between social democratic voters according to their support for, or rejection of, EU membership, with their views along a democratic and/or welfare-nationalist fault line. Similar proportions from both 'Yes' and 'No' camps believed that Sweden's economy could and should continue to be influenced by Swedish politicians, and that controls should be re-imposed upon TNC's. However, they clearly viewed the potential to realise these objectives as furthered by their divergent voting intentions on the question of participation in the EU.

One less investigated difference between the two campaigns related to their resource base, with the 'Yes' campaign receiving an estimated twenty-times more resources than their opponents. Esaisson (1996:33) states that *Ja till EG* spent the same amount on billboard advertising during the final fortnight of the referendum campaign, than it received in total in the form of government funding. Moreover, the 'Yes' groupings benefited from the network of SAP workers who were allowed to campaign for a 'Yes' vote, on full salary.

Perhaps as many as twenty activists took advantage of this scheme to work for the 'Yes' campaign from the Stockholm national headquarters alone, whilst none participated in the 'No' campaign (Aylott, 1999:149). This is failing to count the organisational base provided by the bourgeois parties and the SAF (Twaddle,

1997:208). All of which biased the organisational resources available to the two campaigns. The importance of this imbalance is not lost upon Rokkan (1966:105), who argued that, "votes count, but resources decide the outcome in the end". Thus, the near unanimity of the leading political and social organisations in favour of EU membership, and their willingness to utilise all of their power resources to secure electoral consent for this viewpoint, had a significant influence upon the result of the referendum (Rokkan, 1975:217; Ingebritsen, 1998:167-8).

Table 8-2: Swedish referendum result, EU membership (13 Nov 1994)

Variable	Yes	No
Sex		
Female	47	52
Male	57	42
Age		
18–21	40	59
22–30	52	47
31–64	53	46
64+	58	41
Employment		
Working	53	46
Unemployed	39	61
Early Pension	48	51
Students	55	44
Occupation		
Blue-Collar	37	62
White-Collar	64	35
Agriculture	59	41
Manager	65	44
Political Party Support		
Conservative	86	13
Christian Democratic	41	59
Liberal	81	18
Centre	45	54
New Democratic	34	82
SAP	50	49
Left Party	10	90
Green Party	15	84
Left-Right Spectrum		
Definite Left	31	69
Somewhat Left	40	59
Neither	46	53
Somewhat Right	75	24
Definite Right	86	13
TOTAL	52.2	46.9

Source: Riksdag and Department (1994, No's 36 and 37).

One additional factor which appeared to influence the referendum result, related to the fact that the 'No' campaign failed to develop a mutually acceptable alternative to EU membership. The coalition was therefore fragile, held together by a rejection of EU accession, rather than a shared vision of the future. 'No' supporters preferred an independent, autonomous Sweden, whilst most social democratic voters rejected the MCC and SGP as imposing unemployment and delation upon the European zone.

Nevertheless, the leaderships of the SAP and Centre parties considered such policies to be a necessary basis for a sound Swedish economy, irrespective of EU membership. Therefore, it proved impossible to construct an economic programme that could rival the pro-EU line. Indeed, Aylott (1999) argued that, in view of the importance attached to economic matters during the referendum campaign, the development of such an alternative programme would have been a "crucial prerequisite for success". Rather than forming a historical bloc, the 'No' campaign represented a short-term alliance and this has been suggested to be one factor behind its loss of support during the final days of the campaign.

Sweden in the EU

After successfully completing negotiations in the spring of 1994, and a yes-vote in the referendum on membership in November of the same year, Sweden acceded to the EC on 1 January 1995 (Bieler, 1999:22). The immediate impact of EU membership was that, as a member with a per capita income higher than the EU average, Sweden became a net contributor to the EU, amounting to approximately SEK20bn or 4% of central government expenditure (Aylott, 1999:106). This represented a significant net cost at a time when the government was desperately seeking to reduce the imbalance in public finances. However, in terms of the passionate argument the country had just experienced, little else of substance appeared to occur.

Economic policy had already been realigned to adopt neo-liberal principles, and therefore citizens had become more used to the low inflation and high unemployment, characterising the majority European experience. Taxes did not decline substantially due to EU membership, with the exceptions including changes in alcohol sales, and indeed temporarily increased to plug the budget deficit. Nor did membership result in a massive influx of FDI.

In one respect, however, Swedish membership did appear to make a significant difference, and that was upon the EU itself. Ingebritsen (1997:253) argues that new entrants Sweden and Finland have not passively adapted to the forces of European integration, but have sought to export their corporatist institutions to the EU. One example may include the efforts made by Volvo CEO Pehr Gyllenhammar, in his advocation of the creation of a supra-national employer's federation (Cowles, 1995a). Furthermore, Sweden has participated in the construction of a social democratic response to the neo-liberal orientation of the EU (Ladrech, 2000:2-3). This response included initiatives to include employment issues and economic co-ordination as central elements within EU economic strategy.

The end result was the adoption of the Employment Charter and subsequently the European Employment Pact, in 1999. This required member states to prepare annual national action plans specifying how its policies sought to reduce unemployment via reference to improving the employability and adaptability of the unemployed, stimulating entrepreneurship and being based upon equal opportunities (Ladrech, 2000:113). However non-constraining these measures may be, Dyson (1999:195) claims that they indicate the possibility of "a new axis for policy development". Moreover, Ladrech (2000:2-3) argues that this is "the historic challenge for social democrats".

Despite Dyson's (1999:195) arguments that this agenda represented "a turning-point in the EU's agenda", this may have been over optimistic, as electoral reverses for social democratic parties in France, Austria and Italy have subsequently altered the balance of power in the EU, and has undermined the momentum driving this alternative agenda. Furthermore, even though many social democratic parties would prefer a democratically accountable Europe, complete with the re-introduction of elements of Keynesian economics, most refrain from delegating it the political authority and institutional means of fulfilling this agenda.

EMU

The EU referendum campaign was remarkably silent upon the question of EMU between EU member states, despite the fact that, under the EU's rules (*aquis communitaire*), accession committed Sweden to participation in EMU once it met the required economic convergence conditions. This was partly because the leadership of the SAP, together with the bourgeois parties, had already accepted the implementation of neo-liberal economic policies, including making the central bank independent from government, the pursuit of low inflation and seeking to align its monetary policy closely to the interest rate set by the European Central Bank (ECB). The SAP presented membership of the EU, and potentially EMU, as a means of securing low inflation and growth to the Swedish economy, and thereby a means of reducing unemployment and defending the welfare state (Gould, 1999:166). Indeed, former Social Democratic Minister and present EU Commissioner, Anita Gradin stated:

> Stability is what EMU is about. Stable prices and sound public finance so that budget policy can concentrate on important questions such as jobs instead of interest payments on the national debt (Gradin, 1997).

Acceptance of this new policy stance would immediately remove a considerable degree of opposition from EMU, at least focussing upon the loss of economic autonomy and policy instruments with which to better manage national economies. Moreover, it could be argued that, since the rules governing the operation of EMU were established by international treaty, they could be renegotiated to facilitate greater economic flexibility (Ryner, 1999:47-8). This point appears most unlikely under current conditions, but cannot be ruled out as a future possibility. Nevertheless, even if the negative features of EMU did appear predominant, it was suggested that membership of the Euro is a means to an end – namely, the price to be paid to gain access to the SIM and influence the future shaping of the EMU-zone (Ladrech, 2000:75).

After EU accession, the SAP Finance Minister, Persson, commissioned a panel of economists to investigate the consequences of Sweden's participation in EMU. Lars Calmfors chaired the commission. Its recommendation, delivered in November 1996, was that Sweden should not join in the first wave (in 1999), due to the potential for asymmetric shocks to disproportionately damage the Swedish economy, and because rigidities within the Swedish labour market reduced adaptation to changes in the external environment. The report noted its pessimism concerning the introduction of greater flexibility within nominal wage formation and therefore recommended the retention of national monetary policy to maintain internal balance (SOU, 1996:19-21,399; Calmfors et al, 1998).

The current position is that the Swedish government will conduct a referendum on potential EMU membership if it becomes convinced that the economic problems can be overcome, and that the benefits outweigh the costs. Due to the political sensitivity of this issue, the EU Commission appears ready to concede this strategy, even though, by precedent and treaty obligations, Sweden does not possess a legal veto on the question of EMU.

Chapter 9

Technological Change and the SAF Offensive

Introduction

The ability of the 'Swedish Model' to successfully pursue traditional social democratic objectives – chiefly full employment, economic growth, low inflation, international competitiveness, the development of a comprehensive welfare state, together with the redistribution of income and power – has been called into question by a combination of factors external to the Swedish economy. Globalisation has arguably weakened nationally-located labour movements together with the ability of the state to pursue social democratic-Keynesian policies. Similarly, European integration, itself partly conditioned by globalisation and partly a reaction intended to regulate unfettered capitalism, reinforces the neo-liberal economic orthodoxy presently dominant throughout the international community. Thus, many theorists claim that the future of national economic management is limited, and that Sweden should adapt to these external forces through membership of the EU, potentially including EMU. Indeed, it may do so relatively successfully due to its ingenuity in developing unique institutional arrangements and policy instruments in order that social democratic goals may still be pursued despite limitations upon autonomy of action.

This 'thesis of dispair' is not adopted by this book, however, due to the contradictory nature of the evidence. Moreover, an objective assessment would conclude that national economies retain a far greater freedom of action than is often acknowledged by advocated of the more extreme versions of the 'globalisation thesis'. Nevertheless, it is certainly true that the constraints upon national government action are tighter now than during the Keynesian 'golden era' of the mid-1950s to the mid-1970s.

It is also accurate to conclude that the challenges to the 'Swedish Model' are not only external to the national economy, but additionally include factors that influence developments in the domestic market. Technological change is one very powerful influence upon the development of business strategy, production systems, work organisation, industrial relations and the wider economy. Indeed, it is claimed that the mode of production has shifted from Fordist mass production of standardised goods and services, towards greater diversity in production, including the fulfilling of niche markets, facilitated by the advance of computers and the development of 'flexible-specialisation'. Thus, firms may introduce Japanese-style 'just-in-time' techniques, the contracting out of services previously performed in-house and/or operations being broken down into multiple profit centres. Highly regulated and bureaucratised production may thereby be increasingly superceded by a more flexible, customised and integrated system developing, encompassing the public as well as the private sector (Nilsson, 1996; NUTEC, 1996; Brulin and Nilsson, 1997).

This shift in production technique, to the extent that it has occurred, may be expected to have had a destabilising effect upon an industrial relations system built upon a Fordist model, as smaller, more flexible production units require a multi-skilled and flexible workforce (Nilsson, 1999:462-3). The development of integrated production systems led to an increased concentration of union bargaining activities at the enterprise, not national or sectoral, level. Indeed, centralised wage formation is largely at odds with a more flexible production system.

One explanation for the increasing inflationary bias, denoting wage formation during the latter years of centralised wage bargaining, may have been due to wage drift at local level as employers sought heightened flexibility in workplace. This, in turn, contributed to the loss of legitimacy of the established system of wage formation (Olsson, 1991). At the same time, employers organisations seemed to change strategy, if not adopt a new ideology, which threatened to undermine the Swedish institutions and process of industrial relations (Brulin and Nilsson, 1991; Elvander, 1992; Brulin, 1995; Kjellberg, 1998). This chapter will, therefore, explore the wider consequences of this internal challenge to the Swedish Model.

Post-Fordism

Piore and Sabel (1984:240-2) explain flexible specialisation as:

> ...a strategy of permanent innovation: accommodation to ceaseless change, rather than an effort to control it. This strategy is based upon flexible – multi-use – equipment; skilled workers; and the creation, through politics, of an industrial community that restricts forms of competition to those favouring innovation. For these reasons, the spread of flexible specialisation amounts to a revival of craft forms that were emarginated at the first industrial divide.

It has been increasingly claimed that Fordist mass production is being superseded by post-Fordist, flexible specialisation, representing a "second industrial divide" (Freeman and Perez, 1988). This thesis argues that mass markets are becoming increasingly saturated. This poses a particular problem to a production system based upon the ability to lower costs through increasing economies of scale, and whose technology is dependant upon product-specific machines that result in high overhead costs and the implication of a high cost base if not operated close to capacity. However, that feature of Fordism made it vulnerable to economic downturns.

The chosen solution was to accept, passively or through formal class compromise (as in Sweden), the operation of Keynesianism to maintain full employment through the maintenance of a high degree of capacity for firms. This was reinforced by a wage policy aimed at sustaining mass consumption market for industry's products, and a social policy that socialised consumption and thereby maintained aggregate demand. This combination of policies promoted "intensive regimes of accumulation", which in turn produced non-inflationary growth and increased standards of living, through the subordination of "circulation forms of capital", or finance capital, by productive capital (van der Pjhl, 1984; Lipietz, 1987:24-32). However, as post-Fordism depends less upon nationally generated mass consumption, this reversed the hierarchy of fractions of capital, with finance dominating the economic system through its allocation of economic resources, so that it is regarded as "the pivotal agent in the formation of the emerging global hegemony" (Cox, 1987:267; Ryner, 1999:41-2). Rentier profit has increased in importance relative to profit from production, whilst accumulation is sustained increasingly through a decrease in turnover time and a reduction of labour costs, as opposed to increases in productivity and mass consumption (Harvey, 1990).

A second feature supposedly signifying a shift towards a post-Fordist form of production relates to the observation that consumers are becoming more discerning and utilise their rising living standards to demand goods and services customised to their individual tastes rather than passively consuming uniform, mass produced products. Clark and Fujimoto (1991:2) refer to the growth of "fragmented markets and sophisticated customers". Accordingly, firms endeavour to respond through the provision of a greater diversity in products, utilising new technology to achieve smaller, differentiated production runs. Furthermore, Ryner (1993:20-22) claims that Fordist organisation has become increasingly exhausted and unable to produce satisfactory rates of productivity and technological innovation, thus leading to a resulting rise in the organic composition of capital and ultimately, if left unchecked, stagflation. In contrast, post-Fordism promotes productivity through the reduction in information bottlenecks, and therein facilitates the acceleration of the internationalisation of production (Kaplinsky, 1984). The increasing use of cybernetics both implies a gradual substitution of labour for capital in production, through the creation of 'general purpose' machinery that facilitates economical small batch production (Piore and Sable, 1984:194-280).

Work Organisation

Fordist production was typically associated with a 'Taylorist' hierarchical work organisation and specialised labour force. In contrast, flexible specialisation requires production employees to be competent in several fields, accept periodic re-skilling in order to complete new tasks, and accept greater responsibility and demonstrate initiative in solving problems and improving the production process (Hutchins, 1989). Work is organised in teams, with tasks integrated both horizontally and vertically. The former relating to job tasks like maintenance, internal transport and product control; the latter by the planning of work, the follow-up of production targets, programming and preparatory work, together with managing customer and subcontractor contacts (Nilsson, 1999:468-9).

This 'boundless flow organisation' involves the removal of barriers between occupational groups in order for all to focus upon core production. Thus, blue- and white-collar workers are combined in multi-skilled 'complete teams' (Roos, 1992:68; Brulin, 2000:240). Moreover, there have been tentative discussions about the creation of single status or 'co-worker' agreements, where all employees within a single workplace enjoy the same employment conditions and wage system. This would have significant repercussions for trade unions, which are often organised upon Fordist lines – i.e. in Sweden, the division exists between separate blue- and white-collar worker union movements.

Industrial Relations

Whereas it was rational to set wages centrally, in a standardised, Tayloristic system, a boundless flow system requires individuals to develop in their work, constantly adopt new skills and responsibilities. Therefore, it would seem more rational to set wages and working conditions at workplace level. This does not preclude central agreements setting minimum standards, but these would have to remain flexible enough to allow significant deviation at local level (Nilsson, 1999:469). Brulin (2000:249) argues that unions must adapt to this process, and "become partners in the development processes instead of just negotiating the effects".

The LO appear to have accepted the logic of this position, in their 1995 *Rattvisa* [Equity] report, where they propose that new forms of work organisation require trade unions to strengthen their positions at workplace level in order to ensure that members are indeed given the opportunity to develop in their job (Nilsson, 1999:471). Streeck (1992:101) goes further in arguing for industrial unions to adapt to the new production systems through transformation into "loose federations of workplace and enterprise organisational units". However, it is noted that the increasing heterogeneity of the labour force is a potential problem for trade unions (Vilrokx, 1996).

Impact upon the Swedish Model

The Swedish model was constructed during the Fordist age, and was therefore based upon the assumption of a mass production, high capacity, economies of scale system of industrial production, with centralised wage formation and labour market policy intended to replicate the dominant skills–, not team-based work organisation (Ruggie, 1982). In its early years, the 'Swedish Model' developed within the Bretton Woods international monetary order, whereby significant constraints were imposed upon the freedom of movement of finance in order to maintain a dominance of productive over financial fractions of capital (Patomaki, 2000:126).

The global crisis of Fordism in the 1970s affected Sweden more severely than any other OECD country (Ryner, 1994a:387-392). Furthermore, the perceived requirement for firms to have the ability to respond flexibly to a changing international economic environment may result in the regulation of wages and working conditions associated with co-ordinated bargaining losing its compatibility with efficient corporate strategy (Iversen, 1996:405).

Wilde (1992) claimed that the 'Swedish Model' experienced difficulties because a nationally-based labour movement found it difficult to challenge globalisation and post-Fordist developments, which by their nature enhanced the power of capital. In addition, one of the strengths behind the 'Swedish Model', namely its ability to favour the most efficient corporations through solidaristic wage bargaining and a tax system generous to the reinvestment of profits, tended to concentrate resources in existing industries, based on innovations from the 1930s, rather than redistribute scarce resources to the new flexible specialisation sector (Clement and Mahon,

1994:7). In other words, the 'Swedish Model' "contributed to the locking-in of resources in mature industries" and it is this process, at least in part, that explains the paucity of productivity expansion in the 1980s (Ryner, 1994:171).

Decentralisation of Wage Bargaining

Flexible specialisation requires the construction of a reward structure reflecting non-standard (non-uniform) forms of payment, including quality bonuses, profit sharing, seniority pay, and pension schemes. Thus, the determination of payment becomes an increasingly important management tool to generate incentives for high standards of work performance and inducing workers to invest in firm-specific skill acquisition. To the extent that central wage formation hinders this degree of flexibility, it may equally frustrate the transition towards flexible specialisation. Consequently, Iversen (1996:399) postulates that, in most corporatist countries, including Sweden, technological changes have encouraged the development of "cross-class flexibility coalitions between firms producing high quality goods for fragmented and volatile international markets and groups of highly skilled workers enjoying favourable market positions." This thesis would require a realignment of workers and employers in favour of a new, more flexible system of wage remuneration. Iversen (1996:407) proposes the following characterisations:

Workers

- Privileged sector – workers enjoy powerful market positions, possibly in the sheltered, domestic-orientated sector of production, combining the ability to demand higher wages and externalise the costs.
- Strategic sector – export-orientated workers, enjoying powerful market positions but with the incentive to moderate demands to preserve the competitiveness of their firms which are largely unable to pass on rising costs due to the exogenous determination of prices.
- Weak labour sector – marginal market positions, these workers have little ability to secure above-average benefits, but their organisational resources typically exceed their market resources and so they benefit disproportionally from wage bargaining centralisation (Wallerstein, 1990).

Employers

- Cost-vulnerable sector – do not depend on a highly flexible work force but are exposed to international competition – likely to support centralisation as a means to contain the wage pressure from privileged groups of workers.
- Privileged sector – relatively sheltered from international competition, manufacturing high price, high quality products, requiring a large skill-intensive work force and likely to support decentralisation of bargaining.
- Strategic sector – like their worker counterpart's, these companies face opposing incentives; they want to restrict wage costs to maintain price competitiveness, but they depend on wage flexibility in order to retain their non-price competitiveness.

To the extent that these sectoral classifications are correct, it is likely that bargaining centralisation will be supported by a "redistributive cost-control coalition"; namely workers with little market power combined with those who cannot easily externalise the costs of wage militancy, together with cost-sensitive employers. In contrast, a "high cost, flexibility coalition" would benefit privileged workers, as they would be free to utilise their superior market power in wage negotiations, together with cost-insensitive firms who would derive great benefit from micro-level flexibility (Iversen, 1996:409-410). This scenario therefore places both employers and workers in the strategic sectors, namely those who are sensitive to the flexibility and rising costs, in a pivotal position. Likely to be both wary of centralisation, because of its implications for inflexibility and wage levelling, but also distrusting decentralisations, because of its likely increase in the cost of living, this implies that any successful potential institutional designs need to meet the requirements of this group in order to gain majority support.

The formation of flexibility coalitions, advocating the decentralisation of wage bargaining institutions, is most likely if employers do not fear the inflationary consequences of a privileged sector of employees, or calculate that the inhibition of flexibility through wage levelling and centralisation is less of a problem. Similarly, centralisation coalitions are more likely when privileged groups threaten cost-push inflation and/or when the centralisation of bargaining is disassociated from wage levelling. In Norway, for example, wage bargaining was recentralised during the 1980s due to the inflationary wage militancy of the privileged workers in the petrochemical industry, whilst in Austria, centralised wage formation has remained more or less intact, but for historical reasons this produces little progressive redistribution of income (Iversen, 1996:399). Finally, flexibility coalitions can be encouraged, or their effects mediated, through a choice of macroeconomic policies that facilitate or frustrate the transformation of corporatist institutions.

Problem with the Post-Fordist Explanation

The case for post-Fordism can, however, easily be overstated. Firstly, the theory is often based upon "a historical and erroneous overlaying of its central indicators" (Crouch, 1995; Sheldon and Thornthwaite, 1999:516). Secondly, the literature is unclear on the accuracy of assumptions made concerning the significance of changes in production methods and labour market 'flexibility'. Furthermore, industrial relations studies indicate that national and sectoral cultures and institutions are at least as important in influencing the development of employee relations as 'automatic' effects deriving from changes in technology. Consequently, the strategy pursued by employers' is based upon a calculation, based upon options constrained by historical specific contexts, including the strength of trade unions and the degree of regulation of the labour market.

Another factor relates to the fact that the evidence for market saturation for mass produced consumer goods is not promising (Luria, 1990; Williams et al, 1987). Indeed, Sayer and Walker (1992:192) argue that "whatever the condition of mass production elsewhere, it is alive and well in Japan". Most products associated with Japanese companies, including televisions, cameras, videos and cars, are mass produced products. Furthermore, Streeck (1987:90) rejects the view that Fordism is inflexible, since it designs jobs so that training times are short and employees more easily interchangeable; factors which improve flexibility. However, Wood (1993:540-3) suggests that Fordism suffers from persistent problems of quality and bottlenecks in production caused by unreliability of supply. Thus, just-in-time and total-quality-manufacturing techniques may be adapted as strategies to improve, not replace, Fordism and may "reinforce Taylorism substantively" (Walker, 1989:68).

Costello et al (1989:25) argue that post-Fordist theorists err by concluding that, because new technology *allows* smaller production runs, it therefore necessarily *leads* to smaller and more competitive firms. Instead, extensive R&D is necessary for such technology, and thus it is the largest firms which benefit because they can spread the large fixed costs over a large output. Hence, according to this argument, capitalism will continue to be dominated by large global firms, which may utilise opportunities for specialised production and contract out services to internal profit-centres or external companies in order to minimise market uncertainty to the core enterprise. Nevertheless, these global organisations seek to spread the high costs of technology and future innovation over a large production base, minimising costs close to capacity in much the same way as during Fordism.

The shortening of time horizons in investment, together with the rents paid to the financial sector as payment for risk-taking, may undermine a wholesale transfer to a post-Fordist regime unless effective demand remains high during the transition (Strange, 1986). Consequently, post-Fordism may remain at least partially dependant upon returns to scale and may require 'Keynesian' reflation in order to realise the productive potential that new technology implies. Moreover, there is nothing inherently neo-liberal in the technological change described by Piorre and Sable (1984), who claim that many forms of post-Fordism may occur. Indeed, they concede that mass production could be revitalised through the extension of macroeconomic regulation in order to achieve 'multinational Keynesiansim'. Thus, Borgos (1991:87) claims that the "shift" towards post-Fordism is "by no means inevitable".

Finally, it appears accurate to conclude that TNCs in Sweden, as elsewhere, increasingly gear their payment structures to the requirements of internal rather than national labour markets, and are therefore less inclined to accept responsibility to internal balance through negotiations (Olsson, 1991:36; Burkitt and Whyman, 1994:11-12). Furthermore, it is possible that dividing the workforce into smaller, task-orientated groups may weaken traditional forms of collective consciousness and generate 'microcorporatism' or 'company-corporatism'. This is where firm-centred collaboration between labour and capital replaces class consciousness and national action (Cox, 1981:147-8; Brulin, 1989).

Cox (1987:70-4) argues that 'enterprise corporatism' may seek to integrate core workers through the provision of privileged benefit packages and secure employment. Nevertheless, none of these features need fatally undermine a progressive form of corporatism at national level. Mahon (1991:295) argues that post-Fordism can provide the "material basis for a new historic compromise", transcending Fordist limitations and offering the possibility for workers to embrace industrial democratisation. New technology can increase managerial hegemony, or be used by workers to break down barriers and spread knowledge about productive processes throughout the factory. It can also link workers who are physically separated in ways that would otherwise have been impossible. Therefore, the new technology and innovation in work organisation can be a progressive or regressive feature of future industrial activity, and it is open to the interested parties to discuss and negotiate the optimal balance.

The Employers' Offensive

The impact of technological change, together with the intensified competition generated by globalisation and European integration, affected a significant change in the economic environment in which Swedish firms conducted business. To the extent that national regulation and labour movements are marginalized and weakened by these factors, capital (particularly financial capital) is empowered. Thus, the Swedish business sector faced increased challenges simultaneously with an enhanced ability to adjust strategy and action. Consequently, it is not surprising that this historical context magnified challenge to the class compromise with organised labour that formed an essential component of the Swedish Model. The principle features of this strategic reorientation by the organisation representing Swedish business interests, the Swedish Employers Association (Svenska Arbetsgivareföreningen, SAF), is therefore briefly explored in the remainder of this chapter.

Organised Capital?

The SAF is the pre-eminent business organisation in Sweden, with 45,000 member companies, employing 1.3 million people, and covering manufacturing, construction, commerce, service and transport sectors. The largest of the 35 SAF sub-groups include the engineering sector, with 324,000 employees, the commercial sector (210,000 employees) and construction (85,000 employees), together with a general category (135,000 employees). SAF members employ approximately half of all private sector workers and, although the organisation is dominated by Sweden's large TNCs, a substantial majority of its membership derives from small and medium sized companies. This dominance by large corporations is understandable when considering the oligopolic nature of the Swedish industrial sector, as 57% of manufacturing workers are employed by Sweden's 40 largest manufacturing firms and 25% by its five largest (Eliasson, 1986).

The SAF used to include a negotiations team, who would bargain centrally with representatives from the LO, TCO and sectoral bargaining cartels. During this period, the SAF had considerable penalties it could impose upon members deviating from its line, alongside a substantial lock out fund which could compensate member companies if the SAF instituted a lock out against striking workers during an industrial dispute. Indeed, Skogh (1984:166) suggests that it was the:

> ...ability to compensate loyal members' firms for losses incurred and to penalise others (during lockouts and strikes) for disobedience to its directives, enabled SAF to acquire control over the behaviour of the employers in key areas of industrial relations.

However, the organisation has ceased to perform its wage bargaining function during the last decade. Consequently, the SAF has become more of an information and lobbying organisation and, it is in pursuit of the latter feature of its operations, that it co-operates closely with the other major employer organisations, the Federation of Swedish Industries (Sveriges Industriförbund, SI). The SI more narrowly focuses upon the interests of the larger, industrial companies, although it does include state-owned and co-operative firms in contrast to the private sector SAF.

Changing SAF, Changing Strategy

Domestic-orientated capital[1] dominated the SAF and SI during the 'Keynesian era', from 1932 to 1976 (and arguably 1990), and supported the maintenance of high domestic demand and compromise with trade unions to ensure labour market stability and moderate wage increases. Swedish capitalists were "essential participants" in the development of the Swedish Model (de Geer, 1989:122; Swenson, 1991:515). However, the onset of the 'crisis era', during the mid-1970s, created a number of factors to erode support for the Model (Streeck, 1992; Wadensjö, 1988). These included:

1. Large, export-orientated TNCs became increasingly important in terms of their contribution to the Swedish economy. Thus, during a period when Sweden's share of world exports of industrial goods fell by more 20%, between 1965 and 1986, Swedish TNCs increased their share by 16% (Blomstrom and Lipsey, 1989; Blomstrom, 2000:197). This, together with the increasing dominance of financial capital, due to the transnationalisation of production and finance, resulted in a shift in SAF strategy (Gill and Law, 1989:479). Financial and export-orientated capital loses more than it gains from "a welfarist recovery strategy based upon domestic demand stimulation" (Pontusson, 1987:24). Thus, the change in the balance of power within the SAF weakened support for the Corporatist-Keynesian 'Swedish Model'.

2. Low international demand impelled capital to pursue an alternative accumulation strategy of maximising extraction of surplus product per worker (Ahrne and Clement, 1992:472; Whyman and Burkitt, 1993b:606). The consequences of low international aggregate demand may, therefore, be more

---

[1] Capital is composed of many "distinct (and often conflicting) elements, interests and 'fractions'" with the accumulation strategy pursued by the organisations of capital following the preference of the dominant fraction (Miliband, 1989:13). Export- and domestic-orientated companies are not mutually exclusive since the former require a strong domestic sales platform from which to expand internationally. Nevertheless, potential saturation of the home market caused many companies to concentrate upon export markets. For example, 90% of car production was consumed domestically in the early 1950s whereas this sector is now distinctly export-orientated even though production occurs primarily within Sweden (Olsen, 1992:46).

conducive to the transition towards a post-Fordist, flexible specialisation form of production.

3. Intensified international competition accelerated relocation of productive facilities abroad to secure access to foreign markets (particularly the EU) and establish closer relations with foreign purchasers. The unhibited free movement of capital facilitates the consequences for profits arising from currency movements, allow the company to avoid labour shortages and increase rates of return on investments. Indeed, by 1986, Sweden's seventeen largest companies employed 55% of their total workforce abroad, whilst liberal application of exchange regulations, and their abolition in 1989, enabled Swedish firms to invest more abroad than domestically (Lindbeck et al, 1993:227). This process was eased due to the fact that many enterprises created internal finance companies to increase autonomy from monetary policy and maximise returns from international financial deregulation. Volvo's financial subsidiary *Volvofinans*, for example, possesses liquid assets equivalent to Sweden's sixth largest bank (Olsen, 1991:128).

4. Free movement of capital across national frontiers weakens trade unions and dis-empowers national democracy by restricting governments to actions sanctioned by financial market orthodoxy (Whyman and Burkitt, 1993a:5). Finance capital occupies the "veto position" in the Swedish economy formerly held by the LO (Bergström, 1991:7). Thus, Patomaki (2000:128) notes that, in more recent years, economic policies appeared to be more strongly conditioned by the rapid reactions of short-term financial capital.

5. White-collar trade union growth and militancy, during a period of depressed international demand, caused wage negotiations to became a zero-sum game leading to inter-union rivalry, inflationary pressure and which weakened central negotiation legitimacy (Olsson, 1991:29-37,72).

6. Increased dependence upon human resources necessitated capital competing for employee loyalty by superseding social class with corporate identity, via an individual reward system (Jenson and Mahon, 1993:94). Thus, international and internal labour markets became increasingly important in the determination of remuneration for employees, and national labour markets less significant.

Embeddedness, Voice and Exit

One explanation for this shift in strategy focuses upon a firm's 'embeddedness' in a particular market, the degree of sunk costs in terms of previous fixed investment, and the paucity of exit options (Amin, 1991).

According to Hirschman's (1977) terminology, as the 'exit' options become more costly, due to the embeddedness of productive capital, this motivates capitalists to form collective organisation and use 'voice' in order to protect their investment. The greater the degree of embeddedness, the greater the stability of social interaction over time, and the better the opportunity to establish an institutional framework to facilitate dialogue and enhance production capability (Andersen and Midtun, 1996:135-8). This idea is represented in Table 9-1.

Table 9-1: Dimensions of 'Embeddedness' of Capital

The Economic Dimension	The Sociological Dimension	
	High Social / Legal Constraints	Low Social / Legal Constraints
High Sunk Costs	High level of embeddedness – agriculture, fisheries	Medium level of embeddedness – capital intensive industry
Low Sunk Costs	Medium level of embeddedness – cornerstone enterprises	Low level of embeddedness – finance

Source: Andersen and Midttun (1996:135).

New Leadership, New Strategy

The combination of changing technology, external environment and the perceived threat from the labour movement's reform agenda, caused many small companies to support export-orientated capital in selecting a new SAF leadership prepared to wage a lengthy and vigorous struggle to destroy the social democratic class compromise (de Geer, 1989:174-6; Olsen, 1991:130-1).

The decisive break between the 'old' and 'new' style of labour management occurred in the late 1970s when Curt Nicolin became the new SAF Chairperson, Olof Ljunggren was appointed managing director and a neo-liberal chief editor took control of the SAF newspaper. The new leadership team managed some of the leading companies owned by the Wallenberg family 'sphere' of interlocking directorships.[2] This grouping had accepted the corporatism of the Swedish Model reluctantly, and their leadership signified a shift within the SAF towards direct member representation of entrepreneurs and less discretionary autonomy of officials (Schiller, 1987:124-138). Pragmatic compromise, between participants who had experienced the waste of mass unemployment and depressed markets, was superseded by younger actors determined to impose internal SAF discipline through the "marketing of capitalism" (Whyman and Burkitt, 1993b:606-7).

The "militant pro-capitalist strategy" strategy was not universally popular amongst many industrialists who accepted the SAP as the "party of business" (Isreal, 1978:341-2; Martin, 1992:151). However, the election of the first non-socialist government in almost half a century, in 1976, shifted the balance of political power and thereby reduced the risk involved in what became a "sophisticated" ideological struggle with labour (Olsson, 1988:71). For example,

---

2   The Wallenburg family group controls companies making up approximately 40% of the value of shares on the Stockholm stock market, and including some of the largest Swedish TNC's – i.e. Ericsson, Electrolux, Stora, Asea and Saab-Scania.

considerable effort was employed to frame the language of political discourse to shift public opinion in the SAF's favour (Boréus, 1994:333,350). This sought the replacement of social democratic-Keynesianism with classical free market liberalism, marked by a substantial reduction and marketisation of the welfare state (Ahrne and Clement, 1992:472; Pontusson, 1988:51). Accordingly, capital expended considerable organisational and financial resources, dwarfing those available to the LO, to ensure an unequal struggle for public opinion (Hansson, 1984b:342-5; Bresky et al, 1978:201). The scale of this investment was partially obscured by the discrete use of multiple 'front' organisations (Boréus, 1994:350; de Geer, 1989:326-9).[3] The variety of these initiatives makes the SAF probably the "world's most resourceful employers' organisation" (Piven, 1991:112).

The long-term ideological campaign was complemented by a short-term offensive which focused principally upon:

- Ending corporatist accommodation – involved removal of employer representatives from public boards, winding-up of wage-earner funds and the relaxing of the wave of labour laws introduced during the 1970s, most notably including co-determination procedures (MBL).
- The decentralisation of wage formation.
- The unravelling of the 'Swedish Model' – through adoption of neo-liberal economic precepts, involving the superiority of low inflation targets over full employment, the ending of undue state intervention in the marketplace, the privatisation of state holdings, deregulation of the financial and labour markets, and reliance upon market forces rather than the 'negotiated economy'.

Ending Corporatism

The SAF began to agitate for a series of changes to the industrial relations legislation, but at the centre of all its demands lies the desire for the elimination of the unions' privileged position as employee representative. Thus, the SAF preference is for a revision on the law on employment security to grant workplace rights to individual employees, and not trade unions on behalf of their members (Mahon, 1994:357-8). Furthermore, the SAF delayed negotiations on MBL until it could force concessions from the trade unions such that co-determination became merely a structure to facilitate co-operation at local or plant level (Aspling, 1986:460-4; de Geer, 1989:312-5). The empowerment of workplace determination at local level was, therefore, in accordance with a flexible specialisation strategy and was more consistent with the SAF's policy on the decentralisation of wage bargaining.

In more recent years, the SAF decided to withdraw its representatives from all corporatist bodies, albeit that many of these still have individual business representatives, in the anticipation (correct, as it happened) that the government would be forced to phase out comparable trade union representation. Furthermore,

---

[3] These ranged from numerous research institutes, publishers, a radio station, agencies dedicated to manipulating the media, a schools propaganda section and even a SAF-financed university (Boréus, 1994:112-130; de Geer, 1989:331-6).

Ulf Laurin, then SAF Director, argued that corporatism prevented change, that business representatives often became hostages to majority opinion and that the institutional frameworks and rules of such bodies had been designed contrary to business interests. Therefore, he argued that the "SAF has been too preoccupied with questions that the authorities – rather than enterprises – find important" (Laurin, 1991).

Wage Bargaining Decentralisation

Centralised wage bargaining began to be increasingly questioned by the SAF during the 1970s, when a series of ill-timed wage settlements contributed to an overheating of the economy, before causing a crisis of competitiveness. The negotiation system was becoming increasingly complicated through the inclusion of the white-collar, public sector unions, who were becoming increasingly militant due to the rising problem of wage drift; namely increases in incomes granted at local level in violation to the officially sanctioned distributive norms (see Table 9-2). A degree of wage drift had always existed, and was tolerated because it provided additional rewards for workers with scarce skills.

Table 9-2: Wage drift as % of total wage increases (annual averages)

1966-1970	1971-1975	1976-1980	1981-1985	1986-1991
50.2	42.2	42.3	39.7	60.2

Source: The Swedish Employers' Federation.

By the end of the 1980s, wage drift accounted for almost half of all wage increases, as a result of a growing number of employers seeking to adapt to market forces, escape the constraints on their prerogatives in order to design internal company incentive structures, and/or pay efficiency wages (Calmfors and Nymoen, 1990:412). This generated demands for compensation from workers outside the manufacturing sector, where most wage drift was concentrated. Moreover, it had been argued that multi-tier bargaining systems such as Sweden's – encompassing central, sectoral and local negotiations – has a built-in inflationary bias since it has failed to prevent higher nominal wage increases in Sweden than in other countries (Holden, 1990; Vartiainen, 1998:25). This could be easily solved through allowing the currency to float gently downwards, or via an adjustable peg system. However, this solution was rejected in Sweden as too defeatist (Bosworth and Rivlin, 1987; Lindbeck et al, 1993:226).

The inflationary features of Sweden's centralised wage bargaining system resulted from its operation and were not in any fundamental way indemic of such systems, as corporatist literature will attest (Cameron, 1984; Bruno and Sachs, 1985). Nevertheless, disillusionment with central negotiations and the desire to achieve wage flexibility was magnified by the inability of the SAF to beat the LO during the worst industrial conflict for seventy years, in 1980, and caused decentralisation to become capital's preferred strategy for avoiding rapid cost increases by weakening central union organisations (de Geer, 1989:253-270; Martin, 1992:140-1).

Figure 9-1: Decentralisation of wage bargaining in Sweden, 1965-1993

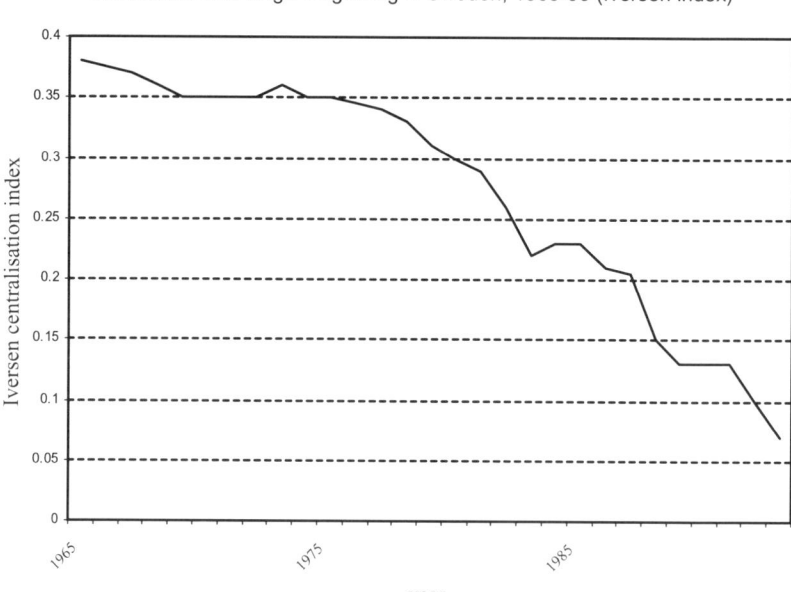

Centralisation of wage bargaining in Sweden, 1965-93 (Iversen index)

In the event, it was increasing heterogeneity within the labour market, and "irreconcilable" rivalries between unions, that enabled the SAF to end three decades of centralised bargaining in the 1983 wage round (see Figure 9-1). The SAF's largest and most important affiliate, the Association of Swedish Engineering Industries (*Verkstads Industrier*, VI), persuaded the SAF to reject centralised negotiations before subsequently enticing the metalworkers' union into an industry-level agreement (Ahlén, 1989:338,344; Bergström, 1991:7; Elvander, 1988:78-138).[4]

The key initiators of the decentralisation drive were the same 'big ten' TNCs who largely determine policy within VI and within the SAF – specifically, this involved the Wallenberg group, including ABB and Ericsson, together with Volvo (Pontusson and Swenson, 1996). As these companies have increasingly

---

[4]   VI was formally known as VF, having changed its name in 1992. However, for clarity and consistency, it is identified as VI in this book, even when discussing events prior to 1992.

concentrated upon the vast majority of their sales which are bound for overseas markets, the domestic market has become less important, and therefore these companies are less willing to determine their management strategies according to stabilising the national labour market. Indeed, the manufacturing sector has been transferring increasing proportion of its production activity outside of Sweden, and employing fewer Swedish workers as a result (Kjellberg, 1992:92-3).

From the perspective of the engineering TNCs that initiated the process of decentralisation, it has been highly successful, reducing bargaining to enterprise and sectoral levels, and increasing flexibility and wage diversion in the process (see Table 9-3). However, decentralised wage formation has caused macroeconomic instability, due to the fragmentation of wage bargaining and competition between unions driving up average wages. Indeed, government imposed 'Rosenbad' and 'Rehnberg' incomes policies during 1986-7 and 1991-2 (Ahlén, 1989:334-341; Martin, 1992:68-9).

Table 9-3: Changes in coefficient of variation of Swedish wage-earners' wages

	Phase I (1962-70)	Phase II (1970-83)	Breakdown (1983-93)
Total variation	-0.34	-0.61	+0.49
Within industry	-0.26	-0.63	+0.39
Within firm	n.a.	-0.60	+0.41
Between industries	-0.50	-0.58	+0.76
Between firms	n.a.	-0.46	+0.56

Source: Vartiainen (1998:27).

The problem, identified in the bargaining literature, is that decentralisation may produce microeconomic wage flexibility but at the expense of higher average wage rises; co-ordinated wage formation is better placed to secure real wage moderation (Faxén et al, 1988). Indeed, many Swedish employers opposed wage decentralisation, particularly the large forestry product companies and many small retail traders, car repair shops and small manufacturers who joined the SAF for the stability and security centralised bargaining provided (Martin, 1992:1). The consequent rise in industrial disputes, together with the increase in real wage growth, at a time of high unemployment, may have caused even the supporters of decentralisation to reconsider their position (Sheldon and Thornthwaite, 1999:524).

The result has been a partial reconsideration of the structure and process of wage formation. For example, the traded goods sector has regained its leadership role in pay formation due to a change of policy by TCO. Moreover, public sector pay formation is no longer tied to outcomes of firm level bargaining in the traded goods sector, wage drift has declined and compensation clauses have disappeared (Pontusson and Swenson, 1996:229). In addition, employers in the traded goods sector and the LO formulated the so-called 'Edin rule' that the sector's total wages bill should be similar to prevailing rates among other EU industrial economies, in order to maintain international competitiveness (LO, 1997). Thus, the ultimate form of wage formation remains indeterminate.

Effect on the SAP

The SAP leadership hesitancy and defensiveness encouraged the SAF to *accelerate* its ideological programme to the extent that, in the aftermath of the 1980 industrial dispute, capital and industrial labour became "irreconcilable" (de Geer, 1989:319; Pontusson, 1988:51). The SAF ideological offensive "deeply affected" the SAP, inducing it to accept private initiatives within the formerly exclusive public sector provision of child care, elderly care and medical care, parental choice in education and adopting the SAF's calls for EU membership (de Geer, 1991INT). After 1982, the SAP maintained the basic thrust of bourgeois economic policy by promoting higher profits to stimulate investment, deregulating capital and foreign exchange markets, introducing a less progressive tax system and accepting the undesirability of further public sector growth (Pontusson, 1987:23). Whilst none of these features necessarily involves the abandonment of traditional social democratic principles, the shift in policy nevertheless is in this direction, and certainly implies the rejection of core elements of the Rehn-Meidner Model. Rather than mounting a challenge to the growing structural power of capital, through modifying existing regulatory frameworks, the SAP dismantled these controls and thereby amplified the ability of capital to dictate to government (Ryner, 1999:49). Indeed, the managing directors of some of Sweden's largest companies have blatantly sought to curb government freedom of action, through:

1. a mass sale of bonds in protest at fiscal policies (McIvor, 1994a);
2. the publication of a joint article in *Dagens Nyheter*, the country's main daily newspaper, immediately prior to the endorsing the de-regulatory policies of the centre-right coalition and stating that investments totalling 50 billion Swedish Kroner would be at risk if taxes were raised (Binding, 1994);
3. the Wallenberg family threatened that, unless sustained reductions were made in public expenditure, several of his companies' headquarters may relocate overseas (McIvor 1994b).

Rehn and Meidner have described such tactics as corporate "blackmail" upon the Swedish government (Wilde, 1992; Wilks, 1996:107). As a result, it appears difficult to foresee the SAP abandoning their acceptance of a neo-liberal, non-accommodating economic policy rule, in favour of the reinstatement of full empoyment as the prime objective of macroeconomic policy. However, in the absence of solidaristic wage-policies and full employment, the Swedish welfare state remains vulnerable to calls for radical reform.

Conclusion

Technological change has, to some extent at least, provided the impetus for the SAF offensive aimed at replacing the 'Swedish Model', and required the labour movement to conceive of new institutional solutions to old problems that allow greater decentralisation and flexibility without undermining social solidarity in the process. This has proved challenging. However, there is nothing inherently negative about the increasing importance of flexible-specialisation. In many regards, it empowers workers and provides for greater variety within work experience. The challenge remains, whether a corporatist arrangement can be developed that can help to stabilise the economy, promote international competition, whilst simultaneously internalising distributional conflict within institutional arrangements and thereby preventing inflationary pressure from destabilising the macroeconomic strategy. There is nothing in the analysis contained within this chapter to suggest that this is impossible, but merely that it will need new solutions to old problems.

PART IV
EVALUATING ALTERNATIVE MACROECONOMIC STRATEGIES

Chapter 10

A 'New Start for Sweden'?

Introduction

The ultimate unravelling of the 1982-91 TWEP was caused, in large part, by the combination of an unsustainable property price 'bubble', a substantial outflow of direct investment leading to capacity constraints for domestic industry, together with the inflationary consequences of high excess profits. In short, the synthesis of neo-liberal policy solutions, together with the remains of the post-Keynesian Rehn-Meidner model, proved to be unsustainable in the medium-term. In addition, the inability of a minority SAP government to get parliamentary support for the timely introduction of an austerity package, designed to reduce the build-up of inflationary pressure on the economy, worsened the over heating.

The collapse in the reputation of the SAP government to successfully manage the Swedish economy provided a clear opportunity for the bourgeois parties to develop a distinctive economic programme rather than feel constrained to provide continuation with social democratic economics. The resulting 'New Start for Sweden' strategy document, agreed between the Moderate and Liberal parties prior to the 1991 election, rejected the 'Swedish Model' and sought to reinvigorate the Swedish economy according to neo-liberal principles.

'New Start' Strategy

The 'New Start' programme was designed to radically restructure the Swedish economy. Its theoretical foundations rested upon neo-classical foundations, ascribing a perceived sluggish growth rate to Eurosclerosis, suggesting that the public sector had grown too large, and was draining the vitality out of the economy. Variants of this approach focus upon the 'crowding out' hypothesis, whereby public sector investment competes with more productive private sector investment opportunities for a relatively fixed level of savings, and in the process causing interest rates to rise in an attempt to ration this excess demand, and thereby depressing the growth rate.

A second element of this approach highlighted the reduction in incentives resulting from the high levels of taxation needed to pay for the public expenditure; corporate taxes may reduce investment and employment, labour taxation may reduce work incentives, savings taxation may reduce the amount of risk capital available to finance productive investment and consumer taxes may increase inflation. Furthermore, to the degree that welfare states truly decommodify workers, this weakens the discipline of the market, creating passive welfare clients who choose not to work, or at least weakening the incentives (positive and negative) employed to increase labour productivity and thereby growth potential. Sweden has the highest share of its GDP accounted for by public sector transfers and expenditure; a fact that is portrayed as both a measure of economic failure, but also a cause of slow growth rates (Henrekson, 1996; Agell, 1996; Dowrick, 1996).

The Eurosclerosis argument is not without its critics, however, who point out that simple associations of statistical data can be misleading, particularly since the ranking of countries depends largely upon the time period from when the data is selected. Moreover, public expenditure has demonstrable beneficial effects upon economic growth. This is particularly noticeable with human capital and physical infrastructure investment. However, it also includes welfare expenditure due to its role as an automatic stabiliser, thereby preventing the economy from suffering a higher degree of capacity reduction than would otherwise occur during a recession (Korpi, 1985; 1996; Barr, 1992).

Endogenous growth theory finds a positive relationship between many aspects of public sector expenditure and economic growth rates (Atkinson, 1999). In contrast, Barro (1990) hypothesised a 'hump shaped' relationship between public goods financed through taxation and economic growth rates, signifying that, beyond an optimal level, the positive association becomes negative, as the Euroslerosis theorists predict. Thus, the conclusions produced by this neo-liberal analysis are clear. Sweden's public sector required reducing in size, its welfare system required reform to reduce dependency, and taxation levels reduced to provide greater incentives to work, save and invest.

The 'New Start', then, sought to realign economic policy in Sweden. The most important objective of macroeconomic policy became a low inflation rate rather than full employment, albeit that the final years of the previous government had seemingly adopted this same stance policy (Finansdepartmentet, 1991:9). This strategy is based upon the theory of the natural rate of unemployment. According to this proposition, government manipulation of aggregate demand can have only short-run effects upon the real economy (i.e. output and employment), with labour market factors determining the natural rate of unemployment in the long-run. Thus, government action will primarily have consequences upon the inflation rate. Thus, rather than stoke up inflationary pressure by trying to reduce unemployment below the natural rate, governments should instead concentrate upon reducing inflation. The theory predicts that this can be achieved at little or no cost, once short term adjustments feed through the system. This strategy is classic monetarism, and represents a rejection of the Keynesian model of the economy, upon which social democratic economic policy has traditionally relied.

In order to achieve the low inflation rate the strategy desired, the 'New Start' involved the maintenance of a tight fiscal policy throughout the entire period of the programme (Finansdepartmentet, 1992:5). The 'Keynesian' use of fiscal policy in order to manage the level of aggregate demand, and thereby seek to influence the level of employment in the economy, was flatly rejected on the grounds that budget deficits thus incurred would generate expectations of future inflation, reduce confidence in economic policy, leading to an increase in the risk premium on interest rates and a weakening of the currency. Thus, "the disadvantages of a generally expansionary fiscal policy...therefore clearly outweigh the advantages which could be achieved by a somewhat higher level of activity in the short term" (Regeringens Propositionen, 1993:19).

According to this approach, the role for fiscal policy is to produce budget surpluses in order to convince the financial markets that economic policy is sufficiently orthodox and anti-inflationary. Confidence in a nation's macroeconomic strategy is expected to result in lower long-term interest rates and a stable currency. Hence, a stable climate for business investment and trading decisions is created.

The important factor in this strategy, therefore, rests upon the assumption that fiscal orthodoxy will engender increased confidence in Swedish economic policy on behalf of the influential managers of investment funds and other significant participants in the global financial markets. In particular, it is increased integration and deregulation of capital flows across borders, which provides these individuals with the power to significantly influence the cost of borrowing (i.e. interest rates) and net capital flows in an economy based upon an assessment of risk and return.

The credibility of any economic package depends at least partially upon the perceptions of the financial market operators. These are, in turn, formed through a typical acceptance of neo-liberal economic theories, and a preference for low inflation as an optimal climate for investment opportunities. This viewpoint over-rides a more balanced view of wider objectives, such as full employment, higher rates of economic growth, trade balance and a more equitable society. Consequently, a tight fiscal policy should generate increased confidence and thereby cause long term interest rates to fall, thus providing a better climate for productive investment, leading to increased employment and higher economic growth.

The pressure on inflation was reinforced through the pegging of the Krona to the European Exchange Rate Mechanism (ERM). The necessity to maintain an external anchor upon the economy was a point of common ground between all major Swedish political parties. Indeed the SAP had actually taken Sweden into the ERM shortly before losing office, as a prelude towards possible future EU membership. The concept of a fixed exchange rate focussed upon the disciplinary effect it would have upon the economic actors. Thus, workers could not demand inflationary wage settlements, nor companies concede them, because this would result in a loss of international competitiveness that could not be easily remedied through depreciation of the currency. Instead, it would involve either a sharper rise in productivity, or a reduction in wage costs, relative to leading competitors, in order to maintain market share and avoid unemployment.

The maintenance of a fixed exchange rate presupposed that this disciplinary effect would be sufficient to secure a moderate wage formation system. This is irrespective of other elements considered to be significant by the Rehn-Meidner model, including the distributional consequences of corporations making excess profits. Furthermore, it depended upon the assumption that any short-term job losses and lost output were relatively insignificant in terms of social costs, or else that these were a price worth paying in order to restrictive expectations in the Swedish economy, and thereby deliver low inflation together with full employment in the medium term.

An additional problem with using a fixed exchange rate as an anchor for the economy concerned the fact that monetary policy would have to be used to maintain the external value of the currency, and could not be used to solve internal problems of unemployment or inflation. However, the 'New Start' programme did not consider this to be a significant loss, because it accepted the argument that the Swedish financial sector had become closely integrated with a single global financial market. Therefore, there no longer existed the possibility for a single nation to set its own interest rates to secure economic objectives. In short, "monetary policy cannot be used to influence domestic demand" and therefore the loss of a non-functioning economic policy instrument had little real costs attached to the policy decision (Finansdepartmentet, 1991:14). Indeed, even assuming the achievement of even a modest upswing in economic activity in the short-term, secured by means of:

> an expansionary monetary policy, involving rapid and dramatic cuts in short-term interest rates which are not based on a credible, long-term budget policy…would risk undermining confidence in the resolution behind the stabilisation policy, and could thus lead to rising long-term interest rates with adverse effects on investments and domestic demand (Regerings Propositionen, 1993:19).

Following the same basic logic, the 'New Start' programme rejected the use of devaluation as an effective strategy (Finansdepartmentet, 1991:22; Vartiainen, 1998:35).

The 'New Start' programme did not simply involve the maintenance of a tight fiscal policy, but it required the composition of taxation and public expenditure to be significantly altered. Specifically, due to the Eurosclerosis arguments discussed earlier, it involved a target to reduce public expenditure as a proportion of GDP in order to free resources for the private sector, which it perceived to be the growth engine of the economy (Finansdepartmentet, 1991:5). The strategy necessitated expenditure strategy involving cuts of between SEK 10-15 billion per year, over the medium term, in order to be able to reduce taxation by a similar amount per year. The urgency of rolling back the state was discussed, in terms of the disincentive effects of taxation, as "an important cause of the poorer economic performance". Thus, the 'New Start' programme involved the use of "strategic tax cuts to promote saving, investment and enterprise" (Finansdepartmentet, 1991:9,13).

Structural reform of the Swedish labour market, the industrial sector and reform of the welfare state, was intended to complement macroeconomic policy by increasing the flexibility of the economy and the responsiveness to market forces. This included further deregulation of the Swedish economy, the privatisation of public owned enterprises, together with the encouragement of more competition in certain sectors of the Swedish economy, principally through the adaptation of the economy to the forces of globalisation. The welfare reforms were intended to "encourage work and saving", "introduce greater personal liability" and reduce the financial burden of the welfare programmes in order to facilitate reductions in taxation (Finansdepartmentet, 1991:6). Underpinning this package, the 'New Start' envisaged EU membership as a means of ensuring that these economic reforms formed part of Sweden's evolution into a 'normal' European society and ending the exceptionalism of the 'Swedish Model' (Eddie, 1993:9).

The final element of the 'New Start' programme, however, is a little surprising when set against the neo-liberal basis for the other measures, namely the retention of the active labour market programmes from the Rehn-Meidner model. One plausible explanation of this fact involves a demonstration of an open-mindedness of Swedish policy-makers to ideas and to drawing from initiatives that seem to work rather well, irrespective of ideological prejudice. However, it could just as easily have resulted from a failure of the government to tackle the growing problem of unemployment, in a country where deviation from full employment had not previously been tolerated.

The bourgeois government greatly expanded the size and number of labour market programmes. Thus, at its height in 1994, approximately 5% of the entire Swedish labour force were participating in such measures, with 1.3% in job development schemes for young people (ungdomspraktik), 1.4% in labour market training (arbetsmarknadsutbildning), and 1.5% in public works and job introduction projects (beredskapsarbeten and arbetslivsutveckling) (Agell et al, 1995:104). This involved a shift away from demand-orientated initiatives, such as public works, whilst skills training programmes were expanded and additional schemes introduced to give the unemployed on-the-job training and maintain their contact with the labour market. One interesting variant of previous labour market programmes involved 'replacement schemes', which provided a state subsidy for a company to temporarily replace a regular employee who is on educational leave, thereby providing the unemployed person temporary employment and updating their work experience, whilst facilitating employers to enhance the skills of their employees (Agell, 1996:70-2).

Crisis, What Crisis?

The 'New Start' for Sweden was, therefore, a radically different type of economic strategy than had been implemented since the rise of Keynesianism in the 1930s. It sought nothing less than to reposition Sweden as a 'normal' European country, by eliminating all elements of the exceptionalist 'Swedish Model', and thereby dramatically restructuring economic institutions and policy. According to its neo-liberal theoretical foundations, the reductions in taxation and reform of the welfare state would strengthen incentives to hard work, savings and investment, whilst the reduction in public expenditure would facilitate a reinvigoration of the Swedish growth engine, private sector industry. The low inflation environment, secured through fiscal orthodoxy and a fixed exchange anchor would alter the expectations and behaviour of economic actors, thereby ensuring lower inflation, interest rates and a stable currency, at little real cost in terms of a temporary rise in unemployment from the natural rate. Thus, the 'New Start' strategy was internally consistent. The problem was that it did not work!

Swedish GDP fell for three years in a row, by 1.7% in both 1991 and 1992, and a further 2% in 1993, thereby totalling a 5.4% reduction in Swedish national income and representing Sweden's deepest recession since the 1930s (EIU, 1994:3). Gross fixed capital formation dropped from 20% at the end of 1990, to 14% by the end of 1993, before recovering slightly to 15% by the end of the following year (Riksbank, 1997:29). Manufacturing output declined by 17%, and real estate building activity by 75%, which amounted to a larger absolute collapse in production than during the 1930s depression (Lindbeck et al, 1993a:221; Lindbeck, 1997:1305). Industrial capacity fell from its typical level of 89-90% in favourable economic periods, to 81% in 1992 (Riksbank, 2002:36). Including the year of slow growth in 1990, industrial output fell by 15%, employment in the tradeables sector dropped by 19% and total employment declining by 11% (EIU, 1993:15; Thomas, 1998:10). Unemployment rose in excess of fivefold during this period, from 1.6% in 1990 to 8.5% in 1993, and with a further 6.5% of the labour market participating in manpower schemes, this meant a total of 15% (Blanchflower et al, 1995:107). Estimates of the output gap, reflecting the difference between what the economy could potentially produce and what it actually currently produces, vary from a substantial 5% to 7.5% of GDP (Riksbank, 2002:36). Moreover, Cerra and Saxena (1999) estimate that the size and duration of this recession led to *permanent* output loss as a result of capacity scrapping, rather than cyclical output loss.

Admittedly, the inflation rate fell sharply during this period, from 10.4% in 1990, to 9.4% in 1991 and 2.2% in 1992. However, this was largely due to the collapse in demand in the depressed Swedish economy, together with the technical matter of the inflationary impact of the 1990 tax reform working its way out of the figures (EIU, 1993:18). Furthermore, the 'New Start' strategy did secure an increase in the profit share of Swedish national income, from 32% in 1991 to in excess of 36% in 1994 (Riksbank, 2001:39). Yet, despite the predictions of neo-liberal theory, this did not automatically lead to an increase in productive investment. Indeed, experience tends to confirm the post-Keynesian prediction that investment depends upon a combination of factors, including current and expected profits, the level of aggregate demand and current capacity utilisation. As all of these other factors were less favourable towards immediate investment, simply redistributing national income in favour of capital owners was insufficient to secure increased capital formation.

The severity of the recession was not, of course, entirely due to the 'New Start' programme. One contributory factor relates to the impact of the international recession upon the export-orientated sector of Swedish industry (Henrekson et al, 1992; Eklund et al, 1993). Moreover, the deregulation of the financial sector and the asset 'bubble' in the late 1980s had encouraged consumers to take on ever increasing personal debt, assisted by banks eager to enhance profits due to new competitive pressures in the sector. According to Lindbeck et al (1993a:222), "in retrospect, credit institutions were not able to deal properly with their new freedom to engage in risky activities" and secured loans on the basis of rising property prices. Therefore, when the asset price bubble burst, most of Sweden's banking sector were technically insolvent, and if not for a rescue package undertaken by the government, equivalent to 4% of Swedish GDP (Lindbeck, 1997:1305).

Despite this public subsidy, net lending by the banking sector contracted sharply in 1993/94, by 20% compared with the previous year, as institutions sought to strengthen their balance sheets by increasing margins and consolidating existing business before taking on new accounts. Thus, at exactly the point where corporations were struggling because of the recession, and the monetary policy stance of the government remained exceptionally tight, the banks further restricted credit, with the obvious negative macroeconomic consequences.

The position of household debt significantly worsened the already poor economic situation. In 1989, household debt stood at 135% of total disposable earnings and savings declined to –4% of household disposable income. Therefore the reduction of this amount to 100% by 1992, together with uncertainty about employment and a reduction in the value of social security benefits, caused household savings to rise dramatically to 8% of disposable income in 1992, and 10% by 1994. This represented a fall in aggregate demand equivalent to 7% of GDP (Lindbeck et al, 1993a:222; Glyn, 1998:9).

The macroeconomic policy legacy from the outgoing SAP government had not been particularly helpful. With the benefit of hindsight, the austerity package that had been delayed from implementation in 1990 due to parliamentary opposition, was finally implemented in 1991, just as the economy was entering recession. Moreover, the 1990 tax reform, a measure supported by the bourgeois parties, had proved to be more inflationary than had been predicted. Thus, a full 6.7% of the 13.3% headline rate of inflation in February 1991 was a direct result of the reallocation of the tax burden from direct to consumption taxation (EIU, 1991:11). Nevertheless, far from ameliorating the deteriorating economic position, the 'New Start' approach made it worse.

Instead of pursuing an expansionary fiscal policy in order to counteract any decline in aggregate demand caused by contraction in the private sector of the economy, the bourgeois government resolved to maintain a tight fiscal stance irrespective of the economic circumstances. Indeed, their policy documents explained that this was to be a deliberate shift from all earlier economic slowdowns, when counter-cyclical Keynesian strategy would have necessitated expansionary fiscal and/or monetary policy policy (Finansdepartmentet, 1991:19). Instead, the three years of the 'New Start' programme involved cuts in public expenditure in excess of SEK 140 billion, with the remainder of a SEK 160 billion total strengthening of public finances arising from targeted tax increases, cumulatively corresponding to more than 10% of GDP (Regeringens Propositionen, 1993:6,36; EIU, 1993:10; 1994:9). Thus, the bourgeois government made a deliberate attempt to adhere to a non-accommodative policy, in which the fixed exchange rate anchored the economy (Calmfors, 1993:53).

This policy, of reducing public expenditure during an economic slowdown, merely exacerbated the situation. The strategy was economically illiterate, having learnt nothing from the experience of the 1930s, when orthodox economic demanded wage cuts and balanced budgets to restore economic growth, but in fact caused a recession to deepen into a world depression, only terminated by the rearmament caused by immediacy of world war. Furthermore, the fiscally orthodox stance did not even meet its own narrow objectives, due to the fact that it contributed towards a higher unemployment rate and lower output, in turn leading to the generation of lower taxation and increase in social security benefit payments.[1] Consequently, central government debt rose from 48% of GDP at the end of 1991 to 80% two years later, whilst the high interest rates maintained by the government further worsened the public finances, as interest payments on this debt amounted to SEK75billion in 1992/3; a level which was equivalent to almost half the budget

---

[1] The significance of Sweden's automatic stabilisers was such that, despite the intentions of the bourgeois government to operate a pro-cyclical fiscal policy, Vartiainen (1998:35) claims that the actual fiscal impact remained expansionary through the years of depression 1992-4.

deficit (EIU, 1994:10). Thereby, one neutral observer of the 'New Start' programme, argued thus:

> Despite much posturing an a series of ineffective austerity measures, Mr. Bildt's
> government has barely even dented the welfare state, with reforms affecting only the
> margins of the system (EIU, 1994:7).

The restrictive fiscal stance did not operate in isolation, however, as it was complimented by a historically tight monetary policy. Interest rates stood at 12.5% at the end of 1992, whilst the depressed economy had chocked inflation off to less than 2%. Thus, at the height of the recession, and with all the problems already discussed exacerbating the situation, monetary policy was extraordinarily tight. Indeed, whilst it was relaxed slightly during the following two years, real interest rates remained between 3.5% to 4% at all times, thereby presenting a severe disincentive to companies that might wish to invest for the future (Riksbank, 1997:5,18).

The tight monetary policy reflects a preference for attracting foreign capital in order to try and keep the exchange rate as high as possible and thereby put pressure on inflation, rather than strengthening the domestic economy and encouraging investment through a 'cheap money' policy. This latter strategy, however, had been ruled out by the theorists of the 'New Start' strategy as impossible in a world of internationalised financial markets. Thus, the combination of tight fiscal and monetary policy led to a general collapse of aggregate demand for domestic output (Lindbeck et al, 1993a:222).

A friendly critic of the 'New Start' strategy, Calmfors (1993:55), suggests that the bourgeois government simply did not recognise the severity of the downturn of the economy. He argued that they overestimated the ability of labour market programmes to be able to absorb the rise in unemployment, which was assumed to be small and short-lived as rapid real wage adjustment would help to stabilise the economy. This approach, which Calmfors describes as "Thatcherism plus a dose of traditional Swedish labour market policy", was incapable of dealing with problems of excess capacity and falling levels of investment (Sachs, 1987). Training workers, to better fulfil the requirements of labour market vacancies, fails to work in the case of demand deficient unemployment when those vacancies are insufficient to absorb almost 15% of the entire labour force. In addition, the government seemingly over-estimated the responsiveness of real wages to unemployment. This fact may have been due to rigidities caused by contract length, ignoring the inflationary consequences of excess profits upon income distribution, or whether due to the ability of insiders to maintain high wages irrespective of competition from unemployed outsiders (Lindbeck and Snower, 1988). Furthermore, Calmfors and Holmlund (2000:129) noted that:

> It is also far-fetched to explain the large rises in unemployment in Sweden and Finland in
> the early 1990s by changes in labour-market institutions. The only plausible explanation is
> the sharp fall in aggregate demand that took place.

1992 Currency Crisis

The deterioration in the Swedish economy, and inability of the non-accommodation strategy to provide a resolution, would be expected to cause a degree of consternation in the foreign exchange markets. However, the combination of a struggling economy, with a tendency for real wages to rise more quickly than its main competitors, but participating in a fixed currency regime, possessed many of the characteristics of interest to speculators. Thus, once similar speculation had already forced Finland to exit the ERM and float the Markka, on 8th September 1992, considerable pressure came to bear upon the Swedish Krona.

The response from the government was to defend the fixed currency link at all costs, in order to demonstrate the credibility of its non-accommodation policy stance. This led to interest rates rising from 16% to 75% and, for a few days, to 502% for new loans, in order to stabilise the market and secure an inflow of footloose capital to ease pressure on the Krona. However, raising interest rates to levels which, if sustained for any period of time, would cripple all economic activity in the country, could never prove to be a sustainable solution. Therefore, due to the fact that the SAP supported the view that the fixed exchange rate should be retained, the government and main opposition party concluded a unique agreement over an emergency economic package designed to revive confidence in the currency.

This package, announced on 20 September 1992, sought to strengthen public finances by SEK40.6bn, over a five year period, representing approximately 3% of GDP, whilst seeking to share the burdens of public expenditure cuts and the postponement of wealth tax cuts (FT 21/9/1992). The degree of political consensus surrounding this compromise did not immediately reduce the immediate pressure on the Krona. However, a second crisis package, announced on 30th September and building upon the budget consolidation detailed in the first, succeeded in stabilising the financial markets. This second crisis package involved a reduction in business costs through shortened holidays and lower payroll taxation, with the cost of these proposals to be funded through an increase in consumption taxation on food, hotel and restaurant services. In total, the second emergency package was estimated to cost households SEK 6000 each, producing a cumulative total of SEK18bn reduction in corporate costs. The LO calculated that this would involve a wage lowering equivalent of 5% (Aftonbladet, 30/9/92).

Ultimately, however, the continuing poor health of the Swedish economy caused persistent speculation, and eventually the Riksbank was forced to concede defeat, although only after depleting its SEK158bn official reserves. Therefore, Sweden left the ERM on 19 September 1992 (Aftonbladet, 20/11/92:6). A desperate final attempt to convince the financial markets of their resolve led to the announcement of a third emergency fiscal retrenchment package. However, this was not supported by the social democrats and, due to its damaging impact upon the economy, would have been unlikely to have done more than delay the inevitable devaluation.

The estimated cost of defending the Krona was put at a minimum of SEK16bn (Dagens Nyheter, 3/11/1996). In the aftermath of the exit from the ERM, the value of the Krona fell by around 20% at the end of 1992, relative to Sweden's main trading partners, thereby boosting the export sector and setting the seeds of the eventual recovery (EIU, 1993:10). In light of the depth of the recession, inflationary pressures were unlikely to be a significant threat to economic fortunes, despite an inevitable increase in import prices.

Why, then, was there such strength of cross-party commitment to maintain fixed exchange rates? Finansdepartmentet (2000:28) suggests that a learning process influences the development of stabilisation policy, with the consequences of the previous 'experiment' uppermost in the minds of those developing the next approach. Thus, policy advisers have the tendency of always 'fighting the previous war' in terms of their reactions to the track record of particular policy options. For example, the common, if not uniform, perception was that the devaluations implemented in the 1970s and 1982 were not as effective in practice as was anticipated, and therefore these theorists were determined to maintain the subsequent fixed exchange rate regime, even when this decision proved damaging to the Swedish economy. Similarly, the failure of this particular example of fixed exchange rate target convinced a new generation of policy advisers that floating rates were preferable.

The collapse of the fixed exchange rate anchor to monetary policy necessitated a reorientation in economic strategy. In the short-term, the government switched to the establishment of an inflation target for the Central Bank, in January 1993, thereby borrowing the policy already being pursued by the central banks of New Zealand, Canada, and the UK. The target for inflation was set at 2%, plus or minus 1% (Lindbeck, 1997:1305; Vartiainen, 1998:37). However, the loss of confidence in the overall economic strategy, following the ejection from the fixed exchange rate mechanism, resulted in the government appointing an ad-hoc commission, chaired by the prominent Swedish macroeconomist, Assar Lindbeck, and charged with considering future strategic options. The results of these deliberations became known as the 'Lindbeck Report'.

Lindbeck Report

The opening sentence of the Lindbeck report noted that, "at some rate moments a nation pauses to reflect on its future" (Lindbeck et al, 1993b:5). Running to over two hundred pages, and with a total of one hundred and thirteen recommendations, the report sought not only to suggest a new design of stabilisation policy, but sought to comment upon structural problems in the economy, potential reform of the labour market and welfare state, together with the impact of the procedures of the political system have upon economic policymaking.[2] For example, the report suggested a strengthening of the budget process within the parliament, in addition to prolonging the election period to four years rather than three, as the latter tended to result in short-termist attitudes and a lack of stability in economic strategy.

The report advocated making the Riksbank independent, and charged with delivering a democratically established inflation target, largely in line with what the government implemented following the failure of ERM membership. The

---

[2] For an English-language version of the main analysis contained within the Lindbeck Report, see Lindbeck et al (1994).

committee recommended stabilising public debt at between 40-50% of GDP, which would require budget strengthening of between SEK60–100bn, principally through expenditure reductions. Nevertheless, the report did suggest a role for active government fiscal policy for 'coarse tuning' the economy, in periods where productive capacity deviated sharply from normal utilisation. It rejected, however, the attempt to 'fine tune' the economy as expecting too much from government action. The report argued for the decentralisation of public sector bargaining, in addition to measures to increase the flexibility of the labour market, welfare reforms and additional infrastructure investments, particularly in education and training.

In terms of its general analysis, the Lindbeck report argued that the 'Swedish Model' had not suddenly encountered problems, but rather that it had never worked in the first place. Repeated devaluations were considered to be unsustainable and had merely postponed the type of structural reform that the report was advocating. Centralised bargaining was dismissed as largely mythical, because bargaining had always taken place on multiple levels, and it was this which had meant that it had become so inflationary. Moreover, labour market policies were criticised because of the difficulty in testing whether they worked very effectively, and in any case, it was reliance upon devaluations and the growth in public sector employment that maintained full employment, not manpower policies (Lindbeck et al, 1993a:252).

Over-Expansion of Public Sector

Under the 'Swedish Model', between 1970 and 1996, Lindbeck (1997:1283-4) noted that GDP per person employed increased by only 1.5% in Sweden compared to 1.7% for the OECD and 2% for European OECD. Intriguingly, total public-sector spending rose by a similar rate during the centre right coalitions in 1976-1982 and 1991-1994, relative to GDP, as during the social democratic years of government (Lindbeck, 1997:1280). Nevertheless, in searching for potential explanations, the Lindbeck report raised the following issues:

1. The size of the public sector – the size of the public sector does appear to be associated with a decline in labour productivity, although this is difficult to accurately substantiate (ESO, 1994:124). However, part of this explanation may be a function of the fact that labour productivity is routinely assumed to be zero in the national accounts. Setting the same figures at 2%, as occurs in certain other countries, would make a significant difference to the overall estimates of Swedish productivity, and go a long way towards closing the perceived gap (Lindbeck, 1997:1286).
2. Technological convergence – the commission considered this to be a partial explanation why the gap narrowed between Sweden and other nations. However, it does not explain why Sweden was subsequently overtaken by some of these nations.
3. Reduced capital accumulation – the neoclassical growth model emphasises the importance of savings and productive investment to explain growth rates. Aggregate investment declined in Sweden from in excess of two percentage points above the OECD average in the 1960s, to a deficit of the same magnitude in the 1980s (Lindbeck, 1997:1288).

4. Investment in human capital – from a strong starting point in 1960s, participation rates in Swedish higher education has lagged other nations. Part of this explanation could involve the disincentive effect upon training and education caused by the narrowing of wage differentials (Sohlman, 1996; Hansson and Lundberg, 1995).

5. Welfare dependency – social security has reduced uncertainty, facilitated risk taking, thereby lessening social and political conflict (Lundberg, 1985:34). However, like (i), it may also lead to Eurosclerosis, as taxes reduce work incentives, welfare payments erode the incentives for private saving, whilst the higher the replacement ratio linked to social security benefits, the weaker market incentives and the more likely to result in dependency upon such benefits (Barro, 1990; King and Rebelo, 1990).

One weakness with this entire approach relates to its dependency upon the selection of time period under investigation. Thus, if concentrating upon the period 1973-85, then Sweden's growth averages 0.25% *above* the OECD average rate, whereas extending the time period until 1990 provides no evidence for the assertion of substantial Swedish underperformance (Dowrick and Nguyen, 1989; Dowrick, 1996). Thus, it is only if studies include data from the atypically severe Swedish recession between 1990 and 1993, that the Swedo-sclerosis case can be made. Indeed, the majority of any perceived "growth lag" occurred during two recession periods, 1976-1978 and 1990-1993 (Lindbeck, 1997:1285).

Uncritical adoption of public expenditure figures provides a misleading comparison between nations. For example, pensions provision in the USA is entirely a private phenomenon, partly funded by current company expenditure and partly by accumulated pension funds. In Sweden, pensions are almost entirely a state-managed phenomenon. Therefore, approximately 10% of the apparent difference between the two countries relates solely to a nominal state administration of Swedish pension funds. Furthermore, if transfer benefits were measured net of income tax paid by the beneficiaries, total public-sector spending as a share of GDP in Sweden would decline by a further 10%, bringing it into line with Belgium, Denmark and the Netherlands (Lindbeck, 1997:1279). Consequently, this element of the Eurosclerosis hypothesis remains unproven.

Why Low Unemployment?

Lindbeck (1997:1308) noted that the research literature identified five possible explanations for Sweden's low unemployment rates during the 'Keynesian' period. These included:

1. *Centralised wage bargaining* – deriving from the sharing of responsibility for an efficiently functioning labour market, on behalf of collective employees and employer organisations, maintained wage moderation in order to secure a narrowing of wage variance and sustaining the conditions for full employment. However, Lindbeck (1997:1390) denies its effectiveness, arguing that "the famous real wage restraint" associated with centralised wage bargaining has

generally only occurred "at very specific occasions of acute crisis immediately after devaluation's of the Swedish krona".

2. *Strict "work requirements" in the unemployment benefit system* – despite the presence of high benefit replacement ratios, the provision of a high quality employment agency became associated with the identification of relevant employment opportunities, and therefore enhancing the job search process. This operated via computerised access to all jobs advertised in Sweden, provision of employment advisors with relatively small caseloads, together with the requirement to undertake training, temporary work or public works programmes, thereby maintaining skills and updating work experience. Academic studies tend to support the argument that the combination of fixed benefit duration and strict work requirements facilitate low unemployment (Layard et al, 1991). However, the rigour of such system's tend to be far harder to enforce during periods of high unemployment, thereby reinforcing the necessity of maintaining full employment, rather than allowing mass unemployment to arise, and then rely on the same techniques to be as effective in its elimination.

3. *Active labour market policy improved the functioning of the labour market* – closely associated with (2), labour market policy (LMP) can certainly contribute towards direct job creation through public works, skills training and employment subsidies. Despite estimates of crowding-out effects of anywhere between half and 80% of unemployed persons who participate in various manpower schemes when the jobs are created in the public sector, there appears no significant problem with jobs created in the private sector (Forslund, 1996; Forslund and Krueger, 1997). Job placement schemes, mobility grants and skills training prove to be the most efficient forms of LMP, and provide a useful function in increasing the efficiency of the labour market. However, the experience of the 1990-93 recession re-emphasised the argument made by the founders of the Rehn-Meidner model, namely that manpower policies should be used to support, not supplant, macroeconomic policy. To be effective, LMP's require a large number of vacancies in order to assist individuals to "swim faster" from unemployment islands to vacancies. Hence, it is not surprising that the economic returns of LMP's fell dramatically under such inhospitable circumstances (Björklund, 1993; Calmfors, 1993).

4. *Periodic devaluations reduced real wages* – devaluation of the Krona boosted employment in the tradables sector of the Swedish economy on a number of occasions. Lindbeck reasoned that this was due to the Keynes' claim that trade unions are more likely to accept cuts in real wages through inflation, since this need not have any impact upon relative wages, rather than nominal wage reductions, based upon the market strength of different groups. Furthermore, Lindbeck (1997:1312) notes that Swedish industrial production is "exceptionally sensitive" to the real exchange rate, due to the dominant position of transnational corporations, which could reallocate production abroad if costs were not contained, but also due to Sweden's production structure, with a significant proportion of the export sector trading in cost-sensitive bulk products.

5. *Public sector acted as employer of last resort* – a rapid increase in permanent public sector employment provided an outlet for enhancing female participation in the labour market, whilst simultaneously maintaining aggregate demand and

thereby employment in the economy as a whole. Indeed, the growth of the Swedish industrial sector peaked in 1965, and thereafter declined by a quarter of a million jobs, whilst public sector employment expanded by about 600,000 workers during the 1970s and 1980s (Rojas, 1998:78,86). With public sector employment approaching 42% of total employment in 1993, its contribution to productivity and approach to wage moderation became increasingly important to the Swedish economy.

Regulation and Rigidity

One further element of the Eurosclerosis hypothesis relates to the over-regulation of European economies, particularly relating to protection granted to workers through government regulation of the labour market. Swedish regulation had increased considerably during the 1970s industrial democracy legislative initiative promoted by the Palme government, and therefore critics claimed that this introduced increased rigidity into the allocation of scarce resources through the ability of Swedish workers to defend their jobs (Mahon, 1994:122). Nevertheless, studies have failed to discover clear evidence that employment protection legislation is an important factor explaining unemployment in the long-run (Nickell and Layard, 1999; OECD, 1999). One explanation involves the impact on inflows into, and outflows from, unemployment largely cancelling each other out, so that there is only a negligible net effect on unemployment (Calmfors and Holmlund, 2000:127). Another relates to the success of labour market policies in terms of facilitating the search process, promoting geographical mobility and skills training better matching the unemployed to job vacancies (Layard et al, 1991:64).

The identification of excessive labour market regulation additionally provides a poor fit to the facts. For example, the open unemployment rate was maintained around an average of 2.4% of the labour force, between 1960 to 1990, and even adding participants on labour market programmes still failed to produce a rate exceeding between 4–5%. Thus, labour market rigidity did not appear to be a particular problem until the onset of a deep, demand-deficient recession, suggesting causes other than empowered employees as contributing to Sweden's problems under its 1991-94 bourgeois government (Gylfason, 1997:36-8).

Welfare Reform

The substantial increase in unemployment during the early 1990s exposed what Esping-Andersen (1990) called the Achilles' heel of the Scandinavian social democratic model, namely regarding the affordability of universal benefits during a period when perhaps 15% of the population are without jobs. However, there are two solutions to this situation. Firstly, follow the Danish example and adjust to the persistence of high levels of unemployment, whilst maintaining the bulk of the welfare state through high contribution rates (Sheldon and Thornthwaite, 1999). Alternatively, Sweden could eliminate the cause of the problem, which is the unemployment, and not the generosity of the welfare system as neo-liberals advise.

Redistribution

The collapse of centralised wage bargaining, the reduction in progressive taxation through the 1990 reform, and the welfare cuts prompted by the budget deficits incurred by the 1991-94 bourgeois government, had consequences for the degree of equality experienced in Swedish society. The Gini coefficient, the internationally recognised measure of equality, had been reduced from 0.28 in the late 1960s to 0.2 in the early 1980s, thereby representing a significant tightening of progressive redistributive measures during this period. However, since the end of the 1980s, this position has been reversed, with the Gini measurement returning to 0.3 by 1994 (Gylfason, 1997:51). Nevertheless, Gottschalk and Smeeding (2000) note that Sweden remains a relatively egalitarian nation, having only the second lowest Gini coefficient amongst twenty-one developed countries, after-taxes and transfers are accounted for, with only Finland producing better figures.

Lindbeck (1997:1295) argued that reductions in wage variance, due to an intensification in the solidarity wage policy, together with a further narrowing of lifetime income due to the progressive tax system, had contributed towards a significant decline in the return on human capital investment. This, in turn, had contributed to a shortfall of highly skilled labour, together with relatively few individuals partaking of postgraduate and postdoctoral programmes. Squeezed differentials had reduced incentives for training and higher education, which Lindbeck postulated was likely to have negative consequences for labour productivity and economic growth.

Lindquist (2000) suggested that the potential gain in terms of economic welfare from removing wage compression, caused by the solidarity wages policy, may be around 4% of GDP. The result would be the demand for low-skill workers rising, as their relative wages fall, and thereby increasing employment. In contrast, Hibbs and Locking (2000) maintain that wage compression between workplaces and industries, can facilitate a greater movement of labour to more productive uses.

Promote Competition

One final recommendation emerging from the Lindbeck report concerned the weak competitive pressure in parts of the Swedish economy, particularly, in the non-tradables sector – constituting about three quarters of the national economy. The combination of a dominant position held by a small number of large firms, together with a the cartellisation of large sectors of the national economy, contributed to high prices and excess profits in many markets, thereby contributing to exploitation of consumers and inflationary tendencies in the Swedish economy (Folster and Peltzman, 1997). Despite Sweden's incorporation into the EU's SIM in 1995, its price level remains approximately one-fifth above the EU average. Although part of this price premium is due to the increased distributional costs associated with a large, lightly populated country on the geographical periphery of Europe, the OECD has estimated that half remains due to an insufficiency in competition in certain sectors of the economy.

Why Change Direction?

The Lindbeck report identified the problems evident in the Swedish economy as arising from a combination of exogenous changes in the economic environment, together with endogenous dynamics of the 'Swedish Model'. The former includes demographic changes, technological development and the internationalisation of the economic system, whilst the latter includes disincentive effects and problems of moral hazard arising from taxation and transfer payments, lack of competition in product markets, ageing institutions and ossified decision-making mechanisms, together with inflexible relative wages (Lindbeck et al, 1993a:220). However, rather than apportion a degree of blame for the policy mistakes made by the bourgeois government, Lindbeck (1997:1311) argued that the increase in unemployment had been postponed by a combination of the public sector as employer of last resort and repeated devaluations, magnified by the impact of a number of large external shocks. The fact that devaluation had been rejected as a viable policy option, and governments had prioritised low inflation over full employment, meant that these options were no longer available and therefore the rise in unemployment would have been inevitable.

In terms of the specific policies pursued by the 'Swedish Model', Lindbeck (1997:1306-7) claimed that:

1. Labour market policies have been successful in reducing unemployment counter-cyclically, but they might lead to inflation due to their role as accommodating the actions of individual actors, which, once anticipated, might enable trade unions and employers to agree inflationary wage increases in the expectation that the negative impact upon employment and profitability will be neutralised by government action. Together with other major policy reforms, this weakened the overall performance of the Swedish economy.
2. The deregulation of capital markets led to a dramatic oscillation in credit flows, which in turn resulted in large fluctuations in asset prices and thereby caused significant liquidity problems for financial institutions. The conclusion drawn is that deregulation should occur with greater care, rather than an appreciation of the role of financial regulation.
3. The volatility in the financial saving rate of households proved to be a destabilising factor for the Swedish economy.
4. Automatic fiscal stabilisers tend to result in budget deficits which "explode" during deep recessionary periods, particularly in nations with well developed welfare states. The traditional view that this helps to prevent even deeper recessions is challenged by a "revisionist" theory, which claims that growing debt will create heightened uncertainty about the ability of the government to meet its financial commitments, amongst private agents. This may raise the precautionary savings rates of households, thereby depressing the economy. Moreover, high existing levels of debt may cause governments to hesitate, even amidst deep recessions, to take expansionary fiscal policy measures.
5. Fixed exchange rates did not prove to be a particularly efficient mean controlling inflation in Sweden, primarily since macroeconomic policy preferred to pursue

full employment rather than maintain a fixed parity, and therefore the economy relied upon devaluation to restore international competitiveness.

Lindbeck's analysis of the Swedish economy, then, raised a lot of topics to consider, both in terms of the orientation of economic strategy, questioning the optimality of using specific policy instruments, and examining the desirability of reform of Sweden's institutional structure. In general, despite Lindbeck's Keynesian heritage, the report accepted uncritically many of the current neo-liberal orthodoxies. Thus, rather than the bourgeois economic experiment proving to be an unwise, and poorly implemented deviation from a relatively successful 'Swedish Model', Lindbeck's view was that Sweden was reverting to becoming a more "normal" West European country again, thereby rejecting the "radical experimentation" of the 1960s and 1970s (Lindbeck, 1997:1314). Membership in the EU was considered likely to accentuate this process. Consequently, the 'Swedish Model' will appear in future textbooks to have been nothing more than a brief historical episode – taking about three decades, from the mid-1960s to the early 1990s.

Chapter 11

'New' Swedish Social Democracy

Introduction

In view of the disastrous performance at the 1991 General Election, the fact that the SAP were returned to office a bare three years later represented a significant triumph for the party and its supporters. Three years of recession under a bourgeois government, a large part of whose economic strategy was undermined by the forced ejection from the ERM in 1992, together with the return of mass unemployment for the first time since the 1930s, meant that the SAP were always going to be favourite to win the election. Moreover, the SAP based their appeal to voters upon traditional social democratic principles of reducing unemployment, a track record in economic management and ability to protect the welfare state (Miles, 2000:232). That the fact that the party received 45.3% of the popular vote reflected a degree of unease with the drift of SAP policy, particularly towards the measures necessary to stabilise public finances. Nevertheless, the fact that the left-green bloc received the support of 56.5% of the electorate, meant that the 1994 election delivered a decisive victory for progressive policies (Petersson, 1994).

The fact that the SAP had not secured a working majority in parliament meant a minority government dependant upon the support of one or more other political parties. Tactically, the SAP rejected an alliance with the Left Party, despite its strong electoral showing, in favour of a working relationship with the Centre Party. It had been a member of the previous bourgeois coalition government but, unlike the Liberal and Moderate (conservative) parties, had not been a signatory to the 'New Start' programme. This partnership had the advantage of association with the previous crisis package which had proved so successful in pulling Sweden out of the 1930s recession. It additionally reinforced the centrist image of the SAP, and provided greater potential for cross-bloc compromise over controversial issues, including the implementation of the 1980 referendum decision to phase out nuclear power by the end of the century. The Centre Party traditionally held a pro-welfare, anti-nuclear viewpoint, and therefore proved a useful ally in terms of reducing the public sector budget deficit without major reductions in welfare expenditure (Aylott, 1999:177).

First Term Priorities (1992-1998)

Despite the reliance upon traditional issues in the campaign, however, the economic strategy advocated by the SAP in 1992 did not involve a wholesale return to the Rehn-Meidner model. Instead, it sought a more stable synthesis of traditional social democratic policies combined with a large dose of neo-liberal economics. Accordingly, the economic strategy focussed upon the following main issues:

- Stable prices – the top priority for government policy;
- Stabilisation of public finances in three years;
- Halving open unemployment in four years.

The priorities of the new government were naturally partly the consequence of the legacy of the previous government. Three years of falling GDP, the return of mass unemployment and government budget deficits seemingly out of control, provided a poor platform for ambitious policy objectives. However, it is still notable that the immediate priorities for the new administration concerned measures consistent with neo-liberal financial orthodoxy, such as stable prices and a desire to balance the budget. The Keynesian goal of full employment, in contrast, was scarcely mentioned, and then only as a long-term desire, to be pursued once all other elements of the economic strategy were secured. Thus, the new SAP macroeconomic framework borrowed a significant degree of its theoretical foundations from the 1990-91 SAP administration, together with adopting a significant proportion of the analysis adopted by the outgoing bourgeois government. Nevertheless, the new social democratic economic programme was not merely reactive, but sought to create optimal conditions for economic growth in addition to solving transitional problems.

Stable Prices

The rejection of the full employment goal in favour of price stability represented a substantial reorientation in economic approach. It involved shifting from a broadly Keynesian, interventionist strategy, based upon the management of aggregate demand, towards a monetarist or neo-classical orthodoxy that rejected almost all forms of active government in favour of the unfettered interaction of market forces. The SAP's justification for this shift in economic prioritisation was expressed, thus:

> Stable prices are a fundamental prerequisite for a successful economic policy. A high rate of inflation, particularly when difficult to foresee, has negative distributional effects. In addition, a high rate of inflation makes for poorer prospects of strong sustained growth, and so undermines the chances of a stable high rate of employment (Regeringens Propositionen, 2002:11).

The distributional impact of unanticipated inflation rates can present a problem to any economic strategy, particularly one that relies upon trade union moderation of wage claims. The longer the wage contract period, the greater the time lag before any unanticipated change in inflation upon real wages can be rectified. Thus, contracts, incorporating wage agreements lasting two or three years, introduce additional stickiness into labour markets characterised by a 'peace obligation', where it is unlawful to re-open negotiations during a contract period. Unofficially, unions could press for local compensation, leading to wage drift outside of the official negotiations, and which, if rising to significant proportions of the overall wage increase, could undermine the formal wage formation system. Alternatively, unions could demand higher wage rises through the central or sectoral bargaining forum, in order to provide a buffer to any unanticipated increase in inflation. However, this undermines the moderating effect of overall negotiations, thereby reducing the international competitiveness of Swedish industry, whilst it may, additionally, contribute towards cost-push inflation, thereby making the possibility of rising prices a self-fulfilling prophesy.

Although inflation can prove problematic to the efficient functioning of co-ordinated wage bargaining systems, the fact remains that most of these problems can be reduced by a process of informed macroeconomic forecasting, together with shorter (annual) contract periods that allow regular up-rating of any sudden change in prices. This would prevent the locking-in of high wage rises as occurred in the early 1970s, when a period of high profits led to wage agreements producing high wage rises simultaneously with the onset of economic recession and the collapse of Swedish market share. Equally, it would avoid unexpectedly high inflation eroding real wages for workers covered by such agreements, whilst professional groups, managers, self-employed and owners of capital could avoid such restrictions and thereby redistribute income in their favour.

The theoretical justification for adopting price stability as the prime policy objective, however, results from the acceptance of the existence of a 'natural' equilibrium rate of unemployment, determined in the labour market. This theorem, associated with the monetarist and 'new' Keynesian schools, discussed in Chapter One, rejected the 'old' Keynesian proposition that government policy could have a lasting impact upon the real economy. Rather than economic policy often having to choose a trade-off between various objectives, the natural rate of unemployment theorem argues that government attempts to reduce unemployment below that rate determined in the labour market will only succeed in the short-run due to a combination of inflationary shock and the time lag involved in the adaptive expectations of economic agents, but importantly cannot succeed in the long-run.

All that happens is that active government macroeconomic policy results in ever-higher inflation rates, with little or no impact upon the real economy. Consequently, the monetarist solution to the high inflation rates, prevalent in the late 1970s involved a sudden deflation of the economy, because any subsequent increase in unemployment would only be temporary, before it returned to the natural rate, and the policy would therefore be almost costless. Of course, the experience of the past two decades has gone a long way to disprove this theoretical approach, as the unemployment resulting from pro-cyclical deflation grew to levels not seen since the 1930s depression, and proved difficult to eliminate once it had risen.

The concept of 'hysteresis' has sought to explain the observed tendency for the equilibrium rate of unemployment to increase if the *actual* rate of unemployment in the *previous* period *exceeds* the *natural* rate pertaining in the former period. First developed by Phelps in 1972, hysteresis proposes that the equilibrium rate of unemployment is *path-dependent*, in that it depends upon the actual history or path of unemployment. In other words, if unemployment rises above the supposed 'natural' rate for any given period of time, this equilibrium rate appears to increase. Similarly, if it is reduced below the natural rate, this rate seems to decline.

Explanations include the impact of capacity scrapping upon the ability of an economy to quickly return to previous rates of unemployment once deflation has caused the collapse of businesses. Alternatively, an increase in demand may give rise to additional investment expenditure, thereby creating additional capacity and thereby enabling the employment of a greater number of people than before the government-sponsored reflation was enacted. Furthermore, duration theories suggest that the depreciation of human capital, together with potential psychological effects upon the unemployed, may cause the long-term jobless to become increasingly unemployable. Indeed, they might, in effect, be viewed as having withdrawn from the labour market. Nevertheless, irrespective of the precise causality, the fact remains that the monetarist or 'new' Keynesian assumption of an equilibrium unemployment rate that is unresponsive to government policy appears to be deeply flawed and contrary to the available evidence.

Monetary Policy – Central Bank Independence

When Sweden abandoned its fixed exchange rate strategy, in late 1992, this was replaced by a nominal anchor, namely direct inflation targeting, thereby adopting the existing practice in New Zealand and the UK. The precise inflation target has been set at 2% (+/- 1%), and is based upon a definition of underlying (not headline) inflation, thereby excluding the direct effects of government economic policy – i.e. interest rates, taxes and subsidies. In theory, the Swedish Central Bank (Riksbank) should react symmetrically irrespective of whether inflation falls below this inflation target, as this may over-deflate the Swedish economy, as if the target is exceeded.

Directly targeting the inflation rate is an improvement over the adoption of a fixed exchange rate regime, in the anticipation that it will slow price inflation through the indirect means of international competition and potential increases in unemployment. However, it appears that this target band was selected more because it met the convergence criteria contained in the Maastricht Treaty on European Union (EU), and in particular relating to the Economic and Monetary Union (EMU) initiative in closer European regional monetary integration, rather than the inflation target being the result of detailed analysis of the rate that would best facilitate full employment. It is therefore quite conceivable that, at some future point, the inflation target will prove an impediment to the elimination of unemployment, if to do so would lead to an inflation rate that would exceed the target range. Of course, this is resolved for the 'new' social democratic economic programme by prioritising price stability ahead of full employment. Nevertheless, the absence of flexibility in macroeconomic targets remains a potential future problem.

The second innovation in monetary policy relates to the Riksbank having been granted its independence from government and parliamentary influence, via changes to the Sveriges Riksbank Act (1988:1385) on 1 January 1999, and thereby being granted autonomous responsibility for monetary policy, subject to the established inflation target (Statskontoret, 1999:23). The changes meant that the Riksbank was no longer required to "consult" with the relevant cabinet minister prior to making any major monetary policy decision, but rather "inform" the government of its decision. Decisions on monetary policy were delegated to an autonomous six-member executive board rather than the former governing board which was dominated by appointees from the main political parties according to their proportionate parliamentary representation. Bank officials were instructed that they "shall not seek or take instructions" in pursuit of their duties, although the bank remained periodically accountable to the Swedish parliament for its actions. The Riksbank does not, however, retain responsibility for the exchange rate; this has reverted to the Finance Ministry, with the Riksbank as advisor and agent charged with the implementation of policy. This is primarily due to the argument that any decision that needs to be taken about EMU, or the return to any future form of fixed exchange rate, is a political and not technical matter.

The granting of the Riksbank its autonomy from the remainder of the government's macroeconomic stance helps to enshrine the price stability goal as the prime institutional objective (Alesina and Summers, 1993). Policy co-ordination become more difficult through the splitting of economic instruments and responsibilities between different agents of government. Moreover, there is at least the suspicion that central bankers, by their very nature, may be more conservative than the average citizen or politician, and thereby respond asymmetrically; more concerned with developing an anti-inflation credibility than the optimal balance between the various goals of a more rounded economic strategy, such as employment, output, growth, balance of payments and the distribution of income (Rogoff, 1985). Furthermore, the whole concept is based upon scant and contradictory evidence (Cukierman, 1992; Posen, 1995; Jordan, 1999).

Notermans (1992:3) claims that:

> even though it is certainly correct that an effective full employment strategy is strongly impeded by an independent central bank, this lesson seems to have been lost even on countries with a strong preference for full employment.

Moreover, he views the collapse of full employment as a central goal of macroeconomic policy arising from the "institutional inability" of Keynesian-social democracy to contain inflationary pressures (Notermans, 1992:3). Whether due to misconceptions about the dominance of globalisation, or a desire to participate in a fixed exchange rate regimes (including European single currency), governments have become convinced that international competitiveness can only be maintained in the long-run by ensuring that inflation rates stay around the level for a country's main competitors. This explicitly rules out devaluation as an alternative, for reasons of strategy or the misguided belief that such policies no longer work. In any case, monetary policy has gradually come to be fully occupied with stabilising the currency and reducing inflation rather than stimulating output and employment through the provision of 'cheap money' (Horngren and Westman, 1991).

Fiscal Policy – Consolidation of Public Finances

The second major elements of the 'new' SAP macroeconomic programme involved a dramatic consolidation of public finances. The reason for this degree of prioritisation stemmed from the fact that the severity of economic downturn, leading to mass unemployment and the consequent rise in social security transfers (net of lower tax revenues), resulted in a budget deficit equivalent to 11.8% of GDP in 1993, and threatening to spiral out of control. The outgoing bourgeois government had, once again, bequeathed the incoming SAP administration with severe budgetary problems (Figure 11-1). However, whereas the problem in 1982 resulted from industrial subsidies paid to prevent an increase in unemployment, the deficit in 1993 arose due to the combination of a weakness in international demand, combined with pro-cyclical deflationary fiscal and monetary policies intended to reduce inflation, but having done so at the cost of the return of mass unemployment not seen since the 1930s.

Figure 11-1: Net lending, public sector, % GDP, 1980-2002

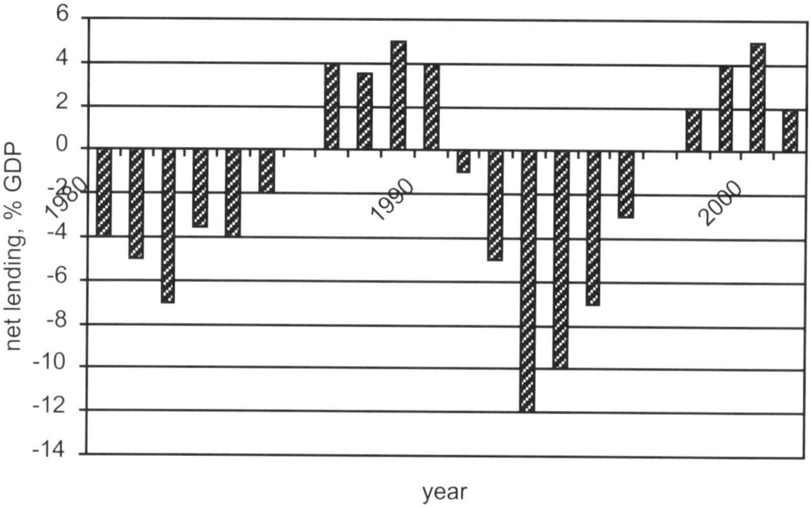

There are a number of reasons why a degree of fiscal consolidation was undoubtedly necessitated by the performance of the Swedish economy. The overhang of successive budget deficits increased total Swedish public sector debt, and therefore interest charges had risen as a proportion of budgetary expenditure. From a neo-liberal perspective, excessive borrowing by the public sector crowded out more productive private sector investment, whilst signalling to the financial markets that taxes might have to rise in the future, thereby reducing the benefits of holding Swedish assets and potentially undermining price stability through exchange rate depreciation.

According to a post-Keynesian viewpoint, however, increased international indebtedness was a negative phenomenon because it had increased the sensitivity of the Swedish economy to the dictates of international financial money markets. Moreover, a large initial budget deficit made it more difficult to implement Keynesian counter-cyclical, deficit financed demand management. Furthermore, the improvement in public finances would considerably improve the confidence in the future of the welfare state amongst the citizenry; perpetual budget deficits give credence to those commentators who claim that welfare programmes are no longer affordable and should be dramatically reduced in scope and generosity.

There is one additional factor, however, that lies behind the desire of the SAP administration to improve public finances within a short period of time, and that relates to the desire to meet the convergence criteria established in the Maastricht Treaty on European Union. According to these rules, established as a means to ensure minimum convergence of economies prior to participating in EMU, applicant countries were supposed to meet the reference targets of budget deficits not exceeding 3% of GDP and public debt remaining below 60% of GDP (EU Commission, 1992).

The latter Stability and Growth Pact (SGP) maintains the budgetary target indefinitely within the Euro-zone, as a condition of membership. Failure to comply, in all but periods of exceptionally deep recessions, defined as where national income declines by at least 0.75% in a given year, would invite censure from the EU Commission, together with fines of 0.5% of GDP, that is if sanctioned by the Council of Ministers. Thus, at least part of the case for fiscal retrenchment involved meeting the minimum requirements for EMU membership.

The fiscal consolidation priority for the SAP government was however not costless. Even if true that structural budgetary reforms are necessary to reduce cyclical deficits, this process could have been pursued according to a more flexible timetable, with reductions occurring only when economies are growing steadily. Cutting public expenditure and/or raising taxes in the middle of a recession would be likely to worsen the economic slowdown, and prove counter-productive as rising unemployment reduces tax revenues and impose additional burdens upon welfare transfer payments. Fortunately for the new SAP administration, the resumption in US economic growth provided an opportune moment for the consolidation of Swedish finances. Thus, the SAP administration benefited from an upsurge in international demand, whereas the previous bourgeois government had been at least partly undermined by a comparable downturn.

The actual fiscal consolidation programme was aggressive in nature, intending to strengthen the government's budgetary position by 7.5% of GDP over a three-year period. The schedule was intended to be front loaded, with 3.5% consolidation to occur in 1995, with a further 2% to come into force in each of 1996 and 1997. Two-thirds of the budget reinforcement involved reductions in public expenditure, particularly in the areas of social transfers and current consumption; the balance being in the form of tax rises. The target was to secure an elimination of the budget deficit by the end of the first term of SAP government, in 1998. These cuts in government spending included a politically controversial reduction in unemployment benefit, in 1995, from 80% to 75% of prior earnings. Moreover, Aylott (1999:167) claims that this programme did little to counter the association between the new economic strategy with economic recession and austerity measures, together with the abandonment of full employment with the desire to participate fully in European integration.

In addition, the fiscal consolidation package benefited from a one-off technical transfer of public assets from the state pension funds through the state budget and being used to pay off a significant proportion of national debt. Altogether this involved a transfer of between 7% and 19% of GDP, and whilst it did not affect the public sector's net asset position, it did improve the EU's calculations of Sweden's national debt, since this figure takes little account of assets held, but rather is only concerned with debt incurred. This is a remarkably short-sighted view, as it would count a mortgage as householder debt but ignore the reality of a house as an asset! Thus, it would appear that this manoeuver was predominantly influenced by the desire to meet the Maastricht convergence criteria, and were little to do with the actual pension fund reform.

Table 11-1: Swedish Public Finances as % of GDP, 1994-2003

	1993	1994	1995	1996	1997	1998	1999	2000	2001	2002*
Expenditure Ratio	70.1	67.3	64.3	62.3	60.5	58.0	57.5	54.7	54.4	54.5
Revenue Ratio	58.3	56.4	56.7	59.3	58.9	60.1	58.8	58.4	59.2	56.3
Budget Balance	-11.8	-10.8	-7.7	-3.1	-1.6	2.1	1.3	3.7	4.8	1.8
Surplus Target					-3.0	0.0	0.5	2.0	2.5	2.0
Net Debt	10.7	21.0	26.1	26.6	24.0	20.6	10.3	2.1	-0.2	-2.1
Gross Debt	73.7	76.2	76.2	76.0	74.5	71.8	64.9	55.3	55.9	53.0

Source: Regeringens Propositionen, 2002:10. * forecast.

The turn-around in public finances was "most remarkable", producing a surplus in 1998 as predicted, with this growing to a budget surplus of 4.8% in 2001, compared to a *deficit* of 11.8% only eight years previously (Gylfason, 1997:46) (see Table 11-1). This was a budgetary position bettered only by Finland with a surplus equivalent to a further 0.1% of GDP (Table 11-2).

The full impact of the consolidation programme is highlighted in Table 11-1, where cuts in spending programmes and a decline in unemployment payments arising from a recovering economy, both contributed towards reducing the public expenditure ratio from its peak of 70.1% of Swedish GDP in 1993 to 54.4% of GDP in 2001. Simultaneously, the combination of tax rises and increasing tax revenues, arising from recovering corporate profits and growing incomes, increased the revenue ratio to 60.1% of GDP, before a slight easing of the tight fiscal stance lowered this figure marginally in more recent years (Regerings Propositionen, 2002:10). Thus, public expenditure had been reduced by a remarkable 15.6% of GDP in under a decade, whereas tax revenues remained more or less constant as a proportion of national income.

Table 11-2: Public sector financial savings in selected nations, 2001-2003

% of GDP	2001
Sweden	4.8
EU average	-0.6
Euro zone average	-1.3
Germany	-2.7
France	-1.4
Italy	-1.4
Finland	4.9
UK	1.1
Denmark	2.5
USA	0.6
Japan	-6.4

Sources: OECD, 2001; Eurostat.

By the end of 1998, Sweden's public expenditure ratio stood just 4% higher than Denmark and France, whilst the OECD average stood at 44% (Statskontoret, 1999:43). Indeed, Sweden was not alone in terms of this reduction in the importance of the public sector in its economy, as public expenditure has fallen as a proportion to GDP, since 1993, in all West European nations (Statskontoret, 1999:39). Nevertheless, the *scale* of the fiscal consolidation programme, resulting primarily from reductions in spending programmes, was impressive in its own terms (Figure 11-2).

The depth and scope of spending reductions were striking, coming as they did from a social democratic government whose electoral support depended in no small part upon defence of the universal welfare state. Persson (1996:8) argued that public acceptance of the fiscal consolidation package was based upon principles that burdens were shared equitably, that the budget strengthening was part of a comprehensive package, and that the process was transparent (see Figure 11-3).

Halving Open Unemployment by 2000

During the summer of 1996, more than one-and-a-half years into their term of office, the SAP and Centre Party agreed a broad policy front aimed at reducing the open rate of unemployment by half, by the end of the century. This policy document noted that the recession of the early 1990s had cost upwards of half a million jobs, with approximately 410,000 lost from the private sector and a further 120,000 from the public sector (PMO, 1996:24). The reductions in public expenditure had contributed to a further reduction in central government administrative jobs, with up to 12% of all such jobs disappearing during the 1990s, affecting 26,000 people (Statskontoret, 1999:17).

Figure 11-2: Revenue and expenditure, general government sector, % GDP, 1980-2002

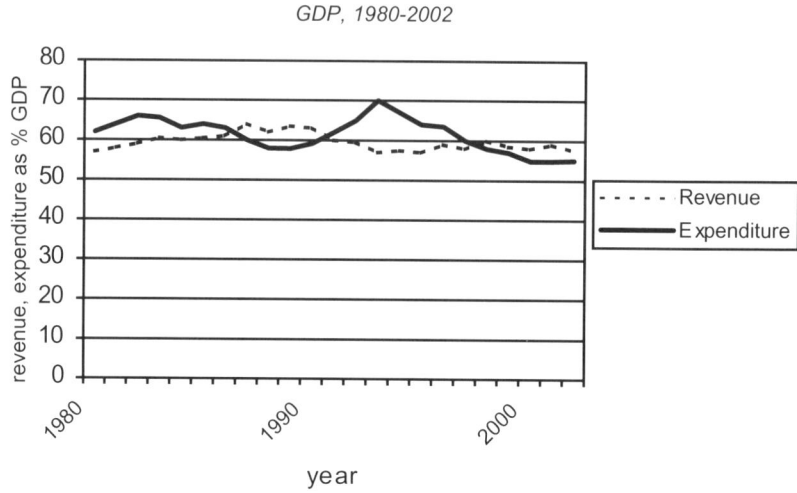

GDP, 1980-2002

Figure 11-3: Share of budget reinforcement contributed by decile

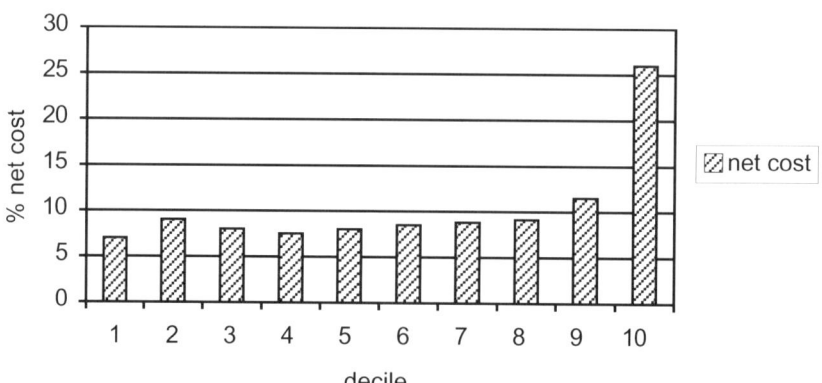

Source: PMO, 1996:48.

When additionally taking into account new entrants to the labour market also seeking jobs, the report notes that considerably more than this number of new jobs would be needed to restore full employment (PMO, 1996:8). Accordingly, the government set itself the rather modest target of reducing the headline rate by 4% over four-and-a-half-years. Estimates made by the government suggested that the current rate of economic growth would deliver a reduction in open unemployment to perhaps 5.7% by the turn of the century, unless additional measures were taken. Hence the initiative.

Specific measures included:

1. Temporary work – awarding 40,000 long-term unemployed temporary work in the municipalities and other areas of the public sector, with wages set at unemployment benefit levels. These were to be increased to 80% of former pay, with the additional cost paid for by limiting the duration of such benefits.
2. Education and traning – expanded adult education by 100,000 places, with priority going to the unemployed with a relatively low-level of basic education, to enable them to increase their core skills and thereby improve their job prospects. Moreover, higher education was expanded by 30,000 places, with at least half of these places for science and technology, and with the regional dispersion of funded places prioritising areas suffering from greater than average unemployment.
3. Grants to firms – small firms benefited from a SEK1bn development and risk capital fund, whilst payroll taxes were reduced by 5% for the first SEK600,000 of the wage bill, again a measure likely to provide disproportionate assistance to small- and medium-sized firms. A further SEK1bn fund was established to facilitate the development of trade and business opportunities in the Baltic Sea region.
4. Targeted tax cuts – stamp duty on houses was reduced to stimulate the real estate market, whilst sales tax on new cars was abolished to stimulate demand in the motor trade.
5. Environmental projects – a SEK1bn was established to fund projects aimed at improving sustainable development.
6. Public sector expansion – the government began a review of the potential for the public sector to renew expanding its workforce, after years of contraction.

In addition, the employment initiative relied upon a flexible use of existing labour market policy resources to ameliorate bottlenecks in the skills base of the labour market and to give assistance to those who experience the greatest difficulty in getting work – i.e. the long-term unemployed, the disabled, and recent immigrants; the latter, particularly with basic language tuition. Furthermore, as part of this process, an *activity guarantee* has been introduced, which requires that, after a maximum two year wait, unemployment people must be offered full time activities until they obtain a job or place in education. The former circulation between open unemployment and participation in labour market measures has been broken by the augmented jobseeker programmes offered under the activity guarantee. Moreover, this initiative is combined with the fact that participation in labour market measures no longer confers renewed eligibility for a further period of unemployment benefits.

The employment initiative additionally noted the importance of amending existing labour legislation in order to provide corporations with greater flexibility, whilst still maintaining protection for workers. A 1995 Labour Law Commission, containing representatives from all major political parties, together with trade union and employer representatives, notably failed to achieve consensus on these matters. Nevertheless, the fact that this topic had been retained as a priority for the SAP administration indicates that the 'new' economic approach has adopted a world-view from neo-liberal economics as concerns the labour market, due to the apparent preference for flexible working conditions. Furthermore, the raft of manpower policies had "increasingly becoming a work and skills principle" as befits a government concerned with maximising the successful participation of all its citizens in the knowledge-intensive global labour market (Regeringens Propositionen, 2000:17).

Wage Formation

The employment initiative began with the words "the government's most important task is to combat unemployment…the struggle for full employment is in the final analysis a struggle for national cohesion" (PMO, 1996:8). For this strategy to succeed, the report noted the necessity for an efficient system of wage formation. However, Notermans (1992:2) argues that the new more restrictive, neo-liberal-influenced macroeconomic policy regime "poses a fundamental threat to the organisational coherence as well as the political role of organised labour". This is partly due to the proposition that the Swedish economy has grown increasingly subject to international competitive pressure, itself resulting in even social democratic governments adopting a more restrictive economic stance in order to prioritise inflation above full employment.

The dramatic increase in unemployment across most of Europe has resulted in a "growing fiscal crisis of the state", allowing neo-liberals to argue for the radical reform and retrenchment of the welfare state. However, this tightening of resources available for public expenditure has led to a reduction in both employment and scale of services, and contributed to a widening of the gap between private and public sector pay. Governments maintain tight fiscal policy in order to squeeze inflationary pressure from the economy, but this merely exacerbates the tension between welfare priorities and the sustainability of provision of these services despite a constant redistribution of resources from public to private sectors. Moreover, restrictive fiscal and monetary policy prevents the accommodation of inflationary wage settlements, thereby making it easier to control wage costs in a decentralised wage formation system.

Deregulation of the financial sector, in particular, has increased competition within the Swedish economy and thereby made employers less willing to award large wage increases due to greater restrictions upon their ability to pass on the resulting cost increases onto consumers via price rises (Iversen, 1996:416). The impact of globalisation and European integration have, additionally, been suggested to have further strengthened competitive market forces, and thereby increasing the price sensitivity of Swedish industry.

The problem with this scenario is that the available evidence suggests that the corporatist and institutionalist analysis is correct, namely that centralised, or co-ordinated, wage bargaining appears to internalise more of the rivalry between unions and produce wage increases that are more consistent with international competitiveness, at least in the absence of compensation through a depreciating exchange rate (Cameron, 1984; Crouch 1985). Nominal wages have been substantially reduced due in a large part to the deep recession experienced by

Sweden in the early 1990s, but real wages have increased significantly, after an initial fall during the years of negative growth rates (see Figure 11-4). Indeed, real wages expanded by an average of 3% per annum between 1994 and 2000, compared to only 0.5% during the 1980s, and with comparative real wage increases in Europe being only 0.7% between 1992 and 1996 (Regeringens Propositionen, 2002:12). Nevertheless, when taking productivity into account, unit wage costs in Sweden would have hardly risen (see Figures 11-4 and 11-5), although continental European industry enjoyed a reduction in unit wage costs as productivity expanded at a rate of approximately 2% per annum between 1992 and 1996 (Pelagidis, 2001b:146).

Figure 11-4: Nominal and real wages, annual % change, 1980-2002

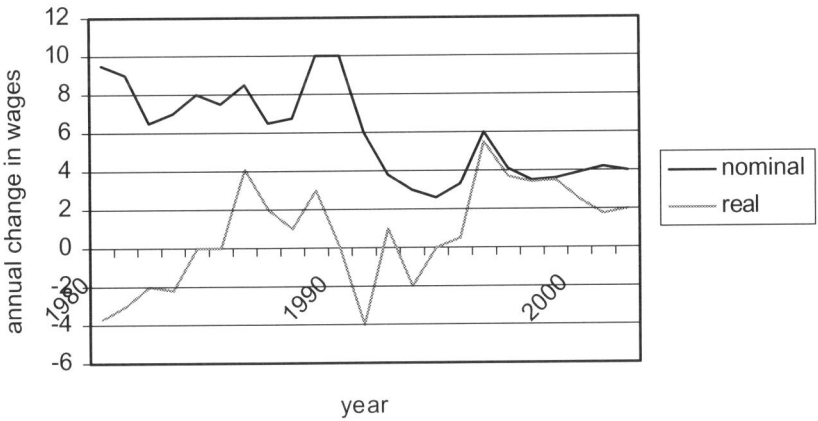

Figure 11-5: Labour productivity, annual change, 1995-2002

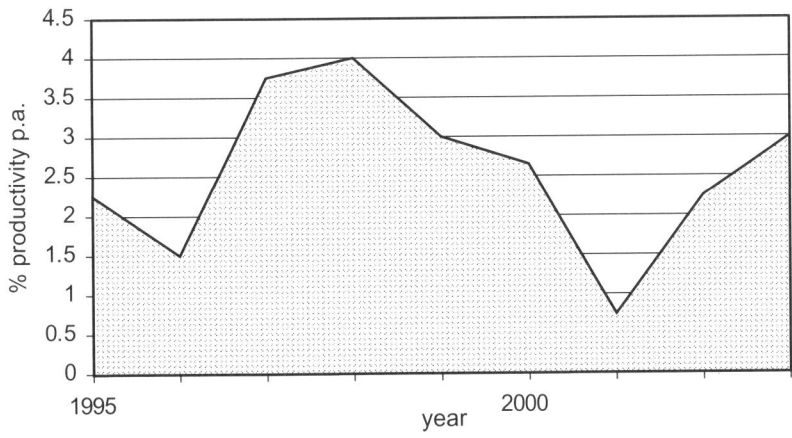

A Competitive Exchange Rate

The forced floating of the Swedish Krona, on 19 September 1992, provided the Swedish export sector with favourable conditions to expand international sales as and when the world economy recovered from its slowdown. Trade-weighted exchange rates remained more than 20% lower than the previous ERM value until the end of 1995, when the value of the Krona appreciated due to the strong export-led growth that Sweden was by then experiencing. Moreover, the exchange rate has remained a minimum of 12% below its former reference value for the entire two terms of SAP administration (see Figure 11-6). Accordingly, the SAP economic strategy pre-supposed the maintenance of this competitive exchange rate, and hence enjoyed a boost to demand from substantial surpluses on the balance of payments, including a then record of SEK35bn in 1995 (PMO, 1996:9,25).

Figure 11-6: Nominal effective exchange rate (SEK), 1994-1998

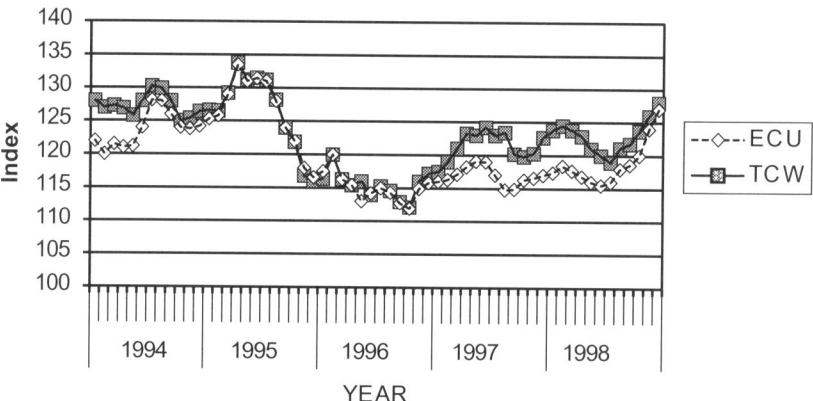

Source: Riksbank, Quarterly Review, No. 4, 1998, p. 98.

The maintenance of a competitive exchange rate, whether by design or a by-product of other economic factors, has assisted the Swedish economy to export its way out of a deep recession, in a similar manner to the earlier 1981-82 recession and the 1930s depression. Moreover, due to the low level of international commodity inflation, declining oil prices, favourable wage settlements, the retention of unused capacity in the Swedish economy and the tightening of macroeconomic stance during the first SAP term of office, the devaluation proved effective in stimulating the economy in the absence of a significant impact upon prices. In the optimum circumstances, devaluation appears to remain a very effective weapon in restoring economic balance, especially when backed by the appropriate set of policy measures to magnify its impact.

Second Term Priorities

The first term SAP administration prioritised public finance consolidation and the establishment of a low inflation economy ahead of the alternative target of full employment. Indeed, it took a year in office before the government published their employment policy, and this only proposed the relatively modest goal of reducing open unemployment by 4% by the turn of the century.

Fiscal policy needed to remain tight, in order to reduce the budgetary problems bequeathed to the government, whilst the independent central bank maintained a restrictive monetary policy, particularly when considering the very low rates of inflationary pressure in the domestic and international economy. Therefore, the major expansionary impulse came from the large depreciation in the exchange rate, immediately prior to the SAP taking office, and whose improvement to industrial competitiveness had filtered through into the real economy by 1994-95. The irony here is that, influenced by neo-liberal theoretical perspectives, the SAP government had officially rejected devaluation as an economic tool, and had collaborated with the previous bourgeois government in their desperate attempts to maintain the ERM fixed-rate peg.

The economic record of the first administration was impressive, in terms of the objectives it had set itself. Inflation fell below 1%, economic growth responded from three years of contraction to an average expansion exceeding 2.5% per annum and the ballooning budget deficit was eliminated. The major omission from this satisfactory record related to unemployment, which remained stubbornly close to its 8% peak. Indeed, by the end of the first administration, in 1998, there remained 10% fewer gainfully employed people than at the beginning of the decade (Statskontoret, 1999:17).

Traditional supporters of social democracy may criticise the record of the first term SAP administration on precisely this point. However, it would be a reasonable defence, certainly in the case of the tight fiscal stance, to claim that the hands of the new government were tied by the mistakes of the previous executive, and that the 'true' programme would be increasingly evident during the second term of office.

Macroeconomic Stance

In examining the second term for a shift in economic approach, the overall strategy would appear little changed. Monetary policy remained in the hands of an independent central bank, albeit that the low levels of inflation allowed interest rates to be reduced to levels between 3.5% to 4%. However, considering the fact that inflation remained around 1%, these real interest rates remained substantial in historical perspective (Figure 11-7). Nevertheless, in international comparison, interest rate premiums declined consistently, compared to US and EU levels, throughout the second term (Figure 11-8).

Figure 11-7: Interest rates ('repo' rates), 1992-2002

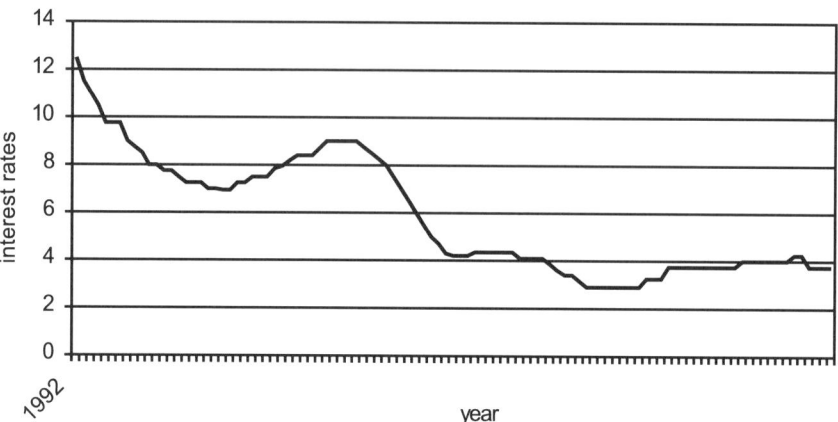

Fiscal policy remained fairly orthodox, with the Finance Minister adopting a medium-term target for public finances of a budget surplus of 2% of GDP, when averaged over the business cycle. This was partly intended to set aside additional resources to cover the consequences of demographic change upon pensions, health and social care, and thereby strengthening the long-term viability of the welfare state. Secondly, a bias towards budget surpluses during good economic periods would "make it possible to pursue an active stabilisation policy without deficits becoming too large" (Regeringens Propositionen, 2002:9). Thus, the fiscal consolidation programme made it possible to combine orthodox financial targets with an expansionary fiscal policy during 2001-2. Automatic stabilisers were thereby enabled to exercise their full effect upon the economy, finance a significant expansion in labour market policies and introduce additional active fiscal measures, all without exceeding the 3% GDP budget deficit as established by the MCC and associated with potential future membership of EMU (Regeringens Propositionen, 2002:68). In this context, the 2002 budget statement states, that:

> A responsible economic policy has created a stable macroeconomic foundation in the form of low inflation and sound public finances. Sweden is therefore able to respond to the weakness of the international economy by offensive measures to safeguard growth and employment (Regeringens Propositionen, 2002:4).

Budget surpluses facilitated significant increases in child allowance – the total value of reforms for children estimated at just under SEK13bn, spread over 4 years (Regeringens propositionen, 2002:14). Moreover, by 2002, the health and social service budgets for local authorities had been increased by SEK30bn over the 1996 level, thereby providing an average SEK5bn extra resources per annum, on a total budget of SEK31.4bn in 2002 (Regeringens Propositionen, 2002:15,33). Thus, irrespective of the maintenance of orthodox fiscal rules, the SAP government utilised its favourable budgetary position to reinforce the financial position of the welfare state. To this extent, at least, the government reverted to more traditional social democratic objectives.

Figure 11-8: Comparative interest rates, 1994-2002

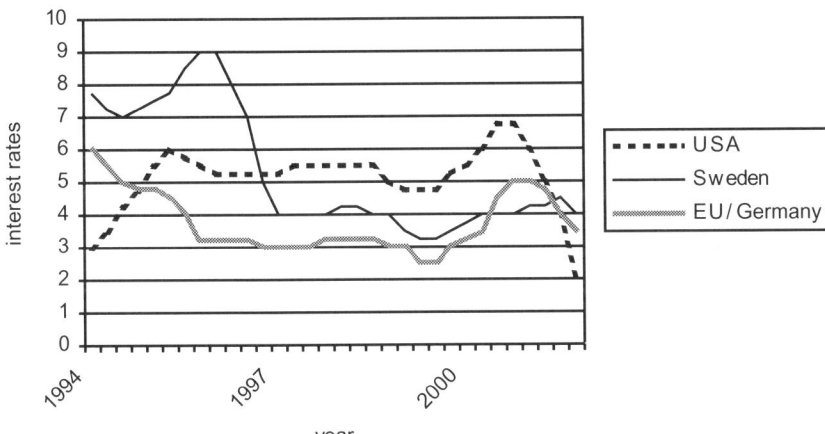

The second term also witnessed an increasing emphasis, on the part of the government, upon designing an economic programme to promote economic growth, employment and social justice. Indeed, the 2002 budget statement even went to so far as to state, that:

> The fight for jobs is at the top of our agenda….in response [to the weak international economic climate], major efforts are being made to restrain any growth in unemployment both by cutting taxes and making more resources available to employ greater numbers of people in the health service, the school system and the social services (Regeringens Propositionen, 2002:4).

And again – "The government's overall objective is full employment" (Regeringens Propositionen, 2002:21).

Miles (2000:235) argues that this change in emphasis was partly the result of a "notable success" enjoyed by the 'traditionalist' wing of the SAP, who defeated the leadership in a party congress debate on the economy, in demanding that full employment be prioritised above the generation of even larger budget surpluses. Miles (2000:239) further argues that this represented a particular setback for the Finance Minister, Erik Asbrink, whose criticism of the motion centred upon the basis that it would send negative signals to the international financial markets.

A second explanation involves the inclusivity adopted by Prime Minister Persson, towards dissenting opinions within his party. Irrespective of his former reputation as an orthodox Finance Minister, Persson has seemingly sought to accommodate criticisms of the neo-liberal slant to the SAP's economic programme.

This had the potential to maintain the support of political allies in the Centre, Green and Left parties, whilst strengthening SAP internal unity (Miles, 2000:232-7).

The social democratic government succeeded in open unemployment to 4%, even though this still relates to an 'augmented' rate of approximately 7% (Figure 11-9). Thus, Sweden remains far from achieving full employment, under any reasonable definition. However, even maintaining the present relatively tight labour markets is likely to prove difficult in the absence of policies and institutional arrangements which facilitate the combination of low levels of unemployment with low inflation, high levels of growth and a satisfactory distribution of income. One option would be to secure a reduction in unemployment through a targeted increase in aggregate demand. This approach is facilitated by the recent decline in productive capacity usage from 90% to 85%, and furthermore by the very low levels of inflation (Figure 11-10). However, it is unlikely that this option will be pursued by the SAP government, because they failed to undertake a similar fiscal boost during their first administration, despite circumstances being more favourable at that point.

Figure 11-9: Open and 'augmented' unemployment, 1980-2002

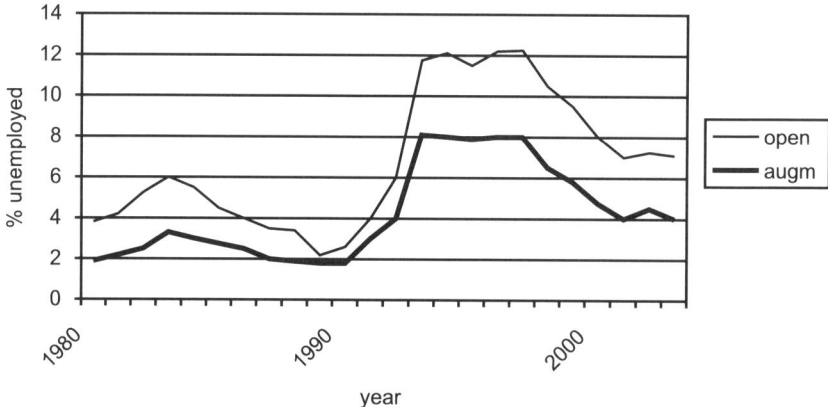

Previous experience has suggested that, without a supportive aggregate demand stance, labour market policy alone will not prove sufficient to eliminate unemployment. Public works schemes can remove individuals from the unemployment claim and provide them with a job, but only on a temporary basis, whilst retraining can help to match the unemployed to available vacancies, but will not by itself create new vacancies. Regional policy initiatives, including the introduction of regional growth agreements in 1998 as a means of adapting policy to local and regional conditions, is a welcome addition to the selective policy instruments in the hands of central and local government. It can provide additional finances for areas with declining populations to ensure that the remaining populations receive adequate public services, whilst simultaneously attracting new jobs through an expansion of higher education and selective tax cuts on employment

Figure 11-10: Percentage capacity utilisation, 1980-2002

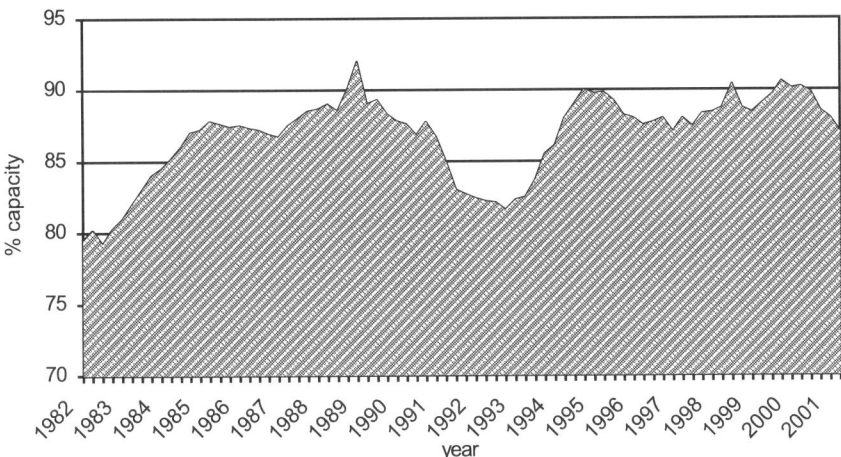

in order to generate sustainable growth in selected regions. However, it is an open question of whether these isolated measures can secure the government's interim goal of an 80% employment rate amongst people aged between 20-64 by 2004. The need for a unified strategy remains a pressing requirement.

Wage Bargaining

One element of a wider strategy would include an efficient system of wage negotiations. This was recognised by the SAP administration, who stated that:

> Efficient wage formation is of crucial importance for sustaining a positive development of the national economy. The long-term goal is full employment (Regeringens propositionen, 2002:12).

The problem remains, however, that the Swedish wage formation system has been decentralised during the 1980s, at the behest of the larger Swedish employers, and therefore the benefits associated with wage co-ordination, and which formed a secure basis for the success enjoyed by the Rehn-Meidner model, are presently not available to the current SAP administration. The only alternative, therefore, is to deal with the consequences of a sub-optimal system of wage formation via the independent central bank creating low inflationary expectations amongst economic actors, and reliance upon the social partners acting in their own medium-term interest.

This situation may, however, be in the process of realignment because the anticipated benefits of a decentralisation have only favoured those trans-national corporations who prefer to determine their own internal labour market reward structures more than the potential gain from industrial peace and restrain the growth in the level of wages at national labour market level. Thus, it has become increasingly possible that a new accommodation could be reached, between union federations who desire wage centralisation, as long as such structures incorporate a greater degree of flexibility at local level than would have been tolerated by unions in the previous centralised system.

The first step in this process may be associated with the agreement, reached between an 'expert' working group composed of representatives from the unions and employers, known as the Edin group, who recommended that wage increases in Sweden should not exceed wages in competitor OECD nations in order to maintain international competitiveness under circumstances where variations in exchange rates will no longer be an option (Elvander, 1997). However, this target 'norm' appears to have had little practical impact in terms of real wage growth in recent years. Moreover, LO members in sheltered sectors, most notably the transport and retail workers unions, together with the foremen's and supervisors' union from the white-collar TCO, have rejected the European norm due to the fact that their members do not typically benefit from the wage drift which occurs in private industry, and can double effective increases in wages over the minimum rate.

Conclusion

The economic programme implemented by the SAP government, during its period in office between 1994 and 2002, is significantly different from previous approaches to the party's management of the Swedish economy. The prioritisation of low inflation as the primary goal of macroeconomic strategy, rather than full employment, denotes the significant shift in priorities, in addition to confirming the neo-liberal theoretical basis for much of current SAP policy. Alongside this feature, the granting of independence to the central bank, dedication of fiscal policy to budget consolidation and rejection of coarse tuning of aggregate demand, all reinforce this conclusion.

Admittedly, the SAP's second term of office did appear to demonstrate a degree more generosity in terms of expenditure towards core welfare state programmes. However, the structure of macroeconomic policy has not changed, and nor does it appear very likely to do so in the near future. It therefore remains to be seen whether this hybrid of neo-liberalism and the remnants of the former Rehn-Meidner model can manage the economy successfully. Post-Keynesian analysis suggests that it will not, and therefore the need to develop an alternative approach, founded upon aggregate demand management, the development of a new system of wage co-ordination, complete with the re-regulation of the financial sector. The plausibility of this alternative approach, together with a more detailed verdict on contemporary SAP macroeconomics, will form the basis of the final chapter.

Chapter 12

Traditional Social Democracy
to 'Third Way'?

Introduction

The Swedish economy, like all others, has undergone a significant transformation during the period of analysis examined within this volume. In part, this reflects industrial change, which is a natural and healthy part of a dynamic market economy. Thus, it is no surprise that macroeconomic policy should evolve in order to maintain its effectiveness in dealing with new challenges provided by emerging industries, shifts in patterns of demand and developments in the international economic environment. Indeed:

> The dominating 'activist' Keynesian philosophy contributed to Sweden becoming a laboratory for stabilisation policy experiments during the last quarter of a century. This laboratory produced a rich harvest of experiments (Finansdepartmentet, 2000:12).

However, the question this book seeks to answer concerns whether the combination of internal and external forces have caused the SAP to re-invent itself as what may be defined as a 'new' form of social democracy, pursuing a 'Third Way' programme embracing many neo-liberal elements, together with a reorientation of traditional social democratic priorities. It is the function of this chapter to draw all of the threads of analysis together, in addition to providing an evaluation of the plausibility of developing an alternative strategy, based more firmly upon traditional social democratic policies and principles.

A 'New Macroeconomics'?

The traditional 'Swedish Model' was founded upon Keynesian macroeconomics, whereby government intervention was considered to be essential to the efficient operation of the economy. Economic policy sought to secure a high growth, full employed economy, operating at near full capacity, complete with relatively low inflation and a managed exchange rate in order to maintain international competitiveness and secure an acceptable balance of payments situation. The prime method was via aggregate demand management, secured through fiscal policy and reinforced through a 'cheap money' accommodating monetary policy. Aggregate demand was set at levels sufficient to employ most workers, with targeted supply-side measures such as labour market policy, utilised to secure full employment and remove bottlenecks of skill shortages within the labour market.

Capital was highly regulated, through a highly developed series of administrative controls and fiscal instruments, in order to prevent investment in non-domestic, non-productive assets from undermining the entire economic programme (Glyn, 1998:2). Co-ordinated, centralised wage bargaining facilitated wage formation without inter-union competition and disributional conflict resulting in inflationary pressure, whilst the provision of inexpensive, collective risk capital to finance industrial investment, completed the Rehn-Meidner, post-Keynesian strategy. These macroeconomic elements facilitated social policy goals, including the development of the Swedish welfare state, reducing social and economic inequality, together with the promotion of social solidarity.

Comparing the present economic programme with this stylised 'Swedish Model', there are a number of significant differences. The most important of these relates to the reordering of objectives established for macroeconomic policy, with the achievement of full employment becoming a secondary and long-term goal, whereas price stability has been advanced to the principle aim of government activity. This change of priorities is often presented as a different means of meeting traditional targets, thus the 1991 economic strategy stated that "a lasting reduction of inflation is the primary means of safeguarding jobs and social security" (Finansdepartmentet, 1991:9). However, this change overturns social democratic practice since the years of the Great Depression, which has seen full employment at the heart of macroeconomic policy (Scharpf, 1991:22).

The re-definition of economic priorities represents more than just a symbolic change of emphasis, but indicates a more fundamental shift in the economic theory from which policy is developed, in addition to a change in belief in the effectiveness of certain policy instruments. It signifies the acceptance of the natural rate of unemployment hypothesis, which holds that government intervention to reduce unemployment is ineffective in the medium term, and only results in a ratcheting-up of the rate of inflation. Not surprisingly, this hypothesis was derived from the work of the leading monetarist theorist, Milton Friedman, and stands in sharp contrast to the theory and practice of Keynesianism.[1]

Derived from the adoption of a neo-liberal model at the heart of SAP policy, the new macroeconomic programme sees little role for even coarse tuning of aggregate demand. Fiscal policy is therefore utilised to secure a surplus in public finances in order to secure future expenditure patterns. Public spending is narrowly conceived as solely fulfilling the social needs to which it is dedicated, thereby ignoring the potential stimulative impact as part of a counter-cyclical economic policy.

Monetary policy is similarly blunted as an effective policy instrument due to the deregulation of the financial sector. The only remaining instrument, interest rates, has been delegated to the central bank, to be utilised in pursuit of an inflation target. Not only does this fracture macroeconomic policy co-ordination, but it leaves the Riksbank as a 'one club golfer', seeking to stabilise the economy around a target

---

[1] 'New' Keynesianism is a synthesis of 'old' Keynesianism and monetarism, in that it accepts the natural rate of unemployment and rational expectations, leaving only a restricted role for government intervention beyond the short-run (Arestis and Sawyer, 2001a:2,9).

rate of inflation (instead of full employment), with only the most limited of measures at its command. Furthermore, because the inflation target was established with no consideration for the wider needs of the economy, it might prove incompatible with the restoration of full employment and desirable rates of economic growth. It also leaves the Swedish trade unions with little ability to influence macroeconomic policy, and therefore having to accept the imposition of a new 'iron law of wages' by a conservative central bank, with no assurance of new job opportunities or capital investment as a result of any wage moderation. Rehn puts this point a little more forcefully:

> The stage we are at now can therefore be characterised by the statement: full employment is no longer permitted. The trade unions should 'learn a lesson' – not to price themselves out of the market….In some cases (eg. the Thatcher government) the policy of restraint-cum-unemployment is quite clearly intended to be not only a deplorable necessity in the fight against inflation but an element of a class war: the power position of trade unions in society is to be destroyed (Rehn, 1987:63-64).

If it had not been for the significant devaluation of the Krona following its ejection from the ERM in 1992, the 'new' SAP macroeconomic strategy would have found it far more difficult to register the growth rates that have been achieved, and with it the rapid consolidation of public finances. Surprisingly, however, the government disapproves of exchange rate management to maintain a competitive economic environment, and prefers to actively pursue participation within the single European currency, the Euro, which would eliminate yet another policy instrument for the successful management of the national economy. Yet, even with the benefit of a substantial devaluation, the Swedish unemployment rate remains stubbornly high and, in the absence of aggregate demand management, the last significant remnant of the former Rehn-Meidner model, namely labour market policies, are unable to solve the unemployment problem on their own.

Discussion of reform of Sweden's labour market regulation is insufficient as a possible solution to this problem, as well as being unlikely to have a significant positive effect upon unemployment (Calmfors and Holmlund, 2000:107). Thus, in the absence of the social partners negotiating a new form of co-ordinated wage formation, in view of the voluntary abstinence from utilising most 'Keynesian' instruments of macroeconomic management, the SAP government has relatively little to say about precisely how it intends to reduce unemployment and meet its own labour force participation targets.

In terms of the once vaunted social policy element of the 'Swedish Model', Ladrech (2000:67) argues this has been reconfigured rather than replaced, with the universal welfare state and income redistribution redefined, not abandoned. Reductions in benefit levels are justified on the basis that "most households can withstand a temporary cut in household income" in order to develop a long-term, sustainable welfare system, whereas the emphasis upon income redistribution "seems to be shifting towards 'redistribution of possibilities'" (Lindgren, 1998:89). Indeed, the SAP administration does appear to have made efforts to reverse some of these former cuts in transfer payments in its second administration, particularly in the area of child support.

Against this, Ryner (1999:39) argues that reductions in social insurance entitlements demonstrates that the Swedish welfare state has been increasingly "hollowed out to facilitate 'self-regulating markets'". It is certainly true that the SAP have adopted the privatisation policies of its predecessor bourgeois administration, with an increasing private sector presence in formerly core areas of public provision – i.e. health and education. This represents a significant marketisation of Swedish society in little over a decade.

The inevitable conclusion, to be reached from this brief summary, is that the 'new' form of SAP macroeconomics is far removed from the traditional 'Swedish Model', and rather closer to the 'Third Way' approach developed in chapter one. According to this account, Swedish social democracy may very well be in crisis, with high levels of unemployment becoming a persistent feature of social democratic Sweden (Ryner, 1999:39). Indeed, many theorists accept this new phenomenon as evidence that the Swedish unemployment rate is adapting itself to more "normal" European levels (Forslund, 1995:17).

External Constraints

In terms of its reaction to external constraints, the 'new' form of Swedish social democracy also seemingly takes an approach similar in emphasis to the 'Third Way' model (Chapter One). Pursuit of the deregulation of the financial sector, now complete, has been a feature of two decades of SAP policy, and as such it has facilitated a substantial capital outflow, leading to more people being employed by nominally Swedish companies outside the domestic economy than within it! Hindsight is a wonderful thing, but it takes only a brief consideration to understand the likely positive effect upon employment, industrial capacity and the level of GDP, had Sweden maintained its controls on the movement of capital and these resources were instead invested in productive capital in the home market. Yet, in practice, the international ownership of Swedish companies has advanced remorselessly, and with it changes in the traditional patterns of work, complete with outsourcing and downsizing (Brulin, 2000:237).

The most significant external constraint upon Sweden's policy autonomy arose due to the rise of neo-liberal economics, together with the international deregulation of international financial markets, thus:

> As the effective sovereignty and subsequently the Keynesian capacity of European nation-states faded, so did corporatism and with it the social-democratic project of politically guaranteed full-employment (Streeck and Schmitter, 1991:145).

Ryner (1999:40) argues that structural change has had a "profound" effect upon social democracy, causing its redefinition. However, this should not be presented as a deterministic effect of external forces beyond the control of social democratic movements. Rather, that the failure of leading members of government and unions to appreciate the ultimate results of their actions, together with an inability to explore alternative strategies, contributed in no small part to the outcome of these events. For example, Ingvar Carlsson is quoted as admitting that the 1982-91 SAP administration underestimated the impact that the growth and international integration of the Swedish financial sector would have upon the effectiveness of macroeconomic policy (Färm, 1991:85). Furthermore, Cornwall (1989) suggests that it was the weakness of European labour movements, and their failure to develop corporatist arrangements that delivered wage moderation, that left nations with little alternative than embrace neo-liberalism and abandon full employment as a viable policy objective.

One potential alternative strategy would be to seek to regain democratic control over capital through supra-national measures. Within the European continent, this may involve the attempt to influence the process of European integration in a social democratic direction. Marks and Wilson (cited in Ladrech, 2000:80) argue that, by the end of the 1980s, "the overwhelming majority of social democrats in established EU member states came to recognise that the European Union was the only game in town, and adjusted their policies accordingly". Unfortunately, this involved the wholesale acceptance of the neo-liberal foundations upon which the process of European integration has been constructed.

The free movement of capital within the SIM empowers capital at the expense of nationally-based governments and trade unions. The operation of the European monetary system has depressed the European economy for a decade or more, resulting in a substantial Keynesian output gap (Gordon, 1987; Solow 1991). Moreover, the convergence criteria, forming the basis of EMU, frustrates counter-cyclical Keynesian policy intervention in order to reduce mass unemployment (Landau, 1995; Vanhoudt, 1999:212-3).

Criticism of the EU is rejected by Smith (1997), who argues that such blame is disingenuous because it deflects consideration that national governments often favour the policy change, and therefore use the EU as a scapegoat for measures they would have pursued in any case. Nevertheless, EU membership locks Sweden into its neo-liberal policy framework, unless or until the social democratic forces within Europe can re-negotiate the international treaties that have established the institutional model for European integration. This can frustrate the development of an alternative, post-Keynesian-social democratic approach to macroeconomics in Sweden.

Can the 'Swedish Model' be Revived?

If the analysis contained within this book is correct, then the contemporary macroeconomic programme being implemented by the SAP can be associated with the 'Third Way' approach, as developed in chapter one. In particular, the SAP's acceptance of the dominating impact of globalisation, and thereby the relative impotence of former Keynesian-social democratic policies, denotes a significant switch from the former 'Swedish Model'. Indeed, the SAP has sought to synthesise neo-liberal economics with protection of progressive social policy in a way that would appear familiar to analysts of New Labour in Britain and Schröder's SPD in Germany.

Apologists for this 'new' version of social democracy would argue that this is the only realistic method to adopt to manage a modern economy. However, the evidence presented in earlier chapters, points to the fact that globalisation is not the dominating phenomenon that many theorists accept. Nor does greater internationalisation necessarily imply the impotence of the nation state.

There remains considerable room for independent economic policy, particularly if skilfully constructed and intelligently implemented, which would allow a social democratic government to pursue traditional objectives of full employment, rapid growth rates, together with social solidarity. Moreover, there is nothing inherent within globalisation that prevents the rediscovery of Keynesian techniques, based upon solid theoretical principles. There is no reason contained in the analysis summarised within this volume to conclude that the 'Swedish Model' itself cannot be revived. Hence, the remainder of this chapter is dedicated to exploring this possibility, and evaluating its likely consequences.

Sustainable Full Employment

Meidner (1997:89) argues that the success of the 'Swedish Model' rested upon the fact that the majority of the Swedish citizenry supported the objectives it sought to achieve, and that the similarity of social and trade union interests made it possible for the strategy to be implemented by an internationally uniquely powerful labour movement. The first part of this basis remains, as most surveys tend to indicate strong political support for a comprehensive welfare state and redistribution policies (Svallfors, 1995; Vartiainen, 1998:22). Indeed, Svllfors (1996) claims that there is "a profound divide between the increasingly neo-liberal paradigm of Swedish elite's and the continued welfarist 'common sense' of the Swedish people". Thus, the first element supporting the revival of the 'Swedish Model' remains intact, namely the degree of popular support for its renewal. Furthermore, although the strength of the Swedish trade unions has declined, largely due to the deregulation of the national economy and subsequent empowerment of footloose capital, membership support for traditional social democratic principles remains firm. Indeed:

> Unions cannot see it as their role to increase the incomes of capital owners at the expense of the workers, and Social Democrats cannot make it their program to dismantle the welfare state in order to lighten the tax burden on business. If they nevertheless did both things, they did so with a bad conscience and more under the cover of darkness than in the full daylight of their programmatic debates (Scharpf, 1991:270).

Meidner (1997:89) further argued that the 'Swedish Model' depended upon the fact that "the means of the model were consistent and mutually supporting." When considering the reformulation of the 'Swedish Model', it is therefore important to firstly establish those elements which contributed to the overall success of the strategy. Accordingly, the evidence presented elsewhere points towards Sweden's ability to maintain low unemployment because it was prepared to persevere with expansionary macroeconomic policies at a time when other countries were pursuing tight money policies to control inflation (Calmfors, 1993; Robinson, 1994). As empathised by the hysteresis approach, the avoidance of incurring high rates of unemployment in itself helped to avoid such high rates persisting and proving difficult to eradicate (Forslund, 1995:20-1).

The problem with this explanation, for those theorists who adopt a neo-liberal or 'new' Keynesian theoretical perspective, arises from the fact that, whilst macroeconomic policies may indeed be accepted as the dominant influence on unemployment in the short-run, these schools of economics assume that the 'equilibrium' unemployment rate is determined by supply side factors in the medium- and longer-term. Consequently, attempts to push unemployment below this level can only lead to rapidly accelerating inflation. Thus, the dominant economic perspectives are forced to rule out the most obvious reasons for Sweden's success in maintaining low rates of unemployment during its 'Keynesian' era (1932-1990), and further explains a significant degree of the dramatic rise in unemployment following the switch of macroeconomic strategies to a pro-cyclical, neo-liberal approach.

The only other realistic explanation for neo-liberals involves the possibility that the transition from an "inflation tolerant" regime to an acceptance of price stability may provoke a deep and persistent recession (Blanchflower et al, 1995:104-5). The alternative, namely that equilibrium unemployment suddenly and for no apparent reason, shifted upwards by as much as 5% in the space of a few months, appears most unlikely, and particularly so since the time period under examination contained a major reversal of macroeconomic strategy (Forslund, 1995:48-9).

A second element in the success of the 'Swedish Model' relates to the distinctive design and role of Swedish institutions in preventing mass unemployment (Layard et al, 1991). These institutional factors most notably include Sweden's active labour market policies and its former co-ordinated wage bargaining system. However, these factors in isolation appear unable to explain Sweden's low rates of unemployment during the 1980s. For example, Denmark had a similar system of centralised wage bargaining, high levels of public employment and utilised a similar system of active labour market policies. However, Denmark additionally operated macroeconomic policies which emphasised fiscal conservatism and price stability rather than full employment as its prime goals, and thereby proved unable of securing low and sustainable unemployment. This suggests that manpower policies and an efficient wage bargaining system are necessary, but not sufficient, for the achievement and maintenance of a full employment policy regime (Blanchflower et al, 1995:106).

Meidner (1997:95-6) reinforces this conclusion, arguing that labour market policy, by itself, "is unable to overcome mass unemployment", and that "full employment can only be regained through a fundamental change of priorities". These will enshrine full employment, not price stability, as the principle objective of government macroeconomic policy. This, in turn, depends upon political considerations, because the SAP could choose to fulfil its commitment to full employment and social equality as core goals of its programme, but instead pursues a neo-liberal platform, and further constrains its own ability to adopt an independent economic line through membership of the EU.

The 'Swedish Model', then, comprised an inter-locking series of individual policy measures. It was conceptualised by its founders, Rehn and Meidner, as an integrated model, with each identifiable element contributing to more than one objective, but each simultaneously reinforcing the operation of all other fundamentals. Aggregate demand management combined with labour market policy and co-ordinated wage bargaining to reduce unemployment without increasing inflationary pressure. Similarly, the maintenance of 'cheap money' through an accommodating monetary policy, together with the provision of collective risk capital, facilitated capital formation without requiring the attraction of excessive profit rates, and thereby facilitating wage moderation by the trade union movement. Tight controls imposed upon the movement of capital helped to push additional resources towards investment in domestic productive capital, thereby stimulating future growth rates, enhanced capacity and more jobs. Thus, the importance of the combination of policies is such that, once they begin to be picked apart, for example starting with liberalisation of capital movements, the remainder of the model ceased to be as effective, and internal tensions became magnified (Ingebritsen, 1998:89).

An Evolving Model?

One factor that 'Third Way' analysts are correct in highlighting relates to the need for macroeconomic strategy to evolve in order to meet new challenges to existing institutions and policy instruments. Boyer and Drache (1996:18) argue that it would be "erroneous" to maintain the same approach to managing the economy, irrespective of the circumstances of the day. For example, Keynes wrote the *General Theory* to deal with the issue of demand deficient mass unemployment and economic depression. However, this does not imply that his basic method of analysis and conceptualisation of discretionary economic management are not equally applicable to circumstances of tight labour markets and inflationary pressure. The Rehn-Meidner post-Keynesian approach proved this point very efficiently. Nevertheless, Boyer and Drache are concerned that technological change, facilitating a post-Fordist mode of production, has undermined the link between mass production and mass consumption upon which the Keynesian system was based. Furthermore, issues of slow growth, low productivity gains and inadequate capital formation require urgent examination, whilst traditional social democratic objectives of redistribution, public ownership and economic democratisation cannot be ignored.

Growth and Capital Formation

One potential weakness demonstrated by the Swedish economy in recent decades has been a decline in its formerly above-average national income per capita, which is arguably due to slower growth rates than major competitor nations. Lindbeck (2000:29) suggests that the 'catch-up hypothesis' may provide one explanation of why other nations have caught up with Sweden's technology, but it cannot explain how other nations passed Sweden between 1970-1990. A second factor may relate to a higher proportion of Sweden's capital being tied up in markets experiencing declining terms-of-trade. This may suggest that the ability of the economy to reallocate scarce factors to newer, dynamic sectors of production is too weak, or that the quality of Swedish products failed to improve as quickly as in competitor nations (Lindbeck, 2000:31).

An apparently more serious problem for the Swedish economy concerns the decline in total factor productivity, from 3.05% per year between 1950 and 1970, to 1.24% between 1970 and 1993. However, these gross figures are misleading, because they disguise OECD estimates that total productivity failed to expand between 1973 and 1979, whereas it rose by 8% per annum during the remainder of the time period, compared to average rates of 1% for the OECD as a whole (Lindbeck, 2000:30). Moreover, one element of this equation relates to the tendency for the public sector to expand, as labour intensive, personal service activities, where 'Baumol's Law' suggests that labour productivity will be generally low and these sectors therefore become relatively costly over time (Baumol and Bowen, 1966). In Swedish national accounting, public sector productivity is generally assumed to be zero, whereas in other nations, it is more typically given a rate of 2% per annum.

More significantly, international comparative studies indicate that 70% of economic growth can be explained by capital accumulation, which is in itself a relatively low figure. However, it emphasises the fact that, if growth rates are to be improved, Sweden will need to accumulate more capital (DeLong and Summers, 1991). Unfortunately, this has been a particular problem for the economy in recent years, with investment as a proportion of GDP declining from 24% in 1965, to 14% in 1995 – a rate below the unweighted world average of 22% (Gylfason, 1997:82). Indeed, Swedish capital accumulation has remained consistently beneath the world average during the last two decades, even at the height of the 1989-90 boom, implying that the growth of domestic productive capacity is one serious problem that has to be tackled by any new macroeconomic strategy.

Figure 12-1: Profit share of national income, manufacturing, 1980-2002

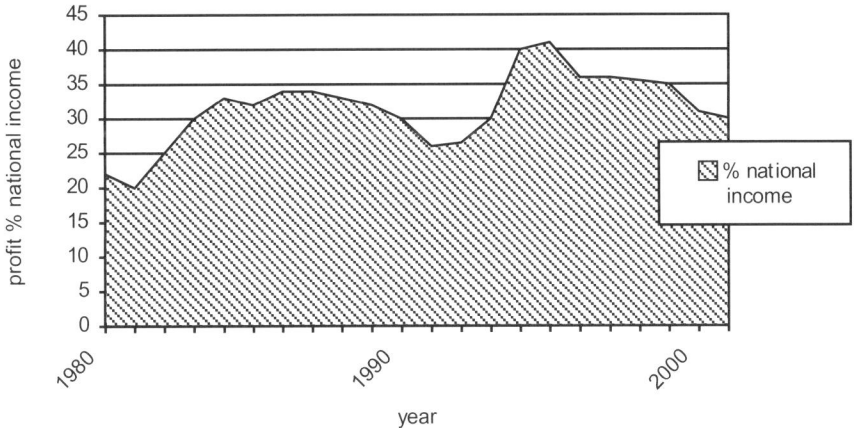

Figure 12-2: Return on capital and profit share – business sector, 1980-2002

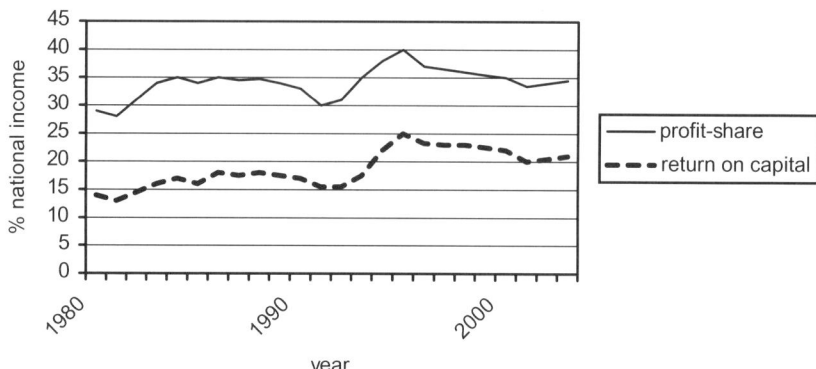

Earlier chapters have already noted that, due to substantial capital relocation outside the Swedish economy, more jobs and investment occurs abroad by nominally Swedish companies than takes place in the domestic economy. This is clearly one substantial cause of slower growth rates and a slower development of capacity than would otherwise have occurred. However, this raises the question of whether the neo-liberal strategy is correct; improve circumstances for business and this will lead to an improvement in growth variables. However, as illustrated in Figure 12-1, Figure 12-2 and Table 12-1, a substantial redistribution of national income from labour to capital together with an upward shift in the return on capital, as a result of neo-liberal policies, has not had the desired effect, namely encouraged an increase in investment, capital accumulation and economic growth rates.

If the neo-liberal strategy of 'paying' capital to reinvest in productive capacity in Sweden does not work, then there is little to be lost in returning to the structure established by the 'Swedish Model'. Reintroduce financial regulation to impose a degree of control on capital movements, together with managing aggregate demand to ensure a reasonable industrial rate of return but not an excessive amount, that could trigger distributional conflict in the labour market. Furthermore, the provision of additional public savings, through budget surpluses, pension funds and other forms of collective savings – these could include WEFs, Renewal Funds, Education Funds, Solidarity Funds and so forth (Whyman, 2002).

Table 12-1: Net saving as a percentage of GDP, annual averages, 1950-1996

	1950-59	1960-69	1970-79	1980-89	1990-96
Household	4.5	3.6	1.8	0.5	3.1
Corporate	4.0	2.6	3.0	4.6	2.7
Govt	3.4	8.4	6.7	-0.4	-4.0
TOTAL	11.9	14.7	11.5	4.7	1.9

Source: Statistics Sweden, National Accounts.

Table 12-2: Percentage of private rates of return to higher education, for men

Year	Before tax	After tax
1969	15.7	11.9
1974	6.9	3.6
1981	4.3	0.5
1984	3.9	1.7
1986	5.3	3.3
1988	4.7	2.7
1991	6.0	4.5

Source: Edin and Holmlund, 1993.

Irrespective of what they are entitled, the decline in availability of public savings to finance productive investments has opened the Swedish economy to influence from international money markets, and therefore, if the 'Swedish Model' is to be reintroduced on a national scale, this dependency has to cease, and savings be generated nationally. In view of the volatility of private and corporate savings ratios, together with the distributional consequences of encouraging private savings through fiscal incentives, this had better be achieved through public controlled funds, as per the Rehn-Meidner approach.

One final factor that has been suggested to have a negative impact upon growth rates relates to declining private rates of return on education (see Table 12-2). A widening income distribution should improve this figure, however concerns for educational wage premiums should be included in any new wage formation system that the social partners in Sweden may be able to negotiate.

Restructuring Wage Bargaining

Centralised, co-ordinated wage formation formed an essential feature of the Rehn-Meidner model. It provided a means for the trade union movement to pursue their solidarity wages policy, thereby promoting fiscal redistribution of income, whilst reinforcing structural change in the economy as a whole. It facilitated real wage moderation and, when operating properly, ensured that wages were established with relation to the maintenance of international competitiveness. However, the SAF offensive in the 1980s shattered this part of the 'Swedish Model', by forcing decentralisation of the wage bargaining system. As a result, with wage bargaining no longer part of the core economic strategy, together with the fact that the current SAP government has forgotten significant lessons learnt during its Keynesian heritage, Meidner (1997:95) claims that "the Swedish Model is in central parts not longer applicable to an economy with high unemployment and new patterns of wage determination".

The previous system of wage formation was not of course perfect. The growth of white-collar unionisation complicated the negotiations system, whilst attempts to impose a rational 'EFO' model to indicate affordable wage increases was undermined by wage drift that only benefited certain workers. Nevertheless, its record in combining real wage flexibility, international competitiveness of Swedish industry, and wage redistribution through the solidarity wages policy, was far superior to the high wage rises, and significant rise in industrial conflict, generated by decentralised wage bargaining. Indeed, the present system is currently locked within a "patently sub-optimal" mid-point between central and workplace wage formation, where the macroeconomic implications of higher wages have ceased to be internalised within the bargaining framework, and with competing actors free-riding on the responsibility of others, results in a price-wage spiral (Friberg and Uddén-Sonnegård, 2001).

Critics of centralised wage bargaining argue that it may be no longer possible in a more heterogeneous world, where firms wish to follow the logic of decentralised work organisation and set wages locally in order to provide incentives for intensified productivity and loyalty to the company. Thus, centralised wage setting could be a feature of particular historical circumstances, for example the Fordist mode of production, and may be unable to function in the absence of these factors (Flanagan et al, 1983; Newell and Symons, 1987). Furthermore, Iversen (1998:64-5) argues that the solidarity wages policy frustrated job growth through expansion of labour-intensive and low-productivity private service due to their being over-priced (Appelbaum and Schettkat, 1994; Iversen and Wren, 1998). The alternatives are therefore to locate job growth in public services (Sweden's solution), leading to an increasing proportion of GDP being accommodated by the public sector, or discouraging participation in the labour market, particularly for married women, older workers and through the repatriation of 'guest' workers (i.e. Austria, Switzerland).

Vartiainen (1988:31) argues that the establishment of a new social compromise between labour and capital will prove difficult due to the destruction of trust in mutual co-operation. Yet, this appears to be precisely what might be happening at present. Friberg and Uddén-Sonnegård (2001) claim that a new bargaining framework is in the basis of development, based upon joint acceptance of the necessity for moderate wage growth, agreement of a set of rules for bargaining, together with the establishment of a National Mediation Office, in 2000, to facilitate the bargaining process. This new system incorporates (Iversen, 1996:422):

* macroeconomic policy stabilisation, resulting in low inflationary expectations;
* pattern-setting of wage bargaining from the exposed sector to the rest of the economy;
* a centralised component to impose macroeconomic wage discipline;
* sufficient room available for follow-up negotiations to reflect local market conditions.

This initiative is based upon the 1997 Agreement on Industrial Development and Wage Formation covering the manufacturing sector, which involves the re-establishment of joint regulation over the labour market to minimise industrial conflict (Sheldon and Thornthwaite, 1999:514). This is particularly significant because VI is one of the eleven employer association signatories of the agreement, despite their former insistence upon the decentralisation of wage bargaining.[2] Expert advice forms the basis for reaching agreement over the room for wage rises, consistent with such factors as competitive conditions and the Maastricht criteria.

In finalising a new system of centralised, co-ordinated bargaining, lessons could be learnt from the more resilient examples throughout Europe. One feature of the Austrian system is that relative wages are determined at sectoral and firm level, and therefore central negotiations are free to focus upon the level of aggregate wages appropriate for the macroeconomy (Iversen, 1996:424). By contrast, in Norway, the re-centralisation of wage bargaining sought to impose discipline upon the inflationary wage demands of petrochemical workers, whilst setting aggregate real wages to improve industrial competitiveness; a similar conjunction of circumstances that inspired the Swedish system of central negotiations (Iversen, 1996:428).

A secondary dynamic in the Norwegian process includes the fact that the leadership in both trade union and employers' associations have developed a good means of communication and conduct negotiations in "an atmosphere of mutual trust" (Gylfason, 1997:60). Finally, in Finland, centralised bargains are imposed with little supplementary wage negotiations, leading to lower wage drift (Eriksson et al, 1990).

Economic Democratisation

One feature of former Swedish social democracy, indeed *the* most significant issue debated within the labour movement for more than a decade, concerns the democratisation of economic life. The Swedish social democratic movement has viewed itself as extending democratic choice into all areas of its citizens lives, and accordingly the broadening of democratic influence into peoples' working lives is a natural progression (Abrahamsson and Broström, 1980). The most significant initiatives in this area were the controversial WEFs, together with the package of industrial democracy reforms introduced in the early 1970s. These sought to provide working people with greater opportunities to influence their own working lives, either through the appointment of worker-directors to company boards, co-determination legislation that required consultation and discussion of major issues before final decisions were made by management, and/or the opportunity to influence strategic corporate decision making through collective shareholding.

None of these measures secured more than marginal improvements in the democratisation of the economic sphere (Whyman, 2002). However, the greater the sophistication of citizens in their role as consumers and electors of representatives in government, local authorities and/or their trade unions, the more it might be anticipated that they will demand ever greater influence over more aspects of their working lives. This desire is in line with new management tools, such as Human

---

2   Small and medium-sized firms, reliant on SAF's facilities, strongly opposed its closure of its bargaining services, although the election of a new SAF President in 1996, marked a reversal of this decision; the SAF was not simply to engage in lobbying and opinion-formation activities, but would provide bargaining services to smaller companies (Sheldon and Thornthwaite, 1999:528).

Resource Management (HRM), which focuses upon productivity-orientated version of employee participation in the work process. Dissatisfaction with an incomplete form of involvement in key decision making will inevitably cause employees and their representatives to reconsider many of the key themes of economic democratisation.

A second feature of the economic democracy debate, within Swedish social democracy, focused upon the ownership of Swedish companies. The SAP has always been reluctant to rely upon large scale nationalisation as a panacea to all inequities in capitalist society. However, the party has noted the enormous concentration of economic power, with only a few families and/or investment groupings, controlling the interests of most large Swedish companies (Skog, 1991). This dominance has been partially altered, by Sweden's EU membership requiring the removal of controls on foreign ownership of Swedish corporate and property assets. Indeed, the foreign ownership of shares quoted on the Swedish stock market has risen from being virtually insignificant a decade ago, to a peak of 38.9% in 2000 (Table 12-3).

Table 12-3: Ownership in companies quoted on the Swedish stock market, by sector, per cent and total value (SEKbn), 1995-2001

	1995	1996	1997	1998	1999	2000	2001
Non-financial enterprises	9.4	8.6	7.8	6.9	6.8	6.7	8.2
Financial enterprises	29.8	30.3	30.3	28.9	29.2	25.8	30.3
Central govt	2.9	4.0	3.0	2.6	1.8	4.9	5.4
Local govt	0.7	0.5	0.5	0.6	0.3	0.3	0.2
ATP	4.3	3.8	4.0	4.5	4.3	4.1	3.7
Households	15.4	14.0	15.3	15.0	15.0	13.1	13.7
Non-profit organisations	7.8	7.3	7.5	6.9	3.6	3.5	3.9
Foreign owners	29.6	31.6	31.6	34.6	38.9	38.9	34.6
Total value (SEKbn)	1145	1651	2123	2285	3259	3637	2909

The shift in ownership has a number of potentially significant effects. Firstly, it increases the proportion of companies operating in Sweden but controlled by international investors who are less concerned about the health of the economy, the state of industrial relations and other factors that impact upon the quality of life for residents of Sweden, and more motivated by the 'bottom line' of short-term profitability and/or expectations of future share price values. This makes Swedish production more dependent upon the 'animal spirits' of speculators in the stock market 'casino economy' that Keynes so criticised as the basis for a modern society, where economic fundamentals are only vaguely associated with stock values at any given time (Jagadeesh and Titman, 1993).

The Riksbank (2002) has noted that it is hard to understand how corporate profits could be rising so quickly, based upon a national economic growth rate of around 2% per annum, that share prices could have risen by an average of 20% – a rate three times the long-term trend. Such growth rates are unsustainable, yet once share prices start to fall, expectations of future losses in value will create a 'bear' market and falling share prices will impede rational investment activity and long-term decision-making. Another significant change involves the loss of the entrepreneur-owner, or at least 'national capitalist', who was integrated into the domestic economy and therefore at least understood the necessity for class compromises with organised labour in order to create a positive climate for business activity.

One further feature inherent in the change in the distribution of ownership of Swedish companies concerns the balance of their activities. For example, one of the arguments in favour of WEFs concerned their reliability in terms of wanting to retain productive activity within the domestic market. However, the expansion of overseas production by Swedish firms has increased dramatically in the aftermath of the removal of financial regulations in the late 1980s, and this has led to the export of skilled jobs by Swedish TNCs, whilst retaining lower-skilled operations in Sweden – a direct reversal of the practice adopted by US TNCs (Blomstrom, 2000:193).

The desire for 'good owners' of Swedish corporations, who are part of society and therefore understand the rationale for social compromise, together with the presumption in favour of production occurring in Sweden rather than being switched elsewhere, has perhaps never been greater. Nevertheless, there are a number of initiatives that government could pursue to improve this position. The reimposition of controls over the movement of capital would significantly alter this balance of ownership, as international investors may prove less likely to dominate the more productive sectors of the Swedish economy, whilst the trend towards locating future production overseas would be severely curtailed.

The loss of a certain degree of investment capital, through smaller inward FDI, could be compensated by the greater use of collective capital investment funds, whether through pension funds and/or introduction of a new form of WEF, to provide cheap finance to companies producing *within* Sweden. Both of these could then advance economic democratisation through the use of voting rights and ability to place individuals on corporate boards. Thus, the Swedish economy could be progressively re-nationalised, in the sense of returned to the ownership and control of its citizens rather than 'faceless' global investors, and in addition a degree of this influence could accrue to working people and their representatives, as advocated in traditional social democratic discourse.

Conclusion

This chapter has sought to evaluate the macroeconomic programme of the contemporary SAP administration, in order to ascertain to what degree it could be classified as part of the 'Third Way' form of 'new' social democracy, that rejects the old Keynesian-corporatist solutions on the basis that globalisation and technological change has rendered these measures impotent. In most essentials, it would appear that the SAP have indeed adopted this new framework, based largely upon neo-liberal theory, complete with the rejection of demand management, exchange rate management, financial sector regulation and the use of collective funds to finance capital formation and steer investment expenditure.

The choice to become a member of the EU, and consideration of participation in an EMU complete with being permanently locked into its monetarist framework, merely reinforces the choice to reject the target and policy instruments capable of securing an economy denoted by sustainable full employment, in favour of becoming just another 'normal' European member state characterised by low growth and high unemployment. Admittedly, the government has retained elements of the Rehn-Meidner approach, including most notably the labour market policies. However, as witnessed during the disastrous 1991-94 bourgeois government, these are incapable of eliminating high levels of unemployment in the absence of a supportive post-Keynesian macroeconomic package.

Apologists for the 'Third Way' claim, rather like British Prime Minister Margaret Thatcher did so memorably when defending her introduction of undiluted monetarism, that 'there is no alternative' to the new synthesis of neo-liberalism and elements of old-style social democracy. This is just as inaccurate a statement now, as it was when Mrs Thatcher built her reputation upon stubborn refusal to consider feasible alternatives.

Close examination of the history of Swedish economic policy in action demonstrates the relative success of the post-Keynesian framework devised by Rehn and Meidner. Even if changing circumstances mean that this cannot be replicated in every detail in today's economy, the essence of post-Keynesian economics is the emphasis upon innovative use of policy instruments to form a strategic intervention in a sub-optimal market economy in order to achieve timeless social democratic goals. These include, full employment, decent rates of growth, low inflation, international competitiveness, the development of a universal welfare state, the redistribution of income and power, and democratisation of all aspects of national life.

Admittedly, certain loose ends remain. Wage bargaining is not yet in a form most suitable to a revised 'Swedish Model', although there are indications that the social partners have established a closer relationship than for a considerable period. Furthermore, it would appear that even the most ideological groups of employers have recognised that co-ordination with a moderate partner is preferable to decentralised competition between firms (for scarce labour) and unions (for member loyalty), with its inflationary consequences and rise in industrial disputes. Consequently, even this aspect of a new form of 'Swedish Model' may prove possible, in the near future, given the desire by all parties to rediscover a compromise solution that secures positive-sum benefits for each of them.

The analysis contained in this book indicates that there is no technical reason why a new form of post-Keynesian, 'Swedish Model' cannot be enacted, it is simply a matter of the political will not existing at present. Whether this remains the last stumbling block preventing the restoration of the 'Swedish Model', only time will tell.

Bibliography

Abrahamsson, B. and Broström, A. (1980), *The Rights of Labour*, Sage Publications, London.

Adelsohn, U. et al (1983), 'Löntagarfonder' [EIFs], *Riksdag Motion 1983/84 No 204* [Moderate Party motion signed by 12 members of parliament], Sveriges Riksdag, Stockholm.

Agell, J. (1996), 'Why Sweden's Welfare State Needed Reform', *Economic Journal*, Vol. 106, No. 439, pp. 1760-71.

Ahlén, K. (1989), 'Swedish Collective Bargaining under Pressure: Inter-union Rivalry and Incomes Policies', *British Journal of Industrial Relations*, Vol. 27, pp. 330-346.

Ahrne, G. (1978), "Middle Way' Sweden at a Cross-Roads: problems, actors and outcomes', *Acta Socialogica*, Vol. 21, No. 4, pp. 317-340.

Ahrne, G. and Clement, W. (1992), 'A New Regime?: Class Representation within the Swedish State', *Economic and Industrial Democracy*, Vol. 13, pp. 455-479.

Albrecht, S.L. and Deutsch, S. (1983), 'The Challenge of Economic Democracy: the case of Sweden', *Economic and Industrial Democracy*, Vol. 4, pp. 287-320.

Alesina, A. and Summers, L. (1993), Central bank Independence and Macroeconomic Performance: Some Comparative Evidence, *Journal of Money, Credit and Banking*, Vol. 25, No. 2, pp. 1-14.

Alogoskoufis, G. et al (1995), *Unemployment: Choices for Europe*, Monitoring European Integration Series, Vol. 5, Centre for Economic Policy Research, London.

Åmark, K. (1988), 'Sammanhållning och intressepolititk: Socialdemokratin och Fackforeningsrörelsen I samarbete på skilda vägar' [Solidarity and Interest Group Politics: The 'Third Way' and The Labour Movement], In: Misgeld, K. et al (eds.), *Socialdemokratins samhalle [Social Democratic Society]*, Tiden, Stockholm, pp. 577-582.

Amin, A. and Thrift, N. (1994), 'Living in the Global', In: Amin, A. and Thrift, N. (eds.), *Globalisation, Institutions, and Regional Development in Europe*, Oxford University Press, Oxford, pp. 1-22.

Amoroso, B. and Jespersen, J. (1992), *Macroeconomic Theories and Policies for the 1990s: a Scandinavian perspective*, Macmillan, London.

Andersson, L., Gustafsson, O. and Yellen, J.L. (1998), 'Structural Change, Competition and Job Turnover in the Swedish Manufacturing Industry, 1964-96', *FIEF Working Paper No. 148*, Trade Union Institute for Economic Research (FIEF), Stockholm.

Andersson, S. (1969), *Vilda Strejker* [Wild-cat Strikes], Rabén & Sjögren, Stockholm.

Andersson, T. (1993) 'Utlandinvesteringar och policy-implikationer' [Foreign Direct Investment and Policy Implications], *IUI Working Paper No. 371*, Industrins utredningsinstiut, Stockholm.

Andersson, T., Fredriksson, T. and Svensson, R. (1996), *Multinational Restructuring, Internationalisation and Small Economies: The Swedish Case*, Routledge, London.

Anderton, B., Riley, R. and Young, G. (2000), *New Deal for Young People: First Year Analysis of Implications for the Macroeconomy*, Report No. 33, Employment Service Research and Development Branch, Sheffield.

Andrén, N. (1991), 'On the Meaning and Uses of Neutrality', *Co-operation and Conflict*, Vol. 26, pp. 67-83.

Arbetsmarknadsdepartmentet (1985), *The Swedish Act on Board representation for the Employees in Joint Stock Companies and Co-operative Associations*, Allmänna förlaget, Stockholm.

Arbetsmarknadsdepartmentet (1988), *The Swedish Act on Co-Determination at Work*, Allmänna förlaget, Stockholm.

Arestis, P. (1986), 'Post-Keynesian Economic Policies: the case of Sweden', *Journal of Economic Issues*, Vol. 20, No. 3, pp. 709-723.

Arestis, P. (1989), 'On the Post-Keynesian Challenge to Neo-Classical Economics: a complete quantitative macro-model for the UK economy', *Journal of Post-Keynesian Economics*, Vol. 11, No. 4, pp. 611-629.

Arestis, P. (1992), *The Post-Keynesian Approach to Economics*, Edward Elgar, Aldershot.

Arestis, P. and Sawyer, M. (2001a), 'Economics of the 'Third Way', in Arestis, P. and Sawyer, M. (eds.), *The Economics of the Third Way: Experiences from Around the World*, Edward Elgar, Cheltenham, pp. 1-10.

Arestis, P. and Sawyer, M. (2001b), 'Economics of the British New Labour: An Assessment', in Arestis, P. and Sawyer, M. (eds.), *The Economics of the Third Way: Experiences from Around the World*, Edward Elgar, Cheltenham, pp. 46-59.

Åsard, E. (1978), *LO och löntagarfondsfrågan – En studie I facklig politik och strategi* [The LO and the question of EIFs – A study of trade union politics and strategy], Rabén & Sjögren, Stockholm.

Åsard, E. (1980), 'Employee Participation in Sweden 1971-1979: The Issue of Economic Democracy', *Economic and Industrial Democracy*, Vol. 1, No. 3, pp. 371-393.

Åsard, E. (1985), *Kampen om löntagarfonderna: Fondsutredningen från samtal till sammanbrott* [The campaign on the EIFs: The Fund Commission from dialogue to breakdown], Norstedts, Stockholm.

Åsard, E. (1986), 'Industrial and Economic Democracy in Sweden: From Consensus to Confrontation', *European Journal of Political Research*, Vol. 14, No's. 1-2, pp. 207-219.

Aspling, A. (1986), *Förtagsdemokratin och MBL: en empirisk och organisationsteoretisk utvärdering av en arbetsrättsreform* [Industrial Democracy and The Co-Determination Act: an empiracle and theoretical organisational evaluation of a labour law reform], PhD Thesis, Ekonomiska Forskningsinstitutet, Handelshögskolan, Stockholm.

Atkinson, A.B. (1972), 'Capital-Growth-Sharing Schemes and the Behaviour of the Firm', *Economica*, Vol. 39, pp. 237-49.

Atkinson, A.B. (1974), *Unequal Shares*, Penguin, London.

Atkinson, A.B. (1999), *The Economic Consequences of Rolling Back the Welfare State*, MIT Press, London.

Atkinson, B., Baker, P. and Milward, R. (1996), *Economic Policy*, Macmillan, London.

Aylott, N. (1999), *Swedish Social Democracy and European Integration: The People's Home on the Market*, Ashgate, Aldershot.

Bäckström, A. (1988), 'The Role of the Automotive Industry for the Swedish Economy and the Labour Market', in Olsen, G.M. (ed.), *Industrial Change and Labour Adjustment in Sweden and Canada*, Garamond Press, Toronto, pp. 242-248.

Bairoch, P. (1996), 'Globalisation Myths and Realities – One century of external trade and foreign investment', in Boyer, R. & Drache, D. (1996) (eds.), *States Against Markets: The Limits of Globalisation*, Routledge, London, pp. 173-192.

Bairoch, P. and Kozul-Wright, R. (1996), 'Globalisation Myths: Some Historical Reflections on Integration, Industrialisation and Growth in the World Economy', *UNCTAD Discussion Paper No. 113*, March.

Barr, N. (1992), 'Economic Theory and the Welfare State: A Survey and Interpretation', *Journal of Economic Literature*, Vol. 30, pp. 741-803.

Barro, R.J. (1990), 'Government Spending in a Simple Model of Endogenous Growth', *Journal of Political Economy*, Vol. 98, No. 5, pp. 103-125.

Baumol, W.J. and Bowen, W.G. (1996), *Performing Arts – The Economic Dilemma*, Twentieth Century Fund, New York.

Bergholm, F. and Jagren, L. (1985), 'Det ulandsinvesterande foretaget-en empirik studie' Trans-National Corporations and Foreign Direct Investment – an empirical study], In: Eliasson, G. (ed.), *De svenska storforetagen* [The Large Swedish Corporations], Indusstrins utredningsinstitut (IUI), Stockholm, pp. 71-160.

Bergman, L., Bjorklun, A., Jakobsson, U., Lundberg, L. and Soderstrom, H.T. (1990), *I samtidens bakvatten* [In a Contemporary Backwater], SNS, Stockholm.

Bergman, L., Jakobsson, U., Persson, M., and Soderstrom, H.T. (1991), *Sverige vid vandpunkten* [Sweden at the Turning Point], SNS, Stockholm.

Bergquist, M. (1969) 'Sweden and the European Economic Community', *Co-operation and Conflict*, Vol. 4, No. 1, pp. 1-12.

Bergström, H. (1987), *Rivstrat? [A Flying Start?]*, Tiden, Stockholm.

Bergström, H. (1991), 'Social Democracy in Crisis', *Current Sweden*, Svenska Institutet, Stockholm, No. 381, May.

Bergström, V. (1980), 'Wage policy, economic growth, and structural change,' paper presented at the *Meidner symposium*, February 1980, Stockholm.

Bergström, V. (1982), *Studies in Swedish Post-War Industrial Investments*, Almqvist & Wicksell, Stockholm.

Bergström, V. (1992), 'Party programme and Economic Policy: The Social Democrats in Government', in Misgeld, K., Molin, K. and Åmark, K. (eds.), *Creating Social Democracy: A Century of the Social Democratic Labour Party in Sweden*, The Pennsylvania State University Press, Pennsylvania, Ch. 5, pp. 131-174.

Bergström, V. (1993), 'Finansplanen och den ekonomiska politiken' [The Budget and the Political Economy], In: Bergström, V. (ed.), *Varfor överge den syenska moddellen?* [Why Abandon the Swedish Model?], Tiden, Stockholm.

Berkling, A. L. (1982), *Från Fram till folkhemmet: Per Albin Hansson som tidningsman och talare* [Forward From the People's Home: Per Albin Hansson as Journalist and Orator], Metodica Press, Stockholm.

Beveridge, W.H. (1944), *Full employment in a free society*, Allen & Unwin Ltd, London.

Bieler, A. (2000), *Globalisation and Enlargement of the European Union*, Routledge, London.

Björklund, A. (1991), 'Evaluation of Labour market Policy in Sweden', in OECD, *Evaluating Labour market and Social Programmes*, OECD, Paris, pp. 73-88.

Blair, A. (1998), The Third Way, Fabian Society, London.

Blair, A. and Schröder, G. (1999), *Europe: The Third Way / Die Neute Mitte*, Joint statement, Labour Party/SPD.

Blanchard, O.J. and Summers, L.H. (1986), 'Hysteresis and the European Unemployment Problem', *National Bureau of Economic Research Macroeconomics Annual*, pp. 15-78.

Blanchflower, D.G., Oswald, A.J. and Sanfey, P. (1996), 'Wages, Profits and Rent-Sharing', *The Quarterly Journal of Economics*, Vol. 111, pp. 227-251.

Blid, H. (1989), *Education by the People – Study Circles*, Arbetarnas Bildingsförbund [Swedish Workers' Educational Association], Stockholm.

Block, F. (1987), *Revising State Theory: Essays in Politics and Postindustrialism*, Temple University Press, Philadelphia, USA.

Blostrÿm, M. (2000), 'Internationalisation and Growth: Evidence from Sweden', *Swedish Economic Policy Review*, Vol. 7, No. 1, pp. 185-211.

Bobbio, N. (1996), *Left and Right*, Cambridge University Press, Cambridge.

Boréus, K. (1994), *Högerväg – Nyliberalismen och kampen om språket I Svensk debatt 1969-1989* [The Right way – new liberalism and the campaign for language in the Swedish debate 1969-1989], Tidens förlag, Stockholm.

Borgos, S. (1991), 'Indusrialist Policy in a Federalist Polity: Microcorporatism in the United States', in Hancock, M.D., Logue, J., and Schiller, B. (eds.), *Managing Modern Capitalism*, Praeger, London, pp. 65-94.

Bosworth, B.P. and Lawrence, R.Z. (1986), 'Economic goals and the policy mix', in Bosworth, B.P. and Rivlin, A.M. (eds.), *The Swedish Economy*, The Brookings Institution, Washington DC, pp. 97-124.

Bosworth, B.P. and Lawrence, R.Z. (1987), 'Adjusting to Slower Growth: The Domestic Economy', In: Bosworth, B.P. and Rivlin, A.M. (eds.), *The Swedish Economy*, Brookings Institute, Washington DC.

Bosworth, B.P. and Rivlin, A.M. (eds.) (1986), *The Swedish Economy*, The Brookings Institution, Washington DC.

Bosworth, B.P and Rivlin, A.M. (eds.) (1987), *The Swedish Economy*, Brookings Institution, Washington DC.

Boyer, R. and Drache, D. (1996) (eds.), *States Against Markets: The Limits of Globalisation*, Routledge, London.

Branting, H. (1926), *Tal och skrifter 1926-1929* [speeches and writings], ll volumes, Tidens förlag, Stockholm.

Brems, H. (1975), *A Wage Earners' Investment Fund – forms and economic effects*, Swedish Institute, Stockholm.

Bresky, J. and Scheman, I.S. (1978), *Med SAF vid rodret – Granskning av en Kamporganisation* [with SAF at the helm – examination of a campaign organisation], Liber förlag, Stockholm.

Broström, A. (1982), 'Industrial and Economic Democracy in Sweden', paper presented at *Bolognia Conference on Industrial and Economic Democracy*, 7-8 May, Bolognia, Italy.

Brulin, G. (1989), *Från den 'svenska modellen' till förtagskorporatism?* [From the Swedish Model to Enterprise Corporatism], Arkiv, Lund.

Brulin, G. (2000), 'The Transformation of Swedish Industrial Relations from Below', *Economic and Industrial Democracy*, Vol. 21, No. 2, pp. 237-251.

Brulin, G. and Nilsson, T. (1991), *Mot en ny syenk model* [For a New Swedish Model], Rabén and Sjögren, Stockholm.

Brulin, G. and Nilsson, T. (1997), *Laran om arbetets ekonomi* [….on labour's economy], Rabén Prisma, Stockholm.

Brulin, H. (1995), "Sweden: Joint Councils under Strong Unionism", in Rogers, J. and Streeck, W. (eds.), *Work Councils – Consultation, Representation and Co-operation in Industrial Relations*, University of Chicago Press, London, pp. 189-216.

Bruno, M. and Sachs, J. (1985), *Economics of Worldwide Stagflation*, Harvard University Press, Boston.

Burkitt, B. (1983a), 'Post-Keynesian Distribution Theory and Employee Investment Funds', *The Economic Studies Quarterly*, Vol. 34, No. 2, pp. 124-132.

Burkitt, B. (1984), *Radical Political Economy*, Wheatsheaf Books, Sussex.

Burkitt, B. (1985), 'The Political Economy of Employee Investment Funds', *Policy and Politics*, Vol. 13, No. 3, pp. 269-279.

Burkitt, B. and Whyman, P. (1994), 'Public Sector Reform in Sweden – Competition or Participation?', *Political Quarterly*, Vol. 65, No. 3, pp. 275-284.

Burkitt, B. and Whyman, P. (1995), 'Full Employment and the Evolution of Keynesian Political Economy – Lessons from Sweden', *Renewal*, Vol. 3, No. 1, pp. 24-36.

Callaghan, J. (1988), *Time and Change*, Collins/Fontana, London.

Calmfors, L. (1984), 'Stabilisation, Policy and Wage Formation in Economies with Strong Trade Unions', In: Emerson, M. (ed.), *Europe's Stagflation*, Oxford University Press, Oxford.

Calmfors, L. (1990), 'Wage Formation and Macroeconomic Policy in the Nordic Countries: A Summary', in Calmfors, L. (ed.), *Wage Formation and Macroeconomic Policy in the Nordic Countries: A Summary*, Oxford University Press, Oxford, pp. 11-62.

Calmfors, L. (1993), 'Lessons from the Macroeocnomic Experience of Sweden', *European Journal of Political Economy*, Vol. 9, No. 1, pp. 25-72.

Calmfors, L. and Driffill, J. (1988), 'Bargaining structure, corporatism and macroeconomic performance', *Economic Policy*, No. 6, April, pp. 13-62.

Calmfors, L. and Forslund, A. (1990), 'Wage Formation in Sweden', in Calmfors, L. (ed.), *Wage Formation and Macroeconomic Policy in the Nordic Countries: A Summary*, Oxford University Press, Oxford, pp. 63-136.

Calmfors, L. and Forslund, A. (1991), 'Real-wage determination and labour market policies: The Swedish experience', *Economic Journal*, Vol. 101, No. 408, pp. 1130-1148.

Calmfors, L. and Holmlund, B. (2000), 'Unemployment and Economic Growth: a partial survey', *Swedish Economic Policy Review*, Vol. 7, pp. 107-153.

Calmfors, L. and Nymoen, R. (1990), 'Real wage adjustment and employment policies in the Nordic Countries', *Economic Policy*, Vol. 5, No. 2, pp. 397-448.

Calmfors, L., Flam, H., Gottfries, N., Matlary, J.H., Jerneck, M., Lindahl, R., Berntsson, C.N., Rabinowicz, E., and Vredin, A. (1998), *EMU – A Swedish Perspective*, Kluwer Academic Publishers, London.

Cameron, D.R. (1984), 'Social Democracy, Corporatism, Labour Quiescence and the Representation of economic interest in Advanced Capitalist Society', in Goldthorpe, J.H. (ed.), *Order and Conflict in Contemporary Capitalism*, Clarendon Press, Oxford, pp. 143-178.

Cameron, D.R. (1996), 'Exchange Rate Policies in France, 1981-83: The Regime Defining Choices of the Mitterand Presidency', in Daley, A. (ed.), *The Mitterand Era: Policy Alternatives and Political Mobilisation in France*, Macmillan, London.

Caporaso, J.A. and Levine, D.P. (1992), *Theories of Political Economy*, Cambridge University Press, Cambridge.

Carlin, W. and Soskice, D. (1990), *Macroeconomics and the Wage Bargain*, Oxford University Press, Oxford.

Carlsson, I. (1994), 'Europasamarbete: ett vansterprojekt' [European Co-operation: A Left Project], in Edberg, R. and Jacobsen, R. (eds.), *På tröskeln till EU* [On the Threshold of the EU], Tidens förlag, Stockholm, pp. 19-20.

Carnoy, M. and Shearer, D. (1980), *Economic Democracy: The Challenge of the 1980s*, M.E. Sharpe, New York.

Cerra, V. and Saxena, S.C. (1999), 'Alternative Methods of Estimating Potential Output and the Output Gap: An Application to Sweden', *IMF Working Paper* No. 59.

Childs, M. (1936), *Sweden the Middle Way*, Yale University Press, New Haven.

CIEC [Commission on Industrial and Economic Concentration] (1976), 'Ownership and Influence in the Economy', in Scase, R. (ed.), *Readings in the Swedish Class Structure*, Permagon Press, Oxford.

Clark, K.B. and Fujimuto, T. (1991), *Product Development Performance*, Harvard Business School, Cambridge, Mass.

Clayre, A. (1980), *The Political Economy of Co-operation and Participation*, Oxford University Press, Oxford.

Clement, W. and Mahon, R. (eds.) (1994), *Swedish Social Democracy – A Model in Transition*, Canadian Scholars Press Inc, Toronto.

Corea, G. (1998), 'More by Default than Design: The Clinton Experience and the Third Way', *Renewal*, Vol. 6, No. 2.

Cornwall, J. (1989) 'Inflation as a Cause of Economic Stagnation: A Dual Model', in: Kregel, J.A. (ed.), *Inflation and Income Distribution in Capitalist Crisis*, New York University Press, New York.

Costello, N., Michie, J. and Milne, S. (ed.) (1989), *Beyond the Casino Economy*, Verso, London.

Cowles, M.G. (1995a), The European Round Table of Industralists, in Greenwood, J. (ed.), *European Case Book on Business Alliances*, Prentice Hall, pp. 225-236.

Cowles, M.G. (1995b), 'Setting the Agenda for a New Europe: The ERT and EC: 1992', *Journal of Common Market Studies*, Vol. 33, December, pp. 501-526.

Cox, R.W. (1981), 'Social Forces, States and World Orders: Beyond International Relations Theory', *Millennium: Journal of International Studies*, Vol. 10, No. 2, pp.126-55.

Cox, R.W. (1987), *Production, Power and World Order: Social Forces in the Making of History*, Columbia University Press, New York.

Cox, R.W. (1993), 'Structural Issues of Global Governance: Implications for Europe', in Gill, S. (ed.), *Gramsci, Historial Materialism and International Relations*, Cambridge University Press, Cambridge, pp. 259-89.

Crouch, C. (ed.) (1979), *State and Economy in Contemporary Capitalism*, Croom Helm, London.

Crouch, C. (1985), 'Corporation in Industrial Relations: A Formal Model', in Grant, W. (ed.), *The Political Economy of Corporatism*, MacMillan, London, pp. 63-88.

Crouch, C. (1995) 'Exit or voice', Two Paradigms for European Industrial Relations after the Keynesian Welfare State', *European Journal of Industrial Relations*, Vol. 1, No. 11, pp. 63-81.

Cukierman, A. (1992), *Central Bank Strategy, Credibility and Independence:....and Evidence*, MIT Press, Cambridge, Mass.

Dahrendorf, R. (1999), 'Whatever Happened to Liberty?', *New Statesman*, 6 September, pp. 25-7.

Daveri, F. and Tabellini, G. (2000), 'Unemployment, Growth and Taxation in Industrial Countries', *Economic Policy*, No. 15, No. 30, pp. 47-104.

Davidson, P. (1997), 'Are Grains of Sand in the Wheels of International Finance Sufficient to do the Job when Boulders are often Required?', *Economic Journal*, Vol. 107, pp. 671-86.

Dawson, G. (1992), *Inflation and Unemployment*, Edward Elgar, Aldershot.

de Geer, H. (1989), I *vanstervind och Högervåg – SAF under 1970–talet* [the 'left-wind' and 'right-way' – SAF during the 1970s], Allmänna förlag, Stockholm.

de Geer, H. (1992), *The Rise and Fall of the Swedish Model: the Swedish Employers' Confederation, SAF, and industrial relations over ten decades*, Carden Publishers, Chichester.

de Groot, H. (1988), *Arbetarrörelsen, Folkpartiet och löntagarfonderna* [the labour movement, the liberal party and the EIFs], Doctoral script, July, Rijksuniversitet Groningen.

Dean, A. Durant, M. Fallon, J. and Hoeller, P. (1990), 'Saving Trends and Behaviour in OECD Countries', *OECD Economic Studies Papers*, No. 14, OECD, Paris.

DeLong, B. and Summers, L.H. (1991), 'Equipment Investment and Economic Growth', *Quarterly Journal of Economics*, Vol. 106, pp. 445-502.

DfEE (1997), *Learning and Working Together for the Future*, Department for Education and Employment, London.

Dowrick, S. (1996), 'Sweden's Economic Performance and Swedish Economic Debate: A View From Outside', *Economic Journal*, Vol. 106, No. 439, pp. 1772-79.

Dowrick, S. and Nguyen, D.T. (1989), 'OECD Economic Growth, 1950-1985', *American Economic Review*, Vol. 79, pp. 1010-30.

Dyson, K. (1999), 'Benign or Malevolent Leviathan? Social Democratic Governments in a Neo-Liberal Euro Area', *Political Quarterly*, Vol. 70, No. 2, pp. 195-209.

Economist, The. (1987), 'A Job for Everyone Who Wants One', *The Economist*, 21 November, SURVEY p. 5.

Eddie, G.D. (1993), 'Sweden: krona crisis stalls 'New Start'', *The World Today*, Vol. 49, No. 1, pp. 9-12.

Edin, P-O. (1981), 'Fonder, tillväxt och lönsamhet' [EIFs, growth and wage formation], *Ekonomisk Debatt*, No. 5, pp. 365-373.

Edin, P-O. (1995), 'EMU maste bli ett vansterprojekt [EMU must be a left-project], *LO-Tidningen*, No. 33.

Edin, P-A. and Holmlund, B. (1993), Avkastning och efterfrågan på högre utbildning [Returns to and Demand for Higher Education], *Ekonomist Debatt*, Vol. 21, No. 1, pp. 31-45.

Edin, P.A., Holmlund, B. and Ostros, T. (1994), 'Wage Behaviour and Labour Market Programmes in Sweden: Evidence from Micro Data', in Tachibanaki, T. (ed.), *Labour Market and Macroeconomic Performance: Europe, Japan and the US*, Macmillan, London.

Edlund, S. and Nyström, B. (1988), *Developments in Swedish Labour Law*, The Swedish Institute, Stockholm.

Eichengreen, B., Tobin, J. and Wyplotz, C. (1995), 'Two Cases for Sand in the Wheels of International Finance', *Economic Journal*, Vol. 105, pp.162-72.

Eidem, R. and Öhman, B. (1979), *Economic Democracy through Wage-Earner Funds*, Arbetslivscentrum, Stockholm.

Eiger, N. (1983), 'The Education of Employee Representatives on Company Boards in Sweden', *In Sweden*, No. 27, May, Swedish Information Service, Stockholm.

EIU (1991), *Sweden: Country Report* – No. 2, EIU, London.

EIU (1993), *Sweden: Country Report* – No. 2, EIU, London.

EIU (1994), *Sweden: Country Report* – No. 1, EIU, London.

Eklund, K.A., Lindbeck, A., Persson, M., Soderstrom, H.T. and Viotti, S. (1993), *Fast kurs med flytande krona* [firm policy with floating krona], Konjlinkturadets rapport, SNS.

Elmeskov, J. (1994), 'Nordic Unemployment in a European Perspective', *Swedish Economic Policy Review*, No. 1.

Elvander, N. (1979), 'Sweden', in Roberts, B.C. (ed), *Towards Industrial Democracy: Europe, Japan and the United States*, Croom Helm, London, Ch. 5, pp. 130-163.

Elvander, N. (1988), *Den Svenska Modellen: löneförhandlingar och inkomstpolitik 1982-1986* [the Swedish model: wage negotiations and incomes policy 1982-1986], Allmänna förlaget, Stockholm.

Elvander, N. (1992), *Lokal lönemarknad – Lönebildning I Sverige och Storbritannien* [Local Labour Market – Wage Formation in Sweden and Great Britain], SNS Förlag, Stockholm.

Elvander, N. (1997), 'The Swedish Bargaining System in the Melting Pot', in *The Swedish bargaining System in the Melting Pot – Institutions, Norms and Outcomes in the 1990s*, Arbetslivinstitutet, Solna.

Eriksson, T., Suvanto, A., and Vartia, P. (1990), 'Wage Setting in Finland', In: Calmfors, L. (ed.), *Wage Formation and Macroeconomic Policy in the Nordic Countries*, SNS and Oxford University Press, Oxford.

Erixon, L. (1984), 'Den svenska modellen I motgang' [The Swedish Model in Adversity], *Nordisk Tidsskrift for Politisk Ekonomi*, No's. 15-16.

Erixon, L. (1985), *What's Wrong with the Swedish Model? An Analysis of Its Effects and Changed Conditions 1974-1985*, Stockholm.

Erixon, L. (2001), 'A Swedish Economic Policy: The Rehn-Meidner Model's Theory, Application and Validity', in Milner, H. and Wadensjö, E. (eds.), *Gösta Rehn, the Swedish Model and Labour Market Policies: International and national perspectives*, Ashgate, Aldershot, pp. 13-49.

Erlander, T. (1976), *Tage Erlander 1955-60*, Tidens förlag, Stockholm.

Esaisson, P. (1996), 'Kampanj pa sparlaga' [Campaign on Low Savings], in Gilljam, M. and Holmberg, S. (eds.), *Ett knappot ja till EU. Valjarna och folkomrostning 1994* [A Narrow Yes to the EU. Voting Patterns in the 1994 Referendum], Norstedts juridik, Stockholm.

ESC (1996), *The Right to Work/Welfare*, Second Report from the Employment Committee, Session 1995-96, HMSO, London.

ESO (Expertgruppen for studier I Offentlig Ekonomi) [Commission to Examine the Public Sector] (1994), *Den offentliga sektorns produktivitetsutveckling 1980-1992* [Productivity in the Public Sector, 1980-1992], Finansdepartmentet, Ds 1994: 133, Almänna Förlaget, Stockholm.

Esping-Andersen, G. (1985), *Politics against Markets: The Social Democratic Road to Power*, Princeton University Press, New Jersey.

Esping-Andersen, G. (1990), *The Three Worlds of Welfare Capitalism*, Polity Press, Cambridge.

Esping-Andersen, G. (1992), 'The Making of a Social Democratic Welfare State', in Misgeld, K., Molin, K. and Åmark, K. (eds.), *Creating Social Democracy: A Century of the Social Democratic Labour Party in Sweden*, The Pennsylvania State University Press, Pennsylvania, Ch. 2, pp. 35-66.

Estrin, S. (1983), *Self-Management: Economic Theory and Yugoslav Practice*, Cambridge University Press, Cambridge.

EU Commission (1992), *Treaty on European Union*, Office for the Official Publications of the European Communities, Luxembourg.

Färm, G. (1991), *Carlsson – en samtalsbok med Ingvar Carlsson*, Tidens Förlag, Stockholm.

Faux, J. (1999), 'Lost on the third way', *Dissent*, Vol. 46, No. 2, pp. 67-76.

Feldt, K-O. (1980), 'Wage-earner ownership and democracy', *International Seminar on Capital and Economic Democracy*, 10-12 September, Stockholm.

Feldt, K-O. (1991), *Alla Dessa Dagar – I Regeringen 1982-1990* [all these days – in government 1982-1990], Pan-Norstedts, Stockholm.

Ferreiro, J. and Serrano, F. (2001), 'The Economic Policy of the Spanish Socialist Governments, 1982-96', In: Arestis, P. and Sawyer, M. (eds.), *The Economics of the Third Way: Experiences from Around the World*, Elgar, Cheltenham, pp. 155-169.

Finansdepartmentet (1983), 'Löntagarfonder i ATP-systemet' [the EIFs in the state pension fund system], *Finansdepartementet*, Ds Fi No. 20, Allmänna förlaget, Stockholm.

Finansdepartmentet (1991), *The Swedish Budget, 1991/92*, Allmänna Förlaget, Stockholm.

Finansdepartmentet (1992), *The Swedish Budget, 1992/93*, Almänna Förlaget, Stockholm.

Finansdepartmentet (2000), *Looking Ahead Through the Rear-View Mirror: Swedish Stabilisation Policy as a Learning Process, 1970-1995*, Allmänna Förlaget, Stockholm.

Finlayson, A. (1999), 'Third Way Theory', *Political Quarterly*, Vol. 70, No. 3, pp. 271-9.

Finn, D. (2000), 'From Full Employment to Employability: A New Deal for Britain's Unemployed?', *International Journal of Manpower*, Vol. 21, No. 5, pp. 384-399.

Fioretos, K-O. (1997), 'The Anatomy of Autonomy: Interdependence, Domestic Balances of Power, and European Integration', *Review of International Studies*, Vol. 23, No. 3, pp. 293-320.

Flanagan, R., Soskice, D., and Ulman, L. (1983), *Unionism, Economic Stabilisation and Incomes Policy: European Experiences*, Brookings Institution, Washington DC.

Folster, S. and Peltzman, S. (1997), 'The Social Cost of Regulation and Lack of Competition in Sweden', in Freeman, R., Swedenborg, B., and Topel, R. (eds.), *Reforming the Welfare State: The Swedish Model in Transition*, NBER and University of Chicago Press, Chicago.

Forslund, A. (1996), *Direkta undantrangningseffekter av arbet-smarknadspolitiska atgarderr* [Report for The Accountants of Parliament], Allmänna Förlaget, Stockholm.

Forslund, A. and Kruegar, A. (1995), 'An Evaluation of the Swedish Labor Market Policy – New and Received Wisdom', *Occasional Paper* No. 65, SNS, Stockholm.

Forslund, A. and Kruegar, A.B. (1997), 'An Evaluation of the Swedish Active Labour Market Policy: New and Received Wisdom', In: Freeman, R., Swedenborg, B., and Topel, R. (eds.), *Reforming the Welfare State: The Swedish Model in Transition*, NBER and University of Chicago Press, Chicago.

Förtagareförbundet (1982), *Fonderna eller Jobben?* [The funds or employment?], Robert Larsson, Stockholm.

Franzen, T. and Horngren, I. (1989), *Devalveringen 1982 och svensk penningpolitik* [The 1982 Devaluation and Swedish Monetary Policy], paper presented at the conference, Devalveringen 1982, Stockholm School of Economics, Stockholm, October 1989.

Freeden, M. (1999), 'The Ideology of New Labour', *Political Quarterly*, Vol. 70, No. 1, pp. 42-51.

Freeman, C. and Perez, C. (1988), 'Structural Crises of Adjustment, Business Cycle and Investment Behaviour', in Dosi, G. et al (eds.), *Technical Change and Economic Theory*, Pinter, London.

Friberg and Uddén-Sonnegård (2001), 'Changed Wage Formation in a Changed Environment?', *Riksbank Economic Review*, No. 1.

George, D.A.R. (1990), 'The Political Economy of Wage-Earner Funds', *University of Edinburgh Economics Discussion Paper*, No. 4, University of Edinburgh, Edinburgh.

Giddens, A. (1994), *Beyond Left and Right*, Polity Press, Cambridge.

Giddens, A. (1998), *The Third Way: The Renewal of Social Democracy*, Polity Press, Cambridge.

Giddens, A. (2000), *The Third Way and its Critics*, Polity Press, Cambridge.

Gidlund, G. (1992), 'From Popular Movement to Political Party: Development of the Social Democratic Labour party Organisation', in Misgeld, K., Molin, K. and Åmark, K. (eds), *Creating Social Democracy: A Century of the Social Democratic Labour Party in Sweden*, The Pennsylvania State University Press, Pennsylvania, Ch. 4, pp. 97-130.

Gill, S. and Law, D. (1989), 'Global Hegemony and the Structural Power of Capital', *International Studies Quarterly*, Vol. 33, No. 4, pp. 475-499.

Ginsburg, H. (1983), *Full Employment and Public Policy: the United States and Sweden*, Lexington Books, Toronto.

Ginsburg, H.L., Zaccone, J., Goldberg, G.S., Collins, S.D., Rosen, S.M. (1997) (eds.), 'Editorial Introduction – Special Issue on: The Challenge of Full Employment in the Global Economy', *Economic and Industrial Democracy*, Vol. 18, No. 1, pp. 5-33.

Gladh, L. and Gustafsson, S. (1981), 'Labour Market Policy Related to Women and Employment', paper given to the *Conference on Regulation Theory of the Labour Market Related to Women*, IIMV/LMP, Berlin, December.

Glyn, A. (1986), 'Capital Flight and Exchange Controls', *New Left Review*, No. 155, pp. 37-49.

Glyn, A. (1995), 'Social democracy and full-employment', *New Left Review*, No. 211, pp. 33-55.

Glyn, A. (1998) 'The assessment: economic policy and social democracy', *Oxford Review of Economic Policy*, Vol. 14, No. 1, pp. 1-18.

Glyn, A. (2001), 'Aspirations, Constraints and Outcomes', in Glyn, A. (ed.), *Social Democracy in Neo-Liberal Times: The Left and Economic Policy since 1980*, Oxford University Press, Oxford, pp. 1-20.

Goldstein, M. and Khan, M.S. (1985), 'Income and Price Effects in Foreign Trade', in Jones, R.W. and Kenen, P.B. (eds.), *Handbook of International Economics*, Vol. 2, North-Holland, Amsterdam.

Gordon, R. (1987), 'Wages Gaps vs. Output Gaps: Is there a Common Story for all of Europe', *NBER Working Paper*, No. 2454, December.

Gould, A. (1999), 'The Erosion of the Welfare State! Swedish Social Policy and the EU', *Journal of European Social Policy*, Vol. 9, No. 2, pp. 165-174.

Gould, P. (1998), *The Unfinished Revolution: How the Modernisers Saved the Labour Party*, Little, Brown and Company, London.

Gourevitch, P., Martin, A., Ross, G., Allen, C., Bornstein, S.L and Markovits, A. (1984), *Unions and Economic Crisis: Britain, West Germany and Sweden*, George Allen and Unwin, London, pp. 189-359.

Gradin, A. (1997), 'EMU är bra för Sverige [EMU is good for Sweden], *Dagens Nyheter*, 23 January.

Graziani, A. (2001), 'The Third Way: Italian Experiments', in Arestis, P. and Sawyer, M. (eds.), *The Economics of the Third Way: Experiences from Around the World*, Edward Elgar, Cheltenham, pp. 106-119.

Green, R. and Wilson, A. (2000), 'Unemployment, Labour Market Deregulation and the "Third Way"', *International Journal of Manpower*, Vol. 21, No. 5, pp. 424-439.

Gros, D. and Thygeson, N. (1992), *European Monetary Integration: From the European System to European Monetary Union*, Longman, London.

Gstohl, S. (1994), 'EFTA and the European Economic Area or the Politics of Frustration', *Co- operation and Conflict*, Vol. 29, No. 4, pp. 333-366.

Guest, D.E. and Pecci, R. (1998), *The Partnership Company*, Involvement and Partnership Association, London.

Gylfason, T. (1990), 'Exchange Rate Policy, Inflation, and Unemployment: The Nordic EFTA Countries', In: Argy, V. and De Grauwe, P. (eds.), *Choosing an Exchange Rate Regime: The Challenge for Smaller Industrial Countries*, IMF, Washington, DC.

Haahr, J. H. (1993), *Looking to Europe: The EC Policies of the British Labour Party and the Danish Social Democrats*, Aarhus University Press, Aarhus.

Haas, A. (1983), 'The Aftermath of Sweden's Codetermination Law: Workers' Experiences in Gothenburg 1977-1980', *Economic and Industrial Democracy*, Vol. 4, No. 1, pp. 19-46.

Hadden, T. (1972), *Company Law and Capitalism*, Weidenfeld and Nicolson, 1977 2nd edition.

Hamilton, M.B. (1989), *Democratic Socialism in Britain and Sweden*, Macmillan, London.

Hanami, T. and Blanpain, R. (1987), *Industrial Conflict Resolution in Market Economies*, Kluwer Law and Taxation Publishers, Deventer, Netherlands.

Hancock, M.D. (1991), 'Industrial Policies in the United Kingdom, Sweden, and Germany: A Study in Contrasts and Convergence', in Hancock, M. D., Logue, J. and Schiller, B. (eds.), *Managing Modern Capitalism – Industrial Renewal and workplace Democracy in the United States and Western Europe*, Praeger, London, Ch. 2, pp. 11-42.

Hancock, M.D. and Logue, J. (1984), 'Sweden: the quest for economic democracy', *Polity*, Vol. 17, Part 2, pp. 248-270.

Hansson, B. (1991), 'The Stockholm School and the Development of the Dynamic Method', in Sandelin, B. (ed.), *The History of Swedish Economic Thought*, Routledge, London, Ch. 7, pp. 168-213.

Hansson, P. and Lundberg, L. (1995), *Fran bas-industri till hogteknologi? Svensk näringsstruktur och strukturpolitik* [From basic industry to high technology – Swedish industrial structure and infrastructure policy], SNS Förlag, Stockholm.

Hansson, S.O. (1984), 'SAFs politiska strategi' [SAF's political strategy], *Tiden*, No's. 5 and 6, pp. 342-8.

Haq, M.ul, Kaul, I. and Grunberg, I. (eds.) (1996), *The Tobin Tax: Coping with Financial Volatility*, Oxford University Press, Oxford.

Harcourt, T. (2001), 'Coping with Globalisation: Austrialian Economic Policy and the Third Way', in Arestis, P. and Sawyer, M. (eds.), *The Economics of the Third Way: Experiences from Around the World*, Edward Elgar, Cheltenham, pp. 201-220.

Harvey, D. (1990), *The Condition of Postmodernity*, Basil Blackwell, Cambridge.

Hashi, I. and Hussain, A. (1986) 'The Employee Investment Funds in Sweden', *National Westminster Bank Quarterly Review*, May, pp. 17-27.

Hasko, H. (1990), 'Employee Investment Funds, The Stock Market And Growth: A Managerial Approach', *Research Report 28*, Labour Institute for Economic Research Publications, Helsinki.

Hay, C. (1997), 'Anticipating accommodations, accommodating anticipations: the appeasement of capital in the moderisation of the British Labour Party, 1987-1992', *Politics and Society*, Vol. 25, No. 2, pp. 234-56.

Hay, C. (1998) 'Globalisation, Welfare Retrenchment and 'the Logic of No Alternative': Why Second-best Won't Do', *Journal of Social Policy*, Vol. 27, Part 4, Oct. 98, pp. 525-532.

Heckscher, G. (1984), *The Welfare State and Beyond*, University of Minnesota Press, Minesota.

Heclo, H. and Madsen, H. (1987), *Policy and Politics in Sweden: Principled Pragmatism*, Temple University Press, Philadelphia.

Helleiner, E. (1994), *States and the Reemergence of Global Finance: From Bretton Woods to the 1990s*, Cornell University Press, London.

Henderson (1993), 'The Role of the State in the Economic Transformation of East Asia', in Dixon, C. and Drakakis-Smith, D. (eds.), *Economic and Social Development in Pacific Asia*, Routledge, London pp. 85-114.

Henley, A. and Tsakalotos, E. (1993), *Corporatism and Economic Performance: A Comparative Analysis of Market Economies*, Edward Elgar, Aldershot.

Henley, A. and Tsakalotos, E. (1995), 'Unemployment Experience and the Institutional Preconditions', in Arestis, P. and Marshall, M. (eds.), *The Political Economy of Full Employment*, Edward Elgar, Aldershot, pp. 176-201.

Henning, R. (1977), *Förtagen i politiken: Om selektiv politik och industrins med staten* [Business in Politics: on Selective Policies and Industry with the State], Studieförbundet Näringsliv och Samhälle [Industry and Society Study Group], Stockholm.

Henrekson, M. (1990), 'Did the devaluations of 1981 and 1982 induce a structural shift in the Swedish Economy?', *Skandinaviska Enskilda Banken Quarterly Review*, No. 4, pp. 90-98.

Henrekson, M. (1991), Devalvering arnas effekter pä den svenska ekonomins struktur [the effects of devaluation upon the structure of the Swedish economy], Research Report No. 34, FIEF, Stockholm.

Henrekson, M. (1996), 'Sweden's Relative Economic Performance: Lagging Behind or Staying on Top?', *Economic Journal*, Vol. 106, No. 439, pp. 1747-59.

Henrekson, M., Jakobsson, U., Persson, M. and Soderstrom, H.T. (1992), *Tillvaxt utan gränser* [Growth without Limits], Konjukturradets rapport, SNS.

Hermansson, C.H. (1965), *Monopol och Storfinans – De 15 Familjerna* [Monopoly and Big Business – The 15 Families], Rabén and Sjögren, Stockholm.

Hibbs, D.A. (1990), 'Wage compression under solidarity bargaining in Sweden', *FIEF Economic Research Parers*, No. 30, FIEF, Stockholm.

Hibbs, D.A. and Locking, H. (2000), Wage Dispersion and Productive Efficiency: Evidence for Sweden', *Journal of Labor Economics*, Vol. 18, No. 4, pp. 755-782.

Higgins, W. (1986), 'Industrial Democracy and the Control Issue in Sweden', in Davis, E. and Lansbury, R. (eds.), *Democracy and Control in the Workplace*, Longman Cheshire, Melbourne.

Higgins, W. and Apple, N. (1983), 'How Limited is Reformism?', *Theory and Society*, Vol. 12, No. 5, pp. 603-630.

Himmlestrand, U. (1981a), 'Sweden: Paradise in Trouble', in Denitch, B. (ed.), *Democratic Socialism: The Mass Left in Advanced Industrial Societies*, Allanheld, New Jersey, pp. 149-162.

Himmlestrand, U. (1981b), *Beyond Welfare Capitalism; in Issues, Actors and Forces in Societal Change*, Heinemann, London.

Hirschman, A.O. (1977), *Exit, Voice and Loyalty*, Harvard University Press, London.

Hirst, P. and Thompson, G. (1996a), *Globalisation in Question: the international economy and the possibilities of governance*, Polity, Cambridge.

Hirst, P. and Thompson, G. (1996b), 'Global myths and National Policies', *Renewal*, Vol. 4, No. 2.

Holden, S. (1990), 'Wage Drift in Norway: A Bargaining Approach', in L. Calmfors (ed.), *Wage Formation and Macroeconomic Policy in the Nordic Countries*, Oxford University Press, Oxford.

Holland, S. (1995), 'Squaring the Circle? The Maastricht Convergence Criteria, Cohesion and Employment', in Coates, K. and Holland, S. (eds.), *Full Employment for Europe*, Spokesman, Nottingham.

Holmlund, B. (1988), 'Arbetsmarknadspolitik och lönebildning' [labour market policy and wage formation], in Björklund, A. (ed.), *90–talets arbetsmarknad* [the labour market in the 1990s], Allmänna förlaget, Stockholm.

Holzhausen, J. (1982), 'Lagen om styrelserepresentation' [The Law on Board Representation], in Persson, H. and Bergnéhr, B. (eds.), *1970–talets reformer i arbetslivet* [The 1970s Reforms in Working Life], Tidens förlag, Stockholm.

Horngren, L. (1993), 'Normer eller discretion: Om Möjliga och omöjliga val I stabiliseringspolitiken' [Norms or Discretion: On the feasibility of choice in stabilisation policy], In: Bergström, V. (ed.), *Varfor överge den syenska moddellen?* [Why Abandon the Swedish Model?], Tiden, Stockholm, pp. 185-201.

Horngren, L. and Westman-Martensson, A. (1991), 'Swedish Monetary Policy: Institutions, Targets and Instruments,' *Sveriges Riksbank Arbetsaport*, No. 2, May, Sveriges Riksbank, Stockholm.

Hufford, L. (1973), 'Sweden: the myth of socialism 1973', *Young Fabian Pamphlets*, No. 33, April, Fabian Society, London.

Huldt, Bo. (1994), 'Sweden and European Community-Building, 1945-92', in Harden, S. (ed.), *Neutral States and the European Community*, Brassey's, London, pp. 104-143.

Hutchins, D. (1989), *Just in Time*, Gower, Aldershot.

Hyman, S. (1975), 'International Politics and International Economics: A Radical Approach', in Lindberg, L.N., Alford, R., Crouch, C. and Offe, C. (eds.), *Stress and Contradiction in Modern Capitalism: Public Policy and the Theory of the State*, Lexington Books, London, pp. 355-372.

IMF (1996), *International Financial Statistics Yearbook*, IMF, New York.

Ingebritsen, C. (1997), 'Coming Out of the Cold: Nordic Perspectives to European Union', In: Caruny, A.W. and Lankowski, C. (eds.), *Europe's Ambiguous Unity: Conflict and Consensus in the Post-Maastricht Era*, Lynne Rienner, London, pp. 239-256.

Ingebritsen, C. (1998), The Nordic States and European Unity, Cornell University Press, Ithaca.

Israel, J. (1978), 'Swedish Socialism and Big Business', *Acta Sociologica*, Vol. 14, pp. 341-354.

Iversen, T. (1996), 'Power, Flexibility and the Breakdown of Centralised Wage Bargaining: Denmark and Sweden in Comparative Perspective', *Comparative Politics*, Vol. 28, No. 4, pp. 399-436.

Iversen, T. (1998), 'The choices for Scandinavian Social Democracy in comparative perspective', *Oxford Review of Economic Policy*, Vol. 14, No. 1, pp. 59-75.

Iversen, T. (1999), *Contested Economic Institutions: The Politics of Macroeconomics and Wage Bargaining in Advanced Democracies*, Cambridge University Press, Cambridge.

Iversen, T., Pontusson, J. and Soskice, D. (eds.) (2000), *Unions, Employers and Central Banks: Macroeconomic Co-ordination and Institutional Change in Social Market Economies*, Cambridge University Press, Cambridge.

Jackman, R. (1994), 'What Can Active Labor Market Policy Do?', *Swedish Economic Policy Review*, Vol. 1, No. 2 1-2, pp. 221-57.

Jacoby, S.M. (1995), "Social Dimensions of Global Economic Integration', in Jacoby, S.M. (ed.), *The Workers of Nations*, Oxford University Press, Oxford, pp. 3-29.

Jagadeesh, N. and Titman, S. (1993), 'Returns to Buying Winners and Selling Losers: Implications for Stock Market Efficiency', *Journal of Finance*, Vol. 48, pp. 65-91.

Jagrén, L. (1986), 'Concentration, Exit, Entry and Reconstruction of Swedish Manufacturing', in Eliasson, G. (ed.), *The Economics of Institutions and Markets: IUI Yearbook 1986-1987*, The Industrial Institute for Economic and Social Research, Stockholm.

Jeerneck, M. (1993), 'Sweden – the Reluctant European?', in Tiilikainen, T. and Petersen, I.D. (eds.), *The Nordic Countries and the EC*, Copenhagen Political Studies Press, Copenhagen, pp. 23-42.

Jenkinson, T. (1987), 'The Natural Rate of Unemployment: Does it Exist?', *Oxford Review of Economic Policy*, Vol. 3, No. 3, pp. 20-6.

Jenson, J. and Mahon, R. (1993), 'Representing Solidarity: Class, Gender and the Crisis in Social Democratic Sweden', *New Left Review*, No. 201, Sept/Oct, pp. 76-100.

Jessop, R. (1994), 'The transition to post-Fordism and the Schumpeterian workfare state', in Burrows, R. and Loader, B. (eds.), *Towards a Post-Fordist Welfare State?*, Routledge, London, pp. 13-37.

Johannesson, J. (1991), *On the Outcome of Swedish Labour Market Policy*, EFA/ Ministry of Labour, Stockholm.

Johannesson, J. and Niklasson, H. (1974), *Att utvärdera arbetsmarknadspolitik* [Evaluating Labour Market Policy], Swedish Ministry of Labour, SOU, No. 29, Allmänna förlaget, Stockholm.

Johannesson, J. and Persson-Tanimura, I. (1978), *Arbetsmarknadspolitik i förändring* [Labour Market Policy in Transition], Swedish Ministry of Labour, SOU, No. 60, Allmänna förlaget, Stockholm.

Johansson, S. (1982), 'When is the time ripe? A question to the Commission on the 1975 Social Democratic Party program', in Zeitlin, M., Esping-Andersen, G. and Friedland, R. (eds.), *Political Power and Social Theory Research Annual*, Vol. 3, JAI Press Inc., London, pp. 113-143.

Johnpoll, B.K. (1972), 'Sweden's Socialists: Hoist with Their Success', *The Nation*, 4 December, p. 553.

Jonung, L. (1986), 'Financial Deregulation in Sweden', *Skandinaviska Enskilda Banken Quarterly Review*, Vol. 4, pp. 109-19.

Jordan, T.J. (1999), Central bank Independence and the Sacrifice Ratio, *European Journal of Political Economy*, Vol. 15, pp. 229-255.

Kaldor, N. (1966), 'Marginal Productivity and the Macroeconomic Theories of Distribution', *Review of Economic Studies*, Vol. 33, pp. 309-19.

Kalecki, M. (1943), 'Political Aspects of Full Employment', *Political Quarterly*, Vol. 14, pp. 322-331.

Kalecki, M. (1971), *Selected Essays on the Dynamics of the Capitalist Economy 1933-1970*, Cambridge University Press, Cambridge.

Kaplinsky, R. (1984), *Automation: New Technology and Society*, International Labour Organisation, Geneva.

Katzenstein, P. (1985), *Small States in World Markets*, Cornell University Press, Ithaca, New York.

Keohane, R.O. (1984), 'The World Political Economy and the Crisis of Embedded Liberalism', in Goldthorpe, J.H. (ed), *Order and Conflict in Contemporary Capitalism*, Clarendon Press, Oxford, pp. 23-31.

Keynes, J.M. (1936), *The General Theory of Employment, Interest and Money*, MacMillan, London, 1973 edition.

Keynes, J.M. (1980), 'The Collected Writings of John Maynard Keynes – Activities 1940-46', *Shaping the Postwar World: Employment, Collected Writings*, Vol. 27, Macmillan, London.

King, R.G. and Rebelo, S. (1990), 'Public Policy and Economic Growth: Developing Neoclassical Implications', *Journal of Political Economy*, Vol. 98, No. 5, pp. 126-151.

Kitschelt, H. (1994), *The Transformation of European Social Democracy*, Cambridge University Press, Cambridge.

Kjellberg, A. (1992), 'Sweden: Can the Model Survive?', in Ferner, A. and Hyman, R. (eds.), *Industrial Relations in the New Europe*, Basil Blackwell, Oxford.

Kleinknecht, A. and Wengel, Jr. (1998), 'The Myth of Economic Globalisation', *Cambridge Journal of Economics*, Vol. 22, No. 5, pp. 637-647.

Korpi, W. (1978), *The Working Class in Welfare Capitalism*, Routledge and Kegan Paul, London.

Korpi, W. (1981), 'Sweden: Conflict, Power and Politics in Industrial Relations', in Doeringer, P.B. (ed.), *Industrial Relations in International Perspective: Essays on Research and Policy*, Macmillan, London.

Korpi, W. (1983), *The Democratic Class Struggle*, Routledge and Kegan Paul, London.

Korpi, W. (1985), 'Economic growth and the Welfare System: Leaky Bucket or Irrigation System?', *European Sociological Review*, Vol. 1, pp. 97-118.

Korpi, W. (1993), 'Medlemskap = Massarbetsloshet' [Membership = Mass Unemployment], in Groning, L. (ed.), *Det nya riket? 24 kritiska röster om Europa-Unionen* [The New Nation? Twenty-Four Critical Opinions on the European Union], Tidens förlag, Stockholm.

Korpi, W. (1996), 'Eurosclerosis and the Sclerosis of Objectivity: On the Role of Values among Economic Policy Experts', *Economic Journal*, Vol. 106, No. 439, pp. 1727-46.

Korten, D. (1995), *When Corporations Rule the World*, Kumarian Press, West Hartford, Conneticut.

Krugman, P. (1991) *Geography and Trade*, MIT Press, Cambridge, Mass.

Kurzer, P. (1993), *Business and Banking: Political Change and Economic Integration in Western Europe*, Cornell University Press, London.

Ladrech, R. (2000), *Social Democracy and the Challenge of the European Union*, Lynne Rienner, London.

Landau, D. (1995), 'The Contribution of the European Common Market to the Growth of Its Member Countries: An Empirical Test', *Weltwirtschaftliches Archiv*, Vol. 131, No. 4, pp. 774-782.

Landgren, K-G. (1960), *Den "nya ekonomin" i Sverige: J.M. Keynes, E. Wigforss, B. Ohlin och utvecklingen 1927-39* [The "new economics" in Sweden: J.M. Keynes, E. Wigforss, B. Ohlin and developments in 1927-39], Stockholm.

Laurin, U. (1991), "Farval till oversatligheten" [Goodbye to authoritarian rule], in SAF (ed.), *Farval till korporatism!* [Farewell to Corporatism!], SAF, Stockholm.

Laursen, F. (1993), 'The Maastricht Treaty: Implications for the Nordic Countries', *Co-operation and Conflict*, Vol. 28, No. 2, pp. 115-141.

Lawrence, R.Z. and Bosworth, B.P. (1986), 'Adjusting to slower economic growth: the external sector', in Bosworth, B.P. and Rivlin, A.M. (eds.), *The Swedish Economy*, The Brookings Institution, Washington DC, pp. 55-96.

Layard, R. et al (1994) *The Unemployment Crisis*, Oxford University Press, Oxford.

Layard, R., Nickell, S. and Jackman, R. (eds.) (1991), *Unemployment: Macroeconomic Performance and the Labour Market*, Oxford University Press, Oxford.

Lazar, F. (1996), 'Corporate Strategies – The costs and benefits of going global', in Boyer, R. and Drache, D. (eds.), *States Against Markets: The Limits of Globalisation*, Routledge, London, pp. 270-296.

Leibenstein, H. (1957), 'The theory of unemployment in backward countries', *Journal of Political Economy*, Vol. 65, pp. 91-103.

Leisink, P. (1999), *Globalisations and Labour Relations*, Edward Elgar, Cheltenham.

Lindbeck, A. (1975), *Swedish Economic Policy*, Macmillan Press, London.

Lindbeck, A. (1983), 'Interpreting income distributions in a welfare state', *European Economic Review*, Vol. 21, pp. 227-256.

Lindbeck, A. (1997), 'The Swedish Experiment', *Journal of Economic Literature*, Vol. 30, pp. 1273-319.

Lindbeck, A. (2000), 'Swedish Economic Growth in an International Perspective', *Swedish Economic Policy Review*, Vol. 7, No. 1, pp. 7-38.

Lindbeck, A., Molander, P., Persson, T., Peterson, O., Sandmo, A., Swedenborg, B. and Thygesen, N. (1993a), 'Options for Economic and Political Reform in Sweden', *Economic Policy*, October, pp. 220-263.

Lindbeck, A., Molander, P., Persson, T., Petersson, O., Sandmo, A., Swedenborg, B., and Thygesen, N. (1994), *Turning Sweden Around*, MIT Press, London.

Lindbeck, A., Persson, T., Petersson, O., Sandmo, A., Swedenborg, B., Thygesen, N. and Molander, P. (1993b), *Nya Villkor för Ekonomi och Politik* [New Conditions for Economics and Politics], SOU No. 16, Allmänna Förlaget, Stockholm.

Lindbeck, A. and Snower, D. (1988), *The Insider-Outsider Theory of Employment and Unemployment*, MIT Press, London.

Lindgren, A-M. (1998), 'Swedish Social Democracy in Transition', in Cuperus, R., and Kandel, J. (eds.), *European Social Democracy: Transformation in Progress*, F. Ebert Stiftung and Wm Beckman, Stichting, Amsterdam.

Lindquist, M.J. (2000), 'Wage Compression and Welfare in Sweden', *Department of Economics Working Paper*, Stockholm University, No. 4.

Lindström, S. and Nordin, S. (1977), *Vem äger storförtagen?* [Who Owns the Large Enterprises?], Tiden, Stockholm.

Lipietz, A. (1987), 'Globalisation of the General Crisis of Fordism', in Holmes, J. and Leys, C. (eds.), *Between the Lines*, Frontyard /Backyard, Toronto.

LO (1951), *Fackföreningsrörelsen och den fulla sysselsättningen* [Trade Unions and Full Employment], LO, Stockholm.

LO (1953), *Trade Unions and Full Employment*, Framtiden, Malmö, 1953 English edition.

LO (1973), *Fackföreningsrörelsen och AP-fonden* [the trade union movement and the AP-Funds], LO, Stockholm.

LO (1976), *Landsorganisation I Sverige Kongress Protokoll 1976* [LO 1976 Congress Protocol – part 2], Tiden, Stockholm.

LO (1986), "Welfare state resources now fully developed – now they must be utilised correctly" [summary of the report '*fackföreningsrörelsen och välfärdsstaten*', presented to the LO congress 1986], LO, Stockholm.

LO (1994), *Trade Unions and the EC: The Trade Union Evaluation of the Membership Negotiations*, Swedish Trade Union Confederation (LO), Stockholm.

LO (1997), *The Solidarity Way: A Modern Wage Formation for Full Employment – Starting-Points and Guidelines*, LO, Stockholm.

LO-SAP (1978), *Löntagarfonder och kapitalbildning – Förslag från LO-SAPs arbetsgrupp* [EIFs and capital formation – report from the LO-SAP working group], Tiden, Stockholm.

LO-SAP (1982), *Arbetarrörelsen och löntagarfonderna – rapport från en arbetsgrupp inom LO och socialdemokraterna* [the labour movement and the WEFs – report from a working group within the LO and the SAP], Tiden, Stockholm.

Luif, P. (1996), *On the Road To Brussels: The Political Dimension of Austria's Finland's and Sweden's Accession to the European Union*, Braumuller, Vienna.

Lundberg, E. (1981), 'The Rise and Fall of the Swedish Model', No's. 1-2, *Skandinaviska Enskilda Banken Quarterly Review*, S-E Banken, Stockholm, pp. 12-19.

Lundberg, E. (1982), 'Perspectives on the Future of the Swedish Economy – Two Extreme Alternatives', in Ryden, B. and Bergström, V. (eds.), *Sweden; Choices for Economic And Social Policy in the 1980s*, George Allen and Unwin, London.

Lundberg, E. (1985), 'The Rise and Fall of the Swedish Model', *Journal of Economic Literature*, Vol. 23, No. 1, pp. 1-36.

Lundberg, E.F. (1996), *The Development of Swedish and Keynesian Macroeconomic Theory and its Input on Economic Policy*, Cambridge University press, Cambridge.

Luria, D. (1990), 'Automation, Markets and Scale: Can Flexible Niching Modernize US Manufacturing', *International Review of Applied Economics*, Vol. 4, No. 2, pp. 127-65.

Mahon, R. (1991), 'From Solidaristic Wages to Solidaristic Work: A Post-Fordist Historic Compromise for Sweden?', *Economic and Industrial Democracy*, Vol. 12, pp. 295-325.

Mahon, R. (1994), 'From Fordism to? New Technology, Labour Markets and Unions', In: Clement, W. and Mahon, R. (eds.), *Swedish Social Democracy – A Model in Transition*, Canadian Scholars Press Inc., Toronto.

Marquand, D. (1997), 'After Euphoria: The Dilemmas of New Labour', *Political Quarterly*, Vol. 68, No. 4, pp. 335-8.

Marquand, D. (1998), 'The Blair Paradox', *Prospect*, May.

Marshall, T.H. (1963), *Sociology at the Crossroads and Other Essays*, Heinemann, London.

Martin, A. (1977), 'In Sweden: a Union Proposal for Socialism', *Working Papers for a New Society*, Summer, pp. 46-58.

Martin, A. (1979), 'The Dynamics of change in a Keynesian Political Economy: the Swedish Case and its Implications', in Crouch, C. (ed.), *State and Economy in Contemporary Capitalism*, Croom Helm, London.

Martin, A. (1984), 'Trade Unions in Sweden: Strategic Responses to Change and Crisis', in Gourevitch, P. et al, *Unions and Economic Crisis*, Allen and Unwin, London.

Martin, A. (1992), 'Wage bargaining and Swedish politics', The Political Implications of the End of Central Negotiations, FIEF, Stockholm.

Martin, H-P. and Schumann, H. (1996), *The Global Trap: Globalisation and the Assault on Prosperity and Democracy*, Zed Books Ltd, London.

McGrew, A. and Lewis, P. (1992), *Globalisation and the Nation States*, Polity Press, Cambridge.

McIvor, G. (1994a), 'Skandia Snub hits Sweden', *The European*, 8-14 July.

McIvor, G. (1994b), 'Wallenberg dynasty demands Swedish chainsaw massacre', in *The Guardian*, 16 September.

Meidner, R. (1975), *Löntagarfonder* [Wage-earner funds], Tidens förlag, Stockholm.

Meidner, R. (1978), *Employee Investment Funds*, George Allen and Unwin Ltd, London.

Meidner, R. (1981), *Tidens debatt om löntagarfonder* [Tiden's debate of the EIFs], Tidens förlag, Stockholm.

Meidner, R. (1983), 'Strategy for Full Employment', Paper presented to the *Public Services International Symposium on The Public Service*, 9-11 September, Stockholm.

Meidner, R. (1985), 'The Role of Manpower Policy in the Swedish Model', paper given to the WZB-Conference *Barriers to Full Employment*, 1-3 October, Berlin.

Meidner, R. (1986), 'Labour market Policy in the Welfare State', in Fry, J., *Towards a Democratic Rationality – Making the Case for Swedish Labour*, Gower, London.

Meidner, R. (1987), 'A Third Way – The Concept of the Swedish Labour Movement', paper presented at the *International Conference on Social Democratic Futures: Learning from Canadian and European Experiences*, University of Ottawa, 18-21 November, Ottawa, Canada.

Meidner, R. (1988), 'Rehn as an LO Economist', *Economic and Industrial Democracy*, Vol. 9, No. 4, pp. 455-74.

Meidner, R. (1991), 'Beyond Wage-Earner Funds', in Hancock, M.D., Logue, J. and Schiller, B., *Managing Modern Capitalism*, Praeger, London, pp. 291-312.

Meidner, R. (1993a), 'Why Did the Swedish Model Fail?', In: Miliband, R. and Panitch, L. (eds.), *Real Problems, False Solutions – Socialist Register 1993*, Merlin Press, London, pp. 211-27.

Meidner, R. (1993b), 'Neutralitet och fullsysselsättning omodernt I ett EG-anslutet Sverige' [Neutrality and Full Employment are Out of Date in a Sweden Integrated with the EU], in Groning, L. (ed.), *Det nya riket? 24 kritiska röster om Europa-Unionen* [The New Nation? Twenty-Four Critical Opinions on the European Union], Tidens förlag, Stockholm.

Meidner, R. (1997), 'The Swedish Model in an Era of Mass Unemployment', *Economic and Industrial Democracy*, Vol. 18, No. 1, pp. 87-97.

Meyerson, P-M. (1978), *Löntagarfonder eller...ägande och demokrati i en marknadsekonomi* [EIFs or...ownership and democracy in a market economy], P.A. Norstedt and Söners förlag, Stockholm.

Micheletti, M. (1985), 'Organising Interest and Organised Protest', *Stockholm Studies in Politics*, No. 29, Department of Political Science, University of Stockholm, Akademistisk avhandling, Stockholm.

Michl, T.R. (1995), 'Assessing the Costs of Inflation and Unemployment', in Arestis, P. and Marshall, M. (eds.), *The Political Economy of Full Employment*, Edward Elgar, Aldershot, pp. 54-78.

Miles, L. (1996), 'The Nordic Countries and the Fourth EU Enlargement', in Miles, L. (ed.), *The European Union and the Nordic Countries*, Routledge, London, pp. 63-78.

Miles, L. (2000), 'Making Peace with the Union? The Swedish Social Democratic Party and European Integration', in Geyer, R. et al (eds.), *Globalisation, Europeanisation and the End of Scandinavian Social Democracy?*, Macmillan, Basingstoke, pp. 218-239.

Miliband, R. (1961), *Parliamentary Socialism*, Allen and Unwin, London.

Miliband, R. (1989), *Divided Societies: class struggle in contemporary capitalism*, Oxford University Press, Oxford, 1991 edition.

Milner, H. (1989), *Sweden: Social Democracy in Practice*, Oxford University Press, Oxford.

Ministry of Finance (1983), *Employee Investment Funds – press release* [includes statement by Minister of Finance Feldt], 13th October, Ministry of Finance, Stockholm.

Ministry of Finance (1984a), 'Finansplanen' [The Budget Plan], Prop. 1984/85: 100 Bilaga 1, Allmänna förlag, Stockholm.

Ministry of Finance (1984b), *Employee Investment Funds*, Ministry of Finance, Allmänna förlag, Stockholm.

Ministry of Finance (1990), *The Medium Term Survey of the Swedish Economy 1990*, Allmänna förlag, Stockholm.

Ministry of Finance (1993), *Economic Policy Statement: Supplementary Budget Bill April 1993*, Allmänna förlag, Stockholm.

Misgeld, K., Molin, K. and Åmark, K. (eds.) (1992), *Creating Social Democracy: A Century of the Social Democratic Labour Party in Sweden*, The Pennsylvania State University Press, Pennsylvania.

Mishra, R. (1996),' The Welfare of Nations', in Boyer, R. and Drache, D. (eds.), *States Against Markets: The Limits of Globalisation*, Routledge, London, pp. 316-333.

Moene, K.O and Wallerstein, M. (1995), 'How Social Democracy Worked: Labour Market Institutions', *Politics and Society*, Vol. 23, No. 2, pp. 185-211.

Molin, K. (1992), 'Party Disputes and Party Responsibility: A Study of the Social Democratic Defence Debate', in Misgeld, K., Molin, K. and Åmark, K. (eds.), *Creating Social Democracy: A Century of the Social Democratic Labour Party in Sweden*, The Pennsylvania State University Press, Pennsylvania, Ch. 12, pp. 375-408.

Möller, G. (1938), 'The Unemployment Policy, *Annals of the American Academy of Political and Social Science 197*, May, pp. 47-48.

Moses, J. (1994), 'Abdication from National Policy Autonomy: What's Left to Leave?', *Politics and Society*, Vol. 22, pp. 125-148.

Newell, A.T. and Symons, J. (1987), 'Corporatism, Laissez-Faire and the Rise in Unemployment', *European Economic Review*, Vol. 31, No. 3, pp. 567-614.

Nickell, S. (1997), 'Unemployment and Labour Market Rigidities: Europe Versus North America', *Journal of Economic Perspectives*, Vol. 11, No. 3, pp. 55-74.

Nickell, S. and Layard, R. (1999), 'Labour Market Institutions and Economic Performance', In: Ashenfelter, O. and Card, D. (eds.), *Handbook of Labour Economics – Vol. 3*, North Holland, Amsterdam.

Nilsson, T. (1996), 'Lean Production and White Collar Work', *Economic and Industrial Democracy*, 17 (3): pp. 447-72.

Notermans, T. (1993), 'The Abdication of Policy Autonomy: Why the Macroeconomic Policy Regime has Become so Unfavourable to Labour', *Politics and Society*, Vol. 21, pp. 133-167.

Notermans, T. (2000), 'Europeanisation and the Crisis of Scandinavian Social Democracy', in Geyer, R. et al (eds.), *Globalisation, Europeanisation and the End of Scandinavian Social Democracy?*, Macmillan, London, pp. 23-44.

NUTEC [Swedish National Board for Industrial and Technological Development], *Towards Flexible Organisations*, NUTEC, Stockholm.

O'Rourke, K.H. and Williamson, J.G. (1999), *Globalisation and History: The Evolution of a Nineteenth-Century Atlantic Economy*, MIT Press, Cambridge, Massachusetts, USA.

Obstfeld, M. (1994), 'Risk-taking, Global Diversification, and Growth,' *American Economic Review*, Vol. 85, pp. 1310-29.

Obstfeld, M. and Taylor, A. (1997), "The Great Depression as a Water-shed: International Capital Mobility over the Long Run", CEPR *Discussion Paper Series*, No. 1633.

Odhner, C-E. (1992), 'Workers and Farmers Shape the Swedish Model: Social Democracy and Agricultural Policy', in Misgeld, K., Molin, K. and Åmark, K. (eds.), *Creating Social Democracy: A Century of the Social Democratic Labour Party in Sweden*, The Pennsylvania State University Press, Pennsylvania, pp. 175-212.

OECD (1963), *Labour Market Policy in Sweden*, OECD, Paris.

OECD (1970), *Workers' Negotiated Savings Plans for Capital Formation*, OECD, Paris.

OECD (1989), *Economic Surveys: Sweden*, OECD, Paris.

OECD (1990), *Economic Surveys: Sweden*, OECD, Paris.

OECD (1992), *Economic Outlook*, OECD, Paris.

OECD (1993), *Main Economic Indicators 1962-1991*, OECD, Paris.

OECD (1996), *Globalisation of Industry*, OECD, Paris.

OECD (1999), *Employment Outlook*, OECD, Paris.

OECD (2001), *Economic Outlook*, OECD, Paris.

Öhman, B. (1985), 'Collective Workers' Savings and Industrial Democracy', *Department of Government Research Report*, No. 1, Örebro University, Örebro.

Olsen, G.M. (1991), 'Labour Mobilisation and the Strength of Capital: The Rise and Stall of Economic Democracy in Sweden', *Studies in Political Economy*, Vol. 34, pp. 109-145.

Olsen, G.M. (1992), *The Struggle for Economic Democracy in Sweden*, Avebury, Aldershot.

Olsen, G.M. (1994), 'Labour Mobilization and the Strength of Capital', In: Clement, W. and Mahon, R. (eds.), *Swedish Social Democracy – A Model in Transition*, Canadian Scholars Press Inc., Toronto, pp. 195-221.

Olsson, A.S. (1991), *The Swedish Wage Negotiation System*, Dartmouth, Aldershot.

Olsson, U. (1993), 'Sweden and Europe in the Twentieth Century: Economics and Politics', *Scandinavian Journal of History*, Vol. 18, No. 1.

Oscarsson, H. (1996), "EU-dimensionen" [The EU Dimension], in Gilljam, M. and Holmberg, S. (eds.), *Ett knappt ja till EU – Valjarna och folkomröstning 1994* [A Narrow Yes to the EU – the 1994 referendum campaign and popular vote], Norstedts juridik, Stockholm.

Padgett, S. and Paterson, W.E. (1991), *A History of Social Democracy in Postwar Europe*, Longman, London.

Palme, O. (1987), 'Sveriges Ekonomi: resultat och nya uppgifter' [Sweden's Economy: Results and Misinterpretations], In: Palme, O. (ed.), *En levande vilja [a living desire]*, Tiden, Stockholm, pp. 102-111.

Panitch, L. (1977), 'The Development of Corporatism in Liberal Democracies', *Comparative Political Studies*, April, pp. 80-81.

Panitch, L. (1994), 'Corporatism in Liberal Democracies', in Lehmbruch, G. and Schmitteer, P. (eds.), *Socialist Register 1994*, Sage, London.

Patel, P. and Pavitt, K. (1991), 'Large Firms in the Production of the World's Technology: An Important Case of Non-Globalisation', *Journal of International Business Studies*, Vol. 22, No. 1, pp. 1-21.

Pauly, L.W. (1995) Capital mobility, state autonomy and political legitimacy, *Journal of International Affairs*, Vol. 48, No. 2, pp. 369-88.

Pedersen, T. (1994), *European Union and the EFTA Countries: Enlargement and Integration*, Pinter, London.

Persson, G. (1996), 'The Swedish Experience in Reducing Budget Deficits and Debt', *Federal Reserve Bank of Kansas City Economic Review*, No. 1, pp. 7-9.

Petersson, O. (1977), *Väljama och Valet 1976* [choice and the 1976 election], Liber förlag, Stockholm.

Petersson, O. (1989), *Maktens Natverk [The Network of Power]*, Carlssons, Stockholm.

Petersson, O. (1994), The Government and Politics of the Nordic Countries, Fritzes, Stockholm.

Petersson, R. (1982), *Behövs löntagarfonder?* [do we need EIFs?], LTs förlag, Stockholm.

Piore, M. and Sable, C. (1984), *The Second Industrial Divide: Possibilities for Prosperity*, Basic Books, London.

Piven, F.F. (1991), *Labour Parties in Postindustrial Societies*, Polity Press, Oxford.

PMO [Prime Ministers Office] (1996), *A Programme for Halving Open Unemployment by 2000* [based upon Riksdagens Propositionen 1995/96, No. 207], Allmänna Förlaget, Stockholm.

Pollin, R. (2001), 'Anatomy of Clintenomics', in Arestis, P. and Sawyer, M. (eds.), *The Economics of the Third Way: Experiences from Around the World*, Edward Elgar, Cheltenham, pp. 60-78.

Pontusson, J. (1984), 'Behind and beyond Social Democracy in Sweden', *New Left Review*, No. 143, January/February, pp. 69-96.

Pontusson, J. (1987), 'Radicalisation and Retreat in Swedish Social Democracy', *New Left Review*, No. 165, September/October, pp. 5-33.

Pontusson, J. (1988), 'Swedish Social Democracy and British Labour: Essays on the Nature and Conditions of Social Democratic Hegemony', *Centre for International Studies Western Societies Programme Occasional Paper No. 19*, Cornell University, New York.

Pontusson, J. (1992), *The Limits of Social Democracy: Investment Politics in Sweden*, Cornell University Press, London.

Pontusson, J. and Swenson, P. (1996), 'Labour Markets, Production Strategies and Wage Bargaining Institutions: The Swedish Employer Offensive in Comparative perspective', *Comparative Political Studies*, Vol. 29, No. 2, pp. 223-250.

Porcano, T.M. (1993), 'Factors Affecting the Foreign Direct Investment Decisions of Firms from and into Major Industrial Countries', *Multinational Business Review*, Autumn, pp. 26-36.

Porter, M.E. (1990), *The Competitive Advantage of Nations*, Macmillan, London.

Posen, A. (1995), *Central bank Independence and Disinflationary Credibility: A Missing Link?* Staff Report 1, Federal Reserve Bank of New York, New York.

Przeworski, A. (2001), 'How Many Ways Can Be Third?', in Glyn, A. (ed.), *Social Democracy in Neo-Liberal Times: The Left and Economic Policy since 1980*, Oxford University Press, Oxford, pp. 312-333.

Ramaswamy, R. and You, J-I. (1992), 'Growth and Structural Change in the Swedish Model', *Department of Applied Economics Working Paper No. 3*, University of Cambridge, Cambridge.

Randquist, M. (1995), 'Regeringkonferensen 1996' [The 1996 government conference], *LO-Tidningen*, No. 33.

Regeringens Propositionen (1993), *Economic Policy Statement*, Propositionen 1992/93, No. 150, Allmänna Förlaget, Stockholm.

Regeringens Propositionen (2000), *Budget Statement – 2000*, No. 1999/2000:1, Allmänna Förlaget, Stockholm.

Regeringens Propositionen (2002), *Budget Statement – 2002*, No. 2001/02:100, Allmänna Förlaget, Stockholm.

Rehn, G. (1948), 'Ekonomisk politik vid full sysselsättning' [Economic Policy in Full Employment], *Tiden*, pp. 135-142.

Rehn, G. (1952), 'The problem of stability: an analysis and some policy proposals', in Turvey, R. (ed.), *Wages Policy under Full Employment*, W. Hodge and Co., London.

Rehn, G. (1957), 'Hata inflationen' [Hate Inflation], *Tiden*, Vol. 49, No. 2, pp. 104-112.

Rehn, G. (1985), 'Swedish Active Labor Market Policy: Retrospect and Prospect', *Industrial Relations*, Vol. 24, No. 1, pp. 62-89.

Rehn, G. (1987), 'Economic Policy and Industrial Relations', *Economic and Industrial Democracy*, Vol. 8, No. 1, pp. 61-79.

Rehn, G. and Viklund, B. (1990), 'Changes in the Swedish Model', in Baglioni, G. and Crouch, C. (eds.), *European Industrial Relations: The Challenge of Flexibility*, Sage, London, pp. 300-325.

Reynolds, P.J. (1987), *Political Economy*, Wheatsheaf Books, Brighton.

Rhodes, M. (1996) 'Globalization and West European Welfare States: A Critical Review of Recent Debates', *Journal of European Social Policy*, Vol. 6, No. 4, pp. 305-327.

Riksbank (1997), *Inflation Report, 1997*, Riksbank, Stockholm.

Riksbank (2001), *Inflation Report, 2001*, Riksbank, Stockholm.

Riksbank (2002), *Inflation Report, 2002*, No. 1, Riksbank, Stockholm.

Riksdagens protokoll (1983), 'Löntagarfonder' [EIFs], *Riksdagens protokoll 1983/ 4*, No's. 53-54, pp. 1-205.

Rivlin, A.M. (1986), 'Overview', in Bosworth, B.P. and Rivlin, A.M. (eds.), *The Swedish Economy*, The Brookings Institution, Washington DC, pp. 1-21.

Robinson, D. (1966), *Non-wage Incomes Policy*, OECD, Paris.

Robinson, D. (1973), *Incomes Policy and Capital Sharing in Europe*, Croom Helm, London.

Robinson, P. (1994), 'The Decline of the Swedish Model and the Limits to Active Labour Market Policy', *Centre for Economic Performance Working Paper* – No. 667, LSE.

Rock, C.P. (1986), *Economic Democracy and Sweden*, Phd Thesis, Cornell University, Cornell.

Rodrik, D. (1998), 'Symposium on Globalization in Perspective: An Introduction', *Journal of Economic Perspectives*, Vol. 12, No. 4, pp. 3-8.

Rogoff, K. (1985), 'The Optimum Degree of Commitment to an Intermediate Monetary Target', *Quarterly Journal of Economics*, Vol. 100, No. 4, pp. 1169-1189.

Rojas, M. (1998), *The Rise and Fall of the Swedish Model*, Profile Books, London.

Rojas, M. (1999), *Millennium Doom*, Social Market Foundation, London.

Rokkan, S. (1966), 'Norway: Numerical Democracy and Corporate Pluralism,' in Dahl, R. (ed.), *Political Oppositions in Western Democracies*, Yale University Press, New Haven.

Rokkan, S. (1975), 'Votes Count, Resources Decide,' in, *Makt og Motiv:Et Festskrift til Jens Arup Seiip* [Power and Motives: A Volume in Honour of Jens Arup Seiip], Gldendal Norsk Förlag, Oslo.

Roos, L-U. (1992), *Handbok I resurssnal production* [Handbook on Lean Production], Almqvist and Wicksell, Stockholm.

Rosenblum, S. (1980), 'Swedish social democracy: at the crossroads', *Contemporary Crises*, Vol. 4, pp. 267-282.

Ross, G. and Jenson, J. (1994), 'France: Triumph and Tragedy', In: Anderson, P. and Camiller, P. (eds.), *Mapping the West European Left*, Verso, London.

Rowthorn, B. and Glyn, A. (1990), 'The Diversity of Unemployment Experience Since 1973', in Marglin, S.A. and Schor, J.B. (eds.), *The Golden Age of Capitalism: Reinterpreting the Post-war Experience*, Clarendon Press, Cambridge, pp. 187-217.

Ruggie, J. (1982), 'International Regimes, Transactions and Change: Embedded Liberalism in the Postwar Economic Order', *International Organisation*, Vol. 36, No. 2, pp. 379-415.

Ruigrok, W. and Tulder, R. van (1995), *The Logic of International Restructuring*, Routledge, London.

Rustin, M. (2001), 'The Third Sociological Way', in Arestis, P. and Sawyer, M. (eds.), *The Economics of the Third Way: Experiences from Around the World*, Edward Elgar, Cheltenham, pp. 11-25.

Ryan, A. (1999), 'Britain: Recycling the third Way', *Dissent*, Vol. 4, No. 2, pp. 77-80.

Ryner, J.M. (1993), 'The Economic "Success" and Political "Failure" of Swedish Social Democracy in the 1980s', *Arbetslivscentrum Research Report*, No. 1, 1993, Stockholm.

Ryner, M. (1994), 'Assessing SAP's Economic Policy in the 1980s: The "Third Way", the Swedish Model and the Transition from Fordism to Post-Fordism', *Economic and Industrial Democracy*, Vol. 15, No. 3, pp. 385-428.

Ryner, M. (1999), 'Neo-Liberal Globalisation and the Crisis of Swedish Social Democracy', *Economic and Industrial Democracy*, Vol. 20, No. 1, pp. 39-79.

Sachs, J. (1987), 'High unemployment in Europe: Diagnosis and Policy Implications', In: Siven, C.H. (ed.), *Unemployment in Europe*, Timbro, Stockholm.

Sainsbury, D. (1993), 'The Swedish Social Democrats and the Legacy of Continuous Reform: Asset or Dilemma?', *West European Politics*, Vol. 16, No. 1, pp. 39-61.

Sandelin, B. (ed.) (1991), *The History of Swedish Economic Thought*, Routledge, London.

SAP [Sveriges socialdemokratiska arbetarparti] (1975), 'Programme of the Swedish Social Democratic Party' (Translated by Tanner, R.G.), SAP, Stockholm.

Sawyer, M. (1995), 'Obstacles to Full Employment in Capitalist Economies', in Arestis, P. and Marshall, M. (eds.), *The Political Economy of Full Employment*, Edward Elgar, Aldershot, pp. 15-35.

Sayer, A. and Walker, R. (1992), *The New Social Economy*, Basil Blackwell, Oxford.

SCB [Statistiska centralbyrån] (1993), *Statistisk Årsbok '93* [statistical yearbook, 1993], Allmänna förlaget, Stockholm.

Scharpf, F. (1991), *Crisis and Choice in European Social Democracy*, Cornell University Press, Ithaca, New York.

Schiebeck, O. (1990), 'The high price of life in utopia! It was nice being Swedish', *The Guardian*, 30 November.

Schiller, B. (1987), *'Det förödande 70–talet'* [the devastating 1970s], Allmäna förlaget, Stockholm.

Schiller, B. (1991), 'The Swedish Model Reconstituted', in Hancock, M. D., Logue, J. and Schiller, B. (eds.), *Managing Modern Capitalism – Industrial Renewal and workplace Democracy in the United States and Western Europe*, Praeger, London, pp. 145-172.

Sheldon, P. and Thornthwaite, L. (1999), 'Swedish Engineering Employers: the search for industrial peace in the absence of centralised collective bargaining', *Industrial Relations Journal*, Vol. 30, No. 5, pp. 514-532.

SI and SAF [Sveriges Industriförbund and Svenska Arbetsgivareföreningen] (1976), *Förtagsvinster, Kapitalförsörjning, Löntagarfonder – Rapport från en arbetsgrupp inom näringslivet* [company profits, capital provision, EIFs – report from an industry working group – The Wallenberg Report], SI and SAF, Stockholm.

Siebert, H. (1997), 'Labour Market Rigidities: At the Root of Unemployment in Europe', *Journal of Economic Perspectives*, Vol. 11, No. 3, pp. 75-94.

Sinclair, R.J. (1994), Between state and market: hegemony and institutions of collective action under conditions of international capital mobility, *Policy Sciences*, Vol. 27, No. 4, pp. 447-66.

SIND (1980), *Ägandet i det privata näringslivet* [Ownership in Private Industry], No. 5, Allmänna förlaget, Stockholm.

Skidelsky, R. (1979), 'The Decline of Keynesian Politics', in Crouch, C. (ed.), *State and Economy in Contemporary Capitalism*, Croom Helm, London, pp. 55-87.

Skog, R. (1991), 'Ägande och inflytande I svenskt näringsliv' [ownership and influence in Swedish industry], in Eidem, R. and Skog, R. (eds.), *Makten över förtagen* [power over the company], Carlssons Bokförlag, Stockholm, pp. 11-26.

Skogh, G. (1984), "Employer Associations in Sweden" in Windmuller, J.P. and Gladstone, A. (eds.), *Employer Associations and Industrial Relations*, Clarendon, Oxford.

Skouras, T. (2001), 'The Greek Experiment with the Third Way', in Arestis, P. and Sawyer, M. (eds.), *The Economics of the Third Way: Experiences from Around the World*, Edward Elgar, Cheltenham, pp. 170-182.

Smith, H. (1962), *The Economics of Socialism Reconsiderd*, Oxford University Press, Oxford.

Smith, J.G. (1997), 'Exchange Rate Instability and the Tobin Tax', *Cambridge Journal of Economics*, Vol. 21, No. 6, pp.745-52.

Smith, M. (1997), 'The Commission Made Me Do It: The European Commission as a Strategic Asset in Domestic Politics', In: Nugent, N. (ed.), *At The Heart of the EU: Studies of the European Commission*, Macmillan, London.

Södersten, J. (1971), 'Förtagsbeskattning och resursfördelning' [Corporation Taxation and Financial Performance], in Lundberg, E. et al, *Svensk Finanspolitik i Theori och Praktik* [Financial Policy in Theory and Practice].

Söderström, H. (1985), 'Union Militancy, External Shocks, and the Accommodation Dilemma', *Scandinavian Journal of Economics*, Vol. 87, No. 2, pp. 335-351.

Söderström, H.T. (1990), 'Stabiliseringspolitiska lärdomar och framtidsperspektiv' [Stabilisation Policy: Past and Future Perspectives], in Södersten, B. (ed.), *Marknad och Politik* [Markets and Policy], Diaglos, Lund, pp. 55-94.

Sohlman, A. (1996), *Framtidens ubildning. Sverige I internationell konkurren* [Future developments – Sweden in international competition], SNS Förlag, Stockholm.

Solow, R. (1979), 'Another possible source of wage stickiness', *Journal of Macroeconomics*, Vol. 1, pp. 79-82.

Solow, R. (1991), *The Labour Market as a Social Institution*, Blackwell, Oxford.

Solow, R. (1998), *Work and Welfare*, Princeton University Press, Princeton.

SOU [Sveriges Officiella Utredningar] (1923), *Den industriella demokratins problem* [the industrial democracy problem], SOU, No's. 29-30, Allmänna förlaget, Stockholm.

SOU [Sveriges Officiella Utredningar] (1968), *Koncentrationsutredningen* [the commission on the concentration of ownership], SOU, Allmänna förlaget, Stockholm.

SOU [Sveriges Officiella Utredningar] (1979), *Löntagarna och Kapitaltillväxten* [Employees and capital growth], Vol's. 8-11], SOU, Allmänna förlaget, Stockholm.

SOU [Sveriges Officiella Utredningar] (1981), *Löntagare och kapitaltillväxten 5. Slutrapport. En rapport från utredningen om löntarare och kapitaltillväxten* [Employees and capital growth 5 – final report – a report from the commission on employees and capital growth], report No. 44, SOU, Allmänna förlaget, Stockholm.

SOU [Sveriges Officiella Utredningar] (1982), 'Ägarstrukturen i börsförtagen' [Ownership Structures in Stock Companies], *Löntagarna och Kapitaltillväxten 9* [Workers and Capital Formation], SOU, No. 28, Allmänna förlaget, Stockholm.

SOU [Sveriges Officiella Utredningar] (1996), *Sveriges och EMU* [Sweden and the EMU], SOU, No. 158, Allmänna förlaget, Stockholm.

Spånt, R. (1980), 'Wealth distribution and its development in Sweden', *Arbetslivscentrum Working Paper*, Arbetslivscentrum, Stockholm.

Spånt, R. (1993), 'SAP – ett slag I luften!' [SAP – a blow in the air], in Groning, L. (ed.), *Det nya riket? 24 kritiska röster om Europa-Unionen* [The New Nation? Twenty-Four Critical Opinions on the European Union], Tidens förlag, Stockholm.

SPD [Grundwertekommission beim Parteivorstand der SPD] (1999), *Dritte Weg – Neue Mitte* [Third Way – New Way], SPD, Berlin.

Standing, G. (1988), *Unemployment and Labour Market Flexibility: Sweden*, International Labour Organisation, Geneva.

Statskontoret [Swedish Agency for Administrative Development] (1999), *The Swedish Central Government in Transition*, Report No. 15A, Publications service, Stockholm.

Stephens, J.D. (1979), *The Transition from Capitalism to Socialism*, Macmillan, London.

Stephens, J.D. (1982), 'The ideological Development of the Swedish Social Democrats', in Denitch, B. (ed.), *Democratic Socialism: The Mass left in Advanced Industrial Societies*, Allanheld, Osmum, pp. 136-148.

Stopford, J. and Strange, S. (1991), *Rival States, Rival Firms: Competition for World Market Shares*, Cambridge University Press, Cambridge.

Strange, G. (1997), 'The British Labour Movement and Economic and Monetary Union in Europe', *Capital and Class*, Vol. 63, pp. 13-24.

Strange, S. (1986), *Casino Capitalism*, Basil Blackwell, Oxford.

Strange, S. (1994), *States and Markets*, Pinter, London, second edition.

Streeck, W. (1987), 'The Uncertainties of Management in the Management of Uncertainty: Employers, Labour Relations and Industrial Adjustment', *Work, Employment and Society*, Vol. 1, No. 3, pp. 281-308.

Streeck, W. (1992), 'Interest Heterogeneity and Organising Capacity: Two Class Logic's of Collective Action, Social Institutions and Economic Performance', *Studies of Industrial Relations in Advanced Capitalist Economies*, Sage, London.

Svallfors, S. (1996), *Välfärdsstatens moraliska ekonomi* [the moral economy of the welfare state], Boréa, Umeå.

Swenson, P. (1989), *Fair Shares: Unions, Pay and Politics in Sweden and West Germany*, Cornell University Press, Ithaca.

Swenson, P. (1991), 'Bringing Capital Back in , or Social Democracy Reconsidered: Employer Power, Cross-Class Alliances and Centralisation of Industrial Relations in Denmark and Sweden', *World Politics*, Vol. 43, pp. 513-544.

Taylor, A. (1996), 'Domestic Saving and International Capital Flows Reconsidered', NBER *Working Paper*, No. 4892.

Taylor, F.W. (1947), *Scientific Management*, Harper and Row, New York.

TCO (1972), *Förtagsbeskattning och löntagarfonder. En debattskrift från TCOs arbetsgrupp för skattefrågor* [company taxation and WEFs – a debate booklet from the TCO's working group on taxation questions], TCO, Stockholm.

Therborn, G. (1984), 'The Prospects of Labour and the Transformation of Advanced Capitalism', *New Left Review*, No. 145, May-June, pp. 5-38.

Therborn, G. (1992), 'A Unique Chapter in the History of Democracy: The Social Democrats in Sweden', in Misgeld, K., Molin, K. and Åmark, K. (eds.), *Creating Social Democracy: A Century of the Social Democratic Labour Party in Sweden*, The Pennsylvania State University Press, Pennsylvania, pp. 1-34.

Thomas, A. (1998), 'The Wage Bargaining Structure in Norway and Sweden and its Influence on Real Wage Developments', *IMF Working Paper*, No. 174.

Thurow, L. (1996), The *Future of Capitalism*, William Morrow and Co., New York.

Tichy, G. (1984), 'Strategy and Implementation of Employment Policy in Austria: Successful Experiments with Unconventional Assignment of Instruments and Goals', *Kyklos*, Vol. 37, Fasc., pp. 363-386.

Tilton, T. (1990), *The Political Theory of Swedish Social Democracy*, Oxford University Press, Oxford.

Tobin, J. (1978), 'A Proposal for International Monetary Reform', *Eastern European Journal*, Vol. 4, pp.153-59.

Tobin, J. (1999), 'A Liberal Agenda', In Freeman, R.B. (ed.), *The New Inequality*, Beacon, Boston, pp. 58-61.

Trehörning, P. (1993), *Measures to Combat Unemployment in Sweden – Labour Market Policy in the Mid-1990's*, SI, Stockholm.

Tsakalotos, E. (2001), 'European Employment Policies: A New Social Democratic Model for Europe?', in Arestis, P. and Sawyer, M. (eds.), *The Economics of the Third Way: Experiences from Around the World*, Edward Elgar, Cheltenham, pp. 26-45.

Turok, I. And Webster, D. (1998), 'The New Deal: Jeapodised by the Geography of Unemployment?', *Local Economy*, Vol. 12, No. 4, pp. 309-328.

Twaddle, A.C. (1997), 'EU or not EU? The Swedish Debate on Entering the European Union, 1993-94', *Scandinavian Studies*, Vol. 69, No. 2, pp. 189-211.

Uhr, C. G. (1977), 'Economists and Policymaking 1930-1936: Sweden's Experience', *History of Political Economy*, Vol. 9, No. 1.

Ullenhag, J. (1971), *Den solidariska lönepolitiken i Sverige* [The Solidaristic Wage Policy in Sweden], Läromedelsförlagen, Stockholm.

UNCAD (1993), *World Investment Directory*, Vol. 3, United Nations, New York.

UNCTAD (1995), *World Investment Report 1995*, United Nations, Geneva.

UNCTAD (1996), *Trade and Development Annual Report*, UNCTAD, New York.

Undy, R. (1999), 'New Labour's 'Industrial Relations Settlement': The Third Way?, *British Journal of Industrial Relations*, Vol. 37, No. 2, pp. 315-336.

Unga, N. (1976), *Socialdemokratin och arbetslöshetsfrågan, 1912-34* [Social Democrats and the Unemployment Question, 1912-34], Arkiv förlag, Lund.

Van der Pijl, K. (1984), *The Making of an Atlantic Ruling Class*, Verso, London.

Van der Pijl, K. (1989), *Restructuring The Atlantic Ruling Class*, Harvester-Wheatsheaf, Hemel Hempstead.

Vanek, J. (1970), *The General Theory of Labor-Managed Market Economies*, Cornell University Press, London.

Vanhoudt, P. (1999), 'Did the European Unification Induce Economic Growth? In Search of Scale Effects and Persistent Changes', *Weltwirtschaftliches Archiv*, Vol. 135, No. 2, pp. 193-220.

Vartiainen, J. (1998), 'Understanding Swedish Social democracy: victims of success?', *Oxford Review of Economic Policy*, Vol. 14, No. 1, pp. 19-39.

Vilrokx, J. (1996) 'Trade Unions in a Post-representative Society', In: Leisink, P., Leemput, J.van and Vilrokx, J. (eds.), *The Challenges to Trade Unions in Europe: Innovation or Adaptation*, Edward Elgar, Cheltenham, pp. 31-51.

von Otter, C. (1986), 'Research and Working Life Science in Sweden', in Fry, J.A. (ed.), *Towards a Democratic Rationality: Making the Case for Swedish Labour*, Gower Publishing Company Ltd., Aldershot.

Wadensjö, E. (2001), 'The Labour Market Policy: Rehn or Rubbestad', in Milner, H. and Wadensjö, E. (eds.), *Gösta Rehn, the Swedish Model and Labour Market Policies: International and national perspectives*, Ashgate, Aldershot, pp. 3-12.

Walker, R. (1989), 'Machinery, Labour and Location', in Wood, S. (ed.), *The Transformation of Work?*, Unwin Hyman, London, pp. 59-90.

Wallerstein, M. (1990), 'Centralised Bargaining and Wage Restraint', *American Journal of Political Science*, Vol. 34, pp. 982-1004.

Waters, M. (1995), *Globalisation*, Routledge, London.

Weir, M. and Skocpol, T. (1985), 'State Structures and the Possibilities for "Keynesian" Responses to the Great Depression in Sweden, Britain, and the United States', in Evans, P.B., Rueschemeyer, D. and Skocpol, T. (eds.), *Bringing the State Back in*, Cambridge University Press, Cambridge, pp. 107-159.

Westerståhl, J. (1945), *Svensk fackföreningsrörelse* [the Swedish trade union movement], Tidens förlag, Stockholm.

Whyman, P. (2001), 'Can Opposites Attract? Monetary Union and the Social Market', *Contemporary Politics*, Vol. 7, No. 2, pp. 113-127.

Whyman, P. (2003), *An Analysis of the Economic Democracy Reforms in Sweden: Background, Operation and Future*, Mellen International Publishers, forthcoming.

Whyman, P. and Burkitt, B. (1993a), 'Restructuring the Labour Process in Sweden: The Offensive of the SAF and the LO Response', *Eleventh Annual International Labour Process Conference*, 31 March-2 April, Blackpool.

Whyman, P. and Burkitt, B. (1993b), 'The Role of the Swedish Employers in Restructuring Pay Bargaining and the Labour Process', *Work, Employment and Society*, Vol. 7, No. 4, pp. 603-614.

Whyman, P. and Burkitt, B. (1993c), 'Employee Investment Funds: Their Potential Contribution to Economic Policy and to a Transformation in Work Organisation', *European Business and Economic Development*, Vol. 1, Part 4, January, pp. 14-19.

Wibe, S. (1993), 'EG och ekonomin' [The EU and the Economy], in Groning, L. (ed.), *Det nya riket? 24 kritiska röster om Europa-Unionen* [The New Nation? Twenty-Four Critical Opinions on the European Union], Tidens förlag, Stockholm.

Widfeldt, A. (1996), 'Sweden and the European Union: Implications for the Swedish party system', in Miles, L. (ed.), *The European Union and the Nordic Countries*, Routledge, London, pp. 101-6.

Wigforss, E. (1922), *Industrins demokratisering* [democratising industry], Tidens förlag, Stockholm.

Wigforss, E. (1941), *Från klasskamp till samverkan* [From Class Conflict to Co-operation], Tidens förlag, Stockholm.

Wigforss, E. (1962), *Frihet och genemskap* [freedom and solidarity], Tidens förlag, Stockholm.

Wilde, L. (1992), 'The Politics of Transition: the Swedish case', *Capital and Class*, Vol. 47, pp. 7-18.

Williams, K., Cutler, T., Williams, J. and Haslam, C. (1987), 'The End of Mass Production', *Economy and Society*, Vol. 6, No. 3, pp. 405-439.

Winch, D. (1966), 'The Keynesian Revolution in Sweden', *Journal of Political Economy*, No. 74, pp. 168-78.

Wood, S. (1993), 'The Japanization of Fordism', *Economic and Industrial Democracy*, Vol. 14, pp. 535-55.

World Bank (1997), *World Development Report 1997 – The State in a Changing World*, Oxford University Press, Oxford.

Wredén, Å. (1976), *Kapital till anställda? – En studie av vinstdelning och löntagarfonder* [Capital to the employees? – A study of profit-sharing and EIFs], Studieförbundet Näringsliv och Samhälle [Research Organisation on Industry and Society], Kugel Tryckeri, Stockholm.

Index